# Managing Outdoor Recreation, 2nd Edition

Case Studies in the National Parks

*To the National Park Service—thanks for all your good work for parks and outdoor recreation.*

# Managing Outdoor Recreation, 2nd Edition

## Case Studies in the National Parks

**Robert E. Manning**

*Rubenstein School of Environment and Natural Resources*
*University of Vermont*
*Burlington, Vermont, USA*

**Laura E. Anderson**

*College of Natural Resources*
*University of Wisconsin – Stevens Point*
*Stevens Point, Wisconsin, USA*

**Peter R. Pettengill**

*Department of Environmental Studies*
*St. Lawrence University*
*Canton, New York, USA*

CABI is a trading name of CAB International

| | |
|---|---|
| CABI | CABI |
| Nosworthy Way | 745 Atlantic Avenue |
| Wallingford | 8th Floor |
| Oxfordshire OX10 8DE | Boston, MA 02111 |
| UK | USA |

Tel: +44 (0)1491 832111
Fax: +44 (0)1491 833508
E-mail: info@cabi.org
Website: www.cabi.org

Tel: +1 (617)682-9015
E-mail: cabi-nao@cabi.org

A catalogue record for this book is available from the British Library, London, UK.

### Library of Congress Cataloging-in-Publication Data

Names: Manning, Robert E., 1946- author. | Anderson, Laura E., author. |
    Pettengill, Peter, 1981- author.
Title: Managing outdoor recreation : case studies in the national parks.
Description: Second edition / Robert E. Manning, Park Studies Laboratory,
    Rubenstein School of Environment and Natural Resources, University of
    Vermont, Burlington, Vermont, USA, Laura Anderson, College of Natural
    Resources, University of Wisconsin Stevens Point, Stevens Point,
    Wisconsin, USA, Peter Pettengill, College of Natural Resources,
    St. Lawrence University, Canton, New York, USA. | Boston : CAB International,
    [2017] | Includes bibliographical references and index.
Identifiers: LCCN 2016048783 (print) | LCCN 2017010213 (ebook) | ISBN
    9781786391018 (paperback : alk. paper) | ISBN 9781786391025 (hardback :
    alk. paper) | ISBN 9781786391032 (pdf) | ISBN 9781786391049 (ePub)
Subjects: LCSH: National parks and reserves--United States--Management--Case
    studies. | Outdoor recreation--United States--Management--Case studies.
Classification: LCC SB482.A4 M264 2017 (print) | LCC SB482.A4 (ebook) | DDC
    333.78/30973--dc23
LC record available at https://lccn.loc.gov/2016048783

ISBN-13: 978 1 78639 101 8 (pbk)
        978 1 78639 102 5 (hbk)

Commissioning editor: Claire Parfitt
Associate editor: Alexandra Lainsbury
Production editor: Tracy Head

Typeset by SPi, Pondicherry, India.
Printed and bound in the UK by CPI Group (UK) Ltd, Croydon CR0 4YY.

# Contents

Preface                                                                                    xiii

Acknowledgements                                                                            xv

PART I   MANAGING OUTDOOR RECREATION                                                        1

1   Parks and Outdoor Recreation                                                            3
    Conceptual Frameworks                                                                   3
        The dual mission of parks                                                           3
        Common property resources                                                           4
        Carrying capacity                                                                   4
        Limits of acceptable change                                                         5
        Indicators and standards of quality                                                 5
        Threefold framework of outdoor recreation                                           6
        Recreation opportunity spectrum                                                     7
    An Outdoor Recreation Management Framework                                              7
    Conclusion                                                                              8

2   Impacts of Outdoor Recreation                                                           9
    Impacts to Park Resources                                                               9
        Soil                                                                                9
        Vegetation                                                                         10
        Water                                                                              11
        Wildlife                                                                           11
        Air                                                                                12
        Natural quiet                                                                      12
        Natural darkness                                                                   13
        Historical/cultural resources                                                      13
    Impacts to the Visitor Experience                                                      13
        Crowding                                                                           13
        Conflict                                                                           14
        Depreciative behavior                                                              15
    Impacts to Facilities/Services                                                         15
        Attraction sites                                                                   15
        Trails                                                                             15
        Campgrounds/campsites                                                              15
        Roads/parking areas                                                                16
        Interpretive facilities/programs                                                   16
    Conclusion                                                                             17

3   Outdoor Recreation Management Practices                                                18
    Management Strategies                                                                  18
    Management Tactics or Practices                                                        20
    Classification of Problem Behaviors                                                    22

Theories of Moral Development    22
Communication Theory    23
Conclusion    24

**4   Evaluating Outdoor Recreation Management Practices**    25

Information and Education    25
   Recreation use patterns    25
   Enhancing visitor knowledge    26
   Influencing visitor attitudes    29
   Depreciative behavior    29
   Related studies    29
   Guidelines for using information and education    30
Use Rationing and Allocation    31
   Five management practices    31
   Fairness    34
   Effectiveness    35
   Pricing    36
   Acceptability    38
   Discrimination    38
   Differential pricing    39
   Principles of pricing    39
Rules and Regulations    39
Law Enforcement    41
Zoning    41
Facility Development, Site Design, and Maintenance    42
Conclusion    44

**5   Applying Outdoor Recreation Management**    45

Management Matrices    45
Observations on the Management Matrices and Appendices    48
Case Studies    51
Conclusion    51

**PART II   CASE STUDIES IN THE NATIONAL PARKS**    53

**6   Treading Lightly on Acadia**    55

Introduction    55
Acadia National Park    55
Managing Hiking in Acadia National Park    56
Further Reading    58

**7   Building a Better Campsite Along the Appalachian Trail**    59

Introduction    59
Appalachian National Scenic Trail    59
Managing Camping Along the Appalachian Trail    59
Further Reading    61

**8   Let There Be Light in Great Smoky Mountains**    62

Introduction    62
Great Smoky Mountains National Park    62
Managing the Viewing of Synchronous Fireflies    63
Further Reading    65

9   How Many Visitors is Too Many at Arches?                        66

    Introduction                                                    66
    Arches National Park                                            66
    Measuring and Managing Carrying Capacity                        67
    Further Reading                                                 69

10  Protecting Biscayne's Underwater Treasures                      71

    Introduction                                                    71
    Biscayne National Park                                          72
    Managing Recreational Boating at Biscayne                       72
    Further Reading                                                 74

11  Saving Bats at Mammoth Cave                                     75

    Introduction                                                    75
    Mammoth Cave National Park                                      76
    Managing WNS at Mammoth Cave                                    76
    Further Reading                                                 78

12  Turning Off the Lights at Chaco                                 79

    Introduction                                                    79
    Chaco Culture National Historical Park                          79
    Managing Natural Darkness above Chaco Canyon                    80
    Further Reading                                                 81

13  Busing Among the Grizzlies at Denali                           82

    Introduction                                                    82
    Denali National Park and Preserve                               82
    The Denali Park Road                                            83
    The Denali Park Wilderness                                      84
    Wildlife as a Park Indicator                                    85
    Further Reading                                                 85

14  Winning the Lottery on the Colorado River                      86

    Introduction                                                    86
    Colorado River Management Plan                                  87
    Intensive Use Demands Intensive Management                      89
    Further Reading                                                 89

15  The Ice Caves are Open, The Ice Caves are Open                  91

    Introduction                                                    91
    Apostle Islands National Lakeshore                              91
    Managing Ice Cave Visitation                                    92
    Further Reading                                                 93

16  The Sounds of Silence in Muir Woods                            95

    Introduction                                                    95
    Muir Woods National Monument                                    95
    Managing the Natural Quiet of Muir Woods                        96
    Further Reading                                                 97

17  Stewarding America's Antiquities at Mesa Verde                 99

    Introduction                                                    99
    Mesa Verde National Park                                        99

Managing Mesa Verde                                                              100
Further Reading                                                                  102

18  **What Goes Up Mt. Whitney Must Come Down**                                  **103**
Introduction                                                                     103
Sequoia National Park and the Inyo National Forest                               103
Managing Recreational Use on Mt. Whitney                                         104
Further Reading                                                                  105

19  **Preventing the Petrified Forest from Disappearing**                        **106**
Introduction                                                                     106
Petrified Forest National Park                                                   107
Managing (and Minimizing) Theft of Petrified Wood                                107
Further Reading                                                                  109

20  **Containing Contaminants at Carlsbad Caverns**                              **110**
Introduction                                                                     110
Carlsbad Caverns National Park                                                   110
Managing Contaminants at Carlsbad Caverns                                        111
Further Reading                                                                  113

21  **Bear Etiquette in Katmai**                                                 **114**
Introduction                                                                     114
Katmai National Park and Preserve                                                114
Managing Visitors and Bears at the Brooks River Area                             115
Further Reading                                                                  117

22  **Don't Pick Up Aquatic Hitchhikers in Voyageurs**                          **118**
Introduction                                                                     118
Voyageurs National Park                                                          118
Managing Voyageurs' Water Resources                                              118
Further Reading                                                                  121

23  **A Mountain with Handrails at Yosemite**                                    **122**
Introduction                                                                     122
Yosemite National Park and Half Dome                                             122
Studying and Managing Use of Half Dome                                           123
This Page is Intentionally Left Blank                                            125
Further Reading                                                                  126

24  **Doing the Zion Shuttle**                                                   **127**
Introduction                                                                     127
Zion National Park                                                               127
Managing Cars at Zion National Park                                              127
Further Reading                                                                  129

25  **The Buzz from Above at Grand Canyon**                                      **130**
Introduction                                                                     130
Managing Overflights in Grand Canyon National Park                               130
Further Reading                                                                  133

Contents

26  Managing Monuments and Memorials at the National Mall          **134**

  Introduction                                                      134
  National Mall and Memorial Parks                                  135
  Managing the National Mall                                        135
  Further Reading                                                   137

27  **Climbing Towards Common Ground at Devils Tower**              **138**

  Introduction                                                      138
  Devils Tower Climbing Management Plan                             139
  Fostering Mutual Respect at Bear Lodge                            140
  Further Reading                                                   141

28  **The Winter Wonderland of Yellowstone**                        **142**

  Introduction                                                      142
  Yellowstone National Park                                         144
  Managing Winter Visitation in Yellowstone                        144
  Further Reading                                                   145

29  **Alternative Transportation at Grand Teton**                   **146**

  Introduction                                                      146
  Grand Teton National Park                                         146
  Promoting Alternative Travel in Grand Teton                      147
  Further Reading                                                   149

30  **No Bad Trip in Glacier**                                      **150**

  Introduction                                                      150
  Glacier National Park                                             150
  Managing Backcountry Camping in Glacier                          151
  Further Reading                                                   153

**PART III   CONCLUSIONS**                                          **155**

31  **Lessons Learned**                                             **157**

  Principles of Managing Outdoor Recreation                         158
    Principle 1: Parks and related outdoor recreation areas must be managed in ways that provide
    outdoor recreation opportunities but also protect park resources and the quality of the
    visitor experience                                              158
    Principle 2: Outdoor recreation management should be guided by a
    management-by-objectives framework                              159
    Principle 3: Outdoor recreation management is an iterative, adaptive process   159
    Principle 4: Outdoor recreation should be managed within a threefold framework
    of concerns: resources, experiences, and management            160
    Principle 5: The Recreation Opportunity Spectrum should be used to help ensure
    diversity in outdoor recreation opportunities                   160
    Principle 6: Outdoor recreation can impact parks and related areas in many
    ways, including park resources, visitor experiences, and park facilities and services   160
    Principle 7: Outdoor recreation can be managed using four basic strategies   161
    Principle 8: Outdoor recreation can be managed using six basic categories
    of management tactics or practices                              162
    Principle 9: Outdoor recreation management problems can be addressed
    by more than one management strategy or practice                163

Principle 10: Outdoor recreation management strategies and practices can address
multiple problems                                                                              163
Principle 11: Outdoor recreation management practices can be used to advance more than
one management strategy                                                                        163
Principle 12: Outdoor recreation management strategies can be advanced by more than one
management practice                                                                            164
Principle 13: Where possible, a reinforcing program of outdoor recreation management
practices should be used                                                                       164
Principle 14: Managers should think systematically, comprehensively, and creatively about
the range of practices that might be used to manage outdoor recreation                         164
Principle 15: Outdoor recreation management practices should not be used simply because
they are familiar or administratively expedient                                                165
Principle 16: Potential unintended and undesirable consequences of outdoor recreation
management practices should be identified and avoided                                          165
Principle 17: Good information is needed to manage outdoor recreation effectively               165
Principle 18: Management of outdoor recreation should be as informed as possible by
understanding the cause of the impact or problem                                               166
Principle 19: Outdoor recreation management decisions should be considered within
the context of larger geographic scales                                                        166
Principle 20: Outdoor recreation management should focus on the impacts of recreation
use, not use itself                                                                            167
Principle 21: Limiting use is generally a last management option in outdoor recreation          167
Principle 22: Limiting or rationing outdoor recreation use requires consideration of how
limited opportunities for use will be allocated                                                167
Principle 23: Indirect outdoor recreation management practices are generally preferred
over direct management practices                                                               168
Principle 24: Intensive outdoor recreation use usually demands intensive management             168
Principle 25: When and where warranted, outdoor recreation management should be
designed to reach visitors before they arrive at parks and outdoor recreation areas            169
Principle 26: The list of outdoor recreation activities and other uses of parks that need
management consideration continues to evolve and expand                                        169
Principle 27: The list of park and outdoor recreation "resources" that need protection
continues to evolve and expand                                                                 169
Principle 28: Variations in outdoor recreation management practices continue to evolve
and expand                                                                                     170
Principle 29: Outdoor recreation management can impact the quality of the visitor
experience both positively and negatively                                                      170
Principle 30: Caution should be used when dispersing visitor use as an outdoor recreation
management practice                                                                            171
Principle 31: Partnerships between park and related outdoor recreation management
agencies and other groups and entities can be helpful in managing outdoor recreation           171
Principle 32: Responsibility for managing outdoor recreation should be shared jointly by
managers and researchers                                                                       171
Principle 33: Quality in outdoor recreation is most appropriately defined as the degree to
which recreation opportunities meet the objectives for which they are managed                  172
Principle 34: Management of outdoor recreation should be conducted proactively,
not reactively                                                                                 172
Principle 35: Managers must exercise their professional judgment in outdoor recreation
management                                                                                     173
Principle 36: A strong program of management is vital to maintaining the quality of parks
and outdoor recreation                                                                         173
Conclusion                                                                                     174

**APPENDIX A    MANAGEMENT PRACTICES**                                            175

Appendix A1    Management Practices for Limiting Use                              177

Appendix A2    Management Practices for Increasing Supply                         187

Appendix A3    Management Practices for Reducing the Impact of Use                193

Appendix A4    Management Practices for Hardening Resources and the Visitor Experience    203

**APPENDIX B    TEACHING AND MANAGEMENT TOOLS**                                   209

Bibliography                                                                      211

Index                                                                             227

This book is enhanced with supplementary resources. To access the teaching and management tools, please visit: http://www.cabi.org/openresources/91018

# Preface

Outdoor recreation continues to grow in popularity in the USA and around the world. Perhaps this is best manifested in the more than 300 million annual visits to the US national parks. While we should celebrate this popular interest in parks and related areas, it also presents the challenging and increasingly urgent issue of how to manage outdoor recreation in ways that protect the integrity of park resources and the quality of the visitor experience. These can be affected in many ways, and it is imperative that impacts be minimized. While parks are established to provide opportunities for outdoor recreation, they must also be protected. Again, the US national parks offer a quintessential example; the 1916 Organic Act creating the US National Park Service dictates that national parks are to be managed "in such manner and such means as will leave them unimpaired for the enjoyment of future generations."

This book addresses the issue of managing outdoor recreation to protect park resources and the quality of the visitor experience. The book is organized into three parts. Part I comprises five chapters that draw on the scientific and professional literature in parks and outdoor recreation to develop a systematic and creative approach to outdoor recreation management. Chapter 1 reviews several conceptual frameworks that can be used to understand the challenges in managing outdoor recreation and to organize thinking about managing outdoor recreation. Chapter 2 identifies and reviews the potential impacts that outdoor recreation can have on park resources, the quality of the visitor experience, and park facilities and services. Chapter 3 outlines the strategies and practices that can be used to manage outdoor recreation, while Chapter 4 assesses the efficacy of a range of management practices. Chapter 5 organizes the information presented in the previous chapters into a series of matrices that can be used to guide a systematic and creative program of outdoor recreation management. The matrices are further elaborated in Appendices A1 through A4.

Part II of the book presents a series of 25 case studies in managing outdoor recreation in the US national parks. The US national park system offers a rich source of successful examples of the application of the range of management practices described in Part I. This system of parks offers the oldest, what may be the most diverse, and one of the largest systems of national parks in the world. National parks in the United States range from urban to rural to wild, span the geography of the country, include natural and cultural resources, and are heavily used by the American people and the international community. The US National Park Service is widely recognized as having a long history and well-developed expertise in successfully managing parks to protect the integrity of natural and cultural resources and the quality of the visitor experience.

But until now, there has been little systematic information on the management practices that have been successful in the national parks—information that can be especially useful to park and outdoor recreation planners, managers, scholars, and students. The 25 case studies presented in Part II span a considerable range of outdoor recreation-related problems and management practices, and a wide spectrum of national parks.

Part III consists of a single chapter designed to extract an emerging set of principles that can be used to guide management of outdoor recreation. These principles draw on both the scientific and professional literature reviewed in Part I and are illustrated with examples from the case studies presented in Part II. These principles are offered to help guide outdoor recreation management in national parks and related areas in the United States and elsewhere.

As we state in the conclusion to Part III, this book is designed to be both helpful and hopeful. While the challenges of managing outdoor recreation are real and urgent, a considerable body of knowledge has been developed to help meet them. Outdoor recreation should be managed by design, not by default. We've prepared this book to guide a proactive management process and program by reviewing the relevant scientific and professional literature on outdoor recreation, constructing a series of matrices that can help organize and stimulate thinking about the range of management strategies and practices, developing a series of 25 case studies of effective management of outdoor recreation in the US national parks, and offering a series of principles that can help guide outdoor recreation management. We trust the information developed and presented in this book can be helpful in managing outdoor recreation and are hopeful about the future of parks and outdoor recreation.

# Acknowledgements

We are grateful to a number of people for their contributions in preparing this book. Michael Rees, Natural Resource Specialist for the National Park Service, arranged meetings with planners at the agency's Denver Service Center and this helped identify good case studies for inclusion in the book. Staff at several units of the US national park system provided information for these case studies and we appreciate this assistance. University of Vermont Park Studies Laboratory staff member William Valliere prepared the book's figures and tables and—along with Graduate Research Assistants Nathan Reigner, Ellen Rovelstad, Vinson Pierce, and Xiao Xiao—helped conduct searches for further reading materials for the case study chapters. Undergraduate student Kai Parker helped prepare the book's references. Staff member Marcie Newland helped prepare the manuscript for submission. We thank CABI editors and staff members Claire Parfitt, Alex Lainsbury and Tracy Head for guiding the manuscript through the publication process, and Anne Wilson for preparing an interactive version of the management matrices.

# Part I Managing Outdoor Recreation

# 1 Parks and Outdoor Recreation

Parks and outdoor recreation are becoming increasingly important in contemporary society. Parks are vital to people in many ways: they offer open, green spaces in our ever-developing world; they're retreats from the hectic lives that many of us lead; and they protect wildlife and other elements of the natural environment, as well as historical and cultural resources that are important markers of society. And, of course, outdoor recreation is also important, offering healthy and satisfying leisure activity; intimate contact with the out-of-doors; opportunities to build family solidarity; enjoyment and appreciation of our natural environment and cultural heritage; and a myriad of other benefits.

National parks may offer the clearest manifestation of the importance of parks and outdoor recreation. Yellowstone National Park, established in 1872, was the first national park in the USA and in the world, the first time a society set aside a large portion of its land for the enjoyment and appreciation of all the people (Runte, 2010; Nash, 2014). American historian and conservationist Wallace Stegner famously called national parks "the best idea we ever had." Now the US national park system includes more than 400 areas across the country: large "crown jewel" parks like Yellowstone, Yosemite, and Grand Canyon, as well as many smaller, historical, and cultural sites such as the Statue of Liberty, Independence Hall, and the birthplace of Martin Luther King, Jr. The US national park system receives more than 300 million visits each year, representing people who come to use, enjoy, and appreciate these places.

## Conceptual Frameworks

Given the importance of parks and outdoor recreation, we should think carefully about how to manage these places and activities. While parks and outdoor recreation are intimately connected, too much recreation or inappropriate recreation activities can threaten the integrity of parks and can degrade the quality of the recreation experience. How can we provide for recreational use of parks and related areas without threatening the natural and cultural resources they were created to protect? And how can we provide opportunities for outdoor recreation that are high in quality and that meet the diverse demands of society? This book answers these questions by identifying, organizing, and illustrating a wide range of park and outdoor recreation management strategies and practices. But before we consider these management strategies and practices, let's examine several conceptual frameworks that can help organize and sharpen our critical thinking.

## The dual mission of parks

Parks are established for two, often competing, purposes: to protect important natural and cultural resources and to offer opportunities for the public to use and enjoy these areas. When parks are used for outdoor recreation, vital natural and cultural resources can be impacted and degraded. Again, the US national parks are a quintessential example of this dual mission. Even though Yellowstone National Park was established in 1872, the National Park Service (the agency charged with managing the national parks) wasn't created by Congress until 1916. In a classic phrase, the legislation creating the National Park Service states that the national parks are to be managed ". . . to conserve the scenery and the natural and historic objects and the wildlife therein and to provide for the enjoyment of the same in such manner and by such means as will leave them unimpaired for the enjoyment of future generations" (US Code, Title 16, sec. 1).

Clearly, national parks are to be used for public enjoyment, but they're also to be conserved. This dual mission creates a fundamental tension: how much and what kinds of use can be accommodated before parks are "impaired"? How can parks be managed for outdoor recreation while conserving them for future generations? Park and outdoor recreation managers must be sensitive to these issues and find ways to manage parks and outdoor recreation that balance the tension inherent in the dual mission of parks—preservation and use.

## Common property resources

Some years ago, a paper entitled "The Tragedy of the Commons" was published in the prestigious journal *Science* (Hardin, 1968). Now a foundational piece of the environmental literature, this paper identified a set of environmental problems—issues of the "commons"—that have no technical solutions but must be resolved through public policy and associated management action. Hardin's ultimate prescription for managing the commons was through "mutual coercion, mutually agreed upon": without such collective action, environmental (and related social) tragedy is inevitable.

Hardin began his paper with an illustration using perhaps the oldest and simplest example of an environmental commons, a shared pasture:

> Picture a pasture open to all. It is expected that each herdsman will try to keep as many cattle as possible on [this] commons . . . What is the utility of adding one more animal?. . . Since the herdsman receives all the proceeds from the sale of the additional animal, the positive utility [to the herdsman] is nearly +1 . . . Since, however, the effects of overgrazing are shared by all herdsmen, the negative utility for any particular . . . herdsman is only a fraction of –1. Adding together the . . . partial utilities, the rational herdsman concludes that the only sensible course for him to pursue is to add another animal to [the] herd. And another; and another . . . Therein is the tragedy. Each man is locked into a system that [causes] him to increase his herd without limit – in a world that is limited . . . Freedom in commons brings ruin to all.
> (p. 1244)

Hardin went on to identify and explore other examples of environmental commons—the atmosphere, the oceans, and ultimately human population growth. However, one of his examples of the tragedy of the commons—one that resonates more urgently each year—is national parks:

> The National Parks present another instance of the working out of the tragedy of the commons. At present, they are open to all without limit. The parks themselves are limited in extent – there is only one Yosemite Valley – whereas population seems to grow without limit. The values that visitors seek in parks are steadily eroded. Plainly, we must soon cease to treat the parks as commons or they will be of no value to anyone.
> (p. 1245)

Management of parks and outdoor recreation represents "mutual coercion, mutually agreed upon" that Hardin suggests is needed to protect parks and the quality of the recreation experience. While these forms of coercion—for example, restricting the amount and type of recreation—may be distasteful because they limit freedom of choice, they are ultimately needed to protect parks and the greater welfare of society. Toward the end of his paper, Hardin suggests that "Freedom is the recognition of necessity" (which he attributes to the philosopher Hegel); only by instituting the mechanisms that will ensure our ultimate well-being will we be truly free to pursue our higher aspirations, both as individuals and as a society. Management of parks and outdoor recreation must include consideration of "mutual coercion, mutually agreed upon" when and where needed.

## Carrying capacity

The term "carrying capacity" has been an important part of natural resources and environmental management for decades. Its emergence can be traced back to a publication entitled *An Essay on the Principle of Population* (Malthus, 1798). This essay reasoned that human population tends to grow at an exponential rate, but that the production of food and other necessary resources grows only arithmetically. In this way, the supply of food and other vital resources presents an ultimate limit to population growth, and if this limit is not respected, the carrying capacity of the earth (or selected geographic regions) will be exceeded, causing what Malthus termed human "vice and misery" and related "positive checks" on human population. Malthus's ideas about carrying capacity and the limits of the earth to support human population growth have become foundational concepts of the contemporary environmental movement. Popular books such as *The Population Bomb* (Ehrlich, 1968), *The Limits to Growth* (Meadows *et al.*, 1972), and *How Many People Can the Earth Support?* (Cohen, 1995) are important examples of this idea.

Scientific applications of carrying capacity were first applied in the fields of fisheries, wildlife, and range management (Hadwen and Palmer, 1922;

Leopold, 1934; Odum, 1953). For example, how many animals can ultimately be supported by a given area of range? Carrying capacity was first applied to parks and outdoor recreation in the 1960s (Wagar, 1964; Lucas, 1964). The initial focus was on the environmental impacts of outdoor recreation: how much use can be accommodated in a park before the area's natural resources are unacceptably impaired? However, it quickly became apparent that there is also a social or experiential component to carrying capacity in the context of parks and outdoor recreation; how much use can be accommodated in a park before the quality of the visitor experience is degraded to an unacceptable degree?

Carrying capacity, or "visitor capacity" as it is sometimes called, has remained an important but challenging issue in the field of parks and outdoor recreation (Graefe *et al.*, 1984; Shelby and Heberlein, 1986; Stankey and Manning, 1986; Manning, 2007, 2011; Whittaker *et al.*, 2011). What is the ultimate capacity of parks for outdoor recreation? How can outdoor recreation be managed to ensure that it does not exceed a park's carrying capacity? These are important questions that must inform park and outdoor recreation management.

## Limits of acceptable change

Research on the application of carrying capacity to parks and outdoor recreation has documented a number of impacts of recreation on park resources and the quality of the visitor experience. For example, park visitors may trample fragile soils and vegetation, and disturb wildlife. And as the number of visitors increases, parks may become crowded. (Impacts of outdoor recreation are described more fully in Chapter 2.) With increasing use of parks comes increasing environmental and social impacts, and at some point these impacts may become unacceptable. But what determines the limits of acceptable change?

This issue is illustrated graphically in Fig. 1.1. This figure illustrates that increasing amounts of recreation result in increasing environmental and social impact (e.g. trampling of soils and vegetation, crowding, the need for more intensive management). As the amount of recreation use increases from X1 to X2, the amount of impact increases from Y1 to Y2. However, the limits of acceptable change are not clear from this relationship; which of the points on the vertical axis—Y1 or Y2, or

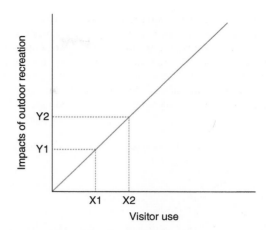

**Fig. 1.1.** The limits of acceptable change.

some other point along this axis—represents the maximum acceptable level of impact? Determining the limits of acceptable change is central to addressing the carrying capacity of parks for outdoor recreation.

To emphasize and further clarify the limits of acceptable change and their relationship to carrying capacity, some studies have suggested distinguishing between the descriptive and prescriptive components of carrying capacity (Shelby and Heberlein, 1984, 1986; Manning 2007, 2011). The descriptive component of carrying capacity focuses on factual, objective data such as the relationships in Fig. 1.1. For example, what is the relationship between the amount of visitor use and perceived crowding? The prescriptive component of carrying capacity addresses the seemingly more subjective issue of how much impact or change is acceptable. For example, what level of perceived crowding should be allowed? Determining acceptable levels of change must form a foundation for park and outdoor recreation management.

## Indicators and standards of quality

Determining acceptable levels of change in parks and outdoor recreation is based largely on management objectives and associated indicators and standards of quality. Management objectives are statements about the desired conditions of parks and outdoor recreation, including the level of protection of park resources and the type and quality of the recreation experience. Indicators of quality are more specific, measurable variables that reflect the meaning or essence of management objectives; they are quantifiable proxies or measures of management objectives. Standards of quality define the minimum acceptable condition of indicator variables.

An example may help to illuminate these ideas and terms. The US Wilderness Act of 1964 specifies that areas designated by Congress as part of the National Wilderness Preservation System are to be managed to provide opportunities for visitor "solitude" (16 US Code 1131–1136). Therefore, providing opportunities for solitude is an appropriate management objective for most wilderness areas. However, solitude is a somewhat abstract concept that is difficult to measure directly. Research on wilderness use suggests that the number of other visitors encountered along trails and at campsites is important to wilderness visitors in defining solitude (Manning, 2011). Thus, encounters with other groups of visitors along trails and at campsites is a potentially good indicator variable because it is measurable, manageable, and can serve as a reasonable proxy for the management objective of wilderness solitude. Research also suggests that wilderness visitors may have normative standards about how many trail and campsite encounters can be experienced before opportunities for solitude decline to an unacceptable degree. For example, a number of studies suggest that wilderness visitors generally find no more than five groups per day encountered along trails to be acceptable and wish to camp out of sight and sound of other groups (Manning, 2011). Therefore, a maximum of five encounters with other groups along trails and no other groups camped within sight or sound may be good standards of quality for managing at least some wilderness areas. Formulating management objectives and expressing them in the terms of quantitative indicators and standards of quality is an important part of managing outdoor recreation.

### Threefold framework of outdoor recreation

Research and practice in the field of parks and outdoor recreation has evolved from an initial orientation toward resource considerations to include a more comprehensive approach that recognizes a threefold framework of concerns. For example, early work on the concept of carrying capacity sought to apply this concept exclusively as it concerns the environmental impacts of outdoor recreation, but quickly expanded to include an experiential component as well. In the preface of his early and influential monograph on carrying capacity, Wagar (1964) wrote:

> The study reported here was initiated with the view that the carrying capacity of recreation lands could be determined primarily in terms of ecology and the deterioration of areas. However, it soon became obvious that the resource-oriented point of view must be augmented by consideration of human values.

Wagar's point was that as more people visit a park or related outdoor recreation area, the quality of the recreation experience is affected as well as the area's environmental resources. The effects of increasing use on recreation quality were illustrated by means of hypothetical relationships between increasing use level and visitor satisfaction.

Wagar's monograph hinted at a third element of park and outdoor recreation management, and this was described more explicitly in a subsequent paper (Wagar, 1968). Noting a number of misconceptions about carrying capacity, it was suggested that carrying capacity might vary according to the amount and type of management. For example, the durability of park resources might be increased through management practices such as fertilizing and irrigating vegetation, and periodic rest and rotation of impact sites. Similarly, the quality of the recreation experience might be maintained or even enhanced in the face of increasing use by means of more even distribution of visitors, appropriate rules and regulations, provision of additional visitor facilities, and educational programs designed to encourage desirable behavior.

Thus, parks and outdoor recreation can be best understood as including three principal components: resources (e.g. soils, vegetation, water, wildlife), experiences (e.g. crowding, conflict), and management (e.g. visitor education, rules and regulations) as shown in Fig. 1.2. Moreover, there are potentially important interactions among the components of this threefold framework. For example, impacts to park resources can affect the quality of the recreation experience, as can the type and level of management. Informed management of parks and outdoor recreation must take into account all components of the threefold framework and the potential interactions among them.

## Recreation opportunity spectrum

The Recreation Opportunity Spectrum (ROS) is a framework to help ensure diversity in parks and outdoor recreation (Driver and Brown, 1978; Brown *et al.*, 1978, 1979; Clark and Stankey, 1979). ROS applies indicators and standards of quality to each of the three components of parks and outdoor recreation—resources, experiences, and management—to illustrate a broad range of recreation opportunities.

Figure 1.3 illustrates a simplified example of ROS. In this example, the presence of wildlife represents the resource component of outdoor recreation and can range from wild to domesticated. Similarly, solitude represents the experiential component of outdoor recreation and this can range from low to high levels. Facility development represents the managerial component of outdoor recreation and this can range from no development to highly developed facilities. These ranges of conditions can be combined into a spectrum of park and outdoor recreation opportunities from wilderness to urban. This structured approach can be used by managers to help ensure

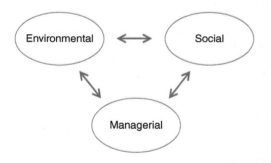

**Fig. 1.2.** The threefold framework of outdoor recreation.

that park and outdoor recreation opportunities meet the diverse demands of society.

## An Outdoor Recreation Management Framework

The conceptual frameworks outlined above have contributed to a management-by-objectives framework that can be used to guide management of parks and outdoor recreation. This approach relies on a series of three primary steps as shown in Fig. 1.4:

**1.** Management objectives and associated indicators and standards of quality are formulated for a park or site within a park. As noted above, management objectives describe desired conditions—the level of resource protection, the type and quality of recreation experiences, and the type and intensity of management—and indicators and standards of quality define these objectives in quantitative, measurable form.
**2.** Indicators of quality are monitored to see if standards of quality are being maintained.
**3.** If standards of quality are violated, then management action is required.

This management framework takes somewhat different forms in alternative contexts. For example, the US Forest Service has conventionally used a framework called Limits of Acceptable Change (LAC) (Stankey *et al.*, 1985), while the US National Park Service developed a framework called Visitor Experience and Resource Protection (VERP) (National Park Service, 1997; Manning, 2001). The VERP framework was ultimately incorporated into the agency's more comprehensive and foundational national park planning process. More recently, an interagency group of park and outdoor recreation managers from six federal outdoor recreation

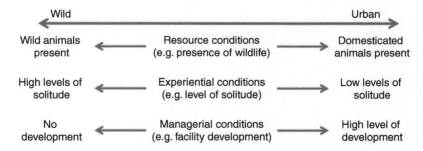

**Fig. 1.3.** A simplified example of the Recreation Opportunity Spectrum (ROS).

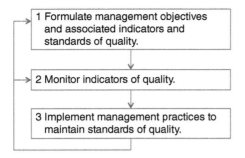

**Fig. 1.4.** An outdoor recreation management framework.

management agencies that includes the US Forest Service and the US National Park Service has developed a common outdoor recreation planning and management framework called Visitor Use Management that incorporates the foundational elements of both VERP and LAC (Interagency Visitor Use Management Council, 2016). While there are some differences in terminology and sequencing of steps, these and related frameworks rely on the three basic steps described above (Manning, 2004). This management framework represents a long-term commitment to management that requires maintaining standards of quality, periodic monitoring of indicators of quality, and reconsideration of management practices based on monitoring data. When circumstances warrant, for example when a management plan has reached the end of its useful life and needs to be revised, management objectives and associated indicators and standards of quality can be reconsidered.

This framework represents a form of "adaptive management" that is in keeping with contemporary environmental management more broadly (Lee, 1993; Stankey *et al.*, 2005). That is, a program of management is implemented based on the best information available, but new information is gathered in an ongoing program of monitoring and research, and management practices are revised in keeping with this new information.

This management framework is built on the concepts outlined in this chapter. It uses management objectives and associated indicators and standards

of quality as quantitative expressions of the limits of acceptable change. These limits of acceptable change define the carrying capacity of parks and related areas, and address the inherent tension between recreational use of parks and protection of park resources and the quality of the visitor experience. The framework requires management actions—"mutual coercion, mutually agreed upon"—as demanded in the context of common property resources. Management objectives and associated indicators and standards of quality can and should be considered for all three of the components of outdoor recreation—the resource, experiential, and management environments—and the configurations of these conditions can and probably should be varied to offer a broad range of park and outdoor recreation opportunities as suggested by ROS.

## Conclusion

The concepts introduced in this chapter suggest the need for a strong and thoughtful program of managing outdoor recreation. Moreover, the importance of managing parks and outdoor recreation plays a central role in the management framework outlined above. Management is required to ensure that standards of quality are maintained and management objectives accomplished. Monitoring of indicators of quality provides a vital test of the effectiveness of management practices; when monitoring of indicator variables finds that standards of quality are in danger of being violated, then changes in management or adoption of new management practices are needed.

Given the importance of management, what can park and outdoor recreation managers do to protect park resources and the quality of the recreation experience? That's what the rest of this book is about. The remaining chapters in Part I describe the potential impacts of outdoor recreation, outline a series of management actions and their potential effectiveness, and then organize these problems and potential solutions into a series of matrices that support an integrated, comprehensive, and thoughtful approach to park and outdoor recreation management.

# 2 Impacts of Outdoor Recreation

Individually, visitors to parks and outdoor recreation areas typically have relatively little impact—they may wander off a maintained trail and on to fragile vegetation, unknowingly disturb wildlife, accidently drop litter, compete with other visitors for limited parking, and unavoidably contribute to a sense of crowding at park attraction sites and campgrounds. These impacts are usually small at the level of the individual visitor. But when this is multiplied by millions of visitors over the course of a year, and the years accumulate into decades, these impacts can become substantive and threaten the integrity of park resources and the quality of the visitor experience. Park managers have become concerned about a wide array of impacts that can be caused by outdoor recreation, and research has begun to document and better understand many of these issues.

Impacts of outdoor recreation fall into three broad categories. First, recreational use can impact park resources: soils, vegetation, water, wildlife, and air are the traditional concerns. More recently, natural quiet and natural darkness are gaining recognition as important park resources that are also threatened and need management attention. And most parks include important historical and cultural resources that can be damaged by too much or inappropriate visitor use. All of these resources must be managed and protected. Second, the quality of the visitor experience may be degraded by too much use or inappropriate use. Of course, the visitor experience may be directly impacted by the aesthetic implications of the resource impacts outlined above, but experiential impacts may also include crowding, conflict among visitors, and depreciative behavior such as littering and vandalism. Third, park facilities and services, including attraction sites, trails, campgrounds, roads and parking lots, and interpretive facilities and programs, may be impacted by outdoor recreation. These are the places and programs in parks that visitors use most intensively, and where the resource

and experiential impacts outlined above are most likely to occur.

## Impacts to Park Resources

Visitor-caused trampling, noise, and pollution can lead to degradation of a park's natural and cultural resources. For example, vegetation can be irreparably harmed under the feet of many hikers. In some settings, even relatively low levels of use can cause significant degradation (Marion and Reid, 2001). Table 2.1 outlines some of the impacts to soil, vegetation, wildlife, and water that can be caused directly or indirectly by outdoor recreation. Noticeable resource impacts can degrade the quality of outdoor recreation for visitors who have come to experience a natural, unimpaired setting. The professional field of "recreation ecology" has emerged to understand the resource-related impacts of outdoor recreation (Leung and Marion, 2000). Most recreation ecology research has been conducted on soils and vegetation (Monz *et al.*, 2010), but water, wildlife, air and other park resources, including natural quiet, natural darkness, and historical and cultural resources, are receiving increasing attention.

### Soil

Providing support for the earth's plant and animal life, soils are complex systems of living organisms, mineral particles, air, water, and light (Hammitt *et al.*, 2015). Pore spaces between soil rock particles allow for the movement of air and water. When soils are trampled, either from human boots, pack animals (such as horses or mules), or recreational vehicles (such as off-road vehicles and mountain bikes), the space between these pores is reduced and soil compaction occurs (Anderson *et al.*, 1998; Leung and Marion, 2000). Low levels of recreation use lead to soil compaction (Hammitt *et al.*, 2015). Dense, compacted soils are less able to absorb

**Table 2.1.** Common types of outdoor recreation-related impacts. (From Leung and Marion, 2000.)

| | Ecological component | | | |
|---|---|---|---|---|
| | Soil | Vegetation | Wildlife | Water |
| Direct effects | Soil compaction | Reduced height and vigor | Habitat alteration | Introduction of exotic species |
| | Loss of organic litter | Loss of ground vegetation cover | Loss of habitats | Increased turbidity |
| | Loss of mineral soil | Loss of fragile species | Introduction of exotic species | Increased nutrient inputs |
| | | Loss of trees and shrubs | Wildlife harassment | Increased levels of pathogenic bacteria |
| | | Tree trunk damage | Modification of wildlife behavior | Altered water quality |
| | | Introduction of exotic species | Displacement from food, water, and shelter | |
| Indirect/derivative effects | Reduced soil moisture | Composition change | Reduced health and fitness | Reduced health of aquatic ecosystems |
| | Reduced soil pore space | Altered microclimate | Reduced reproduction rates | Composition change |
| | Accelerated soil erosion | Accelerated soil erosion | Increased mortality | Excessive algal growth |
| | Altered soil microbial activities | | Composition change | |

water, leading to muddiness, runoff, susceptibility to wind, and erosion (Manning, 1979). Once soils have begun to erode, recovery is difficult even if recreational impacts are removed. Erosion is more pronounced at sites vulnerable to the forces of water and wind. These include: steep slopes, places lacking vegetation cover, and areas with shallow soils (Hammitt *et al.*, 2015). Even less severe impacts to soil, such as loss of the upper litter layer, can lead to a change in the microorganisms that live in the soil and loss of soil fertility (Leung and Marion, 2000). Beyond trampling, soils can be damaged when campers remove large pieces of wood from the ground for fires. Such logs support fungi that allow plants to absorb water and nutrients from the soil. Moreover, extreme heat from camp fires can sterilize the surrounding soils. Soil impacts vary based on recreation activity, soil type, and site factors (Hammitt *et al.*, 2015).

## Vegetation

Recreation activities that impact soils can also impact vegetation, and these two resources are

interrelated as illustrated in Fig. 2.1 (Manning, 1979). Like soils, ground cover vegetation can be damaged or destroyed by trampling. Plants that are damaged from trampling may have less leaf area for photosynthesis, reducing their vigor and ability to reproduce. When soils beneath plants are compacted, plant roots are less able to spread throughout the soil to take in water and nutrients. Likewise, plant seeds may not have enough moisture to incubate in compacted soils (Hammitt *et al.*, 2015). In turn, when plants are destroyed by trampling, exposed soils are left behind that are more likely to erode (Leung and Marion, 2000). Recreationists can damage larger vegetation—shrubs and trees—by using off-road vehicles, driving nails in tree trunks to hang lanterns, peeling bark off trees for kindling, and removing limbs or chopping trees down for firewood or tent poles (Hammitt *et al.*, 2015). Recreationists may also bring invasive plants with them on hiking boots, off-road vehicles, boats, or fishing equipment. Since some plants are more sensitive to these impacts, recreational use can change the composition of plants in an area (Leung and Marion, 2000). As with soil compaction,

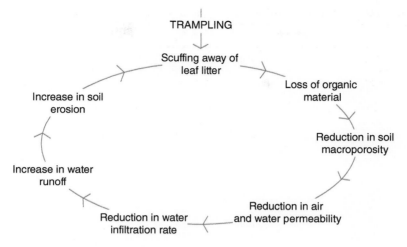

TRAMPLING

Scuffing away of leaf litter

Loss of organic material

Reduction in soil macroporosity

Reduction in air and water permeability

Reduction in water infiltration rate

Increase in water runoff

Increase in soil erosion

**Fig. 2.1.** Soil impact cycle. (From Manning, 1979.)

vegetation cover loss is often seen even at low levels of recreation use (Hammitt *et al.*, 2015). Several recreation ecology studies have noted an asymptotic, curvilinear relationship between recreation use and vegetation impacts. At a new or low-use site, substantial vegetation impacts occur with small increases in use. At moderate-to-high use levels, there is relatively less additional impact from increases in use. Recently, there has been a call to examine other use–impact relationships for vegetation and other resources (Monz *et al.*, 2013).

### Water

Recreation can have a number of effects on water quality and the health of both humans and aquatic ecosystems (Hammitt *et al.*, 2015). Water can be directly impacted when bottles, cans, or other trash are left behind by recreational boaters. Leaked oil from motor boats can damage plankton, plants, and algae, reducing the amount of oxygen in the water, and disrupting the food chain. Likewise, exotic species can be directly introduced through improperly cleaned boats or fishing gear (Leung and Marion, 2000). Water may become muddy or unclear as people disturb sediments through swimming, boating, or wading, or when stream banks erode as a result of trampling (Hammitt *et al.*, 2015). When lakes, ponds, and streams have a high turbidity (many suspended sediments), less light is able to reach aquatic plants and animals, reducing their ability to photosynthesize or to see. Depending

upon location and level of use, camping can also be a source of water pollution, including bacteria from human waste, soap residue, other chemicals, and leftover food (Anderson *et al.*, 1998; Hammitt *et al.*, 2015). Bacterial contamination from humans and other animals is a concern for backcountry visitors relying on natural sources for drinking water and for recreationists who come into direct contact with water (e.g. swimmers). Evidence suggests that wildlife, more often than humans, are the source of bacterial contamination (Hammitt *et al.*, 2015).

### Wildlife

Recreationists can disturb wildlife directly by hunting or harassing animals, or indirectly by modifying wildlife habitat (Hammitt *et al.*, 2015). An outline of many of these impacts is shown in Fig. 2.2. Impacts to wildlife include reduced health and fitness, displacement, lower ability to reproduce, higher death rates, and changes in species composition (Leung and Marion, 2000). However, understanding recreational impacts to wildlife is challenging. Different species have different responses to human activities. Some animals, including bears, deer, and rodents, are attracted to human food, becoming habituated to people when park visitors either intentionally feed animals or improperly store food. Other animals, including shorebirds, eagles, and bighorn sheep, may be easily disturbed by human presence, resulting in

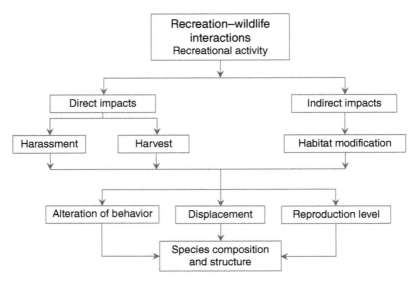

**Fig. 2.2.** Potential impacts of outdoor recreation on wildlife. (Adapted from Hammitt *et al.*, 2015.)

abandonment of nests or home range habitat (Hammitt *et al.*, 2015). Moreover, wildlife disturbance varies by type of recreation activity, and where, when, and how often the activity occurs (Steidl and Powell, 2006). Animals may be especially vulnerable to disturbance during the breeding season, during migration, or in winter, using valuable energy to flee from humans. Stress may be caused when birders or wildlife watchers approach too closely. Alternatively, wildlife may not be able to access important sources of food and water when people camp in these areas. Animals can be directly killed through hunting or fishing (Anderson *et al.*, 1998). By harvesting certain species, hunters and anglers may reduce the amount of food available to other wildlife. In addition, recreation activities can lead to changes in, or loss of, wildlife habitat (Leung and Marion, 2000). For example, removing shrubs to create camping areas may reduce the amount of bird habitat. Compacted soils at campsites or along trails can remove habitat for burrowing animals, or lead to the collapse of established tunnels. Sedimentation of streams and lakes from swimming, wading, and shoreline trampling, may impact fish. Park roads and traffic may cause large mammals to change how they move through a park and where they feed, and vehicles can injure or kill animals through collisions (Hammitt *et al.*, 2015).

### Air

Impacts to vegetation, soil, water, and wildlife can be exacerbated when national parks experience poor air quality. Pollutants carried in the air—including sulfur dioxide, nitrogen oxides, volatile organic compounds, and particulate matter—can damage vegetation, lead to the acidification of streams and lakes, and accumulate in soils (NPS Air Resources, 2016). In turn, wildlife may be negatively impacted by these damaged habitats or by directly breathing, ingesting, or (in the case of frogs and other amphibians) absorbing air pollutants. Likewise, pollution can degrade visitor experiences by reducing visibility, masking the night sky, and causing discomfort to people with respiratory problems. While most air pollution in national parks comes from external sources (e.g. power plants, factories, and city traffic), localized impacts can also result from outdoor recreation. Emissions from automobiles, snowmobiles, and idling tour buses can all contribute to reduced air quality. Additionally, visitor-caused wildfires can be a significant source of pollutants. To a lesser extent, and under certain conditions, pollution from campfires can also have an effect. The National Park Service monitors air quality through its Air Resources Division.

### Natural quiet

In recent years, "natural quiet"—the sounds of nature—has been recognized as another important resource to be protected (Park Science, 2009–2010; NPS Natural Sounds, 2016). Many visitors come to parks expecting to hear running water, birds, wildlife, rustling leaves, and other natural sounds. Natural quiet is also essential to wildlife, which use sound to communicate, navigate, attract mates, avoid predators, locate prey, establish territory, and protect young. Natural quiet can be disrupted through the accumulated noise of many visitors, who may talk loudly or bring with them noise-making technology, such as cell phones, music players, cameras, or car alarms. Visitor transportation, including private automobiles, motorcycles, snowmobiles, motorized boats; and bus, helicopter, airplane, and snowcoach tours, is another source of noise that may intrude on natural quiet. Park operations also introduce unnatural sounds, and include generators, motorized trail maintenance equipment, and park vehicles. Human-caused noise in the natural environment can prevent visitors from fully appreciating parks, including natural sounds. Likewise, wildlife may change behavior and experience increased stress in response to noise. Beyond the natural environment, the National Park Service is also concerned about impacts to cultural and historical soundscapes. Modern sounds (such as ringing cell phones) may interfere with traditional music, historical re-enactments, and historical farming sounds at cultural and historical sites.

### Natural darkness

Another resource that has received increased attention by the National Park Service in recent years is natural darkness (NPS Night Skies, 2016). National parks are some of the last refuges of an unpolluted night sky. Nocturnal animals depend on darkness to hunt, navigate, reproduce, and hide from predators, and many visitors appreciate seeing and experiencing the celestial world as our ancestors did. Impacts to the night sky come mostly from light pollution caused by excessive or poorly designed outdoor lighting (i.e. light that is not directed downward through shielding). Excessive or poorly designed lighting may exist at park facilities, but light from cities as far away as 200 miles can also impact the night sky within parks. In addition, visitors can impact natural darkness by carrying flashlights, building campfires, or by driving at night. While individual sources of light may not cause widespread pollution of the night sky, they can still confuse wildlife and reduce feelings of solitude

among visitors. Air pollution, caused by vehicles within parks and outside sources, can also impact the quality of the night sky. Recent research suggests that amount of light pollution is an important indicator of visitor experience in national parks (Manning *et al.*, 2015).

### Historical/cultural resources

In addition to protecting and managing the natural environment, the National Park Service is responsible for historical, cultural, and archeological sites. Many units of the national park system are historical and cultural sites. Like the natural environment, historical and cultural resources can be damaged through too much or inappropriate visitor use. In many cases, impacts are the result of accumulated wear and tear. Over time, artifacts can be damaged by visitors walking off designated trails and touching, climbing on, or leaning on historical or cultural items. Oils from human skin can damage cultural artifacts, including ancient rock paintings and carvings. Campfires built too close to archeological sites and food consumed near these sites can leave smoke stains and attract rodents. In some cases, visitors may intentionally behave in ways that damage historical/cultural sites. Artifacts may be taken, historical structures defaced through graffiti or carvings, and ancient rock carvings damaged by visitors who take a rubbing of the image (NPS Archaeology Program, 2016).

## Impacts to the Visitor Experience

Much as the field of recreation ecology has emerged to better understand recreational impacts to natural and cultural resources in parks, social science research has examined a number of experiential impacts that can occur in park settings. Many studies of visitors to national parks and related areas have helped to develop an emerging body of knowledge about visitor activities, motivations, and experiences, and how expanding visitor use can affect the quality of the visitor experience (Manning, 2011). Three important issues that can influence the quality of visitor experiences are crowding, conflict, and depreciative behavior.

### Crowding

Crowding in parks and other outdoor recreation areas has long been a concern of managers and researchers. Crowding is a subjective, negative

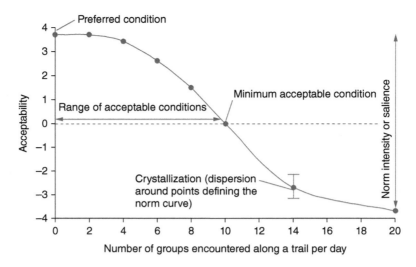

**Fig. 2.3.** A social norm curve showing aggregate evaluations of a range of use levels. (From Manning, 2011.)

evaluation of visitor use levels, and may be experienced by people throughout parks, including at busy visitor centers, attraction sites, campgrounds, popular interpretive programs, heavily visited trails, congested roads, and full parking lots (Anderson *et al.*, 1998; Manning, 1999). Visitor perceptions of crowding may be influenced by personal characteristics of visitors (e.g. previous experience, motivations, expectations, and preferences), the characteristics of others encountered (e.g. group size, mode of travel, perceived similarity), and situational variables (e.g. type of area being visited). For example, a use level that is acceptable at a developed campsite may be seen as crowded at a backcountry camping area. Individuals who experience crowding may cope by visiting less popular locations within a park, by visiting during off-peak times or seasons, by leaving a park altogether, or by changing their perceptions about the park and what they experienced (Manning, 2011). Crowding in parks and related areas is often measured using normative methods as shown in Fig. 2.3. This figure is derived from visitor evaluations of a range of use levels, and identifies a threshold for the maximum acceptable number of encounters with other groups along a trail.

## Conflict

Visitor conflict is another experiential impact that can occur in national parks. Conflict between recreation groups and those participating in different types of activities is well documented in outdoor recreation settings (Graefe and Thapa, 2004; Manning, 2011). Conflict may occur when the behavior of one individual or group interferes with the goals of another individual or group (Jacob and Schreyer, 1980). Goal interference, or interpersonal conflict, occurs when an individual or group directly observes the offending behavior of other recreationists. For example, a group seeking quiet and solitude may experience conflict when encountering a large, rowdy group. However, conflict can still be experienced in the absence of direct interaction. Social values conflict occurs when recreation users hold different beliefs, values, and norms. For example, individuals opposed to hunting may experience conflict in knowing that activity is allowed to occur. There are many possible sources of direct and indirect conflict, including lifestyle tolerance (e.g. use of technology, consumptive activities), degree of activity expertise, level of connection to a park or particular place within a park, the importance of the natural environment to an activity, visitor expectations, and perceptions of safety. Since conflict may be asymmetric (e.g. non-motorized users are likely to object to motorized use, but the opposite may not be true), one consequence of conflict can be displacement of some visitors from an area. In other cases, visitors may not be displaced but have a less enjoyable experience.

## Depreciative behavior

Some visitors engage in behaviors that can negatively impact park resources and other people. Intentionally destructive behaviors include vandalism, litter, graffiti, and tree carving—actions that may be more prevalent in urban or developed park settings (Budruk and Manning, 2006). However, depreciative behaviors also occur in more primitive settings. Campers damage live trees through inappropriate firewood collecting (Hammitt *et al.*, 2015). Hikers on mountain summit trails build cairns that can confuse winter hikers and lead to vegetation loss and soil erosion (Jacobi, 2003). Other visitors feed wildlife or approach wildlife too closely, negatively impacting these animals and creating a potentially hazardous situation for other visitors. Likewise, boisterous behavior (e.g. playing loud music, yelling) may be disruptive to wildlife and other visitors, and can occur in a variety of park settings. Visitors engage in depreciative behaviors for a variety of reasons, including lack of awareness of park rules, lack of knowledge about the consequences of behaviors, response to cues in the environment, a desire to fit in with group members, or as an intentional act (Knopf and Andereck, 2004). News stories connecting social media to graffiti and vandalism in national parks have become increasingly common (Barringer, 2013).

## Impacts to Facilities/Services

Certain areas in parks, including attraction sites, trails, campgrounds and campsites, roads and parking areas, and interpretive facilities and programs, receive especially heavy visitation. Since use is concentrated at facilities and services, these areas experience many of the resource and experiential impacts outlined in the two previous sections. The following section examines how impacts can occur at these places.

### Attraction sites

Attraction sites, such as Old Faithful in Yellowstone National Park, the Statue of Liberty in New York, and the summit of Cadillac Mountain in Acadia National Park, are iconic features where visitors congregate. These areas are managed to accommodate large numbers of people. For example, a boardwalk and benches surround the Old Faithful Geyser. Still, intensive use levels can lead to a number of resource and social impacts, and the natural environment around attraction sites can be impacted when people walk off maintained trails and viewing platforms and feed wildlife. Visitors may experience extremely crowded conditions, may experience conflict with other visitors, and may have to compete for a space at heavily used attraction sites.

### Trails

Trails are an attraction for both casual and serious hikers and may range from those that take visitors into the primitive interior of parks, like Bright Angel Trail in Grand Canyon National Park, to highly developed, hardened trails, like that around Bear Lake in Rocky Mountain National Park. Other trails may be historic, such as the Carriage Roads in Acadia National Park. There are thousands of miles of trails across the many units of the US national park system. In addition, the National Park Service administers 21 national scenic and national historic trails as part of the national trails system (National Trails, 2011).

Trails are susceptible to a number of environmental impacts that result largely from trampling, including erosion, muddiness, trail widening and vegetation loss, soil compaction, loss of habitat for burrowing animals, trail deepening, formation of ruts and grooves, and creation of unofficial "social" trails (Anderson *et al.*, 1998; Leung and Marion, 2000). Different recreation activities can have more or less impact on trails. For example, Fig. 2.4 illustrates the relative impacts on trail tread composition of hiking, horses, and all-terrain vehicles (ATVs). Wildlife may alter their behavior around heavily used trails. In addition, visitors may experience crowding and/or conflict along trails with many, diverse users. For example, conflict may arise when hikers, horse riders, and mountain bikers share a trail.

### Campgrounds/campsites

Millions of people spend the night at campgrounds and campsites in national parks and other units of the national park system each year. (A campsite is designated for a single group of campers, while a campground is a collection of campsites.) An estimated 3.6 million visitors are tent campers, 2.2 million camp in a recreational vehicle, and another 2 million are backcountry campers (NPS Stats, 2016). Like trails, campsites can range from primitive to

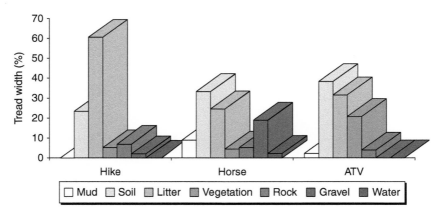

**Fig. 2.4.** Trail tread composition of trails used for hiking, horseback riding, and all-terrain vehicles (ATV). (From Newsome *et al.*, 2004.)

developed. Developed campgrounds for tents and recreational vehicles are located along park roads, such as the Tuolumne Meadows Campground located along the iconic Tioga Road in Yosemite National Park. These sites can offer a number of amenities, such as picnic tables, drinking water, showers, flush toilets, fire rings, wildlife-resistant trash receptacles, and amphitheaters for ranger programs.

Few amenities are offered in the backcountry, where campers hike to their overnight destination, and are often required to obtain and carry a permit. For example, campers visiting backcountry sites in Glacier National Park are required to carry a permit that specifies their trip itinerary, including group size, campground locations, and dates. Backcountry campgrounds have designated places for tents and may have a food preparation area and pit toilet. Other backcountry camping occurs "at-large". For example, overnight visitors to Denali National Park and Preserve acquire a permit to camp in one of the backcountry zones where there are no established trails or camping areas.

There are a number of environmental and social impacts that can occur at campgrounds. Similar to trails, soil compaction can occur on and around campsites, leading to vegetation loss and soil erosion. Impacts to soil, vegetation, and other campsite resources tend to occur relatively quickly even under light levels of use, as illustrated in Fig. 2.5. Over time, campsites may proliferate, increasing in both number and size. Where fires are permitted, soils may be damaged by heat, wood depleted, and trees damaged. Wildlife may be attracted to food at

campsites and become habituated to people. Alternatively, camper activity may cause wildlife to flee from important habitat. Campers may leave behind trash, toilet paper, and human waste. These impacts may degrade the experience of other campers, who may also experience crowding or conflict when encountering large or noisy groups at a campsite.

### Roads/parking areas

People rely on park roads to access natural, cultural, and historic sites within parks, but these roads can also be a central part of the experience for many park visitors. Iconic park roads, including Going to the Sun Road in Glacier National Park, Blue Ridge Parkway in the eastern United States, and the Park Loop Road in Acadia National Park, allow visitors to view spectacular scenery from their cars. However, there can also be impacts on and around park roads and parking areas. During peak seasons, roads can become congested, and parking lots full, leading to conflict and competition for parking spaces. In the absence of established parking spaces, visitors may park along roads, leading to impacts to vegetation on road shoulders. Transportation along roads can be noisy, disturbing both people and wildlife. Emissions from thousands of vehicles can also negatively impact air quality in parks.

### Interpretive facilities/programs

Interpretive facilities and programs in parks include visitor centers, interpretive signs, ranger-led hikes and

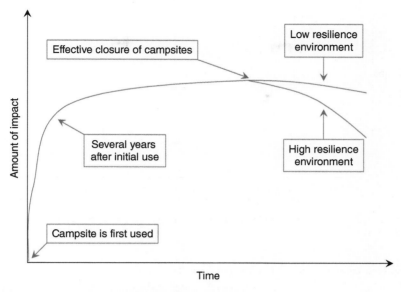

**Fig. 2.5.** Generalized pattern of impact to campsites. (From Cole, 2004.)

talks, campfire programs, and school programs. Popular programs may attract many visitors. Large, noisy, or boisterous groups may be disruptive, making it difficult for visitors to hear rangers or park films. Crowding at visitor centers may make it difficult for visitors to ask questions of park staff and receive the information they need to fully appreciate the park and to behave in a responsible way. Depreciative behaviors, like graffiti, also have the potential to ruin interpretive signs and other resources.

## Conclusion

Outdoor recreation is an important way in which millions of visitors enjoy and appreciate parks and related areas. However, there are a number of environmental and social impacts that can result from outdoor recreation. A considerable body of research has documented many of these impacts, and we've organized this literature into 16 types of impacts representing three basic categories. This organizational approach will be used later in this book as we develop a series of matrices designed to assess the management practices that might be applied to these impacts.

Fortunately, there are a number of management practices that can be employed to address the problems outlined in this chapter. The following two chapters discuss these practices and the research that has been conducted to assess their effectiveness.

# 3 Outdoor Recreation Management Practices

From the previous chapter, it's clear that outdoor recreation can cause a number of problems, and that these problems must be managed to protect park resources and the quality of the visitor experience. Fortunately, a variety of management practices can be applied, and many of these management practices have been found to be effective. It can be useful to organize these practices into classification systems to illustrate the broad spectrum of alternatives available to outdoor recreation managers, and to encourage comprehensive and creative thinking about recreation management. This chapter identifies and discusses a range of management strategies and tactics/practices, and related concepts. Chapter 4 reviews research designed to assess the effectiveness of these management practices.

## Management Strategies

One classification system for outdoor recreation is based on management strategies—basic conceptual approaches that relate to achieving desirable objectives (Manning, 1979, 2011). Strategies describe the ways in which management practices work rather than the management practices themselves. Four basic strategies can be identified, as illustrated in Fig. 3.1. Two strategies deal with supply and demand: the supply of recreation opportunities may be increased to accommodate more use and/or spread use more evenly; or the amount of recreation use may be limited through restrictions or other approaches. The other two basic strategies treat supply and demand as fixed, and focus on reducing the impacts of use by modifying visitor behavior or enhancing the "resistance" and/or "resilience" of park resources and the visitor experience.

Within the first of these basic strategies—increasing the supply of recreation opportunities—there are several distinct sub-strategies. Supply can be increased in terms of time or space. With respect to time, use of parks and related areas is typically highly concentrated in a small percentage of all potentially available days and hours. If some peak use can be shifted to lower use periods, then some of the pressure of overuse might be relieved. This might be accomplished through extension of traditional peak use seasons or encouragement of new off-season activities. Earlier opening and later closing dates, and promotion of winter activities such as ski touring and snowshoeing, are examples of how this strategy might be implemented. Some weekend use might be shifted to weekdays by such means as differential pricing (i.e. charging higher fees for heavily used places and times), while daily use schedules might be expanded by lighted facilities, which are becoming more prevalent in outdoor recreation.

The more traditional way to consider increasing supply is through expansion of the area available for recreation. Both real and effective areas should be considered. Increasing the real area available for recreation refers to acquisition of additional acres of parkland, and this can be done through either expanding an existing park unit or creating an entirely new unit within a park system. Effective area refers to managing existing units more intensively to provide additional opportunities for recreation. This can be approached from the standpoint of a higher level of development (e.g. providing more campsites) or increasing the accessibility of existing facilities (e.g. providing more or better roads and trails).

Reducing recreation demand or limiting the amount of use parks receive is a second basic strategy for managing outdoor recreation. Again, several sub-strategies are available. An overall limit may be placed on all recreational uses. This limit may be approached indirectly through regulation of lengths of stay, in this way excluding as few users as possible, or more directly through imposition of use ceilings. Alternatively, managers may focus on limiting selected types of uses, which can be demonstrated to have high impacts. Recreation

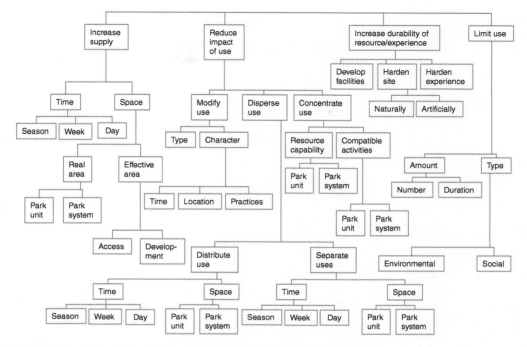

**Fig. 3.1.** Strategies for managing outdoor recreation. (Adapted from Manning, 1979.)

uses with high environmental impacts should be limited or excluded where damage to park resources is apparent, and uses that are high in social impacts should be limited when the quality of the recreation experience declines due to congestion or user conflicts.

A third basic strategy for managing recreational use of parks and related areas treats demand and supply as fixed, at least in the short run, and focuses instead on reducing the impact of recreational use through modifying use patterns or activities. Use patterns might be altered with the idea of encouraging either more concentrated use or more dispersed use. Recreation uses may be concentrated in areas where natural resources such as soil and vegetation are relatively resistant to impacts. Recreation uses may also be concentrated on the basis of compatibility with each other; users with similar activities, values and motivations may be grouped or concentrated together. This may be done on the individual park unit level (e.g. through zoning a park) or by park system (e.g. concentrating compatible uses in selected parks).

The strategy of dispersing recreation use relies on the philosophy of distributing use so that no one area receives damaging amounts of use. Managers may focus on distributing use over either time or space. As with supply, recreation use may be dispersed over time on a seasonal, weekly, or daily basis. It's probably more conventional to think of dispersing use over space or a wider geographical area. Again, this can be done on a park unit or park system basis. Recreation uses may also be dispersed through separation of conflicting uses. As above, this may be accomplished on a temporal basis through seasonal, weekly, or daily units of time, or on a spatial basis by park unit or park system levels.

Modification of recreation activities is a third sub-strategy under reducing the impact of use. Selected recreation activities or user groups may have to be reassigned elsewhere or eliminated from a park altogether due to excessive environmental or social impacts. An alternative is to modify the character of recreation use. In this way potentially damaging activities might not have to be eliminated, but rather altered with respect to their timing (e.g. limited to the dry season), location (e.g. restricted to areas below treeline), or practices (e.g. elimination of campfires).

The last basic strategy for managing recreational use involves enhancing the resistance of parks and/ or the visitor experience. Resources may be hardened to bolster their resistance to recreational impacts. This may be done in a semi-natural fashion, through such means as planting hardier species of vegetation, or in a more artificial way, through engineering practices such as surfacing heavily used sites. An additional sub-strategy involves development of recreation facilities, such as campgrounds and trails, to serve as "lightning rods." In this way recreational use, and its concomitant impacts, are directed away from the resource base and to these developed facilities. A third sub-strategy is to enhance the "resistance" of the recreation experience. This might be done by reducing conflicts among visitors or informing visitors of the conditions they are likely to encounter.

## Management Tactics or Practices

A second classification system for recreation management focuses on tactics or management practices. These are actions or tools applied by managers to accomplish the management strategies described above. Restrictions on length of stay, differential fees, and use permits, for example, are management practices that can be used to advance the strategy of limiting recreation use.

Management practices are often classified according to the directness with which they act on visitor behavior (Gilbert et al., 1972; Lime, 1977; Peterson and Lime, 1979; Chavez, 1996). As the term suggests, direct management practices act directly on visitor behavior, leaving little or no freedom of choice. Indirect management practices attempt to influence the decision factors upon which visitors base their behavior. A conceptual diagram illustrating direct and indirect recreation management practices is shown in Fig. 3.2. As an example, a direct management practice aimed at

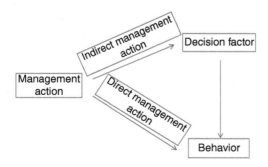

**Fig. 3.2.** Diagram of direct versus indirect management practices. (Adapted from Peterson and Lime, 1979.)

reducing campfires in a wilderness environment would be a regulation barring campfires, and enforcement of this regulation. An indirect management practice would be an education program designed to inform visitors of the undesirable ecological and aesthetic impacts of campfires, and to encourage them to carry and use portable stoves instead. A series of direct and indirect management practices is shown in Table 3.1. Direct and indirect management practices are sometimes referred to as "hard" and "soft" or "heavy-handed" and "light-handed" approaches, respectively (Kuo, 2002).

The relative advantages and disadvantages of direct and indirect recreation management practices have received substantial attention in the outdoor recreation literature. Generally, indirect management practices are favored when and where they are believed to be effective (Peterson and Lime, 1979; McCool and Christensen, 1996). This is particularly true for wilderness and related types of outdoor recreation opportunities (Clark and Stankey, 1979; Lucas, 1982; Hendee et al., 1990). Indirect management practices are favored for several reasons (McCool and Christensen, 1996):

**1.** Legislation and management agency policies applied to wilderness and related areas often emphasize provision of recreation opportunities that are "unconfined" and that allow visitors freedom of choice. Thus, direct regulation of visitor behavior may be inconsistent with such management objectives.
**2.** Recreation is a form of leisure activity connoting freedom of choice in thought and actions. Regulations designed to control visitor behavior can be seen as antithetical to the very nature of recreation. Especially in the context of wilderness and related areas, recreation and visitor regulation have been described as "inherently contradictory" (Lucas, 1982).
**3.** Many studies indicate that, given the choice, visitors prefer indirect over direct management practices (Lucas, 1983).
**4.** Indirect management practices may be more efficient because they do not entail the costs associated with enforcement of rules and regulations.

Emphasis on indirect management practices, however, has not been uniformly endorsed (McAvoy and Dustin, 1983a,b; Cole, 1993; Shindler and Shelby, 1993). It has been argued that indirect practices may be ineffective. There are likely to be some visitors, for example, who will ignore indirect

**Table 3.1.** Example of direct and indirect management practices. (Adapted from Lime, 1977, 1979.)

| Type | Example |
|---|---|
| *Direct* | |
| (Emphasis on regulation of behavior; individual choice restricted; high degree of control) | Impose fines |
| | Increase surveillance of area |
| | Zone incompatible uses spatially (hiker only zones, prohibit motor use, etc.) |
| | Zone uses over time |
| | Limit camping in some campsites to one night, or some other limit |
| | Rotate use (open or close roads, access points, trails, campsites, etc.) |
| | Require reservations |
| | Assign campsites and/or travel routes to each camper group in backcountry |
| | Limit usage via access point |
| | Limit size of groups, number of horses, vehicles, etc. |
| | Limit camping to designated campsites only |
| | Limit length of stay in area (maximum/minimum) |
| | Restrict building campfires |
| | Restrict fishing or hunting |
| *Indirect* | |
| (Emphasis on influencing or modifying behavior; individual retains freedom to choose; control less complete, more variation in use possible) | Improve (or not) access roads, trails |
| | Improve (or not) campsites and other concentrated use areas |
| | Improve (or not) fish and wildlife populations (stock, allow to die out, etc.) |
| | Advertise specific attributes of the area |
| | Identify the range of recreation opportunities in surrounding area |
| | Educate users to basic concepts of ecology |
| | Advertise underused areas and general patterns of use |
| | Charge consistent entrance fee |
| | Charge differential fees by trail, zone, season, etc. |
| | Require proof of ecological knowledge and recreational activity skills |

management efforts, and the actions of a few may hamper attainment of management objectives. It has been argued, in fact, that a direct, regulatory approach to management can ultimately lead to more freedom rather than less (Dustin and McAvoy, 1984). When all visitors are required to conform to mutually agreed-upon behavior, management objectives are more likely to be attained and a diversity of recreation opportunities preserved. There is empirical evidence to suggest that, under certain circumstances, direct management practices can enhance the quality of the recreation experience (Frost and McCool, 1988; Swearington and Johnson, 1995). Moreover, research suggests that visitors are surprisingly supportive of direct management practices when they are needed to control the impacts of recreation use (Anderson and Manfredo, 1986; Shindler and Shelby, 1993).

An analysis of management problems caused by visitors suggests that both direct and indirect management practices can be applicable depending upon the context (Gramann and Vander Stoep, 1987; Alder, 1996). There are several basic reasons why visitors may not conform to desired standards of behavior, ranging from lack of knowledge about appropriate behavior to wilful rule violations. Indirect management practices, such as information and education programs, seem most appropriate in the case of the former, while direct management practices, such as enforcement of rules and regulations, may be needed in the case of the latter.

It has been suggested that there is really a continuum of management practices ranging from indirect to direct (Hendricks *et al.*, 1993; McCool and Christensen, 1996). For example, an educational program on the ecological and aesthetic impacts of campfires would be found toward the indirect end of such a continuum. A regulation requiring campers to use portable stoves instead of campfires would be a more direct management practice; and aggressive enforcement of this regulation with uniformed rangers would clearly be a very direct management practice. This suggests that management practices might also be viewed as ranging along two dimensions, as illustrated in Fig. 3.3 (McCool and Christensen, 1996).

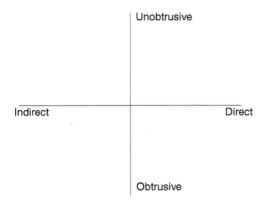

Unobtrusive

Indirect                 Direct

Obtrusive

**Fig. 3.3.** Two dimensions of recreation management practices. (Adapted from McCool and Christensen, 1996.)

Not only can management practices be direct or indirect, they can also be implemented in an obtrusive or unobtrusive manner. It has also been suggested that direct and indirect management practices are not mutually exclusive and that, in fact, they can often complement each other (Alder, 1996; Cole *et al.*, 1997a). For example, a regulation banning campfires (a direct management practice) should be implemented in conjunction with an educational program explaining the need for such a regulation (an indirect management practice).

## Classification of Problem Behaviors

Substantial research and management attention has focused on information and education programs as a recreation management practice, one that is generally seen as an indirect, soft, and light-handed approach. Information and education programs are designed to persuade visitors to adopt behaviors that are compatible with recreation management objectives, usually to reduce the ecological and experiential impacts of outdoor recreation. Research suggests that this approach tends to be viewed very favorably by recreation visitors (Roggenbuck and Ham, 1986; Stankey and Schreyer, 1987; McCool and Lime, 1989; Roggenbuck, 1992; Vander Stoep and Roggenbuck, 1996). Several coordinated national and international information and education programs have been developed in the field of parks and outdoor recreation, including Leave No Trace (LNT) and Global Code of Ethics for Tourism (World Tourism Organization, 2006; Marion and Reid, 2007; Leave No Trace, 2012). The potential effectiveness of these types of programs has been

demonstrated in several studies (Dowell and McCool, 1986; Jones and McAvoy, 1988; Cole *et al.*, 1997b; Confer *et al.*, 2000; Lawhon *et al.*, 2013; Taff *et al.*, 2014a), and this is discussed more fully in Chapter 4.

A conceptual application of information and education to recreation management problems is illustrated in Table 3.2. This classifies problem behaviors in outdoor recreation into five basic types and suggests the potential effectiveness of information and education on each. At the two ends of the spectrum, problem behaviors can be seen as either deliberately illegal (e.g. theft of cultural artifacts; a small number of visitors may steal artifacts even though they know it is illegal) or unavoidable (e.g. disposal of human waste—production of human waste is unavoidable). In both these instances, information and education may have little or no effectiveness. However, the other three types of problem behaviors—careless actions (e.g. littering), unskilled actions (e.g. selecting an inappropriate campsite), and uninformed actions (e.g. using dead snags for firewood)—may be considerably more amenable to information and education programs.

## Theories of Moral Development

A second conceptual approach to the application of information and education is based on theories of moral development and is illustrated in Table 3.3 (Christensen and Dustin, 1989). This approach builds on two prominent theories of moral development (Kohlberg, 1976; Gilligan, 1982). Both theories suggest that people tend to evolve through a series of stages of moral development ranging from those that are very self-centered to those that are highly altruistic and are based on principles of justice, fairness, and self-respect. Individual visitors to parks and recreation areas may be found at any of these stages. Management implications of this conceptual approach suggest that information and education programs should be designed to reach visitors at each stage of moral development by tailoring messages accordingly. For example, to reach visitors at lower levels of moral development, managers might emphasize extrinsic rewards and punishments for selected types of behavior, while communicating with visitors at higher levels of moral development might be more effective by means of emphasizing the rationale for selected behaviors and appealing to one's sense of altruism, justice, and fairness.

**Table 3.2.** Application of information and education to recreation management problems. (Adapted from Hendee *et al.*, 1990; Roggenbuck, 1992; and Vander Stoep and Roggenbuck, 1996.)

| Type of problem | Example | Potential effectiveness of information and education |
|---|---|---|
| Illegal | Theft of cultural artifacts<br>Invasion of wilderness by motorized off-road vehicles | Low |
| Careless actions | Littering<br>Nuisance activity (e.g. shouting) | Moderate |
| Unskilled actions | Selecting inappropriate camping site<br>Building improper campfire | High |
| Uninformed actions | Selecting a lightly used campsite in the wilderness<br>Using dead snags for firewood<br>Camping in sight or sound of another party | Very high |
| Unavoidable actions | Disposal of human body waste, loss of ground cover vegetation in the campsite | Low |

**Table 3.3.** Stages of moral development. (From Christensen and Dustin, 1989.)

| Kohlberg's six stages of moral development | | Gilligan's perspectives on moral development | |
|---|---|---|---|
| Stage | Over-riding concern | Perspective | Over-riding concern |
| Pre-conventional morality | | | |
| 1 | Fear of punishment | 1 | Reference and relation to self; survival; self-oriented; similar to Kohlberg's 1 and 2 |
| 2 | Maximizing pleasure/ minimizing pain | | |
| Conventional morality | | | |
| 3 | What significant others think | 2 | Reference and relation to others; pleasing others is important; somewhat similar to Kohlberg's 3 and 4 |
| 4 | What society thinks | | |
| Post-conventional morality | | | |
| 5 | Justice and fairness | 3 | Reference and relation to self and others; integration of 1 and 2 above; caring is the highest value; departs from Kohlberg at this point |
| 6 | Self-respect | | |

## Communication Theory

Application of communication theory to outdoor recreation suggests that the potential effectiveness of information and education is dependent upon a number of variables associated with visitors and the content and delivery of messages (Roggenbuck and Ham, 1986; Stankey and Schreyer, 1987; Manfredo, 1989; Manfredo and Bright, 1991; Manfredo *et al.*, 1992; Roggenbuck, 1992; Bright *et al.*, 1993; Bright and Manfredo, 1995; Basman *et al.*, 1996; Vander Stoep and Roggenbuck, 1996). For example, visitor behavior is at least partially driven by attitudes, beliefs, and normative standards. Information and education programs aimed at connecting with or modifying relevant attitudes, beliefs, or norms may be successful in guiding or changing visitor behavior. Moreover, the substance of messages and the media by which they are delivered may also influence the effectiveness of information and education programs.

From a theoretical standpoint, information and education can be seen to operate through three basic models (Roggenbuck *et al.*, 1992). The simplest and most direct theoretical model is applied behavior analysis. This approach to management focuses directly on visitor behavior rather than antecedent variables such as attitudes, beliefs, and norms. For example, visitors can be informed of rewards or punishments that will be administered dependent upon their behavior. Since this model does not address underlying behavioral variables, its effectiveness may be short term and dependent upon continued management action.

A second theoretical model is the central route to persuasion. In this model, relevant beliefs of visitors are modified through delivery of substantive messages. New or modified beliefs then lead to desired changes in behavior. While this is a less direct and more complex model, it may result in more lasting behavioral modification.

A third theoretical model of information and education is the peripheral route to persuasion. This model emphasizes non-substantive elements of information and education messages, such as message source and medium. For example, messages from sources considered by visitors to be authoritative or powerful may influence behavior while other messages may be ignored. This model may be especially useful in situations where it is difficult to attract and maintain the attention of visitors, such as at visitor centers, entrance stations, and bulletin boards, all of which may offer multiple and competing information and education messages. However, like applied behavior analysis, the peripheral route to persuasion

may not influence antecedent conditions of behavior and, therefore, may not have lasting effects.

## Conclusion

It can be useful to think about managing outdoor recreation in terms of strategies and tactics/practices. There are four basic strategies for managing outdoor recreation and many management practices that can be used to implement these strategic approaches. Classification of management practices might be based on many factors or concepts. The approaches described above simply illustrate the array of alternatives available for outdoor recreation management. For any given problem, there are likely at least several potential solutions. Explicit consideration should be given to this variety of approaches rather than relying on those that are familiar or administratively expedient. For the purposes of this book, we classify management strategies into four basic categories: increasing the supply of recreation opportunities, limiting use, reducing the impact of use, and increasing the resistance or durability of resources and the visitor experience. And we classify management practices into six basic categories: information/education; use rationing and allocation; rules/regulations; law enforcement; zoning; and site design/facility development/maintenance.

# 4 Evaluating Outdoor Recreation Management Practices

The previous chapter outlined a range of recreation management strategies and practices. Management practices were organized into six basic categories including information/education, use rationing and allocation, rules/regulations, law enforcement, zoning, and facility development/site design/maintenance. A relatively large number of empirical studies have begun to evaluate the effectiveness of these recreation management practices. Much of this work has focused on two areas: information/education, and use rationing and allocation. The other four management practices have received less attention. This chapter reviews and summarizes this body of research.

## Information and Education

Because of the attractiveness of information/education as a management practice (as described in Chapter 3), a relatively large number of empirical studies have examined its effectiveness. These studies fall into several categories, including:

1. Those designed to influence recreation use patterns.
2. Those focused on enhancing visitor knowledge, especially knowledge related to minimizing ecological and social impacts of recreation.
3. Those aimed at influencing visitor attitudes toward management policies.
4. Those that address depreciative behavior such as littering and vandalism.

### Recreation use patterns

Recreation use patterns are often characterized by their uneven spatial and temporal nature; visitor use is often concentrated in peak time periods and at selected locations. If recreation use could be redistributed to some degree, this may reduce problems such as crowding. A number of studies have used computer-based simulation models to document the effectiveness of spatial and temporal use redistribution in reducing contacts among recreation groups (Schechter and Lucas, 1978; Manning and Ciali, 1979; Manning and Potter, 1982, 1984; Potter and Manning, 1984; Underhill et al., 1986; Wang and Manning, 1999; Lawson and Manning, 2003a,b; Cole, 2005; Lawson et al., 2006; Gimblett and Skov-Peterson, 2008; Lawson et al., 2008). It has been shown, for example, that a cut of nearly 20% in total use would be required to achieve the same reduction in contacts obtainable through use redistributions (Potter and Manning, 1984).

Several studies have explored the potential effectiveness of information and education programs as a means of redistributing recreation use (Brown and Hunt, 1969; Lime and Lucas, 1977; Becker, 1981; Lucas, 1981; Roggenbuck and Berrier, 1981, 1982; Krumpe and Brown, 1982; Brown et al., 1992). For example, an early study explored the effectiveness of providing visitors with information on current use patterns as a way to alter future use patterns (Lime and Lucas, 1977). Visitors who had permits for the most heavily used entry points in the Boundary Waters Canoe Area, Minnesota, were mailed an information packet with a description of use patterns, noting in particular heavily used areas and times. A survey of a sample of this group who again visited the study area the following year found that three-fourths of respondents felt that this information was useful, and about one-third were influenced in their choice of entry point, route, or time of subsequent visits.

A study in the Shining Rock Wilderness Area, North Carolina, experimented with two types of information programs designed to disperse camping away from a heavily used meadow (Roggenbuck and Berrier, 1981, 1982). Two treatment groups were created. Both were given a brochure explaining resource impacts associated with concentrated camping and showing the location of other nearby camping areas; one in addition had personal contact with a wilderness ranger. Both groups dispersed their camping activity to a greater degree than a control group, but there was no statistically significant difference between the two groups.

A similar experiment was conducted on trail use in the backcountry of Yellowstone National Park, Montana/Wyoming/Idaho (Krumpe and Brown, 1982). A sample group of hikers was given a guidebook that described the attributes of lesser-used trails prior to obtaining a backcountry permit. Through a later survey and examination of permits, it was found that 37% of this group had selected one of the lesser-used trails compared to 14% of a control group. Results also indicated that the earlier the information was received the more influence it had on behavior. Studies employing user-friendly, micro-computer-based information approaches (e.g. touch-screen programs) have also been found to be effective in influencing recreation use patterns (Huffman and Williams, 1986, 1987; Hultsman, 1988; Harmon, 1992; Alpert and Herrington, 1998).

Hikers in the Pemigewasset Wilderness, New Hampshire, were studied to determine the influence of wilderness rangers as a source of information and education (Brown *et al.*, 1992). Only about 20% of visitors reported that the information received from the rangers influenced their destination within the study area. However, less experienced visitors who reported that they were likely to return to the study area were more likely to be influenced by the information provided, suggesting that the information program may be more effective over time.

Potential problems in using information and education programs to influence recreation use were illustrated in a study in the Selway-Bitterroot Wilderness, Montana (Lucas, 1981). Brochures describing current recreation use patterns were distributed to visitors. Follow-up measurements indicated little effect on subsequent use patterns. Evaluation of this program suggested three limitations on its potential effectiveness:

1. Many visitors did not receive the brochure.
2. Most of those who did receive the brochure received it too late to affect their decision making.
3. Some visitors doubted the accuracy of the information contained in the brochure.

## Enhancing visitor knowledge

A second category of studies has focused primarily on enhancing visitor knowledge through information and education programs, thereby influencing visitor behavior, especially as it applies to reducing ecological and experiential impacts. Two early studies focused on distinct types of users—backpackers in Rocky Mountain National Park, Colorado (Fazio, 1979a), and motorists in a New York state park (Feldman, 1978). The study of backpackers provided information on low-impact camping practices through a series of media: a brochure, a trailhead sign, a slide and sound exhibit, a television program, and a newspaper feature article, though not enough visitors were exposed to the latter two media to evaluate their effectiveness. However, exposure to the slide/sound exhibit, the slide/sound exhibit plus the brochure, and the slide/sound exhibit plus the trailhead sign resulted in significant increases in visitor knowledge. Exposure to the trailhead sign and brochure were not found to be very effective. The study of motorists also found that exposure to two types of information/education media—a brochure and an audio recording—both increased the knowledge level of respondents.

More recent studies have also found significant effects of information and education programs (Echelberger *et al.*, 1978; Dowell and McCool, 1986; Burde *et al.*, 1988; Jones and McAvoy, 1988; Sieg *et al.*, 1988; Dwyer *et al.*, 1989; Manfredo and Bright, 1991; Roggenbuck *et al.*, 1992; Kernan and Drogin, 1995; Cole *et al.*, 1997b; Christenson and Cole, 2000; Stewart *et al.*, 2000; Hendricks *et al.*, 2001; Borrie and Harding, 2002; Duncan and Martin, 2002; Barker and Roberts, 2004; Bradford and McIntyre, 2007; Sorice *et al.*, 2007; Marion *et al.*, 2008; Park *et al.*, 2008). For example, a study of day hikers at Grand Canyon National Park, Arizona, found that an aggressive information/education campaign featuring the message "heat kills, hike smart" presented in the park newspaper and on trailhead posters influenced the safety-related practices (e.g. carrying sufficient water, starting hikes early in the day) of a majority of visitors (Stewart *et al.*, 2000). This study suggests that, when and where warranted, managers may have to be very explicit in their attempts to make visitors more mindful of their surroundings and associated behavior (Moscardo, 1999; Frauman and Norman, 2003).

Bulletin boards at trailheads have also been found to be effective in enhancing visitor knowledge about low-impact hiking and camping practices (Cole *et al.*, 1997b). Visitors exposed to messages at a trailhead bulletin board were found to be more knowledgeable about these practices than visitors who were not; however, increasing the number of messages posted beyond two did not result in increased knowledge levels. Bulletin boards were most effective with hikers and overnight users (as compared to horse riders or day users), probably because of the greater potential utility of the messages to these visitors (McCool and Cole, 2000).

Workshops and special programs delivered to organizations can also be effective in enhancing knowledge levels as well as intentions to follow recommended low-impact practices. The effectiveness of these types of information and education programs have been demonstrated in two studies aimed at Boy Scouts (Dowell and McCool, 1986) and a volunteer group associated with the Boundary Waters Canoe Area Wilderness, Minnesota (Jones and McAvoy, 1988). In both cases, treatment groups scored higher than control groups on tests of knowledge and behavioral intentions administered immediately after the programs and at a later date. Research also suggests that commercial guides and outfitters can be trained to deliver information and education programs that are effective in enhancing visitor knowledge (Sieg *et al.*, 1988; Roggenbuck *et al.*, 1992) and that printed trail guides can also be effective (Echelberger *et al.*, 1978).

A series of visitor surveys conducted at eight wilderness areas also suggest that informative and educational appeals can be effective in encouraging low-impact behaviors (Christensen and Cole, 2000). These studies found that between 51 and 69% of visitors reported that they use cook stoves instead of campfires, and would camp at least 200 feet from lakes as a result of appeals from wilderness managers relating to ecological (e.g. reducing water pollution) and experiential (e.g. reducing crowding) issues. Ecological appeals were more effective than experiential appeals.

Several more recent studies have used potentially powerful field experiments to assess the effectiveness of information and education programs. A study at Mt Tamalpais, California, delivered educational messages to mountain bikers regarding four types of behavior:

1. Yielding when approaching other visitors.
2. Bicycle speed.
3. Behavior upon encountering a closed trail.
4. Crossing a stream (to limit ecological impact) (Hendricks *et al.*, 2001).

Messages were designed to stress a "moral" appeal (a brief description of the ecological and/or experiential consequences of undesirable behavior) or a "fear" appeal (a brief description of fines that are imposed for undesirable behavior). These messages were delivered to mountain bikers in person by either a volunteer patrol hiker, a volunteer patrol biker, or a uniformed hiker. Mountain biker behavior was then unobtrusively observed under experimental and control conditions. Study findings suggest that bikers adopted lower-impact behaviors for three of the four behaviors examined. For example, 59.2% of bikers used recommended, low-impact procedures for crossing streams when they had been exposed to one of the study's educational treatments, and this compared very favorably to only 16.7% of bikers under control conditions. However, the study found no consistent pattern with respect to type of message (moral or fear appeal). Generally, messages delivered by uniformed staff appeared to be less effective than those delivered by non-uniformed volunteers.

Multiple experimental studies have focused on "social" or "visitor-caused" trails—trails that visitors create when they walk off designated trails. One of these studies, conducted at St Lawrence Islands National Park, Canada (Bradford and McIntyre, 2007), applied two types of messages: a simple plea to visitors to stay on designated trails, and a message briefly explaining the impacts of walking off designated trails. These messages (in the form of signs) were placed either at a trailhead or at sites where existing social trails diverged from designated trails. Camouflaged cameras were used to record the behavior of hikers. Under control conditions, 88.3% of hikers were observed using social trails. However, this percentage was reduced to 77% for those who had seen the plea message and 49% for those who had learned of the impacts of walking on the social trails. Signs placed at sites where social trails diverged from the designated trail were substantially more effective than trailhead signs.

A second study of social trails was conducted at Acadia National Park, Maine (Park *et al.*, 2008). One experimental treatment posted signs at a trailhead asking visitors not to walk off the designated trail and briefly explained the reason for this request (to reduce ecological impacts). A second treatment also added ground level reminder signs—simple 4" × 4" wooden blocks with a "no walking" graphic—at all sites where social trails diverged from the designated trail. Visitor behavior was recorded by unobtrusive observers. The first treatment reduced the percentage of visitors who walked off-trail from 73.7% during the control period to 63%, and the second treatment further reduced this to 24.3%.

Another study at Acadia National Park, Maine (Kidd *et al.*, 2015) utilized spatial data analysis to measure the effectiveness of three educational treatments along trails and the summit area of Sargent Mountain. Treatments included an ecological-based message and amenity-based message to encourage visitors to stay on marked trails. A third treatment included a message delivered through personal contact and control conditions included existing trail blazes and rock cairns. Visitors traveling to the mountain summit were asked to carry a GPS unit with them while they hiked. Spatial data collected from these units were analyzed and indicated that sign-based messaging did not significantly influence visitor behavior. Personal contact did, however, decrease the extent to which visitors traveled off trail.

A fourth study using an experimental design examined visitor acceptability of sounds from nearby military aircraft at Sequoia National Park (Taff *et al.*, 2014b). One treatment involved visitors rating the acceptability of a range of audio clips that incorporated the sound of aircraft overflights. The other involved the same listening exercise, but respondents were "primed" with a message regarding the presence of military overflights at the park. Results demonstrated that including an educational message regarding overflights improved acceptability ratings up to 15%, suggesting that distributing information about military overflights may benefit visitor experience.

The final study employing an experimental approach examined wildlife-feeding behavior at Zion National Park, Utah (Marion *et al.*, 2008), using two treatments and a control period. Both treatments asked visitors not to feed wildlife and included a brief explanation of the reason for this request. Treatment 1 used a sign posted near a popular wildlife-feeding area, whereas for treatment 2 a uniformed ranger delivered this message in person at the wildlife-feeding area. Visitor behavior was closely observed during both treatments and a control period. The percentage of visitor groups that intentionally attracted wildlife declined from 24% during the control period to 3% for both treatments. More importantly, the number of groups that intentionally fed wildlife declined from 11% to 3%, and groups that dropped food unintentionally declined from 41% before treatments to 10% for treatment 1 and 6% for treatment 2.

Not all research has found information and education programs to be as effective as indicated in the above studies. A study of the effectiveness of interpretive programs at Great Smoky Mountains National Park, North Carolina/Tennessee, found mixed results (Burde *et al.*, 1988). There was no difference in knowledge about general backcountry policies between backcountry visitors exposed to the park's interpretive services and a control group. However, the former group did score higher on knowledge of park-related hazards. A test of visitor compliance rates with campground regulations in Acadia National Park, Maine, found no difference between time periods when a special brochure was and was not used (Dwyer *et al.*, 1989). A test of a special brochure on appropriate behavior relating to bears in the Boundary Waters Canoe Area Wilderness, Minnesota, found only limited change in actual or intended behavior of visitors (Manfredo and Bright, 1991). Visitors requesting information on wilderness permits were mailed the special brochures. In a follow-up survey, only 18% of respondents reported that they had received any new information from the brochure, and only 7.5% reported that they had altered their actual or intended behavior. A study on the intercoastal waterway of Florida addressed boat speed and collisions with manatees, which injure or kill these animals (Sorice *et al.*, 2007). This study posted signs along the waterway with a graphic of a manatee swimming near the surface of the water and "Watch Your Speed" and "Max Fine $500." The speed of boats during control and treatment conditions was observed, and no statistically significant difference was found. A study of rock climbers in Montana used educational messages on bulletin boards to encourage low-impact behaviors, but little change in behavior was observed between control and treatment periods (though observation of behavior was difficult) (Borrie and Harding, 2002). Finally, a study of diving in St Lucia used two approaches in an effort to reduce damage to coral reefs by divers touching and breaking coral (Barker and Roberts, 2004). A brief message delivered to divers in a pre-dive meeting had no effect, while direct intervention by dive leaders reduced touching by a statistically significant degree. The authors conclude that in heavily used diving areas close supervision of participants may be needed.

The potential effectiveness of information and education is further diminished given the ecological and experiential implications of some types of recreation-related impacts. For example, the studies of off-trail hiking suggest that aggressive information and education programs can reduce off-trail hiking to a range of 25–50% of visitors. While this represents a substantial reduction from control conditions, it may still result in high levels of damage to soils and vegetation. Likewise, from an experiential standpoint, it may take only a relatively small percentage of visitors being boisterous or engaging in other inappropriate behavior to disturb others and detract from the quality of the visitor experience.

## Influencing visitor attitudes

A third category of studies on the potential effectiveness of information and education programs has examined their influence on visitor attitudes toward a variety of management agency policies (Robertson, 1982; Olson *et al.*, 1984; Nielson and Buchanan, 1986; Cable *et al.*, 1987; Manfredo *et al.*, 1992; Bright *et al.*, 1993; Ramthun, 1996; Taff *et al.*, 2014a; Hvenegaard, 2016). These studies have found that information and education programs can be effective in modifying visitor attitudes so they are more supportive of recreation and related park management policies. For example, visitors to Yellowstone National Park, Montana/Wyoming/Idaho were exposed to interpretive messages designed to influence their beliefs about fire ecology and the effects of controlled-burn policies, which influenced both beliefs about fire ecology and attitudes based on those beliefs (Bright *et al.*, 1993).

## Depreciative behavior

A fourth category of studies on the potential effectiveness of information and education as a management practice has focused on depreciative behavior, especially littering. A number of studies have found that a variety of information and education messages and related programs can be effective in reducing littering behavior and even cleaning up littered areas (Burgess *et al.*, 1971; Clark *et al.*, 1971; Marler, 1971; Clark *et al.*, 1972a,b; Powers *et al.*, 1973; Lahart and Bailey, 1975; Muth and Clark, 1978; Christensen, 1981; Christensen and Clark, 1983; Oliver *et al.*, 1985; Christensen, 1986; Roggenbuck and Passineau, 1986; Vander Stoep and Gramman, 1987; Horsley, 1988; Wagstaff and Wilson, 1988; Christensen *et al.*, 1992; Taylor and Winter, 1995; Hwang *et al.*, 2000; D'Luhosch *et al.*, 2009). For example, samples of visitors to a

developed campground were given three different treatments: a brochure describing the costs and impacts of littering and vandalism, the brochure plus a personal contact with a park ranger, and these two treatments plus a request for assistance in reporting depreciative behaviors to park rangers (Oliver *et al.*, 1985). The brochure plus the personal contact was the most effective treatment; this reduced the number of groups who littered their campsite from 67% to 41% and reduced the number of groups who damaged trees at their campsite from 20% to 4%. Types of messages and related purposes found to be effective in a number of studies include: incentives to visitors to assist with clean-up efforts, and the use of rangers and trip leaders as role models for cleaning up litter.

## Related studies

Several other types of studies, while not directly evaluating the effectiveness of information and education, are also suggestive of the potential of this management practice. First, studies of visitor knowledge indicate that marked improvements are possible that could lead to improved visitor behavior. For example, campers on the Allegheny National Forest, Pennsylvania, were tested for their knowledge of rules and regulations that applied to the area (Ross and Moeller, 1974). Only 48% of respondents answered six or more of the ten questions correctly. A similar study of visitors to the Selway-Bitterroot Wilderness Area, Idaho, tested knowledge about wilderness use and management (Fazio, 1979b). The average respondent could answer only about half of the 20 questions correctly. However, there were significant differences among types of respondents, type of knowledge, and the accuracy of various sources of information, providing indications of where and how information and education programs might be channelled most effectively. Visitors to the Allegheny National Forest, Pennsylvania, received an average score of 48% on a 12-item true–false minimum impact quiz (Confer *et al.*, 2000), while visitors to the Selway-Bitterroot National Forest, Montana, scored an average of 33% on a similar quiz (Cole *et al.*, 1997b). A similar study of hikers on the Appalachian National Scenic Trail found that visitors received an average score of 88% on a ten-item quiz (Newman *et al.*, 2002, 2003). Comparisons across the above studies are difficult because they used different measures of knowledge, but they all suggest that there is room (sometimes substantial room) for improvement in visitor knowledge.

Second, several studies indicate that information and education programs could be substantially improved (Hunt and Brown, 1971; Fazio, 1979a; Cockrell and McLaughlin, 1982; Fazio and Ratcliffe, 1989). Evaluation of literature mailed in response to visitor requests has found several areas needing improvements, including more timely response, more direct focus on management problems and issues, greater personalization, more visual appeal, and reduction of superfluous materials. An evaluation of websites for 45 units of the US national park system found that one-third failed to mention the Leave No Trace program, while others addressed it only in administrative documents rather than in ways more accessible to visitors (Griffin, 2005).

Third, a survey of wilderness managers has identified the extent to which 25 visitor education techniques are used (Doucette and Cole, 1993). Only six of these education techniques—brochures, personnel at agency offices, maps, signs, personnel in the backcountry, and displays at trailheads—are used in a majority of wilderness areas. Managers were also asked to rate the perceived effectiveness of education techniques, and generally considered that those based on personnel were more effective than those based on media.

Fourth, a study conducted at Rocky Mountain National Park explored a number of variables likely to influence participation in Leave No Trace practices (Lawhon et al., 2013). Results of the study indicated that perceived effectiveness of Leave No Trace is a significant predictor of future behavior. Therefore, information and education regarding Leave No Trace may be more effective when they explain why practices are effective in reducing impacts.

Related studies have examined the sources of information used by visitors for trip planning (Uysal et al., 1990; Schuett, 1993; Confer et al., 2000). Many respondents report using sources of information that are not directly produced by management agencies, such as outdoor clubs, professional outfitters, outdoor stores, guidebooks, newspaper and magazine articles, and travel agents. This suggests that management agency linkages with selected private and commercial organizations may be an especially effective approach to information and education.

## Guidelines for using information and education

Studies on information and education as a recreation management practice are relatively numerous but highly diverse, employing a variety of message types and media and addressing a variety of issues and target audiences. Generally, these studies suggest that information and education can be an effective recreation management practice. Moreover, a number of guidelines for using information and education can be developed from this literature (Roggenbuck and Ham, 1986; Brown et al., 1987; Manfredo, 1989; Manfredo, 1992; Roggenbuck, 1992; Doucette and Cole, 1993; Bright, 1994; Basman et al., 1996; Vander Stoep and Roggenbuck, 1996; Manning, 2003; Marion and Reid, 2007):

**1.** Use of multiple media to deliver messages is often more effective than use of a single medium.
**2.** Messages may be more effective when delivered repeatedly.
**3.** Some types of messages may be more effective when delivered as close as possible to the time or place where affected behaviors occur (e.g. wildlife feeding).
**4.** Information and education programs are generally more effective with visitors who are less experienced and less knowledgeable. Young visitors may be an especially attractive target audience.
**5.** Brochures, personal messages, and audio-visual programs may be more effective than signs.
**6.** Some messages may be more effective when delivered early in the recreation experience, such as during trip planning (e.g. using a portable camp stove instead of a campfire).
**7.** Messages from sources judged highly credible may be more effective.
**8.** Computer-based information systems can be an effective means of delivering information and education.
**9.** Training of volunteers, outfitters, and commercial guides can be an effective and efficient means of communicating information and education to visitors.
**10.** Providing information on the impacts, costs, and consequences of problem behaviors can be an effective information and education strategy.
**11.** Role modeling by park rangers and volunteers can be effective.
**12.** Personal contact with visitors by rangers or other employees can be effective in communicating information and education.

13. Messages should be targeted at specific audiences to the extent possible. Audiences that might be targeted especially effectively include those that request information in advance and those that are least knowledgeable.

14. Messages delivered from volunteers representing targeted user groups may be especially effective.

15. Information/education programs may be most effective when applied to problem behaviors that are characterized by careless, unskilled, or uninformed actions.

16. Information/education programs should be designed to reach visitors at multiple stages of moral development.

17. Information/education programs designed to connect with or modify visitor attitudes, beliefs, or norms are likely to be most effective in the long run, and to require less repeated application.

18. Information/education can and should be used to complement more direct, heavy-handed, and hard management approaches by explaining the need for such management.

19. Information/education programs should provide simple, interesting, and useful messages.

20. Information/education programs should provide messages that are as consistent and reinforcing as possible.

21. Visitors may be more effectively persuaded by ecological reasons for appropriate behavior rather than experiential reasons.

22. Strongly worded messages and aggressive delivery of such messages can be an effective way of enhancing the mindfulness of visitors, and may be warranted when applied to issues such as visitor safety and protection of critical and/or sensitive resources.

23. Messages at trailheads and bulletin boards should probably be limited to a small number of issues, perhaps as few as two.

24. Non-management agency media, such as newspapers, magazines, and guidebooks can be an effective and efficient means of communicating information/education.

25. Messages should be targeted at issues and behaviors that are least well understood or known by visitors and those that are most important to management.

## Use Rationing and Allocation

Substantial attention has been focused on the management practice of limiting the amount of use that park and recreation areas receive. Use rationing is controversial and is generally considered to be a management practice of last resort because it runs counter to the basic objective of providing public access to parks and recreation areas (Hendee and Lucas, 1973, 1974; Behan, 1974, 1976; Dustin and McAvoy, 1980). However, limits on use may be needed to maintain the quality of the recreation experience and to protect the integrity of critical park resources.

### Five management practices

Five basic management practices can be used to ration and allocate recreation use:

1. Reservation systems.
2. Lotteries.
3. First-come, first-served or queuing.
4. Pricing.
5. Merit (Stankey and Baden, 1977; Fractor, 1982; Shelby *et al.*, 1989a; McLean and Johnson, 1997; Whittaker and Shelby, 2008).

A reservation system requires potential visitors to reserve a space or permit in advance of their visit. A lottery allocates permits on a purely random basis. A first-come, first-served or queuing system requires potential visitors to wait in line (literally or figuratively) for available permits. A pricing system requires visitors to pay a fee for a permit, which may "filter out" those who are unable or unwilling to pay. A merit system requires potential visitors to "earn" the right to a permit by virtue of demonstrated knowledge or skill. It is important to note that there can be variations of each of these five basic approaches to rationing and allocation. For example, lotteries can be weighted to provide some advantage to people who have been unsuccessful in previous lotteries, and pricing can be conducted by means of an auction. Useful syntheses of use rationing and allocation practices have been developed as they apply to river recreation (Whittaker and Shelby, 2008) and wilderness (Cable and Watson, 1998).

Each of these management practices has potential advantages and disadvantages, which are summarized in Table 4.1. For example, reservation systems may tend to favor visitors who are willing and able to plan ahead, but may be difficult and costly to administer. Lotteries are often viewed as eminently fair, but can also be difficult and costly to administer. First-come, first-served systems may

**Table 4.1.** Evaluation of five recreation use rationing practices. (From Stankey and Baden, 1977.)

| | Reservation | Lottery | First-come, first-served | Pricing | Merit |
|---|---|---|---|---|---|
| Clientele group benefitted by system | Those able and/or willing to plan ahead; i.e. persons with structured lifestyles | No one identifiable group benefitted. Those who examine probabilities of success at different areas have better chance | Those with low opportunity cost for their time (e.g. unemployed). Also favors users who live nearby | Those able or willing to pay entry costs | Those able or willing to invest time and effort to meet requirements |
| Clientele group adversely affected by system | Those unable or unwilling to plan ahead; e.g. persons with occupations that do not permit long-range planning, such as many professionals | No one identifiable group discriminated against. Can discriminate against the unsuccessful applicant to whom the area is very important | Those persons with high opportunity cost of time. Also those persons who live some distance from areas. The cost of time is not recovered by anyone | Those unwilling or unable to pay entry costs | Those unable or unwilling to invest time and effort to meet requirements |
| Experience to date with use of system | Main type of rationing system used in both national forests and national parks | None. However, is a common method for allocating big-game hunting permits | Used in conjunction with reservation system in San Jacinto Wilderness. Also used in some National Park Wildernesses | None | None. Merit is used to allocate use for some related activities such as river running |
| Acceptability of system to users[a] | Generally high. Good acceptance in areas where used. Seen as best way to ration by users in areas not currently rationed | Low | Low to moderate | Low to moderate | Not clearly known. Could vary considerably depending on level of training required to attain necessary proficiency and knowledge level |
| Difficulty for administrators | Moderately difficult. Requires extra staffing, expanded hours. Record keeping can be substantial | Difficult to moderately difficult. Allocating permits over an entire use season could be very cumbersome | Low difficulty to moderately difficult. Could require development of facilities to support visitors waiting in line | Moderate difficulty. Possibly some legal questions about imposing a fee for wilderness entry | Difficult to moderately difficult. Initial investments to establish licensing program could be substantial |

| | | | | | |
|---|---|---|---|---|---|
| Efficiency extent to which system can minimize problems of suboptimization | Low to moderate. Under-utilization can occur because of "no shows," thus denying entry to others. Allocation of permits to applicants has little relationship to value of the experience as judged by the applicant | Low. Because permits are assigned randomly, persons who place little value on an opportunity stand equal chance of gaining entry to those who place high value on an opportunity | Moderate. Because system rations primarily through a cost of time, it requires some measure of worth by participants | Moderate to high. Imposing a fee requires user to judge worth of experience against costs. Uncertain as to how well use could be "fine-tuned" with price | Moderate to high. Requires user to make expenditures of time and effort (and maybe dollars) to gain entry |
| Principal way in which used | Reducing visitor numbers. Controlling distribution of use in space and time by varying number of permits available at different trailheads or at different times | Reducing visitor numbers. Controlling distribution of use in space and time by number of permits available at different places or times, thus varying probability of success | Reducing visitor numbers. Controlling distribution of use in space and time by number of persons permitted to enter at different places or times | Reducing visitor numbers. Controlling distribution of use in space and time by using differential prices | Some reduction in numbers |
| How system affects user behavior[b] | Affects both spatial and temporal behavior | Affects both spatial and temporal behavior | Affects both spatial and temporal behavior. User must consider cost of time of waiting in line | Affects both spatial and temporal behavior. User must consider cost in dollars | Affects style of user's behavior |

[a]Based upon actual field experience as well as upon evidence reported in visitor studies (Stankey, 1973).

[b]This criterion is designed to measure how the different rationing systems would directly impact the behavior of users (e.g. where they go, when they go, how they behave, etc.).

favor visitors who have more leisure time or who live relatively close to a park or recreation area, but are relatively easy to administer. Pricing is a commonly used practice in society to allocate scarce goods and services, but may discriminate against potential visitors with low incomes. Merit systems are not widely used, but may lessen the environmental and social impacts of recreation use, although they may also be difficult and costly to administer.

Several principles or guidelines have been suggested for considering and applying use rationing and allocation practices (Stankey and Baden, 1977).

1. Emphasis should be placed on the environmental and social impacts of recreation use rather than the amount of use per se. Some types of recreation use may cause more impacts than others. To the extent that such impacts can be reduced, rationing use of recreation areas can be avoided or at least postponed.

2. As noted above, rationing use should probably be considered a management practice of last resort. Less direct or heavy-handed management practices would seem more desirable where they can be demonstrated to be effective.

3. Good information is needed to implement use rationing and allocation. Managers must be certain that social and/or environmental problems dictate use rationing and that they can assess the effects of alternative allocation systems.

4. Given the advantages and disadvantages of each use-allocation practice, combinations of use-rationing systems should be considered. For example, half of all permits might be allocated on the basis of a reservation system, and half on a first-come, first-served basis. This would serve the needs of potential visitors who can and do plan vacations in advance as well as those whose jobs or lifestyles do not allow for this.

5. Use rationing should establish a linkage between the probability of obtaining a permit and the value of the recreation opportunity to potential visitors. In other words, visitors who value the opportunity highly should have a chance to "earn" a permit through pricing, advance planning, waiting time, or merit.

6. Use-rationing practices should be monitored and evaluated to assess their effectiveness and fairness. Use rationing for recreation is relatively new and is likely to be controversial. Special efforts should be made to ensure that use-rationing practices accomplish their objectives.

## Fairness

A critical element of use-rationing and allocation practices is fairness (Dustin and Knopf, 1989). Parks and outdoor recreation areas administered by government agencies are public resources. Use-rationing and allocation practices must be seen as both efficient and equitable. But how are equity, fairness, and related concepts defined? Several studies have begun to develop important insights into this issue. These have outlined several alternative dimensions of equity and measured their support among the public.

One study identified four dimensions of an overall theory of "distributive justice", defined as an ideal whereby individuals obtain what they "ought" to have based on criteria of fairness (Shelby et al., 1989a). A first dimension is "equality", which suggests that all individuals have an equal right to a benefit such as access to parks and outdoor recreation. "Equity" suggests that benefits be distributed to those who "earn" them through some investment of time, money, or effort. A third dimension is "need"; this suggests that benefits be distributed on the basis of unmet needs or competitive disadvantage. A final dimension is "efficiency", which suggests that benefits be distributed to those who place the highest value upon them.

Insights into these dimensions of distributive justice were developed through a survey of river runners on the Snake River in Hell's Canyon, Idaho (Shelby et al., 1989b). Visitors were asked to rate the five use-allocation practices described above on the basis of four criteria: perceived chance of obtaining a permit, perceived fairness of the practice, acceptability of the practice, and willingness to try the practice. Results suggest that visitors use concepts of both fairness and pragmatism in evaluating use-rationing practices. However, pragmatism—the respondent's perception of his or her ability to obtain a permit—had the strongest effect. These findings suggest that managers have to convince potential visitors that proposed use allocation practices are not only fair, but that they will also provide them with a reasonable chance to obtain a permit.

A second series of studies has examined a more extended taxonomy of equity dimensions that might be applied to provision of a broad spectrum of park and recreation services (Wicks and Crompton, 1986, 1987, 1989, 1990; Wicks, 1987; Crompton and Wicks, 1988; Crompton and Lue,

1992). Eight potential dimensions of equity were identified. A first dimension is compensatory and allocates benefits on the basis of economic disadvantage. The second two dimensions are variations of equality and allocate benefits to all individuals equally, or ensure that all individuals ultimately receive equal total benefits. The fourth and fifth dimensions are based on demand and allocate benefits to those who make greatest use of them or those who advocate most effectively for them. The final three dimensions of equity are market driven and distribute benefits based on amount of taxes paid, the price charged for services, or the least-cost alternative for providing recreation services.

These dimensions of equity were described to a sample of California residents who were asked to indicate the extent to which they agreed or disagreed with each as a principle for allocating public park and recreation services (Crompton and Lue, 1992). A majority of the sample agreed with only three of the dimensions: in decreasing order, demonstrated use, price paid, and equal benefits.

Equity has also been conceptualized as having three basic dimensions:

1. Democratic equity (all people are treated equally).
2. Compensatory equity (distribution of scarce resources is guided by needs).
3. Equity belief (distribution of scarce resources is guided by people's perceptions and beliefs about the situation in question) (Nyaupane *et al.*, 2007).

A survey of residents of Oregon and Washington used a battery of 12 statements to measure the degree to which respondents supported these three dimensions of equity in the context of parks and outdoor recreation. Findings suggest that there is greater support for democratic equity than compensatory equity. Moreover, within the dimensions of compensatory equity, there was more support for discounted fees for the elderly and persons with disabilities than for ethnic minorities and people with low income and/or large families.

### Effectiveness

Despite the complex and controversial nature of use rationing and allocation, many studies have found considerable support for a variety of such management practices among visitors (Stankey, 1973; Fazio and Gilbert, 1974; Stankey, 1979; Lucas, 1980; McCool and Utter, 1981; Utter *et al.*, 1981; McCool and Utter, 1982; Shelby *et al.*, 1982;

Schomaker and Leatherberry, 1983; Lucas, 1985; Shelby *et al.*, 1989b; Glass and More, 1992; Watson, 1993; Watson and Niccolucci, 1995; Fleming and Manning, 2015). Research suggests that even most individuals who have been unsuccessful at obtaining a permit continue to support the need for use rationing (Fazio and Gilbert, 1974; Stankey, 1979; McCool and Utter, 1982). A study of visitors to three wilderness areas in Oregon found that support for use restrictions was based on concerns for protecting both resource quality and the quality of the visitor experience (Watson and Niccolucci, 1995). Support by day hikers was influenced most strongly by concerns with crowding, while support by overnight visitors was influenced by concern with both crowding and environmental impacts. A study of visitors to 13 wilderness areas in Oregon and Washington found broad support for use limits needed to protect ecological resources, but substantially less support for limiting use based on concern over crowding (Cole and Hall, 2008). Similar results were found among visitors to Lake McKenzie on Fraser Island, Australia, where willingness to accept use limits had broad support, especially if it would lead to better environmental outcomes (Fleming and Manning, 2015).

Preferences among alternative use-rationing practices have been found to be highly variable, based on both location and type of user (Magill, 1976; McCool and Utter, 1981; Shelby *et al.*, 1982, 1989b; Glass and More, 1992; Dimara and Skuras, 1998). Support for a particular use-allocation practice appears to be related to which practices respondents are familiar with and whether they believe they can obtain a permit. For example, a survey of visitors to Lakes Cave, Greece, found that a first-come, first-served system was favored by local residents, an admission fee was favored by visitors with higher incomes, and a reservation system was favored by visitors from afar (Dimara and Skuras, 1998). A study of river managers found that first-come, first-served and reservation systems were judged the two most administratively feasible allocation practices and were also the most commonly used (Wikle, 1991).

In keeping with the generally favorable attitude toward use limitation described above, most studies have found visitor compliance rates for mandatory permits to be high, ranging from 68% to 97%, with most areas in the 90% range (Lime and Lorence, 1974; Godin and Leonard, 1977; Van Wagtendonk and Benedict, 1980; Plager and Womble, 1981;

Parsons *et al.*, 1982). Moreover, permit systems that have incorporated trailhead quotas have been found to be effective in redistributing use both spatially and temporally (Hulbert and Higgins, 1977; Van Wagtendonk, 1981; Van Wagtendonk and Colio, 1986).

With the exception of pricing (discussed more fully below), relatively few studies have tested the effectiveness of rationing and allocation. In most cases, it is assumed that once a rationing and allocation system is adopted, it will achieve its primary objective of enforcing a use limit or quota. However, this situation is often more complicated. For example, fee systems require an analysis of demand or willingness to pay to help ensure they will result in desired levels of use. Because lotteries are increasingly used to allocate hunting licenses for popular game species, they have received some research attention to assess their effect on public welfare (i.e. maximize value) and other issues (Akabua *et al.*, 1999; Scrogin *et al.*, 2000; Scrogin and Berrens, 2003; Scrogin, 2005; Little *et al.*, 2006). A study of climbers in Scotland tested the effectiveness of a merit-based approach by lengthening access trails to prime climbing areas (Hanley *et al.*, 2002). An increase in walking time of 2 hours resulted in a 44% reduction in use, though some use was simply redistributed to other, closer climbing areas. The issue of redistribution of use associated with rationing and allocation could be important and should be included in evaluative studies (McCool, 2001).

### Pricing

Among the use-rationing and allocation practices described above, pricing—the primary means of allocating scarce goods and services in a free-market economy—has received special attention in the literature. Economic theory generally suggests that higher prices will result in less consumption of a given commodity or service, and thus pricing may be an effective approach in rationing recreation use. However, park and recreation services in the public sector have traditionally been provided free of charge or priced at a nominal level. The basic philosophy underlying this policy is that access to park and recreation services is important to all people and no one should be "priced out of the market." Interest in instituting or increasing fees at parks and outdoor recreation areas has generated a considerable body of literature—philosophical, theoretical, and empirical.

Interest in pricing has increased substantially in recent years with declining budgets of public park and recreation agencies and a related interest in the revenues that fees might provide. This interest has sparked a number of studies and associated publications on multiple dimensions of pricing in outdoor recreation, including companion special issues of the *Journal of Leisure Research* and the *Journal of Park and Recreation Administration* published in 1999, and an exchange of papers in the *Journal of Leisure Research* (Crompton, 2002; Driver, 2002; Dustin, 2002; More, 2002). An annotated bibliography of fee-related research was published by Puttkammer and Wright (2001), and an extended index of associated scientific and professional literature was prepared under the auspices of the US Forest Service in 2002 (Williams and Black, 2002).

A content analysis of this growing body of literature has identified a number of potential issues as outlined in Box 4.1 (Martin, 1999), and research has begun to address a number of these issues. First, to what extent does pricing influence use of parks and related areas? Findings have been mixed (Manning and Baker, 1981; Fesenmeier and Schroeder, 1983; Becker *et al.*, 1985; Leuschner *et al.*, 1987; Rechisky and Williamson, 1992; Reiling *et al.*, 1996; Lindberg and Aylward, 1999; Marsinko, 1999; Kerkvliet and Nowell, 2000; Hanley *et al.*, 2002; Ready *et al.*, 2004; Schwartz and Lin, 2006; Siderelis and Moore, 2006). For example, a study of day users at six recreation areas administered by the Army Corps of Engineers found that 40% of respondents reported they would no longer use those areas if a fee was instituted (Reiling *et al.* 1996), while a study of climbers in Scotland found that initiation of a parking fee reduced predicted use by 31% (Hanley *et al.*, 2002). A study of visits to 31 heavily used US national parks before and after fee increases estimated that such fees resulted in a significant decline in use (Schwartz and Lin, 2006). Finally, a survey of visitors to a non-fee national forest site in the south-western USA found that half of respondents had chosen the site because it was free, and that one-third had changed their visitation patterns in response to fees implemented in the national forest (Schneider and Budruk, 1999).

Other studies have shown little or no effects of pricing on recreation use levels. For example, a survey of anglers in and around Yellowstone National Park, Wyoming/Montana/Idaho, found that increases in the cost of fishing licenses or park entrance fees were unlikely to reduce fishing activity, at least within a reasonable range of fee levels (Kerkvliet and Nowell, 2000). A study of fees and international visits to three Costa Rican national parks found demand for these parks to be generally inelastic (Lindberg and Aylward, 1999). (Elasticity of demand is discussed more fully below.) This finding is generally consistent with other, similar studies.

The literature suggests that the influence of fees on recreation use is dependent upon several factors, including:

**1.** The "elasticity of demand" for a park or recreation area. Elasticity refers to the slope of the demand curve that defines the relationship between price and quantity consumed. The demand for some recreation areas is relatively elastic, meaning that a change in price has a comparatively large effect on the quantity consumed, while the opposite is true of other areas.

**2.** The significance of the recreation area. Parks of national and international significance, such as Yellowstone National Park, are likely to have a relatively inelastic demand, suggesting that pricing is not likely to be effective in limiting use unless increases are dramatic. Parks that are less significant are likely to be characterized by more elastic demand, and pricing may be an effective use-limiting and allocation practice.

**3.** The percentage of total cost represented by the fee. In cases where the fee charged represents a relatively high percentage of the total cost of visiting a recreation area, pricing is likely to be a more effective use-limiting approach than when the fee charged represents only a small percentage of the total cost.

**4.** The type of fee instituted. Pricing structure can be a potentially important element in determining the effectiveness of fees as a management practice. For example, a daily use fee might be more effective in limiting total use than an annual pass that allows unlimited use opportunities for a flat fee.

## Acceptability

A second issue addressed in the literature is the acceptability of fees to potential visitors (Bowker *et al.*, 1999; Krannich *et al.*, 1999; Trainor and Norgaard, 1999; Vogt and Williams, 1999; Williams *et al.*, 1999; More and Stevens, 2000; Fix and Vaske, 2007). Again, study findings are mixed, though they often suggest that there is a substantial willingness to pay for park and recreation services and that there is general public support for fees. Two national surveys in the USA have addressed public attitudes toward fees for parks and outdoor recreation. A 1995 survey of the American public found that over 95% of respondents reported that outdoor recreation on public lands should be supported wholly or in part by fees (Bowker *et al.*, 1999). A 2000 general population survey focused on US national parks found that, of those respondents who were aware of proposals to increase fees, the vast majority (94%) supported this proposed program (Ostergren *et al.*, 2005).

The literature suggests that the acceptability of fees is at least partially dependent on several factors, including:

1. Dispensation of resulting revenues. If revenues derived from fee programs are retained by the collecting agency and reinvested in recreation facilities and services, then fees are often judged to be more acceptable to park visitors.
2. Initiation of fee or increase in existing fee. Public acceptance of new fees tends to be relatively low compared to increases in existing fees.
3. Local or non-local visitors. Local visitors tend to be more resistant to new or increased fees than non-local visitors. This is probably because fees represent a larger percentage of the total cost of visiting a recreation area for local visitors, who are also likely to visit a given recreation area more often.
4. Provision of comparative information. Visitor acceptance of fees is likely to be greater when information is provided on the costs of competing or substitute recreation opportunities and when visitors are made aware of the costs of providing recreation opportunities.
5. Type of recreation area. Support for fees may be greater in developed parks than in wilderness. Lack of developed recreation facilities in wilderness may suggest that fees are not needed, and fees may be viewed as antithetical to the non-material values conventionally associated with wilderness.

## Discrimination

A third issue concerns the potential for pricing to discriminate against certain groups in society, particularly those who are disadvantaged and/or have low incomes. Once again, research on this issue is mixed (Leuschner *et al.*, 1987; Reiling *et al.*, 1992, 1994; Bowker *et al.*, 1999; Schneider and Budruk, 1999; Schroeder and Louviere, 1999; More and Stevens, 2000; Taylor *et al.*, 2002; Marsinko *et al.*, 2004; Nyaupane *et al.*, 2007; Huhtala and Pouta, 2008). For example, one study examined the socio-economic characteristics of visitors to two similar outdoor recreation areas in Virginia, only one of which charged an entrance fee (Leuschner *et al.*, 1987). No differences were found in income levels, suggesting the fee had no discriminatory effect. A survey of visitors to 14 National Wildlife Refuges found that only 8% of respondents reported that they would be displaced from these areas as a likely response to fee increases (Taylor *et al.*, 2002). Moreover, there was only a weak statistical relationship between displacement and respondent income. Finally, a survey of visitors' evaluations of recreation fees at Flaming Gorge National Recreation Areas, Utah/Wyoming, found a negative relationship between income and support for fees (Fix and Vaske, 2007). However, this relationship was strongly mediated by beliefs about recreation fees (e.g. fees constitute double taxation, recreation is a merit good that should be subsidized), suggesting that such beliefs are more important than income in evaluating the effects of a fee program.

However, a number of studies have found evidence of potential discriminatory effects of fees. For example, two studies of willingness to pay recreation fees at state parks and Army Corps of Engineers day-use areas found that lower-income visitors had a more elastic demand curve than did high-income users (Reiling *et al.*, 1992, 1994). This suggests that pricing may discriminate against lower-income visitors. A survey of Vermont and New Hampshire households found that, although user fees for outdoor recreation are widely accepted, they may substantially reduce participation of lower-income groups in outdoor recreation: 23% of low-income respondents reported they had either reduced use or visited an alternative site in response to recent fee increases, while only 11% of high-income users had made such changes (More and Stevens, 2000). This study also estimated that a US$5 daily fee for use of public outdoor recreation areas affected about 49% of low-income people as compared to 33% of high-income respondents. A 1995 national public opinion survey in the USA found that, although there was broad support for user fees for outdoor recreation (as noted earlier), this support was statistically related to several socio-economic characteristics of respondents, including income, suggesting that fees may have some discriminatory effects (Bowker et al., 1999). A more recent paper also noted fees as a barrier to poorer Americans accessing public recreation opportunities (Scott, 2013), and suggested fee free days and financial assistance programs as means to rectify potential inequities. Discounts for seniors, children, large households, and the unemployed have also been suggested to combat discriminatory effects of fees and have been described in terms of differential pricing (Crompton, 2015).

### Differential pricing

A final issue concerns the use of differential pricing to influence recreation use patterns. Differential pricing consists of charging higher or lower fees at selected times and locations. A number of studies have shown that outdoor recreation tends to be characterized by relatively extreme "peaking:" certain areas or times are used very heavily while other times or areas have relatively light use (Lucas, 1970; Manning and Cormier, 1980; Peters and Dawson, 2005). Can pricing be used to even out such recreation use patterns? Research is suggestive of this potential use of pricing (LaPage et al., 1975; Willis et al., 1975; Manning et al., 1982). For example, studies of experimental differential campsite pricing at Vermont state parks documented significant shifts in campsite occupancy patterns (Manning et al., 1984; Bamford et al., 1988).

### Principles of pricing

It is clear that pricing can be a complex and even contentious issue in parks and outdoor recreation. Fees can be used for multiple objectives, including limiting or redistributing recreation use and raising revenue. Issues of equity are vital. It is important that decisions about pricing be considered and implemented in the context of the primary objectives of public parks and related areas, including ensuring equitable access to outdoor recreation and protecting park resources. This has been described as a "functionalist" approach (More, 1999). A considered

approach to pricing is central to building public trust in fee policies and programs. In an evaluation of outdoor recreation fees in Southern California, "social trust" was the most important predictor of attitudes and impacts related to fees (Winter et al., 1999). While research has not played a strong role in the design and administration of fee programs, managers who have used research findings report that research has been very useful (Absher et al., 1999). A series of evolving principles for designing and administering pricing/fee systems is shown in Box 4.2 (Manning et al., 1996a).

### Rules and Regulations

Rules and regulations are a commonly used recreation management practice, though their use can sometimes be controversial (Lucas, 1982, 1983; Monz et al., 2000). Common applications of rules and regulations in outdoor recreation include group size limitations, assigned campsites and/or travel itineraries, area closures, length of stay limitations, and restrictions on or prohibition of campfires. The importance of encouraging visitors to comply with rules and regulations is emphasized in a study of the US national park system that found that visitors who did not do so caused extensive damage (Johnson and Vande Kamp, 1996).

As noted earlier in this chapter, research indicates that visitors are often unaware of rules and regulations (Ross and Moeller, 1974). This suggests that managers must effectively communicate them to visitors using the principles and guidelines described in the section on information and education programs. In particular, visitors should be informed of the reasons why applicable rules and regulations are necessary, of sanctions associated with failure to comply, and of activities and behaviors that can be substituted for those not allowed.

Only limited research has addressed the effectiveness of rules and regulations as a recreation management practice. The literature suggests that most visitors support limitations on group size, but that group types should also be considered when promulgating such regulations (Roggenbuck and Schreyer, 1977; Heywood, 1985; Watson et al., 1993; Cole et al., 1995; Monz et al., 2000). Group size limits should not be set so low that they affect primary social groups of visitors who may have strong motivations for social interaction. Research suggests that social groups in outdoor recreation tend to be small, but that larger group sizes may be

**Box 4.2. Principles for pricing/fees in outdoor recreation. (From Manning *et al.*, 1996a.)**

**1.** Persons who benefit directly from facilities and services should pay a greater portion of the costs of provision.

**2.** Fees should be designed and administered on the basis of the costs of providing visitor facilities and the impacts of visitors on resources.

**3.** Every user of an agency's facilities and services should pay a fair share of the costs of providing those facilities and services.

**4.** Revenue raised through fee programs should be dedicated to ensuring stewardship of resources and providing public access to those resources.

**5.** Fees and charges represent only a portion of the revenues needed to develop, operate, and maintain recreational resources and opportunities, and are not a substitute for society's investment in its recreational resources and opportunities.

**6.** The design of a fee program should be clearly linked to specific purposes.

**7.** Fee revenues should be shared, with part being retained for use where collected, and the remainder allocated under a clearly stated revenue-sharing policy.

**8.** User fees and charges should be structured and administered in ways that provide incentives for managers to collect fees, and incentives for visitors to pay fees.

**9.** Development and administration of user fees and charges should be accompanied by improvements in cost control, operational efficiency, use of partnerships, and accountability.

**10.** There should be a strong and visible linkage between the fees and charges paid by visitors and the quality of services and benefits they receive.

**11.** Fees and charges should be based, at least partially, on a consideration of private sector fees, and charges and impacts on local communities.

**12.** Managers should be authorized and encouraged to administer user fees and charges with sensitivity to local opportunities, constraints, and issues of social equity.

**13.** Management of visitor use to protect resources and enhance the quality of the visitor experience is a legitimate goal of fee programs and a legitimate use of fee revenue.

**14.** A continuing evaluation program to monitor and analyse the effectiveness of user fees and charges should be conducted, and should be funded by a portion of the revenues obtained through fees and charges.

associated with some minority racial and ethnic groups (Chavez, 2000). Group size limits also have potentially important economic implications for commercial outfitters and non-profit and educational institutions.

Given the trend toward increasing use of group size limits and their controversial nature, a four-step conceptual model to help guide such management decisions has been developed (Monz *et al.* 2000). This model challenges managers and stakeholders to consider the potential costs and benefits of group size limits in alternative contexts as a means of setting a thoughtful, transparent, and defensible maximum group size.

Although group size regulations are conventionally considered in terms of maximum group size, minimums have also been considered and applied.

For example, when grizzly bears are known to be present in portions of Banff National Park, Canada, a restricted access policy is initiated, requiring a minimum group size of six hikers (research demonstrates that larger group sizes are substantially less likely to encounter and be threatened by bears) (Tucker, 2001). Research evaluating this policy found that the vast majority of visitors (81%) expressed support for this policy but that only 60% complied with the regulation.

Regulations limiting or prohibiting campfires are also increasingly common. Campfires can be a cause of wildfires, but can also damage soils, have unsightly aesthetic effects, reduce nutrient recycling through burning of down wood, and lead to environmental impacts associated with gathering firewood. A study of campfire impacts and policies in seven national parks and forests in the USA found three basic regulatory approaches: banning campfires, designating campfire sites, and no regulation of campfires (Reid and Marion, 2005). Findings suggest that banning campfires does not substantially reduce campfire-related impacts but that no regulation results in excessive resource damage. The authors conclude that the regulatory option of designating campfire sites along with banning axes, hatchets, and saws is likely to exercise reasonable control of campfire impacts while preserving the option of campfires, a practice that is highly valued by some visitors.

Research suggests that visitors tend not to support regulations requiring the use of assigned campsites in wilderness or backcountry (Lucas, 1985; Anderson and Manfredo, 1986). An extreme version of this regulation requires backpackers to follow a fixed travel itinerary. Studies of the effectiveness of this regulation have found that visitor compliance rates are relatively low (Van Wagtendonk and Benedict, 1980; Parsons et al., 1981, 1982; Stewart, 1989, 1991). For example, 44–77% of backcountry campers were found not to be in full compliance with their permit itinerary across four zones of Grand Canyon National Park, Arizona (Stewart, 1989). Non-compliance was primarily caused by visitors using campsites other than those specified, or staying in the backcountry more or fewer nights than originally specified.

Research on regulations closing selected areas to public use suggest they are supported by visitors if the underlying reason is clear and justified (Frost and McCool, 1988). Most visitors obeyed a regulation closing selected backcountry campsites for ecological reasons (Cole and Rang, 1983). Regulations closing areas to camping in selected natural areas in Norway have also been found to be effective, although such regulations can substantially threaten and even displace traditional use and users (Vork, 1998). This suggests that regulations should be used cautiously.

## Law Enforcement

Little research has been conducted on law enforcement in outdoor recreation. Most of the literature in this area discusses its controversial nature (Campbell et al., 1968; Bowman, 1971; Hadley, 1971; Hope, 1971; Schwartz, 1973; Connors, 1976; Shanks, 1976; Wicker and Kirmeyer, 1976; Harmon, 1979; Morehead, 1979; Wade, 1979;

Westover et al., 1980; Philley and McCool, 1981; Heinrichs, 1982; Perry, 1983; Manning, 1987). Perhaps the most controversial issue concerns the degree to which law enforcement should take a "hard" approach, as is conventional in most urban and other contexts, versus a "soft" approach that may be more in keeping with the emphasis of parks and outdoor recreation areas on protecting the quality of the visitor experience (Charles, 1982; Carroll, 1988; Cannon, 1991; Forsyth, 1994; Shore, 1994; Pendleton, 1996, 1998). An ethnographic study of law enforcement in Pacific Rim National Park, Canada, illustrates the strategies taken by law enforcement officers that can be seen to represent a spectrum of soft law enforcement that is defined by degree of intervention and symbolic expression (Pendleton, 1998). The "conciliatory" style encourages visitors to comply with rules and regulations by taking a friendly tone, providing the information necessary to facilitate compliance, and suggesting (through uniformed presence, etc.) that harder enforcement is possible. "Bluffing" places greater explicit emphasis on the option for a harder enforcement approach. "Avoiding" is used to ignore enforcement when violations are minor, unintended, or would otherwise be inappropriate. "Bargaining" strikes a deal with violators to abide by applicable rules or face sanctions associated with conventional hard enforcement actions.

Surprisingly little research has addressed the effectiveness of law enforcement in the context of parks and outdoor recreation. A study at Mt Rainier National Park, Washington, found that the presence of a uniformed ranger significantly reduced off-trail hiking (Swearingen and Johnson, 1995). Moreover, visitors tended to react positively to this management practice when they understood that the presence of a ranger was needed for information dissemination, visitor safety, and resource protection. A long-term study of four marine sanctuaries in the Philippines found improved ecological conditions of coral reefs and fish species richness and abundance and attributed this to law enforcement along with enhanced management activities and community support (Walmsley and White, 2003).

## Zoning

Zoning is another basic category of recreation management. In its most generic sense, zoning simply means assigning certain recreation (and other) activities to selected areas (or restricting activities from areas). Zoning can also be applied in a temporal dimension as well as in a spatial sense. It can also be applied to alternative management prescriptions as a way of creating different types of outdoor recreation opportunities (Greist, 1975; Haas et al., 1987). For example, "rescue" and "no-rescue" zones have been proposed for wilderness areas, though this is controversial (McAvoy and Dustin, 1981; Harwell, 1987; Peterson, 1987; McAvoy, 1990).

In its most fundamental form, zoning is widely used to create and manage a diversity of recreation opportunities. The basic concept of zoning is at the heart of the Recreation Opportunity Spectrum (ROS), a concept that has been widely applied in parks and outdoor recreation (Brown et al., 1978; Driver and Brown, 1978; Brown et al., 1979; Clark and Stankey, 1979). Zoning is also used in outdoor recreation to restrict selected recreation activities from environmentally sensitive areas, to separate conflicting recreation uses, and to separate recreation areas from competing and conflicting uses. Zoning can often be interpreted as formal recognition of naturally occurring variability in recreation conditions—diversity in accessibility, distance from population centers, use levels, etc. (Haas et al., 1987).

The concept of zoning appears to have relatively strong support among visitors. A survey of visitors to 12 wilderness areas in the Pacific northwest of the USA found support for zoning within individual wilderness areas and across the system of wilderness areas (Cole and Hall, 2006, 2008). For example, when respondents were asked which of several management options they favored to balance the inherent tension between providing public access versus providing opportunities for solitude, the vast majority of visitors selected zoning options. A large plurality of respondents (44%) favored managing "a few" trails for solitude while allowing for heavier use on remaining trails. The second most popular option (34%) was managing "most" trails for solitude, but allowing for heavier use on remaining trails. Only small percentages favored managing "no" (17%) or "all" trails for solitude (5%). Respondents were asked if they agreed or disagreed with a series of statements concerning potential differences in the ways in which wilderness areas close to population centers should be managed as compared to more remote wilderness areas. Considerable support was found for such differences in management. For example, most respondents reported that in wilderness areas close to population centers it is acceptable to see more

people, visitor behavior should be more restricted, it is more acceptable to manipulate the environment to increase resource durability, and use limits are more likely necessary.

Several recent studies have described the ways in which zoning systems have been developed and applied in a diversity of parks and outdoor recreation areas. For example, a system of four zones has been applied at Koh Chang National Marine Park, Thailand, based primarily on an assessment of the fragility of the area's coral reefs and a survey of visitors regarding preferred use levels and other experiential characteristics (Roman et al., 2007). A similar zoning system has been developed for the Great Barrier Reef Marine Park, Australia (Day, 2002); its objectives are to separate conflicting uses, match types and intensities of uses with inherent resource capability, and provide a range of recreation opportunities. The study concludes that "Zoning has been, and will remain, one of the cornerstones of management," and that "The spectrum of zones set within the framework of a multiple use area allows for a range of reasonable uses to occur in a coordinated way, and provides for broad-area integrated management." A recreation-related zoning system has also been applied to Mount Spil National Park, Turkey, based primarily on ecological considerations (Hepcan, 2000). Buffer zones constitute a special type of zoning designed to separate conflicting uses. For example, a series of buffer zones ranging from 100 to 180 m have been recommended to shield waterfowl from disturbance by selected types of recreational boating (Rodgers and Schwikert, 2002). Parks Canada also has a strong system of zoning that was introduced in the 1970s, although a recent survey of 13 Parks Canada employees suggests it could be updated and improved (Thede et al., 2014).

## Facility Development, Site Design, and Maintenance

A final category of recreation management practices is facility development/site design/maintenance. These practices are primarily designed to protect natural and cultural resources from the impacts of visitor use. Several issues and studies warrant attention. A principal issue in site management is whether recreation use should be concentrated or dispersed. Studies of environmental impacts caused by recreation use have generally found that such impacts can occur quickly even under low levels of use (Hammitt *et al.*, 2015; Leung and Marion, 2000). This suggests that recreation use might best be concentrated on sites that are inherently durable and that can be intensively maintained, and this approach has generally been found to be successful (Spildie *et al.*, 2000; Marion and Farrell, 2002; Reid and Marion, 2004; Cole *et al.*, 2008). However, this strategy may exacerbate crowding and conflicting uses. Alternatively, recreation use can be dispersed, but use levels would have to be kept low to avoid unacceptable aerial expansion of resource impacts. Another basic strategy is "hardening" and otherwise intensively managing recreation sites to minimize environmental impacts; for example, boardwalks and tent pads can be built to shield fragile soils and vegetation from trampling and erosion (Hultsman and

Hultsman, 1989; Doucette and Kimball, 1990). However, such facilities may be considered inappropriate in backcountry and wilderness contexts. Recreation sites can also be designed in ways to minimize environmental impacts (Godin and Leonard, 1976; McEwen and Tocher, 1976; Echelberger *et al.*, 1983; Biscombe *et al.*, 2001). For example, campgrounds might be designed in a "linear layout", illustrated in Fig. 4.1, to minimize the inherent tendency of some visitors to create social trails.

Several literature reviews and studies have addressed and assessed these issues more fully (Hammitt *et al.*, 2015; Leung and Marion, 1999; Marion and Farrell, 2002). For example, redesign of a popular camping area along the Appalachian National Scenic Trail in Maryland closed and

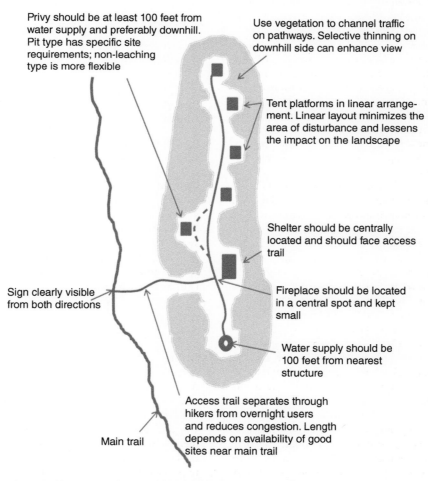

Privy should be at least 100 feet from water supply and preferably downhill. Pit type has specific site requirements; non-leaching type is more flexible

Use vegetation to channel traffic on pathways. Selective thinning on downhill side can enhance view

Tent platforms in linear arrangement. Linear layout minimizes the area of disturbance and lessens the impact on the landscape

Shelter should be centrally located and should face access trail

Sign clearly visible from both directions

Fireplace should be located in a central spot and kept small

Water supply should be 100 feet from nearest structure

Main trail

Access trail separates through hikers from overnight users and reduces congestion. Length depends on availability of good sites near main trail

**Fig. 4.1.** "Linear layout" of backcountry campground. (Adapted from Fay *et al.*, 1977.)

rehabilitated large, heavily impacted campsites in flat areas. These were replaced with smaller sites in sidehill locations that offered more privacy and discouraged campsite expansion, reducing the total area of environmental disturbance and resulting in higher visitor satisfaction (Daniels and Marion, 2006). Another study used symbolic rope fencing along the margins of trails in Acadia National Park, Maine, to discourage visitors from walking off-trail (Park et al., 2008). This approach was found to be substantially more effective than several information/education practices.

## Conclusion

A large and growing body of scientific and professional literature has explored the potential effectiveness of a range of recreation management practices. Most of this work has been focused on six basic categories of management practices:

1. Information/education.
2. Use rationing/allocation.
3. Rules/regulations.
4. Law enforcement.
5. Zoning.
6. Facility development/site design/maintenance.

Much of this research suggests that all of these management practices can be used to reduce the environmental and experiential impacts of outdoor recreation. Special care must be exercised when rationing and allocating use to ensure that no groups are being discriminated against, especially when using fees as a management practice.

# 5

# Applying Outdoor Recreation Management

Chapters 2 through 4 take a systematic approach to inventorying and describing problems that can be caused by outdoor recreation, as well as the range of management strategies and practices that can be employed to address these problems. Problems caused by outdoor recreation were categorized into 16 types organized into three basic categories: park resources, the visitor experience, and park facilities and services. Management practices were categorized in two ways: strategies and tactics/practices. Four basic strategies were defined and six categories of management practices can be employed within each of the four strategies.

## Management Matrices

This systematic way of thinking about problems and management strategies and practices offers the basis for constructing an organized and comprehensive approach to managing outdoor recreation. This approach relies on a series of matrices such as the one shown in Fig. 5.1. In this figure, the 16 types of problems that can be caused by outdoor recreation are arrayed across the top of the matrix, and the four strategies and six practices that can be used to manage these problems are arrayed along the side of the matrix. Since there are four strategies with six categories of practices under each, this requires use of four matrices (one for each of the four strategies). The matrix in Fig. 5.1 is for the strategy of limiting use. The other three strategies—increase the supply of recreation opportunities, reduce the impact of use, and harden the resource/experience—are shown in Figs. 5.2, 5.3, and 5.4, respectively.

Each matrix includes 96 cells—the intersections of problems and management practices—as numbered and shown in the figures. Each cell has the potential to include one or more specific management practices (that fall within the management strategy and the category of management practices defined by that row of the matrix) that might be used to address the problem defined by that column of the matrix. For example, cell number 1 in Fig. 5.1 is defined by the column labeled **Impacts to resources (Soil)**. Moreover, it is also defined by the row labeled **Information/Education** under the strategy of **Limit use**. In other words, cell number 1 should include the ways in which information and education could be used to limit use of an area suffering from excessive impacts to soil caused by outdoor recreation. There are at least three management practices that could be used:

**1.** Information and education could be used to promote use of alternative sites, either within the park in question or at other parks. This could reduce the amount of use at the site or park in question by dispersing some use to other sites or parks.
**2.** Information and education could be used to promote alternative times to use the site or park in question. For example, soils are often wet and more vulnerable to compaction in the spring.
**3.** Information and education could be used to inform potential visitors of current impacts and resource conditions (e.g. excessive soil compaction and erosion) at the site or park in question in the hope that this might encourage potential visitors to refrain from using the site or park.

These three management practices are labeled 1a, 1b, and 1c, respectively, and are included in a listing of management practices in Appendix A1. Appendix A1 is a listing of management practices associated with Fig. 5.1, falling under the strategy of limiting use and employing all six categories of management practices to reduce recreation-related impacts and associated problems.

Figure 5.2 is the matrix for the strategy of increasing the supply of recreation opportunities. By increasing the supply of opportunities, recreation use—and associated impacts—might be dispersed across a greater number of sites and parks,

| Management practices | Problems | | | | | | | | | | | | | | | |
|---|---|---|---|---|---|---|---|---|---|---|---|---|---|---|---|---|
| **Strategies** Practices | Impacts to resources | | | | | | | | Impacts to experience | | | Impacts to facilities/services | | | | |
| Limit use | Soil | Vegetation | Water | Wildlife | Air | Natural Quiet | Natural Darkness | Historical/Cultural | Crowding | Conflict | Depreciative behavior | Attraction sites | Trails | Campgrounds/Campsites | Roads/Parking | Interpretive facilities/Programs |
| Information/Education | 1 | 7 | 13 | 19 | 25 | 31 | 37 | 43 | 49 | 55 | 61 | 67 | 73 | 79 | 85 | 91 |
| Rationing/Allocation | 2 | 8 | 14 | 20 | 26 | 32 | 38 | 44 | 50 | 56 | 62 | 68 | 74 | 80 | 86 | 92 |
| Rules/Regulations | 3 | 9 | 15 | 21 | 27 | 33 | 39 | 45 | 51 | 57 | 63 | 69 | 75 | 81 | 87 | 93 |
| Law enforcement | 4 | 10 | 16 | 22 | 28 | 34 | 40 | 46 | 52 | 58 | 64 | 70 | 76 | 82 | 88 | 94 |
| Zoning | 5 | 11 | 17 | 23 | 29 | 35 | 41 | 47 | 53 | 59 | 65 | 71 | 77 | 83 | 89 | 95 |
| Facility development/Site design/Maintenance | 6 | 12 | 18 | 24 | 30 | 36 | 42 | 48 | 54 | 60 | 66 | 72 | 78 | 84 | 90 | 96 |

**Fig. 5.1.** Management matrix for the strategy of limiting use.

thereby limiting the amount of impact at one site or park. As in the other matrices, cell number 1 is the intersection of the column relating to the problem of impacts to soil and the row relating to the management practice of information and education. In this matrix the management strategy is increasing the supply of recreation opportunities. There are at least two management practices that could be used:

**1.** Information and education could be used to inform visitors of the full range of recreation areas and opportunities that are available, helping to disperse recreation use.
**2.** Information and education could be used to promote visitation to low-use areas, helping to disperse use and lower associated impacts.

These two management practices have been labeled 1a and 1b, respectively, and are included in a listing of management practices in Appendix A2. Appendix A2 is a listing of management practices associated with Fig. 5.2: management practices that fall under the strategy of increasing the supply of recreation areas and opportunities and employ information and education to reduce recreation-related impacts and associated problems.

Figure 5.3 is the matrix for the strategy of reducing the impact of use. It will be remembered from Chapter 3 that this strategy does not try to change the amount of use, but focuses on reducing the amount of impact per visit or visitor. As in the example above, cell number 1 is the intersection of

the column relating to the problem of impacts to soil and the row relating to the management practice of information and education. However, in this matrix the management strategy is reducing the impact of use rather than reducing the amount of use. There are at least six management practices that could be used:

**1.** Information could be used to promote use of alternative sites to disperse use (either within the park in question or to other parks). Note that the objective here is to disperse use, and not limit it. While this might seem like a subtle difference, it has important implications for meeting the demand for recreation among the public.
**2.** Information and education could be used to promote alternative times to use the site or park in question. Again, this is similar to the second management practice described above, but is intended to disperse use, not to limit it.
**3.** Information and education could be used to promote use of sites or parks that are more resistant and/or resilient to soil compaction and erosion or which have been hardened against these types of impacts (i.e. concentrate recreation use on sites or parks that are more capable of withstanding heavy use).
**4.** Information and education could be used to inform visitors of acceptable and unacceptable recreation activities. For example, in areas where soils are especially vulnerable to compaction and erosion,

| Management practices | Problems | | | | | | | | | | | | | | | |
|---|---|---|---|---|---|---|---|---|---|---|---|---|---|---|---|---|
| **Strategies** Practices | Impacts to resources | | | | | | | | Impacts to experience | | | Impacts to facilities/services | | | | |
| **Increase supply** | Soil | Vegetation | Water | Wildlife | Air | Natural Quiet | Natural Darkness | Historical/Cultural | Crowding | Conflict | Depreciative behavior | Attraction sites | Trails | Campgrounds/Campsites | Roads/Parking | Interpretive facilities/Programs |
| Information/Education | 1 | 7 | 13 | 19 | 25 | 31 | 37 | 43 | 49 | 55 | 61 | 67 | 73 | 79 | 85 | 91 |
| Rationing/Allocation | 2 | 8 | 14 | 20 | 26 | 32 | 38 | 44 | 50 | 56 | 62 | 68 | 74 | 80 | 86 | 92 |
| Rules/Regulations | 3 | 9 | 15 | 21 | 27 | 33 | 39 | 45 | 51 | 57 | 63 | 69 | 75 | 81 | 87 | 93 |
| Law enforcement | 4 | 10 | 16 | 22 | 28 | 34 | 40 | 46 | 52 | 58 | 64 | 70 | 76 | 82 | 88 | 94 |
| Zoning | 5 | 11 | 17 | 23 | 29 | 35 | 41 | 47 | 53 | 59 | 65 | 71 | 77 | 83 | 89 | 95 |
| Facility development/Site design/Maintenance | 6 | 12 | 18 | 24 | 30 | 36 | 42 | 48 | 54 | 60 | 66 | 72 | 78 | 84 | 90 | 96 |

**Fig. 5.2.** Management matrix for the strategy of increasing the supply of recreation opportunities.

| Management practices | Problems | | | | | | | | | | | | | | | |
|---|---|---|---|---|---|---|---|---|---|---|---|---|---|---|---|---|
| **Strategies** Practices | Impacts to resources | | | | | | | | Impacts to experience | | | Impacts to facilities/services | | | | |
| **Reduce the impact of use** | Soil | Vegetation | Water | Wildlife | Air | Natural Quiet | Natural Darkness | Historical/Cultural | Crowding | Conflict | Depreciative behavior | Attraction sites | Trails | Campgrounds/Campsites | Roads/Parking | Interpretive facilities/Programs |
| Information/Education | 1 | 7 | 13 | 19 | 25 | 31 | 37 | 43 | 49 | 55 | 61 | 67 | 73 | 79 | 85 | 91 |
| Rationing/Allocation | 2 | 8 | 14 | 20 | 26 | 32 | 38 | 44 | 50 | 56 | 62 | 68 | 74 | 80 | 86 | 92 |
| Rules/Regulations | 3 | 9 | 15 | 21 | 27 | 33 | 39 | 45 | 51 | 57 | 63 | 69 | 75 | 81 | 87 | 93 |
| Law enforcement | 4 | 10 | 16 | 22 | 28 | 34 | 40 | 46 | 52 | 58 | 64 | 70 | 76 | 82 | 88 | 94 |
| Zoning | 5 | 11 | 17 | 23 | 29 | 35 | 41 | 47 | 53 | 59 | 65 | 71 | 77 | 83 | 89 | 95 |
| Facility development/Site design/Maintenance | 6 | 12 | 18 | 24 | 30 | 36 | 42 | 48 | 54 | 60 | 66 | 72 | 78 | 84 | 90 | 96 |

**Fig. 5.3.** Management matrix for the strategy of reducing the impact of use.

visitors might be asked to restrict their activities to pedestrian uses only and refrain from motorized use. **5.** Information and education could be used to inform visitors of acceptable and unacceptable behavior. For example, visitors could be encouraged to stay on maintained trails. **6.** Visitors could be educated about why selected activities and behaviors are unacceptable, in an effort to discourage these activities and behaviors. For example, visitors could be educated about how walking off maintained trails can damage fragile soils through compaction and erosion.

These six management practices are labeled 1a through 1f, respectively, and are included in a listing of management practices in Appendix A3. Appendix A3 is a listing of management practices associated with Fig. 5.3: management practices that fall under the strategy of reducing the impact of use and employ all six categories of management

| Management practices | Problems | | | | | | | | | | | | | | | |
|---|---|---|---|---|---|---|---|---|---|---|---|---|---|---|---|---|
| **Strategies** Practices | Impacts to resources | | | | | | | | Impacts to experience | | | Impacts to facilities/services | | | | |
| **Hardening the resource/experience** | Soil | Vegetation | Water | Wildlife | Air | Natural Quiet | Natural Darkness | Historical/Cultural | Crowding | Conflict | Depreciative behavior | Attraction sites | Trails | Campgrounds/Campsites | Roads/Parking | Interpretive facilities/Programs |
| Information/Education | 1 | 7 | 13 | 19 | 25 | 31 | 37 | 43 | 49 | 55 | 61 | 67 | 73 | 79 | 85 | 91 |
| Rationing/Allocation | 2 | 8 | 14 | 20 | 26 | 32 | 38 | 44 | 50 | 56 | 62 | 68 | 74 | 80 | 86 | 92 |
| Rules/Regulations | 3 | 9 | 15 | 21 | 27 | 33 | 39 | 45 | 51 | 57 | 63 | 69 | 75 | 81 | 87 | 93 |
| Law enforcement | 4 | 10 | 16 | 22 | 28 | 34 | 40 | 46 | 52 | 58 | 64 | 70 | 76 | 82 | 88 | 94 |
| Zoning | 5 | 11 | 17 | 23 | 29 | 35 | 41 | 47 | 53 | 59 | 65 | 71 | 77 | 83 | 89 | 95 |
| Facility development/Site design/Maintenance | 6 | 12 | 18 | 24 | 30 | 36 | 42 | 48 | 54 | 60 | 66 | 72 | 78 | 84 | 90 | 96 |

**Fig. 5.4.** Management matrix for the strategy of hardening the resource/experience.

practices to reduce recreation-related impacts and associated problems.

Figure 5.4 is the matrix for the strategy of hardening the resource or the park experience. Again, as we saw in Chapter 3, this strategy is designed to shield park resources and/or the quality of the visitor experience from the potential impacts of outdoor recreation. As in the first three matrices, cell number 1 is the intersection of the column relating to the problem of impacts to soil and the row relating to the management practice of information and education. In this matrix the management strategy is hardening the resource or the park experience. Unfortunately, information and education cannot be used to harden soil from the potential impacts of outdoor recreation. But information and education could be used to help "harden" the visitor experience by shaping realistic visitor expectations for park conditions. Research demonstrates that visitor expectations can play an important role in determining visitor satisfaction; if visitors expect to encounter park conditions that are less than pristine, they are likely to be less dissatisfied than if they expect to see little park degradation (Manning, 2011). Therefore, information and education designed to inform visitors of current park conditions such as soil compaction and erosion may "harden" the quality of the visitor experience. This is the only potential application of information and education in hardening either

soil or the quality of the visitor experience as affected by soil impacts. This management practice is labeled 1 and is included in a listing of management practices in Appendix A4. Appendix A4 is a listing of management practices associated with Fig. 5.4: management practices that fall under the strategy of hardening the resource or the park experience and employ all six categories of management practices to reduce recreation-related impacts and associated problems.

## Observations on the Management Matrices and Appendices

The management matrices presented in this chapter, along with their associated appendices, offer a systematic and comprehensive way of thinking about managing the potential impacts of outdoor recreation. They build on the categories of management problems developed in Chapter 2 (the 16 problems comprising resource, experiential, and managerial concerns) and the categories of management practices (the six categories of management practices for each of the four management strategies) developed in Chapters 3 and 4. By combining this organizational approach into a series of four matrices, explicit consideration can be given to all possible management practices as they apply to the full spectrum of management problems.

Each of the four management matrices results in 96 potential interactions between problems and management practices. Collectively, the four matrices represent 384 potential ways in which management practices might be used to address management problems. Moreover, in many cases there are multiple ways in which management practices might be employed within each of the matrix cells. This illustrates the large number and wide variety of ways in which the potential problems associated with outdoor recreation might be managed.

Appendices A1 through A4 represent an attempt to fill in the cells of each of the four management matrices—to brainstorm the ways in which the four management strategies and six categories of management practices might be used to address the 16 management problems. This is a daunting task and the appendices should be used as working documents, illustrative of the variety of management approaches that can be brought to bear. Readers are encouraged to continue the process of expanding these appendices. An interactive electronic version (Appendix B) can be found at http://www.cabi.org.openresources/ 91018.

The management matrices and associated appendices can be approached and used in several ways. For example, they can be "entered" through the type of problem encountered. What are the potential management practices that can be used to address selected resource-related problems such as soil compaction and erosion? What are the potential management practices that can be used to address selected experiential problems such as crowding? What are the management practices that can be used to address problems at selected facilities and services such as trails? These enquiries can be made at the broad level of all potential management practices, or those that represent selected management strategies and practices, such as information and education designed to reduce the impact of use.

The management matrices and associated appendices can also be entered through the type of management practice. How broadly applicable are the four basic management strategies? How can alternative categories of management practices be used to solve management problems? The management matrices and associated appendices can also be used broadly or specifically. For example, what is the array of management practices—considering all management strategies and practices—that can be used to address a management problem such as soil compaction and erosion? Or, more specifically,

how can information and education designed to reduce use be employed to address soil compaction and erosion?

The two "sides" of the management matrices can also be used in different ways. The classification of management problems is divided into three categories of problems: resource, experiential, and facilities/services. It will be remembered from Chapter 2 that the first two categories of problems represent the basic types of impact to park resources and the quality of the visitor experience that can result from recreation use. The third category—facilities and services—are the basic categories of places or contexts in which these impacts occur. The matrices and associated appendices can be entered through either the basic resource and experiential impacts, or through the places and contexts in which these impacts occur. Similarly, the classification of management practices is based on both strategies and tactics/practices, and the management matrices and associated appendices can be entered through either of these approaches.

The lists of specific management practices contained in the appendices may seem to include some duplication in places, at least at first glance. But there are often seemingly subtle, but important differences in what may appear to be similar management practices. For example, information and education can be used to inform visitors of conditions at recreation sites (e.g. soil compaction and erosion, crowding). However, this can be used to accomplish very different objectives or strategies: to encourage visitors to use other sites/parks, or to "harden" the visitor experience by appropriately preparing visitors for the conditions they are likely to experience. In this way, using information and education to inform visitors of conditions at recreation sites can be seen to be two quite different management practices based on the context in which they are applied.

Finally, there is no practical limit to the amount of detail that can be included in the management matrices and associated appendices. The 16 categories of problems that can be caused by recreation could be extended into finer divisions; for example, impacts to wildlife could be broken down into terrestrial and aquatic. Similarly, the six categories of management practices could be broken into finer divisions: for example, information and education can be delivered in person and by print and other media. Readers are encouraged to make these finer divisions as they find them useful.

**Table 5.1.** Management problems, strategies, and practices addressed in the case studies in Part II.

| Case studies | Soil | Vegetation | Water | Air | Wildlife | Natural Quiet | Natural Darkness | Historical/Cultural | Crowding | Conflict | Depreciative behavior | Attraction sites | Trails | Campgrounds/Campsites | Roads/Parking | Interpretive facilities/Programs | Limit use | Increase supply | Reduce impact of use | Harden resource/experience | Information/Education | Rationing/Allocation | Rules/Regulations | Law enforcement | Zoning | Facility development/Site design/Maintenance |
|---|---|---|---|---|---|---|---|---|---|---|---|---|---|---|---|---|---|---|---|---|---|---|---|---|---|---|
| | | | | | | | | | | | | | | | | | | | | | | | | | | |
| | **Impacts to resources** | | | | | | | | **Impacts to experience** | | | **Impacts to facilities/services** | | | | | **Management strategies** | | | | | | **Management practices** | | | |
| Treading Lightly on Acadia | ✓ | ✓ | | | ✓ | | | | ✓ | ✓ | ✓ | ✓ | ✓ | | | | | | ✓ | ✓ | ✓ | | ✓ | | | ✓ |
| Building a Better Campsite Along the Appalachian Trail | ✓ | ✓ | | | | | | | ✓ | ✓ | ✓ | ✓ | | ✓ | | | | | ✓ | ✓ | ✓ | | ✓ | | | ✓ |
| Let There Be Light in Great Smoky Mountains | ✓ | ✓ | | | | | | | | | | | | | | ✓ | | | ✓ | ✓ | ✓ | | ✓ | | | ✓ |
| How Many Visitors is Too Many at Arches? | ✓ | ✓ | | | ✓ | | | | ✓ | ✓ | ✓ | ✓ | ✓ | | | | ✓ | | ✓ | ✓ | ✓ | ✓ | ✓ | ✓ | ✓ | ✓ |
| Protecting Biscayne's Underwater Treasures | ✓ | ✓ | ✓ | | ✓ | | | | | | | ✓ | | | | | | | ✓ | ✓ | ✓ | | ✓ | ✓ | ✓ | ✓ |
| Saving Bats at Mammoth Cave | | ✓ | | | | | ✓ | | | | | ✓ | | | | | | | ✓ | ✓ | ✓ | | ✓ | ✓ | ✓ | |
| Turning off the Lights at Chaco | | | | | | ✓ | | | | | | ✓ | | | | | | | ✓ | ✓ | ✓ | | ✓ | | | |
| Busing Among the Grizzlies at Denali | | | | | ✓ | | | | ✓ | ✓ | | ✓ | | | ✓ | | ✓ | | ✓ | | ✓ | ✓ | ✓ | | ✓ | ✓ |
| Winning the Lottery on the Colorado River | | | | | ✓ | | | | ✓ | ✓ | | ✓ | | ✓ | | | ✓ | | ✓ | | ✓ | ✓ | ✓ | | ✓ | |
| The Ice Caves are Open, The Ice Caves are Open | | | | | | | | ✓ | | | | ✓ | | ✓ | | | | ✓ | | | ✓ | | ✓ | ✓ | | ✓ |
| The Sounds of Silence in Muir Woods | | | | | | ✓ | | | ✓ | | | | | | | | | | ✓ | ✓ | ✓ | | ✓ | | | |
| Stewarding America's Antiquities at Mesa Verde | ✓ | | | | ✓ | | | ✓ | ✓ | | | ✓ | ✓ | | | ✓ | | | ✓ | | ✓ | | ✓ | ✓ | | ✓ |
| What Goes Up Mt Whitney Must Come Down | ✓ | ✓ | | | | | | | | | | | ✓ | | | | ✓ | | ✓ | | ✓ | ✓ | ✓ | ✓ | | |
| Preventing the Petrified Forest from Disappearing | | | | | | | | ✓ | | | ✓ | | | | | | | | ✓ | | ✓ | | ✓ | ✓ | | |
| Containing Contaminants at Carlsbad Caverns | | | | | | | | | | ✓ | | | | | | | | | ✓ | | ✓ | | ✓ | | | ✓ |
| Bear Etiquette in Katmai | | | | | ✓ | | | | ✓ | ✓ | | ✓ | ✓ | | | | | | ✓ | ✓ | ✓ | | ✓ | | | ✓ |
| Don't Pick up Hitchhikers in Voyageurs | | | ✓ | | | | | | | ✓ | | | | | | | ✓ | | ✓ | | ✓ | | ✓ | ✓ | | |
| A Mountain with Handrails in Yosemite | | | | | | | | ✓ | ✓ | ✓ | | | ✓ | | | ✓ | | | ✓ | ✓ | ✓ | | ✓ | | | ✓ |
| Doing the Zion Shuttle | ✓ | ✓ | ✓ | ✓ | ✓ | | | | ✓ | ✓ | | | | ✓ | ✓ | ✓ | ✓ | ✓ | ✓ | ✓ | ✓ | ✓ | ✓ | | ✓ | ✓ |
| The Buzz from Above at Grand Canyon | | | | ✓ | ✓ | ✓ | | | ✓ | ✓ | | | | | ✓ | ✓ | ✓ | | ✓ | | ✓ | | ✓ | ✓ | ✓ | ✓ |
| Managing Monuments and Memorials at the National Mall | ✓ | ✓ | | | | | | ✓ | ✓ | ✓ | ✓ | ✓ | | ✓ | ✓ | | | | ✓ | ✓ | ✓ | | ✓ | ✓ | | ✓ |
| Climbing Towards Common Ground at Devils Tower | | | | | | | | ✓ | | ✓ | | ✓ | | | ✓ | | | | ✓ | | ✓ | | ✓ | | | |
| The Winter Wonderland of Yellowstone | ✓ | ✓ | ✓ | ✓ | ✓ | ✓ | | | ✓ | ✓ | | | | | | | ✓ | | ✓ | ✓ | ✓ | | ✓ | ✓ | ✓ | ✓ |
| Alternative Transportation at Grand Teton | ✓ | ✓ | ✓ | ✓ | ✓ | ✓ | | | ✓ | ✓ | | | ✓ | | ✓ | ✓ | | ✓ | ✓ | ✓ | ✓ | | ✓ | | ✓ | ✓ |
| No Bad Trip in Glacier | ✓ | ✓ | ✓ | ✓ | ✓ | ✓ | | | ✓ | ✓ | | | | | | ✓ | ✓ | ✓ | ✓ | ✓ | ✓ | ✓ | ✓ | | ✓ | ✓ |

## Case Studies

To illustrate how the management matrices and associated appendices can be used, 25 case studies are presented in Part II of this book. These case studies are drawn from successful management approaches used in the US national park system. The case studies were selected to represent as many of the 16 categories of management problems and the four management strategies and six categories of management practices as possible. At the beginning of each case study, the management problems, strategies, and practices employed are specified. Additionally, Table 5.1 has been developed to illustrate the management problems, strategies, and practices represented in each of the 25 case studies presented in Part II of the book. Figure 5.5 shows the geographic distribution of the parks represented in these case studies.

## Conclusion

The systematic approach to describing and organizing the resource and experiential impacts of outdoor recreation and the management approaches designed to minimize these impacts can be arrayed to form a series of management matrices as shown in Figs. 5.1 to 5.4. These matrices can be used to help think comprehensively and creatively about the full range of potential management solutions to the impacts caused by outdoor recreation. Appendices A1 to A4 illustrate the diverse ways in which these management matrices can be used, while Appendix B leads readers to an interactive version of these management matrices. Finally, a series of 25 case studies in the US national parks presented in Part II of this book illustrate the ways in which management problems have been successfully addressed in the context of the management matrices.

1 - Acadia National Park
2 - Appalachian National Scenic Trail
3 - Great Smoky Mountains National Park
4 - Arches National Park
5 - Biscayne National Park
6 - Mammoth Cave National Park
7 - Chaco Culture National Historical Park
8 - Denali National Park and Preserve
9 - Colorado River (Grand Canyon National Park)
10 - Apostle Islands National Lakeshore
11 - Muir Woods National Monument
12 - Mesa Verde National Park
13 - Mt. Whitney (Sequoia and Kings Canyon National Park)
14 - Petrified Forest National Park
15 - Carlsbad Caverns National Park
16 - Katmai National Park and Preserve
17 - Voyageurs National Park
18 - Yosemite National Park
19 - Zion National Park
20 - Grand Canyon National Park
21 - National Mall
22 - Devils Tower National Monument
23 - Yellowstone National Park
24 - Grand Teton National Park
25 - Glacier National Park

**Fig. 5.5.** Geographic distribution of parks represented in the case studies.

# Part II   Case Studies in the National Parks

# 6 Treading Lightly on Acadia

On peak summer days, thousands of hikers can be found along the extensive and diverse trail system in Acadia National Park. The collective use by so many visitors can take a toll on trail resources. Some visitors alter and build rock cairns; walk off-trail to avoid rocks, roots, and wet spots; and hike with unleashed dogs. These behaviors can compromise hiker safety, lead to soil erosion and vegetation loss, and threaten wildlife (**Impacts to trails; Impacts to soil; Impacts to vegetation; Impacts to wildlife; Depreciative behavior**). Relying on the strategy of **reducing the impact of use**, a group of seasonal "ridgerunners" intercepts visitors on trails to inform them about these issues and to promote low-impact hiking practices (**Information/Education**).

## Introduction

Each individual hiker has relatively little impact on the environment. But **when you multiply this impact by millions of hikers each year, there can be important consequences that may begin to threaten the ecological integrity of parks.** The collective impact of recreation on the natural environment has been a concern of the National Park Service for several decades. As the number of visits to parks and related areas grows, so do impacts to plants, soils, and wildlife. Behaviors of seemingly little consequence at the individual level (e.g. walking around a puddle on a trail) become problematic when repeated many times over the course of a hiking season. To make matters worse, impacts to vegetation and soils can occur even at relatively low levels of use. To address this problem, the National Park Service often develops regulations on visitor behavior to help protect the natural environment and the experience for all visitors. However, managers at Acadia National Park recognized that regulations alone would be inadequate to address visitor impacts. Such regulations would be difficult to enforce, and doing so could be disagreeable to visitors. More importantly, many visitors were likely unaware of park regulations and the potential impacts of their behavior.

Following these considerations, the National Park Service partnered with the National Outdoor Leadership School and other agencies to promote outdoor education on a national scale. Known as Leave No Trace (LNT), the program promotes a consistent national message based on scientific understanding. **At the heart of LNT are seven principles:**

1. **Plan ahead and prepare.**
2. **Travel and camp on durable surfaces.**
3. **Dispose of waste properly.**
4. **Leave what you find.**
5. **Minimize campfire impacts.**
6. **Respect wildlife.**
7. **Be considerate of other visitors.**

Training courses, workshops, and contacts with park managers, outfitters and guides, scouting and other outdoor groups, and the public are used to spread the LNT message. The organization has developed a series of "Skills and Ethics" booklets targeted at specific environments and activities, reference cards for various activities, and provides promotional materials on its website (http://www.lnt.org). While initially focused on backcountry settings, the program has expanded to address recreation impacts in more accessible park contexts. As one of the most visited parks in the USA, Acadia National Park has drawn on the principles of LNT to address visitor-related impacts along its extensive trail system.

## Acadia National Park

Located on the coast of Maine, Acadia National Park encompasses rocky ocean shoreline, sand beaches, mountain summits, inland ponds and

**Fig. 6.1.** Acadia National Park may be the most intensively used national park in the USA, concentrating 2.5 million annual visits on to less than 50,000 acres. (Photo by Robert Manning.)

lakes, wetlands, and woodlands (Fig. 6.1). Historic carriage roads, horse stables, and a lighthouse reflect the cultural history of the first national park to be established in the eastern USA. While modest in size at just over 47,000 acres, Acadia contains more than 140 miles of hiking trails. Trails were purposefully designed to connect visitors with scenic vistas and provide access to the diverse coastal and island landscapes within the park. Much credit for the early trail system belongs to the planning, building, and private fundraising efforts of village improvement associations of the early 1900s. Subsequently, trails have been further developed and maintained by the Civilian Conservation Corps and through the Acadia Trails Forever program, a partnership between the National Park Service and the non-profit group Friends of Acadia. **An estimated 5000 visitors explore some portion of the park's trail system each day during the peak summer months of July, August, and September.**

## Managing Hiking in Acadia National Park

With over 2 million visitors per year and an extensive, easily accessible trail system, Acadia National Park has drawn on LNT principles and outreach to address visitor-created impacts along trails (Fig. 6.2). In particular, the park has proactively addressed three issues. Following the principle "leave what you find," visitors are encouraged not to disrupt cairns and rocks along mountain trails. The message "travel on durable surfaces" is used to discourage hikers from walking off-trail. Finally, the park has given special attention to the issue of dogs, reminding visitors to keep dogs on leash through the principle "be considerate of others."

Visitor modification of cairns along mountain trails can damage soils and vegetation, threaten hiker safety, and degrade the character of the natural environment. Cairns are rock structures that are constructed to mark trails in treeless landscapes. They are used for way finding and may be essential to keeping hikers on track in winter or during low visibility conditions. Despite this, some visitors in Acadia alter cairns by adding or removing rocks from the structures. In some cases, new cairns or other types of rock formations are constructed. When rocks are removed from the ground to create these structures, fragile mountain soils erode quickly, leading to vegetation loss. Further, when many rock structures are present, the natural character of the landscape is compromised, degrading the experience for hikers who have come to experience a natural setting.

Visitors walking off-trail is another behavior that has concerned park managers for many years, and can have significant consequences for Acadia's natural environment. Soils and vegetation can be

**Fig. 6.2.** The National Park Service has partnered with the non-profit organizations Leave No Trace and Friends of Acadia to educate hikers and reduce the impact of outdoor recreation on the trail system at Acadia National Park. (Photos by Charlie Jacobi.)

damaged when visitors step off trail to avoid mud, puddles, roots, or rocks. As a consequence, trails may widen or new paths may form. A more recent issue for the park relates to visitors traveling with pets. Acadia is recognized as a dog-friendly park, where visitors are allowed to hike with dogs on most trails. However, some owners fail to keep dogs on a leash at all times, as required. When dogs are allowed to run freely, other hikers, particularly children, may feel unsafe. Further, loose dogs may scare or kill park wildlife, including ground nesting birds. Finally, dogs themselves can become lost or may be injured during a run-in with a porcupine or an animal with rabies.

To address these issues, Acadia enlists the help of four seasonal ridgerunners to interact with visitors and promote an LNT message. Ridgerunners have worked in the park since 1997, and are currently supported by an endowment established through Acadia Trails Forever. The endowment also supports Acadia Youth Conservation Corps seasonal trail crews. For 12 weeks each summer, ridgerunners perform a variety of tasks for park managers, including monitoring trail use, repairing cairns along mountain trails, and administering questionnaires. But **the most important task of ridgerunners**

**is to talk with visitors about low-impact hiking behaviors in the park.**

Ridgerunners use a variety of approaches to engage hikers in conversation. One is to intercept visitors at popular trailheads using posters that illustrate the day's message. To discourage walking off-trail, trails with significant braiding or widening are shown. Historic and current pictures of Bubble Rock, a popular hiking destination, demonstrate the loss of vegetation over a 40-year time period. Ridgerunners also use time spent maintaining cairns as an opportunity to talk with visitors about these rock structures. To further address the cairn issue, they may display a poster that shows a mountain summit littered with cairns and exposed pockets of soil. Alternatively, ridgerunners may simply talk with visitors out on the trails, starting conversations by asking people where they're from or by commenting on a favorite sports team.

These informal conversations allow the park to educate visitors about low-impact issues in a friendly and proactive manner, an approach that may differ from summit steward programs that focus primarily on correcting visitor behavior. For example, while ridgerunners inform hikers with loose dogs about park regulations, they also thank hikers walking with leashed dogs for complying with these regulations. Children's hang tags listing the seven LNT principles are handed out to willing recipients. This proactive approach also involves supplementing ridgerunner contacts with other education and information efforts. The park has spread the message about cairns through the local newspaper, on public radio, and in an LNT video distributed to outing clubs, nearby camps, and sporting goods shops, and has also created a patch for children that says "Leave the Rocks for the Next Glacier."

While the park acknowledges that there is a need to study and better understand the effectiveness of the ridgerunner program on visitor behavior, the message of LNT in Acadia has reached a sizeable audience. Over the course of several seasons, **ridgerunners have interacted with thousands of visitors, recording 4500 "substantive contacts" in 2010 alone.** A reliable funding source and the park's commitment to the LNT message suggest that ridgerunners will be standing by to greet Acadia visitors for many years to come.

## Further Reading

Acadia National Park (2002) Hiking trails management plan. US Department of the Interior, Acadia National Park, Maine, 1–56.

Acadia National Park (2016) Available at: http://www.nps.gov/acad (accessed 9 September 2016).

Acadia Trails Forever (2016) Available at: https://friendsofacadia.org/what-we-do/trails-and-carriage-roads/acadia-trails-forever/ (accessed 9 September 2016).

Jacobi, C. (2003) Leave the rocks for the next glacier - Low impact education in a high use national park. *International Journal of Wilderness* 9, 30–31.

Leave No Trace (2016) Available at: http://www.lnt.org (accessed 20 October 2016).

Leung, Y. and Marion, J. (2000) Recreation impacts and management in wilderness: A state-of-knowledge review. USDA Forest Service Proceedings RMRS-P-15-Vol-5, Ogden, Utah.

Marion, J. and Reid, S. (2001) Development of the United States Leave No Trace program: A historical perspective. In: Usher, M. (ed.) *Enjoyment and Understanding of the Natural Heritage*. The Stationery Office Ltd, Scottish Natural Heritage, Edinburgh.

# 7 Building a Better Campsite Along the Appalachian Trail

Years of uncontrolled use at a camping area along the Appalachian Trail resulted in widespread damage to soil, trees, and other vegetation; a decimated firewood supply; and visible signs of human waste (**Impacts to campsites; Impacts to soil; Impacts to vegetation**). The camping area was also crowded and sometimes rowdy, making it unattractive to many long-distance hikers (**Crowding; Conflict; Depreciative behavior**). To deal with these issues, new "side-hill" campsites were constructed (**Harden resource; Facility development/Site design/Maintenance**) and campers were informed of group size limits (**Limit use; Rationing/Allocation**) and bans on alcohol and campfires (**Reduce the impact of use; Rules/Regulations**) through signs and an on-site caretaker (**Information/Education**).

## Introduction

There's a tradition among experienced backpackers to limit their impact on the natural environment. Care is taken to stay on designated paths, camp on durable surfaces, not disturb wildlife, leave what is found, remove waste, and respect other visitors. However, not all campers ascribe to these principles. **Left unchecked, insensitive camping practices can scar the landscape.** In once-vibrant ecological systems, vegetation is trampled or missing, soils hardened or eroded, human garbage left behind. The impacts of unregulated camping were particularly apparent at one camping area along the Appalachian National Scenic Trail. Through a multi-faceted management approach, the campground was transformed from a place to be avoided to a celebrated backcountry destination.

## Appalachian National Scenic Trail

Envisioned by regional planner Benton MacKaye in the mid 1920s and completed in 1937, **the Appalachian Trail stretches 2175 miles from Springer Mountain in Georgia to Mount Katahdin in Maine** (Fig. 7.1). In 1968, the Appalachian Trail became one of the first national scenic trails in the USA and part of the national park system. Designated through Acts of Congress, national scenic trails protect continuous long-distance hiking corridors for the public in nationally significant scenic areas. Crossing through 14 states, the Appalachian Trail is maintained through partnerships between public agencies and private organizations. Volunteer efforts of local clubs are coordinated by The Appalachian Trail Conservancy, a non-profit organization that also raises funds to support ongoing management. Among the resources maintained by these groups are shelters and other camping areas that provide respite for long-distance hikers, weekend backpackers, and other visitors.

## Managing Camping Along the Appalachian Trail

Annapolis Rocks is located in western Maryland, less than ¼ mile from the Appalachian Trail and about 2 miles from a parking area on US Route 40. With a scenic sunset view, climbing rocks, natural spring, and large level area, the site—previously a parcel of private land—became a popular camping destination for climbers and casual visitors. On busy weekends, 100 or more people gathered at the flat camping area. Crowded conditions were accompanied by lively social interactions, large bonfires, and alcohol consumption. Years of heavy, unregulated use led to significant degradation of the camping area. The site experienced widespread vegetation loss and soil compaction. Where vegetation remained, informal trails cut through the landscape. Logs covered with charcoal residue, patches of sterile land, and a decimated firewood supply resulted from numerous campfires. Likewise, live trees were damaged as some campers sought new sources of campfire fuel. In the absence of sanitation facilities and low-impact practices, toilet paper scraps and partially burned cans, bottles, and other trash could be seen throughout the site. **These conditions made Annapolis Rocks—once called "the worst campground along the Appalachian Trail"—unattractive to long-distance hikers** (Fig. 7.2).

Following land purchases at Annapolis Rocks by the Maryland Department of Natural Resources and the National Park Service, an ambitious suite of management actions was implemented to redevelop the site for low-impact camping. Using plans drafted by the Maryland Appalachian Trail Management Committee, the original camping area, which included 19 visitor-created campsites, was closed. In its place, 14 smaller campsites were

**Fig. 7.1.** The Appalachian Trail runs nearly 2200 miles between Springer Mountain, Georgia, and Mt. Katahdin, Maine, offering hikers an epic journey. (Photo by Jeff Marion.)

**Fig. 7.2.** Campsites at the Annapolis Rocks area along the Appalachian Trail were badly degraded, but a new campsite location and design have substantially improved conditions. (Photo by Jeff Marion.)

constructed on nearby sloping land. Campsite development involved excavating material from upslope and placing it behind a retaining wall below to provide a flat camping surface. **This type of design, known as "side-hill" campsite construction, can prevent the spread of soil and vegetation disturbance.** The new campsites were distributed among healthy vegetation and spaced 100 feet apart—a distance at which normal conversations are not easily heard—to allow for more private camping experiences. Further, the new location moved campers away from rock cliffs at the site, improving visitor safety. In conjunction with the new sites, group sizes were limited to ten people, the total number of campers per night was capped at 75, and alcohol and campfires were prohibited. In addition, two self-composting toilets were installed on either side of the camping area.

Several steps were taken to inform campers about the new facilities and rules. The old camping area, closed for rehabilitation, was fenced. Signs reminded visitors of the closure and directed them to camp at the side-hill sites. New rules and regulations were posted by a map of the camping area at two kiosks. The first was located at the trailhead parking lot and the second near the camping area. In addition, two trail ridgerunners were hired to supervise the campsite and surrounding area during the peak visitation season. One of the ridgerunners served as a caretaker, living at the campsite from April to October. The caretaker directed visitors to the new campsites, informed them of group size limits, bans on fire and alcohol, and Leave No Trace practices (see the case study Treading Lightly on Acadia, Chapter 6, p. 55).

Monitoring of campsite conditions at Annapolis Rocks demonstrated the success of the management program. **With the closure of the old campsites, the area of vegetation and soil disturbance was reduced from around 40,000 square feet to just over 3000 square feet.** Native vegetation returned to the original camping area and the amount of exposed soil was reduced. In surveys conducted before and after the management changes, visitors to the new campsites said that they were more satisfied with campsite privacy, noise levels at campsites, and spacing between groups. Likewise, side-hill campers were more satisfied with the condition of trees, the amount of vegetation, and the naturalness of the site than visitors to the original unmanaged campsites.

While the management actions taken were largely successful in meeting trail objectives, there were some other consequences to the changes at Annapolis Rocks. Most apparent is the likelihood that some visitors were displaced due to restrictions on campfires, alcohol, and large groups. Among campers who were not displaced, a few concerns have emerged about the new campsite design. Visitors to side-hill campsites expressed somewhat lower satisfaction with being able to select a preferred campsite than visitors to the pre-management site, and said that they would prefer smoother tent pads, more campsites, and larger campsites. Fitting with the latter finding, monitoring of side-hill campsites revealed a slight expansion in their size (8%) during the first year. However, project managers concluded that the campsites may have been too small in the first place, and subsequent measures have not revealed any additional expansion at the new sites.

Though located just a few steps from the Appalachian Trail, the camping area at Annapolis Rocks faced both ecological degradation and a party atmosphere that made it unattractive to many long-distance hikers. A multi-faceted approach involving site design, restoration, education, and monitoring succeeded in rehabilitating the site into an area suitable for primitive, backcountry camping. Formal recognition of this success came in 2004 when the Annapolis Rock Hiker Campground and Trail was designated as a national recreation trail.

## Further Reading

Appalachian National Scenic Trail (2016) Available at: http://www.nps.gov/appa (accessed 20 August 2016).

Daniels, M. and Marion, J. (2006) Visitor evaluations of management actions at a highly impacted Appalachian Trail camping area. *Environmental Management* 38, 1006–1019.

Jenner, J. (2004) Curbing campground chaos: Innovative AT tent sites stem sprawl, offer more privacy. *Appalachian Trailway News* 65, 14–22.

Marion, J. (2003) Camping impact management on the Appalachian National Scenic Trail. American Trail Conference, Harper's Ferry, West Virginia.

Maryland Appalachian Trail Management Committee (2001) Management plan for a proposed hiker campground to be developed at Annapolis Rocks, Maryland Appalachian Trail Management Committee.

National Park Service (2005) Appalachian Trail vital signs. US Department of the Interior Technical Report NPS/NER/NRTR - 2005/026, Boston, Massachusetts.

# 8 Let There Be Light in Great Smoky Mountains

A wondrous display of synchronous fireflies at Great Smoky Mountains National Park draws many visitors to the park each spring. However, the small viewing area and limited number of days over which this natural event takes place challenges the National Park Service to prevent associated resource impacts caused by cars parking along the margins of the park road (**Impacts to soil; Impacts to vegetation**) and potential impacts to firefly habitat and behavior (**Impacts to wildlife**). Given the demand to see this natural event, there is also great potential for too many people at the event, diminishing the quality of the visitor experience (**Crowding**). The National Park Service has responded to these potential problems through two basic strategies: **Limiting visitor use** and **Reducing the impact of use**. For example, a required permit and associated lottery system have been initiated (**Rationing/Allocation**), visitors must ride a shuttle bus to the viewing area to reduce the impacts of parking (**Rules/Regulations; Facility development/Site design/ Maintenance**), and visitors may not catch fireflies (**Rules/ Regulations**), and visitors have been asked to restrain their use of flashlights (**Information/Education**).

## Introduction

Great Smoky Mountains National Park offers one of the most unusual and interesting phenomena of nature—synchronous fireflies. Most people, especially children who have grown up in rural areas, have known the joy of fireflies or "lighting bugs," as they're often called. Really beetles, they arise from the forest after dark to display their short, seemingly random bursts of light. Relatively easy to catch, they're often gathered in Mason jars to watch them more closely. **There are many fireflies in Great Smoky Mountains National Park—at least 19 species—but** *Photinus carolinus* **is the only one in which swarms of these fireflies flash in a striking synchronous pattern.**

The production of light by living organisms is called "bioluminescence." A number of species have this capacity, including selected fungi, fish, shrimp, jellyfish, plankton, glowworms, snails and springtails. Bioluminescence is a chemical reaction that causes the release of light with little or no emission of heat. This unusual light is referred to as "cold" light; nearly 100% of the energy emitted is light, in contrast with an incandescent light bulb, which emits 90% heat and only 10% light. Maybe these beetles have a lot to teach us!

Entomologists believe that the light fireflies emit is part of their mating process. Males fly and emit light as a way to attract females on the ground; perhaps it's the brightness or length of the light that favors the mating success of the males. But no one is quite sure about why (or how) *Photinus carolinus* emit their light in a synchronous pattern. Everyone agrees, however, that it is a wonder of nature. These fireflies don't always flash in unison—they may flash in waves across hillsides and at other times flash randomly; synchrony occurs in short bursts that end with abrupt periods of darkness.

At Great Smoky Mountains National Park, these fireflies display this behavior for only about two weeks in late May to mid-June (Fig. 8.1). The largest populations and most exuberant displays are found near the park's popular Elkmont Campground where the habitat is especially conducive to the needs of these fireflies. And that's the problem—many visitors travel to the park each spring to watch this marvel of nature, resulting in them converging at a specific location in a concentrated period of time. **Without proper management, there would be chaos in which the fireflies and their habitat might be damaged and there would be unacceptable levels of crowding, thereby diminishing the quality of the visitor experience.**

## Great Smoky Mountains National Park

Great Smoky Mountains National Park was established by Congress in 1934 and straddles the ridges of

**Fig. 8.1.** The magical phenomenon of synchronous fireflies at Great Smoky Mountains National Park draws in an over-abundance of visitors each spring. (NPS Photo by Radium Schreiber.)

the Appalachian Mountains between North Carolina and Tennessee. The park includes 16 mountains that are higher than 6000 feet. John D. Rockefeller, Jr., made a substantial contribution to help the federal government acquire land for the park. The park comprises more than half a million acres and is one of the largest protected areas in the eastern USA. Primarily because of its location near large centers of population, the park is perpetually the most visited in the nation.

**The park is especially significant for its remarkable biological diversity.** It includes more than 200 species of birds, over 100 species of trees, more than 1400 species of flowering plants, 66 species of mammals including a thriving black bear population, 50 species of fish, 39 species of reptiles and 43 species of amphibians. The park is 95% forested, including large areas of old-growth forests. This biodiversity is largely the result of a variety of elevations, abundant rainfall, high humidity, and the old-growth forests. Moreover, plants and animals common in the southern USA occupy the lowlands of the park, whereas species in the northeastern USA find an appropriate habitat at

the park's higher elevations. Scientists estimate that there may be an astounding 30,000–80,000 species in the park, most of them as yet uncatalogued.

The park also has a rich human history, beginning with occupation by the Cherokee Indians. Cade's Cove is an especially popular visitor attraction with a cluster of restored buildings—including log cabins, barns, a grain mill, and churches—representative of white settler communities in the 18th and 19th centuries.

Today, the park is a great recreation attraction for many visitors. There are 850 miles of trails and unpaved roads for hiking, including 70 miles of the Appalachian Trail. A short trail leads to the summit of Clingman's Dome, where there are spectacular views of the park and surrounding mountains.

## Managing the Viewing of Synchronous Fireflies

As this phenomenon of synchronous fireflies has grown in popularity, the National Park Service has developed a suite of management actions to protect firefly habitat and provide the opportunity for visitors to experience this event in a way that is in keeping with the naturalness of the park whilst allowing a high-quality viewing experience. The agency has adopted two primary management strategies: limit the amount of use and reduce the impact of use.

Limiting the amount of use is based primarily on available parking at the nearby Sugarlands Visitor Center. Here, visitors must leave their cars and board a shuttle bus for transport to the viewing area; this is the only way to access the viewing area (Fig. 8.2). Visitors can receive parking permits through a lottery system managed on a government website (www.recreation.gov) that handles most National Park Service reservations for campsites and other services. A lottery system is used because the demand for parking permits far exceeds capacity, and a lottery helps ensure that all visitors have an equal chance of receiving a permit. Visitors should read the Firefly Event webpage at the website noted above. The website is available each spring as soon as the National Park Service announces what they believe will be the eight peak viewing nights (the peak period of synchronous firefly activity varies a little each year, depending on the environmental conditions). A parking pass covers a maximum of six people per car, although a few parking passes are available for larger vehicles with more passengers. There is a nominal fee for parking permits and riding on the shuttle bus. This permit, lottery and shuttle bus system eliminates roadside parking at the viewing area and the damage this inevitably causes to soil and vegetation along the margins of the park road. It also addresses the visitor safety concerns associated with driving and parking large numbers of cars in close proximity to one another, especially after dark. And, of course, it also limits the number of visitors at the viewing area in a way that offers a high-quality viewing experience.

The National Park Service is also trying to reduce the impacts of use through an aggressive information and education campaign and a set of rules and regulations. This information is presented on the

**Fig. 8.2.** Visitors are required to ride a shuttle bus to see the synchronous firefly displays as a way to limit their impact. (Photo by NPS staff.)

website where visitors can apply for the parking permit, and by rangers at the Visitor Center and the viewing site. To help protect the fireflies, visitors are not allowed to catch fireflies, and are required to stay on maintained trails at all times and to pack up and take away their trash. To enhance the quality of firefly viewing, the park has developed a "light show etiquette" that it asks visitors to abide by so fireflies are not disrupted and visitors' night vision is not impaired. These behaviors include covering flashlights with red or blue cellophane, using flashlights only when walking to the viewing site, turning off flashlights after reaching the viewing site, and pointing flashlights down (at the ground) when walking.

## Further Reading

Faust, L.F. (2010) Natural history and flash repertoire of the synchronous firefly *Photinus carolinus* (Celeoptera: Lampyridae). *Florida Entomologist,* 93(2), 208–217.

Faust, L.F. and Weston, P.A. (2009) Degree-day prediction of adult emergence of *Photinus carolinus* (Coleoptera: Lampyridae). *Environmental Etomology,* 38(5), 1505–1512.

National Park Service (2015) Park Announces Synchronous Firefly Viewing Event Dates. Available at: https://www.nps.gov/grsm/learn/news/fireflies-2015.htm (accessed 21 October 2016).

National Park Service (2016) Synchronous Fireflies. Available at: https://www.nps.gov/grsm/learn/nature/fireflies.htm (accessed 21 October 2016).

# 9

# How Many Visitors is Too Many at Arches?

Visitor use of Arches National Park has grown dramatically in the past few decades and now exceeds 1 million visits annually. But this use has had several important impacts in the park, including trampling of fragile soils and vegetation (**Impacts to soil; Impacts to vegetation**) and crowding on trails and at attraction sites (**Crowding; Impacts to trails; Impacts to attraction sites**). The National Park Service developed and applied its Visitor Experience and Resource Protection framework to measure and manage carrying capacity at Arches. The resulting management regime employed two management strategies (**Limit use; Reduce the impact of use**) and included division of the park into a series of spatial zones (**Zoning**), visitor education about when and where to visit, and appropriate visitor behavior (**Information/Education**), sizing of parking lots to limit crowding and fencing to discourage walking off maintained trails (**Facility development/Site design/Maintenance**), regulation and enforcement of overflow parking (**Rules/Regulations; Law enforcement**), and mandatory permits for use of some park attractions (**Rationing/Allocation**), including those accessed through popular ranger-led tours (**Impacts to interpretive facilities/programs**).

## Introduction

Carrying capacity was one of the conceptual frameworks introduced in Chapter 1. In its most generic form, carrying capacity is the amount and type of recreational use that can be accommodated in a park without unacceptable impacts to park resources or the quality of the visitor experience. Carrying capacity is a long-standing and increasingly urgent issue in national parks and related areas. The National Park Service is required by the National Parks and Recreation Act of 1978 to develop plans for each park that include "identification and implementation commitments for visitor carrying capacities" (P.L 95-625). The centrality of carrying capacity is derived from its linkage to the twofold mission of parks: to protect park resources and the quality of the visitor experience, while providing for public use. The increasing urgency of this issue in national parks is driven by long-term increases in recreational use; the number of visits to the US National Park System now exceeds 300 million annually.

**Arches National Park is a poster child for the issue of carrying capacity.** It is a relatively small national park, but has experienced sustained growth in attendance over the past several decades, eclipsing the 1 million mark in 2010.

This popularity has come with a number of challenges, including trampling and degradation of fragile soils and vegetation, and crowding on trails and at attraction sites. Arches was the first national park to address carrying capacity using the management-by-objectives framework outlined in Chapter 1.

## Arches National Park

Arches National Park was established in 1929 in south-east Utah. It comprises 77,000 acres of high elevation desert that is part of the vast Colorado Plateau. Elevations range from just over 4000 feet to about 5600 feet and the area receives less than ten inches of precipitation per year. The park's distinctive sandstone landscape has been eroded by water, wind, and temperature into a series of canyons, expansive formations of "slickrock," towering monoliths and "hoodoos," sandstone "fins," and distinctive stone arches (Fig. 9.1). Over 2000 arches have been documented (arches must have an opening of at least 3 feet), representing the highest density of these geologic features in the world. **Delicate Arch has become the scenic symbol of the park and the American Southwest more generally, and the three-mile round-trip trail to Delicate Arch is one of the most famous trails in the US National Park System.**

**Fig. 9.1.** Arches National Park features impressive slickrock formations, including a collection of natural stone arches. (Photo by Robert Manning.)

Other distinctive features and visitor attractions include Balanced Rock, The Windows, the Fiery Furnace, and Devil's Garden.

Most of the park's soil is sandy and develops a distinctive biological crust called "cryptobiotic soil." This soil crust comprises bacteria, moss, lichens, fungi, and algae and it is vital to the desert ecosystem as it stabilizes the soil, stores water, and fixes nitrogen. It is easily disturbed by visitors walking off maintained trails and can take up to 250 years to recover from such damage.

The park and surrounding area also has an interesting human history. It was used by Native Americans for about 10,000 years before European settlement and this is manifested in rock art and other physical evidence. The historic cabin at Wolfe Ranch is an example of early American attempts to settle the area. Edward Abbey, a famous American nature writer, worked as a seasonal ranger in the park in the late 1950s and his definitive book, *Desert Solitaire*, is based on this experience.

## Measuring and Managing Carrying Capacity

The National Park Service developed its management-by-objectives framework—Visitor Experience and Resource Protection (VERP)—for measuring and managing carrying capacity in the 1990s. This framework was first applied at Arches and the resulting plan was the first in the National Park System to address carrying capacity in a comprehensive, park-wide manner. As described in Chapter 1, this management framework consists of three primary steps:

**1.** Formulation of management objectives and associated indicators and standards of quality.
**2.** Monitoring indicators of quality.
**3.** Managing the park to ensure that standards of quality are maintained.

Since this plan was applied to the whole park, an initial step was to divide the park into a series of zones that ranged from "developed" (small areas that include roads, parking lots, a visitor center, and a campground) to "primitive" (large areas of the park that have no facilities and are relatively undisturbed).

To support formulation of indicators and standards of quality for each zone, a program of natural and social science was conducted. Natural science focused on the effects of trampling of the park's fragile soils and vegetation. The cryptobiotic soil crust noted above is found extensively throughout the park. Ecological research documented the extent and location of this soil crust, the relationship between recreational use and damage to soil crust, and developed a soil crust monitoring protocol.

Social science focused on understanding the quality of the visitor experience. An initial phase of study included focus groups with visitors and other stakeholders (e.g. residents of communities outside the park, park staff). Several indicators of quality were identified, including crowding on trails and at attraction sites and the aesthetic implications of impacts to the microbiotic soil crust caused by visitors walking off maintained trails. A second phase of the social science research administered a survey to park visitors. As part of the survey, visual simulations were prepared of a range of visitor use levels on trails and at attraction sites and a range of impacts to soil and vegetation. For example, a series of computer-edited photographs was prepared illustrating a wide range of visitor use levels at Delicate Arch (see Fig. 9.2). Visitors who had just completed a hike to Delicate Arch were asked to rate the acceptability of these photographs based on the number of visitors shown. Average acceptability ratings were computed and graphed, and the graph for Delicate Arch is shown in Fig. 9.3.

For Delicate Arch, average acceptability ratings fall out of the acceptable range and into the unacceptable range at about 30 people-at-one-time (PAOT), and this was established as a standard of quality for Delicate Arch. Crowding-related standards of quality were established for all park zones based on this research and related information.

The park is now being managed to help ensure that standards of quality are being maintained. This includes several management practices. For example, the parking lots serving the park's three main visitor attraction sites—Delicate Arch, the Windows, and Devil's Garden—were sized to help ensure that crowding-related standards of quality are not violated. This sizing was based on simultaneous counts of the number of cars in parking lots and the number of visitors at attraction sites such as Delicate Arch. Statistical models were then developed to estimate the maximum number of cars that could be accommodated in parking lots without violating crowding-related standards of quality. Parking lots were stripped to designate authorized parking spots, natural rock barriers were placed around parking lots to discourage

**Fig. 9.2.** How many visitors is too many? A set of visual simulations allows survey respondents to see the results of varying levels of visitor use. (Images by Wayne Freimund, Dave Lime, and Robert Manning.)

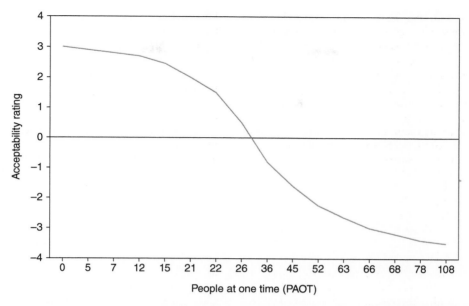

**Fig. 9.3.** Social norm curve for the acceptability of seeing visitors at Delicate Arch. (Adapted from Manning *et al.*, 1996b.)

overflow parking, a regulation against overflow parking was adopted and communicated in signs, and the regulation against overflow parking was enforced when needed.

Permit systems are used to control the amount of use in some areas. For example, a day-use permit is required for the Fiery Furnace and the number permits is limited. Visitors must watch an educational film on how to minimize impacts to soil and vegetation before being issued a permit. The only other way to access the Fiery Furnace is on a ranger-led tour. These tours are very popular and reservations may be made up to 6 months in advance. Permits are also required for overnight use of the primitive zone of the park. The park employs an extensive system of information and education to guide visitor use, including suggestions about where and when to visit to avoid crowding and advising against walking off maintained trails, including why visitors should abide by this advice. Information and education are delivered on the park's website, in the park newspaper that is given to all visitors, on signs in the park, in the park visitor center, on ranger-guided activities, and on social media such as Facebook and Twitter. Where social trails begin to appear, small, ground-level posts are installed reminding visitors to stay on maintained trails. Finally, low wooden fences

have been erected in strategic places at major park attractions to discourage off-trail hiking and development of social trails.

In accordance with the VERP framework, the park must monitor indicators of quality to ensure that standards of quality are being maintained. This includes measuring the amount of disturbance to soil and vegetation and the number of visitors on trails and at attraction sites. Monitoring is costly, however, in terms of both money and staff time, and the park has struggled to maintain this activity. The VERP plan formulated and implemented at the park suggested that the National Park Service should dedicate staff time to this activity, but there are many competing demands for staff time and monitoring remains a challenge.

### Further Reading

Abbey, E. (1968) *Desert Solitaire; A Season in the Wilderness*. McGraw-Hill, New York.

Arches National Park (2016) Available at: http://www.nps.gov/arch (accessed 21 October 2016).

Belnap, J. (1998) Choosing indicators of natural resource condition: A case study in Arches National Park, Utah, USA. *Environmental Management* 22, 635–642.

Cox, R. (2000) Protecting the national parks. *CQ Researcher* 10, 521–544.

Lawson, S. and Manning, R. (2001) Solitude versus access: A study of tradeoffs in outdoor recreation using indifference curve analysis. *Leisure Sciences* 23, 179–191.

Manning, R. (2000) Crowding and carrying capacity in outdoor recreation: From normative standards to standards of quality. In: Jackson, E. and Burton, T. (eds) *Leisure Studies: Prospects for the Twenty-First Century*. Venture Publishing, Inc., State College, Pennyslvania, pp. 323–334.

Manning, R. (2001) Visitor experience and resource protection: A framework for managing the carrying capacity of national parks. *Journal of Park and Recreation Administration* 19, 93–108.

Manning, R. (2004) Recreation planning frameworks. *Society and Natural Resources: A Summary of Knowledge*. Modern Litho, Jefferson, Missouri, pp. 83–96.

Manning, R. (2011) *Studies in Outdoor Recreation: Search and Research for Satisfaction*, 3rd edn. Oregon State University Press, Corvallis, Oregon.

Manning, R., Lime, D. and Hof, M. (1996) Social carrying capacity of natural areas: Theory and application in the U.S. National Parks. *Natural Areas Journal* 16, 118–127.

Manning, R., Freimund, W., Lime, D. and Pitt, D. (1996) Crowding norms at frontcountry sites: A visual approach to setting standards of quality. *Leisure Sciences* 18, 39–59.

National Park Service (1995) Visitor experience and resource protection implementation plan Arches National Park - Utah. US Department of the Interior, Denver, Colorado, pp. 1–71.

Smith, C. (1995) A delicate question: When is an arch crowded? In: *High Country News*, March 6. Moab, Utah.

# 10 Protecting Biscayne's Underwater Treasures

Visitors to Biscayne National Park have the opportunity to explore globally important, biologically diverse underwater habitats. However, when recreational boaters cross though shallow waters, anchor, or become grounded on seagrass meadows or coral reefs, significant resource damage can occur (**Impacts to soil; Impacts to vegetation; Impacts to water; Impacts to wildlife**). These problems are magnified by the park's high level of visitation (**Crowding; Conflict**) and the presence of boaters unaccustomed to navigating in shallow waters (**Depreciative behavior**), with many impacts occurring in certain "hotspot" areas (**Impacts to attraction sites**). To address these issues, the park maintains markers and mooring buoys (**Facility development/Site design/Maintenance**), prohibits beaching and anchoring in sensitive areas (**Rules/Regulations**), educates visitors about responsible boating behaviors (**Information/Education**), assesses fines to visitors who damage underwater resources (**Law enforcement**), and works to restore damaged habitats (**Facility development/Site design/Maintenance**). No-take, slow speed, idle speed, and noncombustible engine zones have been established and expanded to further protect underwater habitats in vulnerable areas (**Zoning**). These management practices are designed to advance the management strategies of limiting the impact that visitors may have (**Reduce the impact of use**) and hardening park resources through maintenance and restoration (**Harden resource/experience**).

## Introduction

**Some of the world's most diverse and productive ecosystems lie under the sea.** Off the coast of southern Florida, marine life abounds in seagrass meadows and coral reefs. Close to shore, shallow, clear waters support meadows of flowering plants, seagrasses that provide food for sea turtles, manatees, sea urchins, and a nursery for young fish, lobsters, and shrimp. Rooted within the sands below, these life-sustaining meadows form vegetative mats that protect coastlines from erosion and storm damage, maintain water clarity, and absorb carbon from the atmosphere. A bit further from shore, vibrant reef tracts are home to dozens of species of living corals; they include brain, star, elkhorn, and staghorn corals, sea fans, and sea whips. Colorful reef fish—gobies, parrotfish, and damselfish, to name a few—live among the coral structures, along with a diversity of other sea creatures.

Despite their ecological, economic, and recreational importance, these rich benthic ecosystems face numerous threats. Shoreline development, pollution, climate change, and overfishing are problems that occur on regional and global scales. But the direct impact of recreational use can also be significant. **Habitat degradation from recreational boating is a major cause for concern in Biscayne National Park** and in nearby protected waters. When boats cross through shallow waters, anchor, or become grounded on seagrass beds or corals, habitat recovery may take years, if not decades. In some cases, recovery may not be possible. Severely damaged seagrass beds and coral reefs may never grow back, instead becoming sand bars.

The extent of damage that can result from the collective actions of boaters is revealed in aerial images. Long white scars crisscross through green seagrass beds, a result of boat propellers dragging along the bottom of a shallow sea. Damage also occurs when anchors strike seagrass habitat, or when chains from anchors drag along the ocean floor. When a boat becomes grounded, the problem can be made much worse when an operator attempts to "power off" from the situation and creates a large gash in the submerged earth. In the absence of vegetation, exposed sand is churned up by waves, reducing water clarity. When these impacts occur on coral reefs, the damage opens a pathway for disease, and the cost, effort, and time needed for restoration is magnified.

About 100 boat groundings are reported each year in heavily visited Biscayne National Park, and many more groundings go unreported, the consequences of which are left to be discovered by resource managers. Ninety percent of reported groundings occur in seagrass habitat. To address impacts to benthic habitats from recreational boating, Biscayne has engaged in a multi-faceted campaign of education, monitoring, enforcement, and recovery, and has established new protections through management zones to further address the problem.

## Biscayne National Park

Situated at the doorstep of Miami, Florida, Biscayne National Park stretches 22 miles from Key Biscayne to Key Largo. **The submerged aquatic habitats of Biscayne comprise 95% of the park's 173,000 acres** (Fig. 10.1). The remainder of the park protects tropical hardwood and mangrove forests on undeveloped keys and coastal lands. Each year, 500,000 visitors flock to Biscayne to relax on boats, to swim, snorkel, dive, kayak, and fish, to take a glass-bottom boat tour, and to camp on one of the undeveloped keys. Special accommodations are made for the busy Columbus Day weekend, an event that draws hundreds of boats to the park and a lively group of visitors who gather to enjoy the festive, party-like atmosphere.

The only hiking trail in Biscayne—a remnant of the 7-mile-long "spite highway" bulldozed into the landscape by area landowners prior to the park's creation—reflects Biscayne's rocky origins. While developers saw opportunities to establish new roads, cities, a seaport, and an airport in the undeveloped northern Florida Keys, national support for the area's protection led to its designation as a national monument in 1968. Set aside to protect "a rare combination of terrestrial, marine, and amphibious life in a tropical setting of great natural beauty," the monument was expanded and redesignated as a national park in 1980.

## Managing Recreational Boating at Biscayne

In Biscayne, the marine landscape is wide open, a feature that distinguishes it from most other units in the US national park system. While some visitors pass through the Dante Fascell Visitor Center on the mainland, most arrive by boat. **With individual vessels dispersed across thousands of acres of water, reaching, informing, and monitoring visitors is a daunting task.** A modestly sized Visitor Protection Division is responsible for patrolling the entire seascape. Despite the challenge, the park has used both visitor education and site design to prevent damage to benthic habitats in the park.

**Fig. 10.1.** Most of Biscayne National Park is underwater and features coral reefs, sea grass beds, and abundant marine life. (National Park Service photo by John Brooks.)

On the park website, at boat docks, and in press releases, the importance of seagrass beds and coral reefs is emphasized, and boaters are provided with tips on how to avoid damaging these habitats (Fig. 10.2). Among the items highlighted are: being able to read and use nautical charts; reviewing these charts before heading out; knowing how to use electronic navigation equipment; and being aware of the tides. (In the shallow waters of Biscayne, tides can greatly influence the likelihood of becoming grounded.) In addition, boaters are encouraged to wear polarized sunglasses in order to better read water conditions. Mariner rhymes provide guidance about how to proceed based on these conditions. The phrase "brown, brown, run aground!" refers to the brown color of water that occurs when seagrass beds and reef formations are near the surface; boaters are advised to avoid these areas. In contrast, "blue, blue, cruise on through" indicates that waters are deep and safe for boating.

Markers and buoys also help boaters avoid fragile, shallow habitats and alert visitors to park rules and regulations. Markers take various forms and serve different purposes. Lighted structures aid in navigation and are permitted and maintained by the US Coast Guard. Day markers, poles, and pilings are used to mark sensitive habitat, shallow areas, and prohibited areas, and to post park regulations. Floating buoys, which are tethered to an anchor, are also used for navigation and to prevent damage to marine habitat. In particular, white mooring buoys are located near coral reefs to help protect this fragile resource. By tying a boat to a mooring buoy, the chances of damaging corals with anchors or anchor chains is reduced. When all mooring buoys are occupied, visitors are allowed to anchor in sandy areas near reefs, and are advised to anchor downwind from the reef to avoid having the anchor chain drag across the reef.

Eventually, anchoring will be prohibited in the park's newly established marine reserve zone. Additional mooring buoys will be added to the zone, which protects about one-third of Biscayne's coral reef habitat. Established in the park's 2015 General Management Plan, the marine reserve zone aims to protect the coral reef ecosystem and restore reef fish populations. While fishing is prohibited within the zone, a variety of other recreational uses are allowed, including swimming, snorkeling, scuba diving, and glass-bottom boating. The plan also expands zones that limit speed and combustion engine use. Limits on high-speed propellers and speed of travel reduce the likelihood of direct

**Fig. 10.2.** Accidental boat groundings at Biscayne National Park can seriously damage coral reefs and seagrass beds. (Photo by Amanda Bourque.)

damage to seagrass beds. Moreover, less sediment will be disturbed under the new restrictions, leading to higher water clarity, and healthier seagrass.

While markers, mooring buoys, speed and vessel restrictions, and educational efforts help reduce damage to underwater habitats, boat groundings still occur. Additional measures are needed to prevent groundings during the busy Columbus Day weekend. To help accommodate navigation during this time of high visitation, shoal markers were added along the shallow Featherbed Bank. Visitors are required to anchor within a "mandatory anchorage area" and are prohibited from doing so elsewhere in the park. Additional law enforcement officers and medical staff are on patrol, and the US Coast Guard enforces a reduced speed limit on the Intracoastal Waterway.

**When boat groundings or anchoring on reefs occur, visitors face a hefty fine.** Further, under the Park System Resource Protection Act, boaters may be responsible for the costs of habitat restoration. After a boat grounding, the park's Damage Recovery Program team assesses the extent of the damage through mapping, measuring, and photography, and designs a restoration project. Once a site is restored, the site is monitored over several years. Of course, restoration is not easy, and imposing large fines on visitors is not a preferred approach for interacting with the public.

To help minimize the damage when boat groundings do occur, Biscayne advises visitors about what to do if found in this unfortunate situation. First, boaters should turn motors off; attempts to "power off" can lead to significant habitat damage, in some cases creating a "blow hole" in the sea floor about the size of the boat's hull. (A boat's engine may also be ruined in the process.) Instead, visitors are advised to attempt to push or pole the boat off manually, backing out the way the boat approached. Another alternative is to wait for the high tide to return to allow the boat to drift off the sea bottom. When these approaches fail, boaters are told to call for commercial assistance. The park offers a free Boating Education class for the general public and for boaters who receive a citation while in the park.

Much of Biscayne's "great natural beauty" can be found under the sea. The future of these underwater treasures will depend upon careful planning, monitoring, and recovery efforts, as well as the behaviors of citizens well beyond park boundaries.

## Further Reading

Biscayne National Park (2015) Final general management plan/environmental impact statement. National Park Service. US Department of the Interior.

Biscayne National Park (2016) Available at: http://www.nps.gov/bisc (accessed 10 August 2016).

Duarte, C. (2002) The future of seagrass meadows. *Environmental Conservation* 29, 192–206.

Janiskee, B. (2008) Threats to the parks: Biscayne National Park. *National Parks Traveler*, June 20.

Tilman, J., Canzanelli, L., Clark, R., Curry, R., Graham, B., Mayr, M., Moulding, A., Mulcahy, R., Viehman, S. and Whittington, T. (2004) Restoration of coral reef habitats within the national park system. In: Harmon, D., Kilgore, B. and Vietzke, G. (eds) *Proceedings of the 2003 George Wright Society/National Park Service Joint Conference*. The George Wright Society, Hancock, Michigan.

US Coral Reef Task Force (2016) Available at: http://www.coralreef.gov/ (accessed 10 August 2016).

Warnken, J. and Byrnes, T. (2004) Impacts of tourboats in marine environments. In: Buckley, R. (ed.) *Environmental Impacts of Ecotourism*. CAB International, Wallingford, UK.

# 11 Saving Bats at Mammoth Cave

Bats are one of many intriguing features that draw visitors to Mammoth Cave National Park each year. But visitors can contribute to the spread of white-nose syndrome (WNS), a disease that has devastated bat populations throughout the eastern and central USA (**Impacts to wildlife**). Park managers have responded to this emerging threat through the strategies **Limit use** and **Reduce the impact of use**. The park has closed access to colonial bat roosting sites, placing gates at entrances to caves occupied by threatened or endangered bats (**Facility development/Site design/Maintenance**). Law enforcement rangers patrol closed cave entrances for evidence of illegal entry (**Law enforcement**). Visitors entering the cave on ranger-led tours are prohibited from wearing or carrying items that have been in another cave and that have not been disinfected (**Rules/Regulations**). Upon completing tours, visitors must walk across a bioremediation mat to remove and disinfect spores from the fungus associated with WNS (**Facility development/Site design/Maintenance**).

## Introduction

Beneath the forested hills and valleys of south central Kentucky lies the world's longest known cave. Its presence is suggested from above by the region's karst topography—limestone outcrops, sinkholes, and disappearing streams. **The 400+ mile cave formed over hundreds of millions of years from a shallow sea.** Layers of sandstone, shale, and limestone were deposited on the sea floor. The waters receded, the land lifted, and rivers emerged. Over time, acidified rainwater seeped through cracks in the limestone, dissolving the limestone and creating the vast network of underground passages known today as Mammoth Cave.

Caverns decorated with stalactites and stalagmites, flowstones, dripstones, and gypsum flowers have drawn visitors to Mammoth Cave for 200 years. Modern tour names—"Frozen Niagara," "Domes and Dripstones"—highlight these features, formed by the precipitation of minerals from water dripping, trickling, and running through the cave. Within this impressive geologic setting lives a rich diversity of cave wildlife. Some animals are simply visitors, living mostly on the surface, while other creatures spend their entire lives underground. Deep within the cave, species of fish, shrimp and beetles, in the absence of necessity, have no eyes or skin pigmentation.

In recent years, one type of cave creature has garnered the urgent attention of Mammoth Cave National Park managers. The park is home to nine species of cave-associated bats, including two that are federally endangered—Indiana and Gray (Fig. 11.1). While often cast in an unfavorable light in popular culture, bats are ecologically essential to human well-being. These flying mammals consume copious amounts of crop-destroying, disease-spreading insects and pollinate fruits and vegetables.

Bat populations in the USA have been devastated by the arrival of white-nose syndrome (WNS). First discovered in New York State in 2006, the disease has spread to caves throughout the central and eastern USA, leading to the death of millions of bats. WNS is named after a non-native, cold-tolerant fungus that can be seen in white patches around the face, ears, and wings of infected bats. The fungus impacts bats during hibernation, causing them to wake up and move about, burning fat reserves. Without a winter food supply, infected bats die from starvation or dehydration.

**The disease is likely transmitted directly from bat to bat, but also by cave visitors who can carry fungus spores from cave to cave on clothing and gear.** As WNS has spread, and knowledge of the disease has grown, Mammoth Cave has adapted its management of cave visitors to best address this emerging threat.

**Fig. 11.1.** Mammoth Cave National Park is home to nine species of cave-associated bats, including the federally endangered Indiana bat. (US Fish and Wildlife Service photo.)

## Mammoth Cave National Park

Mammoth Cave National Park was authorized by Congress in 1926, established in 1941, and formally dedicated in 1946, following World War II. It has since received designations as a World Heritage Site (1981) and International Biosphere Reserve (1990). Above ground, the 53,000-acre park supports an abundance of traditional recreational activities, including camping, hiking, biking, fishing, canoeing, and horseback riding. The park contains an extensive above-ground trail network, two biologically rich rivers, developed and primitive campgrounds, and a visitor center.

The main draw, of course, is below the surface. Each year, 400,000 visitors participate in ranger-led cave tours in the park. Fourteen miles of developed trails can be found within Mammoth Cave. During peak summer visitation, ten different cave tours are offered, and these range in difficulty and duration. Tours cater to different aspects of the cave, from natural geologic features to historical uses to caving adventure.

## Managing WNS at Mammoth Cave

Following initial detection in New York, WNS spread quickly, arriving in Kentucky in 2011 and to caves within the park in 2013. In conjunction with growing scientific knowledge about the disease and how it is spread, **the park has adapted its management of visitors to minimize the spread of the disease.** Initial efforts primarily focused on preventing introduction of WNS to Mammoth Cave. More recently, managers have sought to prevent its spread between caves in the park and to other caves outside the park, and to protect visitors in light of changes in bat behavior associated with the fungus.

Given the sensitive nature of cultural and natural resources within the cave system, including bats, human access is highly regulated. An underground visit to Mammoth Cave requires participation in a ranger-guided tour, research permit, or special permit. Visits outside of tours are limited to research, education, and cave restoration activities, or rescue. Even by permit, access is restricted to a list of approved people and groups. Independent recreational caving has not been allowed in Mammoth Cave since the mid-1990s.

With the threat of WNS looming, the park placed further restrictions on access to colonial roosting sites. These are places where large numbers of bats gather to hibernate in winter and to rest or raise young in summer. (Other non-colonial bats hibernate and roost in caves or other places as individuals.) Since 2008, these caves have been closed to all but WNS bat research and monitoring activities, even when bats are not present. Guided tours already occurred away from hibernacula and roosts.

To ensure that visitors don't enter vulnerable areas underground, including bat habitat, the park has gated access to several caves. Most gates are "bat friendly," allowing bats to freely enter and exit the cave, and permitting air exchange with the surface. At some constructed entrances, gates are sealed in an effort to restore natural conditions. In places where a gate might draw attention to an otherwise unnoticeable entrance, the cave is left un-gated, and the park refrains from promoting the

location of these entrances. Law enforcement rangers monitor gates and un-gated areas to detect illegal access, and also observe and intercept visitors above ground who have come to the park with private caving gear.

By far, most cave visitation occurs through ranger-led tours. For the purposes of managing WNS, cave tours fall into two categories: (i) those that involve minimal contact with cave sediments (walking tours); and (ii) those that involve extensive contact with cave sediments (wild cave tours). The vast majority of visitors participate in walking tours. Less than 2% take a wild cave tour, in which they climb and crawl through tight cave spaces. (Wild cave tour participants must be 42 inches or less in body width.)

**Several measures are taken to address WNS as visitors arrive to, participate in, and depart from their tours.** Educational materials about bats and WNS are included on the park website, in the visitor center, and on the tour brochure. As tour groups gather, they are screened for previous cave activity. Any person who has visited a cave or mine

**Fig. 11.2.** To help prevent the spread of white-nose syndrome, a fungal disease deadly to bats, wild cave tour participants wear caving gear provided by the park. (National Park Service photo.)

since 2005 is asked to visit the White-Nose Syndrome Station in the visitor center. Clothing or items that have been in a cave or mine since that time are not allowed on the tour. If shoes cannot be changed, they are cleaned with a disinfectant. Visitors not willing to comply with these requirements are offered a refund. Given increased contact with cave sediments, wild cave tour participants are required to wear caving gear provided by the park (Fig. 11.2).

As visitors finish their tour, they must walk over a bioremediation mat, an intervention that was introduced following the arrival of WNS in Kentucky. The mats consist of a length of carpet/artificial turf followed by a section containing cleaning solution. The mats work by physically removing spores from visitors' shoes and disinfecting any remaining spores. Gear worn during the wild cave tour is collected and cleaned by park staff for the next tour.

Although WNS is not considered harmful to people, changes in bat behavior since the disease's arrival has become a recent concern. The park has seen an increase in the number of bats flying into visitors in winter months, likely due to being awakened from hibernation by WNS. While there haven't been a large number of human–bat contacts, the park has become concerned about visitor health, in particular the potential for exposure to rabies. Visitors are advised to never touch a bat, to wear long-sleeved shirts, pants, and a hat, and to notify a ranger if they come in contact with a bat.

Monitoring efforts are underway to understand when and where these contacts occur, and tour schedules may be modified as this information is gathered.

The ultimate impact of WNS on bats in Mammoth Cave and beyond remains to be seen. Early estimates suggest an 80% population loss of some bat species in the park in the few short years since WNS arrived. As understanding of WNS continues to evolve, so too will the approach to managing visitors to Mammoth Cave.

## Further Reading

Fish and Wildlife Service (2011) A national plan for assisting states, federal agencies, and tribes in managing white-nose syndrome in bats. US Department of the Interior.

Mammoth Cave National Park (2016) Mammoth Cave National Park website. Available at: www.nps.gov/maca (accessed 8 June 2016).

National Park Service (2011) White-nose syndrome response plan. Mammoth Cave National Park. US Department of the Interior.

Toomey, R., Thom, S., Gillespie, J., Carson, V. and Trimboli, S. (2013) White-nose syndrome at Mammoth Cave National Park: Actions before and after its detection (February 14, 2013). *Mammoth Cave Research Symposia*. Paper 13.

Zanarini, G., Anderson, N., Clark, C., Shultz, L., Toomey, R, and Trimboli, S. (2016) Continuing measures in response to white-nose syndrome at Mammoth Cave National Park. (April 18, 2016). *Mammoth Cave Research Symposia*. Paper 18.

# 12 Turning Off the Lights at Chaco

Artificial lighting within and outside of Chaco Culture National Historical Park has reduced the ability of visitors to experience "natural darkness" and the celestial sky as seen by the Chacoan people thousands of years before (**Impacts to natural darkness**). "Light pollution" can also impact wildlife and vegetation (**Impacts to wildlife; Impacts to vegetation**). Within Chaco, mercury vapor lights shined brightly outside the visitor center (**Impacts to attraction sites**). The park retrofitted its lighting structures (**Facility development/Site design/Maintenance**) and informed the public about the issue through night sky programs at an observatory they constructed (**Information/Education**). This program of management is designed to pursue two management strategies: expanding opportunities to experience natural night (**Increase supply**), and reducing light pollution related to park visitation (**Reducing the impact of use**). The leadership of Chaco Culture and other southwest parks inspired legislation that is reducing light pollution in the region.

## Introduction

In the north-west corner of New Mexico, visitors to Chaco Culture National Historical Park can peer into the same night sky seen by the Chacoan people 8000 years before. **It's an experience that most people in the developed world never have.** The artificial lights of cities, towns, roads, factories, and refineries mask the billions of stars and planets of the Milky Way galaxy. And since darkness is also wildlife habitat, the impacts of light pollution extend beyond the ability of people to see constellations. Nocturnal animals, such as bats, owls, fireflies, and hatchling turtles depend on natural darkness to hunt, navigate, reproduce, and hide. Plants take their cues from the natural rhythm of night and day, showing signs of stress when exposed to continuous light.

**National parks are some of the last dark places in the USA.** Many are found in the American Southwest, in patches of night-time blackness that can be identified in pictures from space. Yet, even remote parks aren't immune from light pollution. Lighting from visitor centers, campgrounds, nearby attraction sites, and gateway communities may interfere with natural darkness. Air pollution from transportation and industrial sources can obscure the view on an otherwise clear night. Even the curved glow of cities can be seen from as far away as 200 miles. **Protecting the night sky requires working beyond park boundaries.** Chaco Culture

has been a leader in addressing night resources, both within the park and on a broader scale.

## Chaco Culture National Historical Park

Located in the semi-arid desert landscape of the San Juan Basin, Chaco Culture National Historical Park contains the relics of an ancient civilization (Fig. 12.1). Between 850 and 1250 AD, the Chacoan people chose the canyon valley—surrounded by sandstone mesas, slickrock outcrops, and side canyons—as the setting for a center of culture and commerce. People gathered in multi-story "great houses" for trading, business, and ceremony. Containing hundreds of rooms, these public buildings were purposefully planned and constructed, and connected with distant great houses by a sophisticated road system. **The importance of the sky to the Chacoan people is reflected in the alignment of buildings to the movements of the sun and moon, and in drawings of celestial events on cliff walls.**

First designated as a national monument in 1907, the 33,960-acre site became a national historical park in 1980. Nearly 4000 archeological sites have been identified in the park. In 1987, Chaco Culture was recognized for its internationally significant prehistoric buildings and architecture, becoming one of just 20 World Heritage Sites in the USA. Today, archeoastronomy—the study of how ancient people understood the sky—is a key

**Fig. 12.1.** Chaco Culture National Historical Park celebrates prehistoric Native American culture, including remarkable stone architecture and astronomical observations and associated building alignments. (National Park Service photo.)

part of the park's interpretive program. Astronomy programs are offered at an observatory three nights a week, with special programs held during solstice and equinox. More than 3000 visitors attend astronomy programs annually. In 2013, Chaco was named an International Dark Sky Park.

## Managing Natural Darkness above Chaco Canyon

Sixty miles from the nearest town, Chaco Canyon is very dark by US standards. However, by the early 1990s, park officials became concerned about protecting and promoting natural night. The ability of visitors to experience conditions viewed by the ancient Chacoan people was threatened by lighting within Chaco Culture and activities outside of the park. In 1993, night sky was listed as a natural resource in the park's general management plan, giving the issue of darkness equal weight to other important natural and cultural resources.

A first step in protecting Chaco's night sky was to address lighting issues within the park. Mercury vapor lights, one of the most inefficient and polluting light sources, shined brightly outside the visitor center. The park replaced the fixtures with shielded incandescent bulbs. Shielding directs light downward where it is needed, while preventing beams from escaping sideways and upward into the sky. Where possible, motion sensors were installed so lamps would illuminate only when needed. In addition, unnecessary lighting was removed. **A relatively inexpensive action for the park, the new lighting led**

to a 30% reduction in electricity costs. Through a regional night sky initiative, similar efforts took place at parks throughout the Southwest. By 2001, lighting across the US national park system was addressed in the National Park Service Management Policies, which direct parks to light areas only when necessary, to use minimal lighting techniques, and to shield lights as appropriate. As a result, 99% of Chaco is now designated as a "natural darkness zone," with no permanent lighting structures.

While important efforts are taking place across the national park system, effective protection of the night sky requires action beyond park boundaries. One approach to inspiring such action is through visitor education. Chaco Culture first offered night programs in 1987, and a few years later began hosting biannual star parties in partnership with the Albuquerque Astronomical Society (AAS). Hundreds of amateur astronomers were drawn to the region during the darkest nights of the year. Donation of astronomy equipment led to the construction of an observatory in the park, and subsequent volunteer-led astronomy programs. **Night sky programs at the observatory allowed many visitors to experience a natural dark sky for the first time** (Fig. 12.2). Armed with a new awareness of the issue, visitors had the power to address lighting in their own back yards, and to support night sky protection efforts in their own communities. The New Mexico Night Sky Protection Act is a good example of legislation that can result from park leadership and public support. Following the efforts at Chaco Culture and other parks in the region, national park managers promoted night sky protection in southwest newspapers. The New Mexico Heritage Preservation Alliance declared the night sky to be the state's most endangered historic place, and the National Parks Conservation Association released a report on light pollution in national parks, drawing even more attention to the issue. Passed in 1999, the New Mexico law prohibits sale of mercury vapor lights in the state and requires that lights be shielded when it is time to replace them. While political necessity exempted outdoor advertisers, farms, and ranches from the requirements, light pollution from street lighting in cities and towns across the state has been addressed through the legislation.

A final approach to protecting the night sky at Chaco Culture and other national parks is to quantify light pollution so that it can be monitored and managed over time. **A group of National Park**

**Fig. 12.2.** The National Park Service has constructed an observatory at Chaco to help visitors appreciate the beauty and importance of night skies. (National Park Service photo.)

Service scientists, known as the **Night Sky Team**, is conducting assessments of light pollution across the national park system. High-grade camera and computer equipment is set up on clear, moonless nights to measure each park's darkness level. The inventory will not only provide a record of current conditions, but also help to identify sources of light pollution. Further, data will be shared with the public to support collaboration with other agencies, organizations, and interest groups.

The steps taken to protect natural darkness at Chaco Culture and throughout the US national parks have helped raise public awareness of natural night. This leadership has inspired action beyond park boundaries. Through continuing efforts and partnerships, future generations may also have the opportunity to experience the dark sky of the ancients.

## Further Reading

Chaco Culture National Historical Park (2016) Available at: http://www.nps.gov/chcu (accessed 9 September 2016).

International Dark-Sky Association (2016) Available at: http://www.darksky.org (accessed 9 September 2016).

National Parks Conservation Association (1999) Vanishing night skies. *National Parks* 73, 22–25.

Natural Lightscapes (2012) Available at: http://www.nature.nps.gov/air/lightscapes (accessed 20 January 2012).

Rich, C. and Longcore, T. (eds) *Ecological Consequences of Artificial Night Lighting*. Island Press, Washington, DC.

Rogers, J. and Sovick, J. (2001) Let there be dark: The National Park Service and the New Mexico Night Sky Protection Act. *The George Wright Forum* 18, 37–45.

Shattuck, B. and Cornucopia, G. (2001) Chaco's night lights. *The George Wright Forum* 18, 72–76.

# 13 Busing Among the Grizzlies at Denali

Denali National Park and Preserve offers visitors the premier opportunity in North America to see large concentrations of charismatic wildlife, including grizzly bears and wolves. The park is managed in ways that allow visitor access but guard against wildlife disturbance (**Impacts to wildlife**) and other potential impacts (**Crowding; Impacts to attraction sites; Impacts to campgrounds/campsites; Impacts to roads/parking**). The primary management strategies used to minimize wildlife disturbance include caps on visitor use (**Limit use**) and guiding where and how visitors may use the park (**Reduce the impact of use**). Visitor use is limited along the Denali Park Road and in the large wilderness portion of the park (**Rationing/Allocation**). The number of permits for wilderness camping varies across a system of wilderness zones (**Zoning**). A bus system has been implemented on most of the Denali Park Road (**Facility development/Site design/Maintenance**) and visitors are required to ride on park buses, backcountry campers must obtain a permit and use bear resistant food containers, and pets are not allowed (**Rules/Regulations**). An ambitious visitor education program (**Information/Education**) is aimed at backcountry campers, including a Backcountry Information Center (**Facility development/Site design/Maintenance**) designed to encourage hiking and camping behaviors that minimize conflict between visitors and wildlife.

## Introduction

Denali National Park and Preserve is a "crown jewel" of the US national park system. However, prior to 1972, visitation was relatively low because of its remote location in Alaska and its lack of good road access. That changed with completion of the George Parks Highway in 1972, a modern paved road that helped open much of interior Alaska to visitors. **Given the fragile character of much of Denali, particularly its diverse and stunning wildlife—grizzly and black bears, caribou, moose, wolves, and Dall sheep—how might the park welcome substantially more visitors while protecting its wildlife?** The park responded with a bold approach that reaches all visitors, ensuring reasonable public access, but protecting sensitive wildlife.

## Denali National Park and Preserve

"Denali" means "the high one" in the native Athabaskan language and generally refers to the mountain that is the centerpiece—both literally and figuratively—of the park. At 20,320 feet, this is the highest mountain in North America. The mountain was officially named Mount McKinley in the late 19th century after the American president, but many people, especially Alaskans, continued to refer to it

as Denali. In a 2015 order from the US Interior Secretary, the mountain was officially re-named "Denali." Charles Sheldon visited the area in the early 20th century and became concerned that settlers and eventually visitors might threaten indigenous wildlife, especially Dall sheep. Shortly thereafter, Mount McKinley National Park was established by Congress in 1917, included approximately 2 million acres, and was established as a "game refuge." However, much of the parkland was in the higher elevations of the Alaska Range of mountains and excluded a considerable amount of the area's wildlife habitat. In 1980, the area was redesignated as Denali National Park and Preserve and expanded to 6 million acres, an area larger than many states in the "lower 48." One of the primary purposes of establishing the larger reserve was to "maintain sound populations of, and habitat for, wildlife species." The moniker of "Preserve" indicates that most of the land that was added to the park can be used for "subsistence" purposes under regulations established by the State of Alaska.

Today, Denali National Park and Preserve is visited by 400,000 people each year, with these visits compressed into the short summer months of June through the first half of September. The park is a mix of landscapes, including some forests in the lower elevations; vast swathes of tundra; long, braided rivers; and snow fields, rock, and glaciers at the higher elevations. Most visitors to the park hope to see Denali (the mountain)—lost in the clouds most of the time—and the park's famous wildlife, particularly grizzly bears and other "charismatic megafauna." **Nowhere else in America can such concentrations of these large mammals be observed in such an accessible natural environment.** The park also includes rich habitat that attracts birds from all over the world. Access to the park for nearly all visitors is through the historic 91-mile Denali Park Road, which runs along the foot of the Alaska Range and dead-ends at the abandoned mining village of Kantishna. Some visitors also backpack through the 2 million acres of the park that are designated as wilderness. The National Park Service manages both the road and the wilderness to minimize impacts on park wildlife.

## The Denali Park Road

As the George Parks Highway was nearing completion in the early 1970s, the National Park Service anticipated a sharp increase in visitation and decided to institute a mandatory bus system on most of the Denali Park Road (Fig. 13.1). The road goes deep into the heart of the park and offers outstanding opportunities to view wildlife. Visitors may drive their cars on the first 15 miles of the road, but all travel after that point must be on buses. Some of these are conventional sightseeing buses, but these don't go very far into the park. Visitor Transportation System (VTS) buses—much like conventional school buses—travel the whole road, and visitors can ride as far as they wish. The road is not paved and is narrow and rough, sometimes skirting high cliffs, and travel is slow and long. But most visitors are richly rewarded with sightings of many of the park's "big five": bears, caribou, moose, wolves, and Dall sheep. Buses are operated by the park's concessionaire and charge a fee. The number of bus trips along the road is capped, based on consideration of wildlife and other issues. Bus drivers are experienced and knowledgeable and help "interpret" the park to visitors, as well as keep a sharp eye out for wildlife. Buses stop whenever wildlife is seen. All VTS buses depart from and return to the park's Wilderness Access Center, which includes many informational and educational displays.

The bus system was implemented to minimize the impacts of visitors on wildlife. Since buses carry many passengers, this substantially reduces the number of vehicles on the road, so limiting disturbance

**Fig. 13.1.** The park's extensive shuttle bus system takes visitors deep into Denali National Park and offers striking views of Mt. McKinley (now renamed Denali) and the park's world-class wildlife. (Photo by Robert Manning.)

of wildlife. Drivers are trained how to operate their vehicles in a manner that will not disturb wildlife. The bus system also helps control human–wildlife interactions that might be dangerous for both wildlife and visitors. Bus passengers are under the control of the driver and must follow park rules and driver instructions. Visitors may not leave the bus when wildlife is present, must keep their arms inside the bus at all times, and may not feed or harass wildlife in any way. The buses also present an opportunity for drivers to educate visitors about wildlife and other park features, and this is often a highlight for many visitors.

## The Denali Park Wilderness

While the Denali Park Road allows all visitors to see wildlife, **the nearly 2 million acres of wilderness in the park offers hikers and backpackers a much more intimate opportunity to experience the park and its wildlife** (Fig. 13.2). Because the amount and types of wilderness use were increasing, the National Park Service recently developed a new Backcountry Management Plan, and protection of wildlife was one of its major considerations. A number of management practices are employed to help ensure that wilderness use does not endanger either wildlife or visitors. First, like many wilderness areas, use is limited through a permit system. Permits are not needed for day hiking, but are required for overnight use. The wilderness is divided into a number of zones, and these zones represent a range of allowed use levels based on wildlife and other resource considerations, and to provide visitors with a range of opportunities.

Second, the park conducts an ambitious program of information and education for backcountry hikers. Of course, the official website for the park includes a number of pages of material about the wilderness portion of the park. In addition, the National Park Service maintains and staffs a Backcountry Information Center just inside the park; this is where visitors can obtain their backcountry camping permits and consult with rangers and staff. Backcountry visitors are advised to:

1. Make a noise while hiking to alert bears of their presence.
2. Be alert for bears and alter activities to avoid them.
3. Never run from a bear.
4. Refrain from feeding wildlife or allowing wildlife to obtain human foods.
5. Maintain a minimum ¼ mile distance from bears.
6. Refrain from approaching or following wildlife.
7. Remain alert for bears while cooking and be ready to pack up and move quickly.
8. Move away from animals if the presence of visitors alters an animal's behavior.

**Fig. 13.2.** Hikers at Denali National Park find their own way in this largely trail-less wilderness, but they must be careful not to disturb wildlife, including grizzly bears. (Photo by Robert Manning.)

Visitors are allowed to carry pepper spray as a potential defense against bears, but are advised that this is a last resort in the case of an emergency, and should not be viewed as a substitute for proper backcountry behavior. The park's permit system for backcountry camping provides an important means for communicating information to visitors.

Third, a number of rules and regulations have been adopted to guide wilderness use. For example, **backcountry campers must use bear resistant food containers in most of the wilderness zones and store them at least 100 yards from cooking areas and tent sites.** Several types of containers have been approved by the National Park Service and listed on the park's website, and most of them are constructed of a very hard plastic and cannot be opened by bears or other wildlife. Containers are loaned to backcountry campers free of charge at the Backcountry Information Center. Other rules and regulations address pets and closure of sensitive areas. No pets are allowed in the backcountry as they can disturb wildlife. Selected areas of the wilderness portion of the park are closed temporarily or permanently due to sensitive denning or nesting habitat, and for predators that are protecting a kill site. It is the responsibility of visitors to avoid closed areas by checking with staff at the Backcountry Information Center before each trip. Like all other park visitors, backcountry campers must ride the park buses to and from the portions of the park in which they hike. VTS buses will stop anywhere along the park road to drop off or pick up hikers, and special buses (with extra storage space) are provided for backcountry campers.

## Wildlife as a Park Indicator

The new Backcountry Management Plan includes a number of indicators and standards of quality.

As described in Chapter 1 of this book, indicators and standards are used to quantify management objectives for the park and guide subsequent park management. The new plan includes indicators and standards for wildlife. Wildlife are actively monitored, and if statistically significant changes occur in the number, distributions, and demographics (e.g. age structure, gender ratios) of wildlife, and these changes can be correlated with changes in visitor use, the National Park Service will implement practices to alter the level and/or type of visitor use. The management practices that can be used are outlined in the Backcountry Management Plan and include many of the practices discussed in Chapter 5 of this book.

## Further Reading

Denali National Park and Preserve (2006) Denali National Park and Preserve final backcountry management plan. National Park Service, US Department of the Interior, Denali Park, Alaska, 1–179.

Denali National Park and Preserve (2012) Denali Park Road Vehicle Management Plan and EIS webpage. Available at: http://www.nps.gov/dena/parkmgmt/roadvehmgteis.htm (accessed 26 October 2016).

Denali National Park and Preserve (2016) Available at: http://www.nps.gov/dena (accessed 9 September 2016).

Manning, R. and Hallo, J. (2010) The Denali Park Road experience: Indicators and standards of quality. *Park Science* 27, 33–41.

Morris, T., Hourdos, J., Donath, M. and Phillips, L. (2010) Modeling traffic patterns in Denali National Park and Preserve to evaluate effects on visitor experience and wildlife. *Park Science* 27, 48–57.

Phillips, L., Hooge, P. and Meier, T. (2010) An integrated study of road capacity at Denali National Park. *Park Science* 27, 28–41.

Phillips, L., Mace, R. and Meier, T. (2010) Assessing the impacts of traffic on large mammals in Denali National Park and Preserve. *Park Science* 27, 42–47.

# 14 Winning the Lottery on the Colorado River

The Colorado River is the heart of Grand Canyon National Park and offers visitors a world-class whitewater river trip. However, use of the river was causing impacts to the limited number of campsites along the shore (**Impacts to campsites**), many of the area's iconic side canyons and other attraction sites (**Impacts to attraction sites**), and some of the canyon's archeological and historical sites (**Impacts to historical/cultural resources**). The growing amount and diverse types of use were also causing crowding at campsites and on the river (**Crowding**), and conflict between motorized and non-motorized boaters (**Conflict**). A new management plan is relying on the twin strategies of **Limiting use** and **Reducing the impact of use**, and has implemented a coordinated suite of management practices, including spatial and temporal zoning of the river (**Zoning**), regulation of the number and type of boating trips (**Rules/Regulations; Rationing/Allocation**), ranger patrols to enforce regulations (**Law enforcement**), a lottery system to allocate permits to non-commercial boaters (**Rationing/Allocation**), and an intensive program of public education (**Information/Education**).

## Introduction

Grand Canyon is one of the "crown jewel" national parks in the USA, and its status as a World Heritage Site ratifies this importance on a global scale as well. It's famous, of course, for its massive gash in the earth—about 275 miles long, between 5 and 15 miles wide, and 1 mile deep—revealing much of the geologic history of the earth. The rocks exposed at the bottom of the canyon are estimated to be nearly 2 billion years old. Most visitors are awestruck the first time they see the canyon, its jaw-dropping scale and complexity seemingly beyond human imagination. **But the Colorado River is the living heart of the canyon** (Fig. 14.1). For the past 6 million years the river has eroded and exposed the canyon as the vast Colorado Plateau has been uplifted several thousand feet by tectonic forces, a process that is ongoing. The river has been a vital source of water for local Native American tribes for 12,000 years, provided inspiration to artists and writers, and been the focus of some of the most intensive environmental controversies in American history. And in recent years, the Colorado River has also become a mecca for whitewater boating, boasting over 100 major rapids, some of them at the very top of the difficulty scale.

The first documented river-running trip on the Colorado River through Grand Canyon was led by John Wesley Powell in 1869, one of the great American adventure stories. Powell was a one-armed Civil War veteran turned scientist who was interested in mapping the scarce water resources of the American Southwest. At that time, the Grand Canyon region was little more than a blank spot on the map and there were stories about the mysteries of the canyon, including huge rapids and giant waterfalls. Powell and his group of ten men and four wooden boats set off from Green River, Wyoming and traveled nearly 1000 miles, emerging from the Grand Canyon after 2 months and many hardships. The river saw little use after that for nearly 100 years, until surplus rubber rafts from World War II and rapidly growing interest in the environment and outdoor recreation conspired to make this river trip one of the most iconic and popular adventures in the world. In 1955 the National Park Service estimated that about 70 people rafted the river; by 1972 the number was more than 10,000. With use—and associated environmental and experiential impacts—starting to spin out of control, the National Park Service "froze" use and began a planning process to manage river use more carefully. **A new plan was developed and implemented in 2006 which has brought to bear a new suite of management practices,** including a lottery for the limited number of private or non-commercial float trips allowed each year.

**Fig. 14.1.** The Colorado River offers rafters a world class float trip featuring whitewater, geologic wonders, and striking side canyons. (Photo by Robert Manning.)

## Colorado River Management Plan

The Colorado River flows through Grand Canyon National Park for 277 miles from Lee's Ferry (just below Glenn Canyon Dam) to Lake Mead (the reservoir created by Hoover Dam). This is one of the longest free-flowing sections of the river and it offers boaters many attractions, including thrilling whitewater adventure, striking geologic scenery, many remote and intimate side canyons to explore, hundreds of archeological and historical sites, remarkable plant and animal communities, and a vast wilderness to enjoy and appreciate. The problem, of course, is that so many people want to enjoy and appreciate it! And that has led to the new Colorado River Management Plan.

First, a few facts about running the Colorado River. All river trips launch at Lee's Ferry at the eastern end of the park; this is the only road access in this portion of the park and Lee's Ferry is designated River Mile 0. There is no more road access until River Mile 226 at Diamond Creek on the Hualapai Indian Reservation and this where most river trips end. However, the river continues until River Mile 277 where it leaves the confines of Grand Canyon National Park and enters Lake Mead. Because this stretch of river is long, river trips are also relatively long, ranging from several days to as long as 30 days. There are four basic types of river trips. Commercial trips are conducted by companies licensed by the National Park Service and participants pay a fee to take part. Non-commercial trips comprise private individuals who conduct their own trip. Both commercial and non-commercial trips may be either motorized or non-motorized.

**The objective of the Colorado River Management Plan is to "conserve park resources and visitor experiences while enhancing river running recreational activities."** This requires addressing the fundamental issue of the carrying capacity of the river for recreation: how much and what types of recreation can be accommodated before there are unacceptable impacts to the park's environmental and cultural resources and the quality of the visitor experience (the issue of carrying capacity is discussed in Chapter 1). A program of research, planning, and public involvement identified and assessed the following information in addressing the carrying capacity of the Colorado River for outdoor recreation:

1. Physical variables, including the number, size, and distribution of camping beaches.
2. Resource variables, including the number, types, and condition of natural and cultural resources.

3. Social variables, including on-river and attraction site encounters, competition for campsites, number of trips-at-one-time (TAOT) on the river, and number of people-at-one-time (PAOT) in the river corridor.

Several important issues were identified, including:

- the number of river trips that can be accommodated on the river;
- allocation of these trips between commercial and non-commercial groups and between motorized and non-motorized groups;
- environmental impacts to campsites and attraction sites including popular side canyons;
- ability of groups to camp out of sight and sound of other groups;
- number of other groups seen on the river each day;
- impacts to historical and cultural sites;
- welfare of threatened and endangered species; and
- conflict between motorized and non-motorized boaters (Fig. 14.2).

The plan incorporates a suite of management practices, including rules and regulations, law enforcement, zoning, and education. Through the planning process it was determined that recreational use of the river will be limited by means of a set of regulations on the maximum number of groups that can launch from Lee's Ferry each day. Moreover, the number of groups allowed to launch each day varies by season (from 1 in the low, winter use season to 6 in the first half of September) to provide a range of experiences on the river. The total number of launches allowed each year is 1101 and this allows for an estimated maximum of 24,567 users each year resulting in an estimated 228,986 user days (the presence of one user for any part of a day). The National Park Service regularly publishes a "Launch Calendar" that specifies how many and what types of groups are allowed to launch each day. Type of group includes commercial and non-commercial, motorized and non-motorized, maximum length of trip, and maximum group size. Commercial groups are allocated just over half (54%) of all launches, but account for a much greater percentage of all use because their group size tends to be much larger than non-commercial groups. This level of use and its distribution has been determined to be the maximum amount and types of use that can be accommodated while conserving park resources and the quality of the visitor experience.

**Fig. 14.2.** Rafters camp on sand beaches and must be careful to limit their impact, including litter, attracting wildlife, and avoiding crowding and conflict with other groups. (Photo by Robert Manning.)

Additional regulations are designed to address equity, visitor safety, and resource protection. For example, visitors are allowed only one river trip per year (to help ensure that as many people as possible have access to the river); commercial passengers must be accompanied by a National Park Service-approved guide on all trip-related hikes (to help ensure visitor safety); boats are not allowed to enter the Little Colorado River; and visitors are not allowed to use upper Elves Chasm from March through October (to protect threatened and endangered species). Periodic ranger patrols on the river are designed to enforce rules and regulations, as well as educate boaters and provide a search and rescue service.

Allocation of launches is managed differently for commercial and non-commercial users. Commercial use is allocated among qualified companies based largely on historic use levels. However, non-commercial use is allocated based on what is called the "weighted lottery system." Prior to the 2006 plan, non-commercial use was allocated using a waitlist system: boaters put their name on a list (which required a nominal fee) and waited until a launch was available. However, **by 2000 the waitlist had grown to an estimated 20 years** and this proved to be impractical. The weighted lottery system requires potential non-commercial boaters to file an application each year with preferred launch dates for the following year, and applications are selected at random. However, the chances of being selected are enhanced if potential trip leaders have not boated the river in recent years. This is designed to help ensure that boaters who are unlucky in the lottery system are more likely to be selected in future years.

The plan also uses a zoning system, dividing the river into three spatial "zones" designed to offer different types of recreation experiences. Most of the river—from River Mile 0 to 226 (Lee's Ferry to Diamond Creek)—is designated a "Primitive Zone" emphasizing relatively low use levels, a predominately natural environment, and little management presence. A "Semi-Primitive Zone" extends from River Mile 226 to River Mile 260 (Diamond Creek to Quartermaster) and is characterized by moderate levels of use, natural to modified natural-appearing environment, and a low level of management presence including infrequent ranger patrols. A "Rural Natural Setting Zone" extends from River Mile 260 to River Mile 277 (Diamond Creek to the park boundary) and is characterized

by relatively high levels of use, a modified natural-appearing environment, and routine ranger patrols. A temporal zoning system was also established to address the issue of motorized versus non-motorized use; motorized use is allowed only from 1 April through 15 September.

Finally, the plan relies heavily on a sophisticated and intensive program of information and education. The National Park Service maintains a website to help potential visitors plan their trip (http://www.nps.gov/grca/planyourvisit/whitewater-rafting.htm). This website explains how the river is managed, outlines rules and regulations, and describes low-impact behaviors. It includes an orientation video, audio and video podcasts, and a slide show. Commercial use of the river is managed by contracts with river-running companies that require intensive training of guides who are then responsible for the behavior of their clients. A DVD was produced and is used to educate non-commercial boaters. Non-commercial boaters are also given a personal orientation by a ranger at Lee's Ferry before they launch.

## Intensive Use Demands Intensive Management

The Colorado River through Grand Canyon National Park is a world-class recreation resource and it shouldn't be surprising that there is enormous interest in "running" the river. The National Park Service has worked hard to help ensure that as many people as possible get to enjoy and appreciate the adventure that this river offers. But park resources must be protected in the process and the quality of the visitor experience must be maintained at a high level. The management plan for the river allows nearly 25,000 people to boat the river each year and this represents nearly 250,000 user days. To allow this much use requires the National Park Service to employ an intensive management program that includes limits on the amount and type of use, rules and regulations, law enforcement, contractual relationships with commercial companies, a lottery system for non-commercial users, and a sophisticated information and education program.

## Further Reading

Engle, J. (2006a) Lottery replaces list for canyon rafting. *Los Angeles Times*, October 1.

Engle, J. (2006b) Lottery prize: The Colorado River. *Los Angeles Times*, September 24.

Grand Canyon National Park (2016a) Available at: http://www.nps.gov/grca/parkmgmt/crmp.htm (accessed 26 October 2016).

Grand Canyon National Park (2016b) Available at: http://www.nps.gov/grca (accessed 26 October 2016).

Grand Canyon National Park River Permits Office (2016) Grand Canyon River Statistics presentation slides. Available at: http://www.rrfw.org/sites/default/files/documents/NPS_review_of_2006_to_2010_data.pdf (accessed 26 October 2016).

Grand Canyon River Outfitters Association (2016) Available at: http://www.gcroa.org (accessed 26 October 2016).

Shelby, B. (1980a) Crowding models for backcountry recreation. *Land Economics* 56, 43–55.

Shelby, B. (1980b) Contrasting recreational experiences: Motors and oars in the Grand Canyon. *Journal of Soil and Water Conservation* 35, 129–131.

Whittaker, D. and Shelby, B. (2008) Allocating river use: A review of approaches and existing systems for river professionals. River Management Society, Missoula, Montana.

# 15 The Ice Caves are Open, The Ice Caves are Open

In recent years, record numbers of visitors have gathered at Apostle Islands National Lakeshore to see its now famous ice caves. The lakeshore has adapted quickly to high visitation during the normally quiet winter season, accommodating challenges associated with visitor safety, crowded conditions, parking availability, provision of essential services, and potential impacts to ice cave structures (**Crowding; Impacts to roads/parking; Impacts to attraction sites**). The lakeshore has used communication to manage visitor expectations and behavior (**Information/Education**). This reflects the strategies of **Reduce the impact of use** and **Harden experience**. Road plowing and a shuttle service help to **Increase supply** of visitation opportunities (**Facility development/Site design/Maintenance**). Visitors are prohibited from engaging in activities that could damage ice, and endanger themselves and other visitors (**Reduce impact of use; Rules/regulations**).

## Introduction

In winter, Apostle Islands National Lakeshore (Apostle Islands) can be a quiet place. By early fall, lighthouse tours and campfire programs conclude, island cruises and water taxis make their final lake outings, and visitor centers close. But in winter 2014, the lakeshore was far from quiet. Images of frozen waterfalls, ice columns, and caverns dripping with icicles entered the public consciousness through news stories and social media posts. In the midst of a long, bitter cold season, visitors from across the USA and beyond poured into Bayfield Peninsula in northwest Wisconsin, doubling annual visitation to the lakeshore in just 2 months. They were coming to see the ice caves.

Over millennia, red sandstone sea caves at Apostle Islands formed through natural forces—ancient braided rivers, glaciers, lake waters, and cycles of freezing and thawing. **Ice caves are sea caves decorated by freezing waves and running water, with ice formations sometimes cast in blue or pink** (Fig. 15.1). When temperature and wind conditions allow the formation of stable ice on Lake Superior, visitors may access ice caves on foot. However, as climate has changed, opportunities to see the caves have become less certain. The record-breaking 2014 season followed 5 years of no cave access.

Accommodating the trek of thousands of visitors across lake ice is a multi-faceted management challenge. Visitor safety must be considered in light of cold, slippery, and changeable ice and weather conditions. For an uncertain number of weeks, large numbers of visitors are in need of basic services, from parking and restrooms to information, park staff presence, and rescue. As these many visitors venture out onto the ice, the caves and ice formations themselves need to be protected. Park staff adapted quickly to the influx of visitors, effectively managing the ice-cave sensation by promoting visitor awareness of what to expect and by working with partners.

## Apostle Islands National Lakeshore

**Apostle Islands consists of 21 islands and 12 miles of mainland on Lake Superior, the world's largest lake by surface area.** The boundaries of the 69,500-acre lakeshore extend ¼ mile into the lake. Eighty percent of the park is designated as federally protected wilderness. The mainland offers visitor centers and a hiking trail, but the primary attractions—wilderness hiking trails and campsites, sandy beaches, lighthouses, sandstone cliffs, and sea caves—require a trip on the lake. A concessionaire, Apostle Island Cruises, and several private companies provide boat tours, hiker shuttles, water taxis, charter trips, and kayak and boat rentals to support visitor access to these attractions.

**Fig. 15.1.** In winter, frozen waterfalls, ice columns, and icicles transform red sandstone sea caves at Apostle Islands National Lakeshore into ice caves. (National Park Service photo.)

## Managing Ice Cave Visitation

A core responsibility in managing ice cave visitation at Apostle Islands is to designate the caves as open or closed. Caves are open to the public only when ice conditions are deemed low risk. (Park staff emphasizes that ice can never be considered completely safe.) **Ice caves are declared open when ice meets a minimum thickness and the ice sheet is locked between known land points.** There must not have been any "through-ice incidents" or major weather events in the past week. The park emphasizes that conditions can change quickly, and updates visitors on the current status of the caves through their website, Facebook page, and the Ice Line—a telephone number with a recording indicating whether the caves are open or closed. While ice caves can be found on some of the park's islands, Apostle Islands only monitors ice conditions for public access along the mainland caves.

Once the caves are declared open, the lakeshore communicates with visitors in a number of ways to manage expectations and encourage safe and appropriate behavior. The park posts detailed information about visiting the ice caves on their website; shares this information with partners, including local chambers of commerce; and communicates directly with visitors at the Apostle Islands Visitor Center, which is opened when the caves are accessible.

Much information is targeted at helping visitors develop realistic expectations for the amount of effort and preparation needed to visit the caves. Visitors are told to plan for a 2.5–6-mile round trip on ice from the nearest parking lot, with additional miles added by the need to park further away on busy days (Fig. 15.2). Protective clothing, including multiple layers, waterproof boots, and spiked footwear are encouraged. Links to websites

**Fig. 15.2.** Ice cave visitors are encouraged to wear layered clothing, waterproof boots, and spiked footwear on the 2.5–6-mile round trek on lake ice. (National Park Service photo.)

with the latest weather conditions and wind chill factors are provided. Visitors are alerted to the lack of food, water, shelter, and cell phone reception on site.

Visitors are also informed of the potential for encountering many other people on-site. To help manage use, those with flexible schedules are encouraged to visit on a weekday and to carpool. Beyond this, **partnerships have made increased winter use possible.** For example, funding for portable toilets was provided by local chambers of commerce. Roadside plowing that increases available parking has been provided by a local town. A regional transit service has added a shuttle service to and from more distant parking areas for a small fee. To help cover the costs associated with ice cave visitation, the park has imposed a special recreation permit fee of US$5 per day.

**While much emphasis has been placed on accommodating and protecting visitors, there are also rules/regulations in place to protect the ice caves.** Visitors are prohibited from climbing or rappelling from ice cliffs, a potentially dangerous activity that can also damage ice structures. The ice—ephemeral and increasingly rare—is, after all, what visitors have come to discover.

## Further Reading

Apostle Islands National Lakeshore (2016) Apostle Islands National Lakeshore website. Available at: www.nps.gov/apis (accessed 15 June 2016).

Burnett, J. (2014) Winter of 2014 brings record crowds to view ice caves at Apostle Islands National Lakeshore. (February 17, 2014). *National Parks Traveler*. Available at: http://www.nationalparktraveler.com/2014/02/winter-2014-brings-record-crowds-view-ice-caves-apostle-islands-national-lakeshore24670 (accessed 29 June 2016).

Donnelly, C. (2016) Climate change threatens national parks. (March 16, 2016). *Medill Reports Chicago*.

Available at: http://news.medill.northwestern.edu/chicago/climate-change-threatens-national-parks/ (accessed 27 June 2016).

Feldman, J. (2011) The need for legible landscapes: Environmental history and NPS management at Apostle Islands National Lakeshore. *The George Wright Forum* 28, 148–160.

Feldman, J. (2011) *A Storied Wilderness - Rewilding the Apostle Islands*. University of Washington Press, Seattle, Washington.

# 16 The Sounds of Silence in Muir Woods

Large numbers of visitors resulted in substantial noise at Muir Woods National Monument, and this limited the opportunity for visitors to hear the sounds of nature along trails and at Cathedral Grove (**Impacts to natural quiet; Impacts to trails; Impacts to attraction sites**), and may have affected sensitive wildlife (**Impacts to wildlife**). Using the management strategy of **Reducing the impact of use**, signs (**Information/Education**) were placed in the park designating Cathedral Grove a "Quiet Zone" (**Zoning**) and encouraging visitors to reduce the noise they make.

## Introduction

There's something almost spiritual about old-growth forests. The massive trunks of 200- and 300-foot tall trees remind many visitors of the columns that support the world's great churches. And the age of the trees—often hundreds or even thousands of years—are an even more direct link to the origins of the great religions. **Like churches, old-growth forests tend to be quiet places.** In these forests, only the muted sounds of nature are heard—wind softly blowing through the leaves, streams burbling along the valley bottoms, and the occasional call to worship by ravens, Steller's Jays, and other inhabitants of the forest. Many visitors almost instinctively begin to speak in hushed tones when they enter an old-growth forest.

But this behavior isn't universally shared. Visitor-caused noise—including cell phones, the electronic whir and clicks of digital cameras, and the sometimes boisterous behavior of commercial and school groups—can, when magnified by thousands of visitors each day, begin to drown out the sounds of silence, disturbing wildlife, and degrading the quality of the visitor experience. To address this problem, the National Park Service initiated an educational program to sensitize visitors to noise at Muir Woods National Monument, focusing particularly on an area aptly called Cathedral Grove. This educational program was tested on an experimental basis. On "treatment" days, signs were placed at the park entrance and again as visitors approached Cathedral Grove, designating this area a "quiet zone" and asking visitors to reduce the noise they made. Sound monitoring equipment found that noise levels

in Cathedral Grove were substantially lower on treatment days compared to "control" days (days when the signs were not posted). Moreover, a visitor survey found that respondents consciously reduced the noise they made at Cathedral Grove during treatment days and strongly supported designation of this area as a quiet zone. The educational program is now a permanent part of managing the park.

## Muir Woods National Monument

Muir Woods National Monument lies just north of San Francisco, California. It's a popular tourist destination, attracting over 750,000 visits annually. The park comprises less than 600 acres—small by national park standards—but includes 240 acres of old-growth Coast Redwoods (*Sequoia sempervirens*), one of few such stands remaining in the San Francisco Bay area (Fig. 16.1). Most of the redwoods in the park are between 500 and 1200 years old, and the tallest tree is 258 feet. **Many of the largest and oldest redwoods are located in Cathedral Grove, the heart (or soul) of the park.** The park was declared a national monument in 1908 by President Theodore Roosevelt, and was named in honor of John Muir, a colorful naturalist and pioneer of conservation and widely considered the "father" of the US national park system. Cathedral Grove hosted an important gathering of delegates from 50 nations who met in San Francisco to draft and sign the United Nations Charter. President Franklin Roosevelt was to have opened the conference, but died shortly before it convened. A commemorative ceremony in his memory was held in Cathedral

**Fig. 16.1.** Muir Woods National Monument offers visitors to the San Francisco Bay area a chance to experience an old-growth redwood forest. (Photo by Robert Manning.)

Grove on 19 May 1945, and a plaque was placed there in his honor. Most visitors walk along the park's main mile-long trail, which traverses Cathedral Grove.

## Managing the Natural Quiet of Muir Woods

The National Park Service and other park and outdoor recreation management agencies work hard to reduce the impacts that visitors often have. These concerns have conventionally addressed important natural resources, including soils, vegetation, water, and wildlife, or "landscapes" more broadly. More recently, parks are being recognized as having important "soundscapes" as well—the mix of natural and cultural sounds in a park. "Natural quiet," the sounds of nature undisturbed by human-caused noise, is being recognized as an increasingly scarce resource that needs to be protected.

Concern about human-caused noise in parks and outdoor recreation areas was originally driven by issues of wildlife disturbance. Human noise can have obvious effects on wildlife, such as disturbance of habitat. Sometimes these effects are not as apparent, such as disruption of communication among insects. More recently, concern has arisen about the ways in which noise can detract from the quality of the visitor experience. Of course, disturbance of wildlife reduces the chances of visitors seeing and hearing wildlife; it also diminishes the "peace and quiet" that many visitors seek in parks and related areas. Research has shown that visitors value the tranquility of parks, and that noise can annoy visitors, interrupt interpretive programs, and generally interfere with enjoyment, relaxation, and appreciation of parks.

**Many national parks and related areas are experiencing problems of unwanted and excessive human-caused noise.** High-profile examples include snowmobiles in Yellowstone National Park and air tours at Grand Canyon National Park (these examples are described in two other case studies). In response, the National Park Service has revised its policies to address soundscape-related issues more directly. These policies state that the agency "will restore to the natural condition wherever possible those park soundscapes that have become degraded by unnatural sounds (noise) and will protect natural soundscapes from unacceptable impacts." To further this policy, the agency created its Natural Sounds Program Office in 2000 to "articulate National Park Service...policies that will require, to the fullest extent practicable, the protection, maintenance, or restoration of the natural soundscape resource in a condition unimpaired by inappropriate or excessive noise."

Concern about noise at Muir Woods National Monument began more than 20 years ago and was focused on human disturbance of the Northern Spotted Owl, an endangered species. More recent concern has addressed the impacts of noise on the quality of the visitor experience. In a survey of park visitors, "peacefulness," "quiet," and "the sounds of nature" were found to have a positive influence on the quality of the visitor experience, and "noisy visitors," "loud talking," and related issues were found to substantially degrade the quality of the visitor experience. A follow-up survey incorporated a series of audio clips with increasing levels of visitor noise overlaid on a recording of natural sounds in the park, and visitors rated the acceptability of these audio clips. Findings suggested that visitors found human-caused noise above 37 decibels to be unacceptable, and that noise in Cathedral Grove sometimes exceeded this level. Based on these

**Fig. 16.2.** The National Park Service has designated Cathedral Grove in Muir Woods as a "Quiet Zone" to allow visitors to hear the sounds of nature. (Photo by Robert Manning.)

findings, the park instituted the educational program described above. Signs on treatment days were posted at the park entrance and as visitors approached Cathedral Grove, designating this area a "quiet zone" and asking visitors to turn off cell phones, speak in a lowered voice, and encouraging children to walk quietly (Fig. 16.2). A sophisticated sound-monitoring device was placed in Cathedral Grove (out of sight from visitors) and recorded sound levels on a continuous basis on ten randomly selected treatment and control days. A visitor survey was also conducted on treatment days to explore visitor reactions to the quiet zone designation.

Sound monitoring found that noise levels in Cathedral Grove were substantially lower—to a statistically significant degree—during treatment days. The lower sound level has a substantial effect on the park's soundscape and the quality of the visitor experience. For example, the lower sound level associated with the educational program is the equivalent of a nearly 30% reduction in visitor use levels without the signage system. The lower noise level is also the equivalent of a nearly 100% increase in the "listening area" for the park—the size of the area in which visitors can hear the sounds of nature. Findings from the visitor survey

were also encouraging. Nearly all respondents reported seeing the signs asking visitors to be quiet, and the vast majority (over 95%) reported that they consciously limited the amount of noise they made in the park because of this educational program. Nearly all visitors supported designation of Cathedral Grove as a quiet zone.

**The relatively simple educational program at Muir Woods was remarkably effective in "quieting" the park**, thereby reducing the impacts of visitor use and enhancing the quality of the visitor experience. As a result, the National Park Service has permanently designated Cathedral Grove a quiet zone and has institutionalized its associated program of visitor education and signage. This designation was formally declared on 19 May 2008 in honor of the day in 1945 when the United Nations delegates met in Cathedral Grove.

### Further Reading

Hempton, G. and Grossmann, J. (2009) *One square inch of silence: One man's quest to preserve quiet.* Free Press, New York, New York.

Muir Woods National Monument (2016) Available at: http://www.nps.gov/muwo (accessed 27 October 2016).

Nash, R. (1967) John Muir, William Kent, and the conservation schism. *Pacific Historical Review* 36, 423–433.

Natural Sounds Program (2016) Available at: http://www.nature.nps.gov/naturalsounds (accessed 27 October 2016).

Park Science (2009–2010) Special issue: Soundscapes research and management - Understanding, protecting, and enjoying the acoustic environment of our national parks. *Park Science* 26, 1–72.

Pilcher, E., Newman, P. and Manning, R. (2009) Understanding and managing experiential aspects of soundscapes at Muir Woods National Monument. *Environmental Management* 43, 425–435.

Rothman, H. (2004) *The New Urban Park: Golden Gate National Recreation Area and Civic Environmentalism*. University Press of Kansas, Lawrence, Kansas.

Stack, D., Newman, P., Manning, R. and Fristrup, K. (2011) Reducing visitor noise levels at Muir Woods National Monument using experimental management. *Journal of the Acoustical Society of America* 129, 1375–1380.

# Chapter 16

# 17 Stewarding America's Antiquities at Mesa Verde

Mesa Verde National Park in southwest Colorado was established in 1906 to protect ancient archeological sites of Ancestral Puebloan people, abandoned 800 years ago. The area includes world-famous cliff dwellings such as Cliff Palace. But these sites are fragile, were vandalized and looted before establishment of the park, and can be damaged by too much or inappropriate visitor use (**Impacts to historical/cultural resources; Depreciative behavior**). These cultural resources are protected by a program of management, including site closures (**Rules/Regulations**) and stabilization of ruins (**Facility development/Site design/Maintenance**), access to sites only in the presence of a uniformed ranger (**Rules/Regulations; Law enforcement**), limits on the number of visitors allowed on ranger-led tours (**Rationing/Allocation; Impacts to interpretive facilities programs**), division of the park into two primary use zones providing alternative types of visitor experiences (**Zoning**), and information and education about the significance of the area in the form of interpretive programs (**Information/Education**). This management program is based on the strategies of **Limiting use, Reducing the impact of use, and Hardening the resource**.

## Introduction

On 18 December 1888, cowboys Richard Wetherill and Charlie Mason were rounding up stray cattle in an area called Mesa Verde in southwest Colorado. As they peered over the edge of the mesa top they saw something startling: the remains of a large collection of interconnected buildings made of stone tucked into a shallow cave. **Upon closer inspection, they realized they had discovered the improbable and impressive dwellings of a former civilization.** Wetherill called the site Cliff Palace, and he and his family continued to explore the area over the ensuing years, finding many other dwelling sites and unearthing scores of artifacts.

But the discovery of the cliff dwellings brought many visitors who vandalized the structures and looted the ancient treasures. Walls and roofs were knocked down in the process, large areas were excavated in a haphazard way, and roof beams were burned as firewood. Even the early archeologist, Gustaf Nordenskiold, excavated the sites in ways that modern archeologists would consider destructive. In 1906, Congress reacted by establishing Mesa Verde National Park, as a way to protect this important cultural area.

## Mesa Verde National Park

Mesa Verde National Park comprises 52,000 acres of land in the Four Corners region of the American Southwest. Mesa Verde is Spanish for "green table," and describes a large, irregular, and mostly flat area at about 7000 feet above sea level. This area was the home of an ancient civilization of Native Americans popularly called the Anasazi, but more correctly called the Ancestral Puebloan people. Evidence suggests the area was inhabited from 550 to 1300 AD. The park includes nearly 5000 archeological sites, including nearly 600 cliff dwellings (Fig. 17.1). **These are the largest and most impressive cliff dwellings in North America and constitute the premier archeological site in the USA.** The park has been designated a World Heritage Site.

For more than 700 years, Native Americans lived and flourished here, farming and hunting. At first, they lived in primitive pit houses on the mesa tops. Later, they built elaborate pueblos made of adobe. In the late 12th century they began to build cliff dwellings in caves and under outcroppings in the cliffs of the mesas. In the late 13th century, the inhabitants began to move away from the area, eventually deserting their home sites entirely. The reason they abandoned the area is unknown, but may have been caused by a prolonged drought and

**Fig. 17.1.** Cliff Palace is the largest cliff dwelling in Mesa Verde National Park and is an iconic visitor attraction. (National Park Service photo by Flint Boardman.)

associated crop failure or invasion of foreign tribes from the north. Former inhabitants migrated south into New Mexico and Arizona, and today's 24 Native American Nations (the pueblo people along the Rio Grande River, the Zuni in New Mexico, and the Hopi in Arizona) regard Mesa Verde as their ancestral home.

The cliff dwellings are the primary visitor attraction because of their dramatic character and because they represent the height of the civilization. Several of the largest cliff dwellings are open to the public, including Cliff Palace, Long House, and Balcony House. Cliff Palace is the largest cliff dwelling, having over 150 rooms, and thought to have been home for more than 100 people at any one time. Several large pueblo sites are also accessible to the public, including Sun Temple, Far View House, Cedar Tree Tower, and Badger House Community. The park's museum and research collection includes 3 million artifacts and archives. Archeological sites open to the public are found in two areas of the park known as Chapin Mesa and Wetherill Mesa. The park accommodates over 500,000 visits annually.

## Managing Mesa Verde

Park managers are challenged at Mesa Verde with making the park's cultural resources accessible to the public in ways that will protect these resources for future generations. The program of management comprises several practices, including site closures; rules and regulations; law enforcement; site management; rationing and allocation; information and education, with a special emphasis on what the National Park Service conventionally calls "interpretation;" and zoning.

First, **the law creating the park in 1906 forbids visitors from entering any cliff dwelling without the presence of a uniformed ranger** (Fig. 17.2). (Congress also passed the historic Antiquities Act the same year in an effort to protect cultural resources on all public lands; this Act is still in use today.) The purpose of this rule is to ensure that these fragile archeological sites are not damaged and that artifacts are not disturbed. The National Park Service takes three approaches to implementing this rule:

**1. Most of the park and its cultural resources are closed to visitor use.** Much of the park has yet to be fully surveyed and many of the known archeological sites have not been studied or stabilized. These areas are too fragile to accommodate public use at this time. Visitors must remain in developed areas of the park and may not wander off maintained trails.

**2.** Several of the largest cliff dwellings, including Cliff Palace, Balcony House, and Long House, can only be seen on daily tours led by park rangers.

**3.** One cliff dwelling, Step House, is self-guiding with rangers present to monitor use and answer questions. Spruce Tree House has historically been available for self-guided tours, but rock falls led

**Fig. 17.2.** Visitors may tour several of Mesa Verde's cliff dwellings, but only in the presence of a park ranger. (Photo by Robert Manning.)

park managers to close the area in 2016 for safety reasons. Stabilization work may lead to reopening in the future.

In addition to the law requiring the presence of a uniformed ranger, the National Park Service has established several additional regulations, including forbidding visitors to "sit, stand, climb, or lean on fragile archeological structures" and prohibiting "removal, collection, and/or disturbance of any natural or cultural resources."

Ranger-led tours are limited in size to ensure that visitors can hear the tour narrative and ask questions, and to limit the possibility of damage to the sites. Tickets for these tours must be purchased in person at the park's Visitor Center. **During the peak use season, visitors may purchase a ticket for either Cliff Palace or Balcony House, but not both on the same day, to help ensure that access to these sites is available to as many visitors as possible.**

The park's archeological sites are managed in a variety of ways to allow public access while protecting the integrity of the sites. As noted above, most sites are closed to the public because they have not yet been studied or stabilized. Other sites, such as the major cliff dwellings noted above, have been studied and stabilized to enable visitor use. Some sites, such as a few of the mesa-top pueblos, have been more heavily stabilized using cement mortar;

this enables these sites to be used by visitors without constant monitoring by rangers or other park staff.

Park management places a heavy emphasis on information and education in the form of interpretation. Interpretation is presentation of information to visitors in ways that informs them about the park and enhances their enjoyment and appreciation of its resources, and does this in a way that engages visitors. A large corps of interpretive rangers conducts the tours of Cliff Palace, Balcony House, and Long House, and is stationed at Step House, as well as at the park's Visitor Center. In addition, several special tours to sites normally closed to visitors are conducted each year in association with the Mesa Verde Museum Association, a non-profit organization that helps support the park. The park's major concessionaire also conducts guided bus tours. **These interpretive programs are designed on the principle articulated by pioneering National Park Service interpreter Freeman Tilden: "through interpretation, understanding; through understanding, appreciation; through appreciation, protection."**

Finally, the park is zoned into two distinctive areas. Chapin Mesa is most easily accessible and includes the most popular visitor attractions such as Cliff Palace and Balcony House. This area is heavily visited. Wetherill Mesa is accessible by a narrow, winding 12-mile road, and a paved trail system provides visitors access to the area's principal attractions, including Long House. The area is designed for visitors who enjoy walking, biking, and a more relaxed atmosphere.

## Further Reading

Cook, S. (2011) Mesa Verde a model for saving cultural resources – Subcommittee discusses hurdles for national parks. In: *Durango Herald*, November 6.

Fiero, K. (2002) Preserving dirt-walled structures in Mesa Verde National Park. *Conservation and Management of Archaeological Sites* 5, 55–62.

Lowenthal, D. and Binney, M. (eds) *Our Past Before Us: Why Do We Save It?* Maurice Temple Smith Ltd, London.

Mesa Verde National Park (2016) Available at: http://www.nps.gov/meve (accessed 18 August 2016).

NPS Archeology Program (2016) Available at: www.nps.gov/archeology (accessed 18 August 2016).

# 18 What Goes Up Mt. Whitney Must Come Down

As the highest mountain in the "lower 48," Mt. Whitney is a favorite destination for many hikers in the USA and beyond. However, this popularity has led to a number of management problems, including impacts associated with very large numbers of visitors on the trail and summit and improper disposal of human waste (**Crowding; Impacts to attraction sites; Impacts to trails; Impacts to soil; Impacts to vegetation**). Portions of Mt. Whitney lie in Sequoia National Park and the adjacent Inyo National Forest, and the National Park Service and US Forest Service have cooperated in managing recreational use of the mountain in several important ways. This coordinated program of management is based on the strategies of **Limiting use** and **Reducing the impact of use** and includes: **1.** designating a Mt. Whitney Zone where special regulations apply (**Zoning**); **2.** requiring a permit for both overnight and day use (**Rationing/Allocation**); **3.** promulgating a special set of regulations that apply to visitors in the Mt. Whitney Zone, including a requirement that visitors remove their solid human waste (**Rules/Regulations**); **4.** a program to inform visitors about special regulations (**Information/Education**); and **5.** enforcement of these regulations (**Law enforcement**).

## Introduction

While there is some uncertainty about the exact height of Mt. Whitney in California, there is no disagreement about the fact that it's the highest mountain in the contiguous USA. The brass plaque at the summit of the mountain lists its elevation as 14,494 feet, but recent measurements have found its height as 14,505 feet. **Mt. Whitney's distinction as the highest mountain in the lower 48 states, along with a well-maintained trail to the summit, has made it a prized destination of many hikers.** Though there are several trails that approach the mountain, the Mt. Whitney Trail up the east side of the mountain is the most popular, and is the only one that offers access to the summit by a day hike. However, it's a demanding hike covering a 22-mile round trip and requiring over 6000 feet of elevation gain. Despite the grueling nature of the hike, hundreds of visitors used to gather at the trailhead at Whitney Portal well before dawn to attempt the climb. This resulted in very large numbers of hikers on the trail and at the summit, exceeding use levels that many people felt were appropriate for a wilderness environment. Disposal of human waste was a special problem, given that much of the trail is above tree line and where there is little or no soil to accommodate conventional waste burial guidelines. These and related problems have led to implementation of a suite of new management practices.

## Sequoia National Park and the Inyo National Forest

The summit of Mt. Whitney marks the boundary between Sequoia National Park and the Inyo National Forest (Fig. 18.1). These areas are managed by the National Park Service and the US Forest Service, respectively. There has been a long history of bureaucratic rivalry between these agencies; the National Park Service has its genesis in efforts to preserve scenic areas, while the Forest Service has its origins in a more utilitarian approach to natural resource management. Nevertheless, the two agencies have adopted a strong partnership in their joint efforts to manage recreational use of Mt. Whitney in a responsible manner.

Sequoia National Park is adjacent to Kings Canyon National Park and these two national parks are administered together. Sequoia is sometimes referred to as "the land of giants" because of its signature groves of sequoia trees, the world's largest living things. The Inyo National Forest is also monumental, including nearly 2 million acres of the Sierra Nevada and Great Basin Mountains. Landforms range from semi-arid deserts to lush meadows and high-elevation lakes to alpine summits. It includes nine wilderness areas that offer a staggering array of recreational opportunities.

© R.E. Manning, L.E. Anderson and P.R. Pettengill 2017. *Managing Outdoor Recreation: Case Studies in the National Parks*, 2nd Edition (R.E. Manning *et al.*)

**Fig. 18.1.** Mt. Whitney is the highest mountain in the continental USA and is jointly managed by the National Park Service and the US Forest Service. (National Park Service photo.)

## Managing Recreational Use on Mt. Whitney

Management of recreational use on Mt. Whitney includes a suite of coordinated actions. First, the mountain and its immediate surroundings have been designated as the "Mt. Whitney Zone." This calls attention to the importance of this area and the need for special management focus. An important component of this program of management is the cooperative approach of the National Park Service and the US Forest Service. It would not be possible to manage recreational use of the mountain in a coherent and effective way without this type of coordination. An important manifestation of this cooperative approach is the Eastern Sierra Interagency Visitor Center. This facility is staffed by both agencies and offers a program of information and education on the special character of Mt. Whitney and guidelines for use of this area. In addition to providing information to visitors about use of Mt. Whitney, it sends a strong message to potential visitors: **"To preserve its wilderness character, all visitors must be committed to extremely high standards of conduct."**

Given the especially high demand for access, use has had to be limited through a permit system. On the popular Mt. Whitney Trail, 60 overnight visitors and 100 day-use visitors are allowed each day during the peak use period from 1 May to 1 November. For trips in May, June, and July, visitors must apply by 20 April. For trips in August, September, and October, applications are due by 27 April. A lottery is used to select successful applications. If there is space left after the lottery has been conducted, permits may be obtained in person the day before the permit entry date at the Interagency Visitor Center. Permits must be attached to the outside of backpacks so as to be visible to rangers who patrol the area. If visitors do not have a permit, they will be fined up to US$100 and asked to leave the area.

The combination of high use and the need to preserve the wilderness character of this area means that all visitors must abide by a number of regulations. For example, from Memorial Day weekend through 31 October, all food, food-related trash, and scented items (e.g. toothpaste, deodorant) must be stored in bear-proof containers (most hikers use plastic "bear canisters" that are carried in backpacks). Moreover, at the trailhead, food-related items must be taken out of cars and stored in the bear-proof lockers provided. These regulations are designed to discourage bears from frequenting this area and becoming aggressive with hikers on the trail or at campsites. Bears are adept at breaking into cars to get food; if this happens, visitors may be fined (as well as having to deal with the damage to their cars!).

**Perhaps the most demanding regulation is that visitors must pack out all solid human waste.** Conventional burial of human waste is not feasible given high use levels and lack of soil at higher elevations. Hikers receive a waste allocation and gelling (WAG) bag with their permits (Fig. 18.2). This is a plastic bag with a urine-activated powder to encapsulate and deodorize solid waste. The bag includes a zip-lock seal, but extra bagging is recommended. WAG bags can be disposed of in dumpsters at the trailhead. WAG bags are now used in an increasing number of specialized outdoor recreation areas such as mountain climbing sites.

The coordinated, multi-agency program of recreation management on Mt. Whitney employs a suite of management practices designed to protect both the area's extraordinary resources and the quality of the visitor experience. At iconic places such as Mt. Whitney, both managers and visitors must be prepared to accept increasingly intensive management.

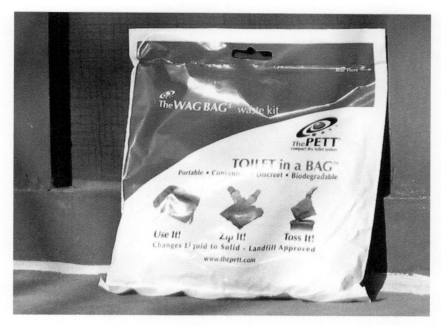

**Fig. 18.2.** Hikers on Mt. Whitney must carry out their own solid human waste because soils in the area are too shallow for burial and decomposition. (National Park Service photo.)

## Further Reading

Barringer, F. (2007) No more privies, so hikers add a carry-along. *The New York Times*.

Cleanwaste (2016) Available at: http://www.cleanwaste.com/wag-bag (accessed 27 October 2016).

Climburg, A., Monz, C. and Kehoe, S. (2000) Wildland recreation and human waste: A review of problems, practices, and concerns. *Environmental Management* 25, 587–598.

Inyo National Forest (2016) Available at: http://www.fs.usda.gov/recmain/inyo/recreation (accessed 27 October 2016).

MacDonald, D. (2008) Packing out waster: You can take it with you. *Backpacker Magazine*, June.

Oye, G. and Spitek, B. (2008) Mount Whitney case study. Available at: http://www.nps.gov/yose/parkmgmt/upload/Oye%20Briefing%20Sheet.pdf (accessed 27 October 2016).

Sequoia and Kings Canyon National Parks (2016) Available at: http://www.nps.gov/seki (accessed 27 October 2016).

# 19 Preventing the Petrified Forest from Disappearing

Visitors to Petrified Forest National Park have the opportunity to walk among the crystallized remains of trees that lived more than 200 million years ago. However, a small percentage of visitors threaten the preservation of these Mesozoic structures by taking petrified wood from the park (**Depreciative behavior; Impacts to historical/cultural resources**). To address this challenging problem, the park has promulgated a strict rule against removing petrified wood (**Rules/ Regulations**) and established a robust education and outreach program that alerts visitors to this rule and the importance of leaving petrified wood in its place. Information is shared through a visitor center film, at entrance gates, in the visitor guide, on the park website, on signs at trailheads, and through interpretive displays (**Information/Education**). Park rangers and uniformed volunteers monitor popular sites, and visitors pass through a check station as they leave the park; anyone caught taking, moving, or damaging petrified wood is fined (**Law enforcement**). Real and fake cameras have been used to monitor heavily used sites and discourage theft (**Facility development, site design/maintenance**). Additionally, petrified wood from outside sources is sold by a park concessionaire for visitors wanting a souvenir. These management practices are designed to **Reduce the impact of use** by diminishing theft, and to **Increase the supply** of souvenirs by using sources of petrified wood from outside the protected area of the park.

## Introduction

More than 200 million years ago, trees floated down the corridor of an ancient river system in what is now northeastern Arizona. Stripped of their limbs and bark during the journey, the trees collected in log jams, and were quickly buried in sediment. Without oxygen, logs decayed slowly, absorbing minerals from volcanic ash, their woody structure replaced over hundreds of years by quartz crystals. **Through the forces of geologic time, the trees became petrified wood.**

Today, quartz log "forests" shimmer in the sunlight in Petrified Forest National Park, reflecting the colors of the rainbow through impurities of iron, carbon, and manganese (Fig. 19.1). These remarkable structures have endured through the age of dinosaurs and through ancient human civilizations. They outlasted commercial interests of the late 1800s—though not entirely unscathed—that sought to mine petrified logs for amethyst or to pulverize them for industrial abrasives. **But in modern times, these relics of the Mesozoic era face a new threat: the allure of the souvenir.**

Unfortunately, national parks aren't immune from irresponsible, thoughtless, selfish, or ill-intentioned human behaviors. Disregard for park rules and regulations, even among a small minority of visitors, can have a major impact on park resources. In some cases, depreciative visitor behaviors, such as graffiti, vandalism, and litter, may be simply unsightly and costly to clean up or repair. But the problem can be much worse when cultural artifacts, historic objects, or geological features are involved. When these items are damaged, moved, or stolen, the consequences can be devastating. In many cases, the harm is irreparable, since the value of these resources is greatly diminished when taken out of context, even if the item is returned.

In Petrified Forest National Park, just a small percentage of visitors (perhaps only 1%) elect to take petrified wood from the park. However, when this percentage is multiplied over hundreds of thousands of visitors each year, the magnitude of the impact is considerable. Though difficult to quantify, it is estimated that tons of petrified wood are taken from Petrified Forest each year. Once removed, the wood cannot be replaced, and a piece of scientific knowledge is forever lost. For these reasons, preventing theft of petrified wood is a major concern for park managers, who have introduced an aggressive suite of management actions to address the problem.

**Fig. 19.1.** Petrified Forest National Park features large concentrations of petrified wood that is fossilized trees from the Late Triassic period about 225 million years ago. (National Park Service photo by T. Scott Williams.)

### Petrified Forest National Park

In 1906, President Theodore Roosevelt created Petrified Forest National Monument though the Antiquities Act, citing the need to protect petrified wood for the public good. The area was designated a National Park in 1962, and greatly expanded in 2004 to encompass more than 200,000 acres. Though known for its geologic namesake, the park also contains over 800 archeological and historic sites, 50,000 acres of designated wilderness, and hundreds of species of shortgrass prairie plants and wildlife. A 27-mile road links the north and south ends of the park, and connects visitors with several attractions, including the Painted Desert Visitor Center; Rainbow Forest Museum; scenic overlooks with views of the Painted Desert; archeological sites, including Puerco Pueblo and Newspaper Rock; the historic Painted Desert Inn; and several short trails through concentrations of petrified wood, including Crystal Forest, Giant Logs, and Blue Mesa. While overnight backpacking is allowed in the Petrified Forest National Wilderness Area, the remainder of the park is only open during daylight hours. Approximately 800,000 people visit the park each year, with most of this visitation occurring during the summer.

### Managing (and Minimizing) Theft of Petrified Wood

The regulations regarding petrified wood, and other natural and cultural resources in Petrified Forest National Park, are clearly stated: "Do not remove any natural or cultural object from the park, including fossils, rocks, animals, plants, and artifacts." "Do not relocate objects within the park." **Visitors who take, move, or damage petrified wood face a minimum fine of $325.**

To promote and enforce these regulations, the park interacts with visitors throughout their time in Petrified Forest (Fig. 19.2). Even before visitors arrive, they may encounter messages on the park's website about petrified wood, its importance, and the problem of theft. As visitors arrive at one of the two visitor centers—Painted Desert Visitor Center and Rainbow Forest Museum—they may elect to watch a film in which the petrified wood issue is highlighted. Those who read the park visitor guide will find the issue addressed on the front cover by the Superintendent. Here he writes: "One of the biggest dangers our park faces is the illegal removal of park resources, particularly petrified wood. With the help of visitors, this selfish act can diminish." Additional reminders about petrified wood are placed throughout the guide—in a list of park

**Fig. 19.2.** The National Park Service delivers an extensive visitor information and education program to visitors that includes a strong message about why pieces of petrified wood should not be taken from the park. (National Park Service photo.)

regulations, in text describing park trails, and in a tribute to park volunteers who help monitor petrified wood trails.

Passing through the entrance gate, visitors are greeted by an attendant who reminds them about the importance of park resources and emphasizes the illegal nature of taking wood and other natural and cultural objects. Park entrances are always staffed while the park is open, meaning that all visitors entering the park will receive this message. Further, the park is only open during daylight hours, in part to discourage the temptation of collecting petrified wood in the evenings. At the gate, visitors are asked if they are carrying any petrified wood from sources outside the park (where collecting is legal). If so, the wood is tagged at the gate so that it can be identified as legal by park staff. As visitors exit the park, they are stopped once again and asked whether they have taken anything from the park. **Signs posted ½ mile from each exit alert visitors to the check station ahead. Park rangers have collected many pieces of petrified wood along these stretches of road where visitors have pitched their cache out the window before reaching the exit.**

At one time, the park gave each visitor a piece of petrified wood (from outside sources) as they left Petrified Forest. By doing so, it was hoped that people would be discouraged from taking petrified wood, knowing that that they would receive this souvenir upon their departure. This practice is no longer followed, but a similar approach currently exists in allowing the park concessionaire to sell petrified wood in gift shops within the park. Visitors who purchase the crystallized wood are told that it comes from outside of the park, and the purchase is specially boxed and tagged.

In another approach, the park recently highlighted a visitor legend in a display at the Rainbow Forest Museum. While the origins of the legend are unknown, many visitors have claimed to suffer misfortune after taking petrified wood from the park. In letters accompanying returned wood crystals, visitors relay woeful tales of sickness, divorce, and disaster experienced after returning home with their prized memento. In some cases, people return wood that parents or spouses had taken, hoping to improve their luck, based on a legend that has taken on a life of its own. Of course, once the wood has been removed from its original location, its ecological and scientific value is greatly diminished.

The park has taken additional measures to prevent theft along trails and in places where there are heavy concentrations of petrified wood. Signs use a variety of messages to appeal to different types of visitors, ranging from the directive of "DO NOT steal petrified wood" to explanations of why it is important to follow this rule. These messages are incorporated into interpretive programs and hikes that take place in these areas. Park rangers and roving interpreters are stationed at these sites as financial resources allow, to monitor visitor behavior. A more cost-effective approach has been to place uniformed volunteers at the sites. In addition, the park has used both real and fake cameras to further discourage petrified wood theft.

Research has shown that these types of management actions can be effective in addressing the problem. A study demonstrated that three interventions—the presence of a uniformed volunteer, an interpretive sign, and a signed pledge—were all equally effective in reducing the rate of petrified wood theft. However, the interventions did not stop everyone from taking a piece of petrified wood. Interviews with park visitors revealed that people who had taken a piece of petrified wood rationalized their behavior (e.g. discounting the importance of a small chip), despite acknowledging that it is wrong to take petrified wood as a general principle.

It simply may not be possible to convince a very small percentage of visitors to change their behavior. It is a frustrating and perplexing problem that has demanded creativity and innovation on the part of the park, and for which there is no fool-proof solution. However, **through a persistent and wide-ranging effort to inform, educate, and monitor visitors, Petrified Forest National Park has helped** to ensure that the trees of the dinosaurs can be seen by many generations to come.

## Further Reading

Burn, S. and Winter, P. (2008) A behavioral intervention tool for recreation managers. *Park Science* 25, 66–68.

Christensen, H. and Clark, R. (2009) Increasing public involvement to reduce depreciative behavior in recreation settings. *Leisure Sciences* 5, 359–379.

Cialdini, R.B. (2003) Crafting normative messages to protect the environment. *Current Directions in Psychological Science* 12, 105–109.

Gramann, J., Bonifeld, R. and Kim, Y. (1995) Effect of personality and situational factors on intentions to obey rules in outdoor recreation areas. *Journal of Leisure Research* 27, 326–343.

Janiskee, B. (2008) Petrified Forest National Park is still being stolen one piece at a time. *National Parks Traveler*, December.

Petrified Forest National Park (2016) Available at: http://www.nps.gov/pefo (accessed 20 August 2016).

Thompson, R. (2014) *Bad Luck, Hot Rocks: Conscience Letters and Photographs from the Petrified Forest.* The Ice Plant, Los Angeles, California.

Widner, C. and Roggenbuck, J. (2000) Reducing theft of petrified wood at Petrified Forest National Park. *Journal of Interpretation Research* 5, 1–18.

Widner, C. and Roggenbuck, J. (2003) Understanding park visitors' response to interventions to reduce petrified wood theft. *Journal of Interpretation Research* 8, 67–82.

# 20 Containing Contaminants at Carlsbad Caverns

Decorated by natural wonders that have taken millennia to develop, the underground chambers of Carlsbad Caverns likely appear pristine and protected to most visitors. However, research has revealed that even the innermost reaches of the park's subterranean resources may be threatened by outside contaminants associated with visitor use (**Impacts to water; Impacts to air, Impacts to attraction sites**). In light of these scientific discoveries, managers chose to **Reduce the impact of use** and, in some cases, **Limit use** to protect fragile park resources. The park has removed, replaced, and installed infrastructure to prevent pollutants from seeping below ground and has even developed an annual "lint camp" to help remove unwanted airborne debris (**Facility development/Site design/Maintenance**). Many of the caves' iconic attraction sites are managed for high levels of use and accessibility, while backcountry caving opportunities are limited through a strict permit system (**Rules/Regulations; Rationing/Allocation; Zoning**).

## Introduction

In the midst of the Guadalupe Mountains of Texas and New Mexico exists an extraordinary network of caves. Unlike most caves, the caverns of Carlsbad were formed by a forceful "sulfuric acid bath." Beginning millions of years ago, hydrogen sulfide from petroleum reservoirs below advanced upward and met with groundwater. The blending of the two formed sulfuric acid that aggressively dissolved the area's limestone bedrock. As the groundwater receded and the "acid bath" drained, immense chambers were left behind.

With the collapse of a hillside in the last million years, a natural entrance to Carlsbad Caverns was created (Fig. 20.1). This opening allowed air to flow and mix with precipitation percolating from above, and a variety of *speleothems* (underground geologic features) were formed (Fig. 20.2). Mineral-laden water ran down sloped ceilings and created sheet-like, often folded, *draperies*. *Stalactites*, formed from mineral-laden water dripping from ceilings and in some cases eventually met *stalagmites* (formed from build-up of minerals on cave floors); this has resulted in impressive *columns* throughout caverns. Thin, hollow *soda straws* grew from single rings of calcite, bunches of *popcorn* formed on walls indicating past airflow direction, and *helictites* disregarded gravity by arching and coiling without explanation. **Critical to the continued growth of these awe-inspiring adornments are** uncontaminated sources of water and air. Unfortunately, visitors can bring contaminants with them into the caves.

## Carlsbad Caverns National Park

First established as a national monument by President Calvin Coolidge in 1923, Carlsbad Caverns were bestowed national park status by Congress in 1930. In 1995, the park received a World Heritage Site designation for its rare speleothems and their continued growth as part of an ongoing geologic process. It is perhaps best known for its highly accessible "show cave," Carlsbad Cavern. Carlsbad Cavern includes elevator transport and about two thirds of its Big Room Route is wheelchair accessible. Information in the cavern is provided by exhibits, park rangers, and an audio guide. It also includes an underground rest area with accessible bathrooms.

The park includes 119 other known caves and 46,766 surface acres including 33,000 acres of designated Wilderness. Surface ecosystems of the park include Chihuahuan Desert with Pinyon-Juniper forests at higher elevations. More than 750 plant species may be found above ground, as well as a number of mammals, birds, amphibians, and reptiles. There are 17 species of bats that make the park home, including a colony of Brazilian Free-tailed bats that roosts in Carlsbad Cavern and has an estimated population of 400,000.

**Fig. 20.1.** The natural entrance of Carlsbad Caverns has not only played a role in forming delicate natural wonders, but has also provided access to millions of visitors. (National Park Service Photo by Peter Jones.)

Approximately 400,000 visitors explore the park's caves, roads, and trails each year. A 7-mile paved entrance road with wayside exhibits leads to the visitor center and the Walnut Canyon Desert Loop provides a more rugged scenic drive on a gravel road. While there is no developed campground at Carlsbad Caverns, backcountry camping permits are available and allow visitors to explore over 50 miles of minimally maintained aboveground trails.

## Managing Contaminants at Carlsbad Caverns

In 1996, Carlsbad Cavern's General Management Plan described initiation of a study of groundwater infiltration at the park. Moreover, it noted a need to "better understand and mitigate human-induced changes in the cave ecosystem." The study identified parts of the cave that were impacted, or likely to be impacted, by contamination from surface facilities. Runoff from public parking lots, including motor oil and antifreeze, and leaks in sewer lines were sources of pollution. Unnaturally high concentrations of aluminum, zinc, total organic carbon, and nitrate within Carlsbad Cavern were attributed to these sources and their potential to impact water quality and human health was documented.

With the threat of hazardous spills endangering cave ecosystems and even public health, park managers chose to act. Parking was removed from above the cavern and the area was re-vegetated with tiered beds of native plants, new above ground sewer lines replaced leaking old below ground sewer lines, and oil/grit separators were installed to collect and treat runoff in other parking areas. The rehabilitation project has been hailed a success and was awarded a certification for sustainable landscape design in 2013.

However, water is not the only resource at risk in Carlsbad Caverns. As visitors pass through the subterranean show caves of the park, they shed hair and dead skin cells as well as tiny fibers from their clothes. Known collectively as lint, these materials may breakdown into particles small enough to float through the air and attach to cavern walls.

**Fig. 20.2.** Carlsbad Caverns contains fragile formations known as speleothems such as the soda straw stalactites and columns pictured here. (National Park Service Photo by Peter Jones.)

While micro-litter from a single visitor may not seem like a serious impact, consider its accumulation over the course of the park's existence; more than 43 million visits have been made to the park since 1924. The breakdown of lint has been shown to generate acids that may dissolve calcite and support microbes that outcompete native microbe populations, changing the very nature of the caves themselves.

In 1988, park managers and a group of volunteers decided to tackle lint head on. Armed with tweezers, brushes, and spray bottles, 25 individuals removed 25 pounds of lint over the course of 600 hours. Thus, the first "lint camp" was born. This labor-intensive abatement program has been repeated at the park almost every year since and has led to an estimated removal of over 443 pounds of lint. Rock walls have also been established along cave trails to help trap lint and keep it from flowing through the air. These trails are vacuumed twice a year to help mitigate impacts.

Active lint containment and clean-up has focused primarily on the highly accessible Carlsbad Cavern, but the park also includes outstanding opportunities

to visit other caves. Wild caves in the park may be entered with a permit from the Cave Resource Office and may require vertical caving techniques and specialized knowledge and equipment. Permits are issued on a first-come, first-served basis and visitation limits vary from three trips per week to two trips per month depending on the cave. All trips include a minimum group size limit of three for visitor safety, while maximum group sizes permitted range from four to ten to minimize visitor-caused impacts. Non-marking boots are required to prevent scuff marks on rocks and some routes in caves are designated by flagging tape to reduce impacts to sensitive formations. The park actively monitors wild caves and states that "caves impacted by careless users will be closed."

Some caves have been restricted to specific uses. For example, Lechuguilla Cave is limited to National Park Service approved scientific research and exploration. The cave contains rare speleothems including cave pearls, hydromagnesite balloons, and 20-foot gypsum chandeliers. Pools in the cave have also been found to contain rare forms of bacteria, some of which have been examined in laboratories and may play a role in developing treatments for human diseases such as cancer and HIV.

After discovering that native microbes in these pools were devastated by even a small number of contacts with cavers, some areas were closed to study how long it may take for microbe populations to recover. Where research and exploration continues, cavers are required to sleep and eat on drop cloths so that any dropped materials will be captured. And, when a new pool is found, scientists approach the area with Tyvek protective suits and deploy slides that will be collected five years later for the purpose of investigating bacteria under a microscope in a lab.

When Carlsbad Caverns was proclaimed a national monument, it was set aside because "beyond the spacious chambers that have been explored, other vast chambers of unknown character and dimensions exist." **The unknown still exists deep below the Guadalupe Mountains.** How Carlsbad Caverns National Park is managed will play a role in how much we may learn from it in the future.

## Further Reading

Burger, P.A. and Pate, D.L. (2001) Using science to change management perspectives at Carlsbad Caverns National Park. In: Kuniansky, E.L. (ed.) *U.S. Geological Survey Karst Interest Group Proceedings, Water-resources Investigation Report 01-4011*, pp. 47–51.

Carlsbad Caverns National Park (2016) Carlsbad Caverns National Park website. Available at: www.nps.gov/cave (accessed 4 August 2016).

Marech, R. (2014) Fighting fluff. *National Parks Conservation Association*. Available at: https://www.npca.org/articles/950-fighting-fluff (accessed 4 August 2016).

National Park Service (1996) General management plan. Carlsbad Caverns National Park. US Department of the Interior.

National Park Service (2006) Cave and karst management plan/Environmental assessment. Carlsbad Caverns National Park. US Department of the Interior.

Northup, D.E. (2011) Managing microbial communities in caves. In: van Beynen, P.E. (ed.) *Karst Management*. Springer, Utrecht, Netherlands, pp. 225–240.

Pate, D.L. (2013) Moving the national park service cave and karst program forward – identifying and understanding park resources. In: Land, L. and Joop, M. (eds) *NCKRI Symposium 3: Proceedings of the 20th National Cave and Karst Management Symposium*, pp. 111–115.

# 21 Bear Etiquette in Katmai

Visitors to Katmai National Park and Preserve have the opportunity to view brown bears at close range as they gather to feast on migrating salmon. But increasing demand for viewing opportunities, coupled with the large concentration of bears found in the area, has led to concerns about visitor safety, crowding on platforms (**Crowding; Impacts to attraction sites**), and disturbance of bears (**Impacts to wildlife**). To address these concerns, the park has constructed additional viewing platforms and an elevated boardwalk (**Harden the resource**), installed several web cameras at the most popular viewing area (**Increase supply**), and erected an electric fence around the campground (**Facility development/Site design/Maintenance**). All visitors are required to attend "Bear Etiquette" training (**Reduce the impact of use; Information/Education**) and to follow bear safety rules (**Rules/Regulations**). Time and use limits are placed on the viewing platform closest to the falls (**Limit use; Rationing/Allocation**).

## Introduction

Each summer, as many as 100 brown bears gather along the Brooks River in southwest Alaska. **Weighing up to 900 pounds, these massive coastal mammals are part of the largest population of protected brown bears in North America.** The normally solitary bears are brought together for one common purpose: to pluck migrating salmon from the river's falls and devour them on the spot. Fish fortunate enough to make it through the gauntlet of bears will have their spawned-out bodies consumed on the return trip. The annual ritual takes place in an expansive wilderness, a place so remote that it is accessible only by float plane or boat. But these bears are not alone in their fishing expedition; as many as 40 human visitors crowd on to a viewing platform to watch the spectacle. Many more wait on nearby platforms, eager for the chance to have a closer look. It is a complex and challenging management scenario, having so many people so close to so many bears, but it is one that plays out each summer in Katmai National Park and Preserve.

## Katmai National Park and Preserve

Katmai National Park and Preserve is located on the Alaska Peninsula about 300 miles south-west of Anchorage. In June 1912, a powerful volcanic eruption shook the area, causing the peak of Mount Katmai to collapse, and burying a nearby valley in hundreds of feet of superheated ash. In the aftermath, a National Geographic expedition team discovered the "Valley of Ten Thousand Smokes." A geologic marvel, thousands of plumes of "smoke"—steam vapor from water trapped below—escaped through vents in the valley floor. The group lobbied for the valley's protection, and in 1918 Katmai National Monument was created. Though the fumaroles have long since cooled, visitors still tour the remnants of the massive volcanic eruption on guided bus tours. In 1980, Katmai was designated a National Park and Preserve as part of the Alaska National Interest Lands Conservation Act. Today, Katmai protects 4.7 million acres of land, and is part of a larger network of protected areas that includes Aniakchak National Monument and Preserve, the Alagnak Wild River, and the Becharof and Alaska Peninsula National Wildlife Refuges.

While a vast wilderness is open to exploration by Katmai visitors, the majority of visitor activity is concentrated in the Brooks River Area. Its namesake, the Brooks River, runs about a mile and a half between Lake Brooks and the largest lake in the National Park system, Naknek Lake. A National Historic Landmark, the area is culturally significant with a human history that dates back more than 4000 years. But it was a fishing camp established in the 1950s that set the stage for the area's development. Today, facilities include

© R.E. Manning, L.E. Anderson and P.R. Pettengill 2017. *Managing Outdoor Recreation: Case Studies in the National Parks*, 2nd Edition (R.E. Manning *et al.*)

a developed campground, ranger station, visitor center and auditorium, concessionaire lodge, fish-freezing building, and elevated boardwalks and viewing platforms. **It is these boardwalks and platforms that take visitors to what is now the area's main attraction: the opportunity to view large concentrations of brown bears at close range** (Fig. 21.1).

Getting to Brooks River is not particularly easy. Most visitors take a commercial flight from Anchorage to the park's administrative headquarters in King Salmon and then ride on an air taxi float plane to cover the last 30 miles to Brooks Camp. Despite the remoteness, an estimated 10–15,000 visitors travel to the Brooks River each year to view bears and to explore the area's other natural and cultural elements. This level of visitation is remarkable considering the small size of the Brooks River Area and the fact that visitation takes place over only three and a half months, with park facilities open from early June to mid-September each year. Moreover, the best chances of seeing bears occurs during just two months: in July when bears gather at the six-foot Brooks Falls to catch salmon migrating upstream, and in September after spawning is complete and bears feed throughout the lower river.

## Managing Visitors and Bears at the Brooks River Area

The challenges presented by having so many people and so many bears in such a small area are manifold. In any other context, decisions about how to accommodate large numbers of enthusiastic visitors around a limited resource would be challenging enough. But at Brooks Camp, the limited resource involves several hundred pound predators with four-inch claws. With an abundant food source, normally solitary bears tolerate people and other bears, but individual bears could behave in unpredictable ways if provoked. Certainly, visitor safety is a priority. In turn, the park must be concerned with how people affect bears. The legislation that designated Katmai National Park and Preserve requires that brown bears and their habitat be protected.

A primary approach to accommodating visitor viewing experiences in relative safety has been to construct elevated platforms and walkways (Fig. 21.2). Currently, Brooks River Area includes three bear viewing platforms, a staging platform, and an elevated boardwalk. The two original platforms include "Falls Platform," located adjacent to Brooks Falls, and "Lower River Platform," located near the mouth of the Brooks River. The former provides

**Fig. 21.1.** The annual gathering of brown bears that come to feed on salmon as they spawn in the Brooks River in Katmai National Park is a remarkable natural phenomenon. (National Park Service photo by Peter Hamel.)

**Fig. 21.2.** The National Park Service has constructed viewing platforms to allow a limited number of visitors to watch and photograph brown bears. (National Park Service photo by Peter Hamel.)

the best view of bears during the July salmon migration, while the latter provides viewing opportunities during the September feast. However, conditions on the two platforms were frequently crowded and visitors often had to wait their turn to get a good view. Further, the mile-long trail to the Falls Platform set up a potentially hazardous situation. Visitors shared the trail, which was routed through dense spruce forest, with the bears.

To address these issues, the park constructed two new platforms and replaced the trail with an elevated boardwalk. The first new viewing structure—named Riffles Platform—is located about 300 feet downstream from the Brooks Falls Platform, while the second new "staging" platform lies slightly away from the river in between the Brooks Falls and Riffles platforms. When the Falls Platform reaches capacity, the two new platforms provide alternative places to view wildlife while waiting—and the covered staging platform provides some protection from the weather.

A maximum of 40 people is allowed on the Falls Platform at one time; when capacity is reached, visitors are limited to 1 hour of viewing time at Brooks Falls. **To increase the bear viewing capacity at the falls, the park installed a webcam at Falls Platform in 2009.** In its first year, an additional 3000 virtual visitors were able to view bears in Homer, Alaska where park rangers interpreted bear actions "in

real time." Since then, Katmai has partnered with explore.org to provide several additional webcams, including an underwater camera. Park rangers offer online talks, forum discussions, and blog postings to keep virtual visitors informed. Both virtual and on-site visitors are encouraged to share their experiences with one another on Twitter.

Back at the river, the three Brooks Falls area platforms are connected by the new, elevated boardwalk. The boardwalk separates people from bears, increasing safety, and provides additional viewing opportunities. However, some concern has been raised about how the new structures, which cross over bear trails and daybeds, impact the bears. A study conducted in the years before and after the new construction found that overall bear activity in the area did not decline. However, bears avoided crossing under the new structures, particularly during times of heavy visitor use. The study cautioned that any additional construction could be problematic, since bears may have to travel further to route around the structures. Additionally, it was suggested that education, outreach, and visitor monitoring efforts be targeted towards disruptive visitor behaviors, such as loud noises.

In fact, education is another key component of managing visitors among bears at Brooks River Area. **Upon arrival at Brooks Camp, all visitors are required to attend a "Bear Etiquette" training** course at the visitor center. Visitors are taught about bear safety and reminded of park regulations. Among the regulations in place to protect visitors and bears in the Brooks River Area are prohibition of food and drink outside of buildings or designated picnic areas, prohibition of pets, a requirement that gear be carried at all times (to prevent curious bears from acclimating to human belongings), and a requirement that visitors maintain a distance of 50 yards from bears. Nature photographers are encouraged to follow the ethical field practices of the North American Nature Photography Association, and those who elect to stay at Brooks Camp Campground are required to store food and garbage in a central cache and spend the evening surrounded by an electric fence designed to deter bears from entering. Anglers must take additional precautions to prevent bears from becoming "food-conditioned," removing or cutting their line and moving away slowly if a bear approaches them while fishing, and immediately freezing any fish that they wish to keep.

The approach to managing people and bears along the Brooks River continues to evolve over time as the park engages in ongoing study and monitoring to help assess and inform management efforts. The Brooks River Area Development Concept Plan provides guidance about development along the Brooks River that will protect resources and improve visitor experiences. The plan proposes that all park facilities be relocated to the south side of the Brooks River, that day use limits be set for the area, and that the interpretive program be improved. Over time, elements of the plan have been amended and implemented. For example, as a result of recent planning, the park will replace the seasonal floating bridge at the mouth of the Brooks River with an elevated bridge and boardwalks. As with the existing elevated boardwalks, the change will serve to separate bears and people. It is expected that removing the floating bridge will also improve the movement of bears along the river. With careful planning and continued adaptation, perhaps people and bears will continue to gather in Katmai for many years to come.

## Further Reading

Anderson, L., Manning, R., Valliere, W. and Hallo, J. (2010) Normative standards for wildlife viewing in parks and protected areas. *Human Dimensions of Wildlife* 15, 1–15.

DeBruyn, T., Smith, T., Proffitt, K., Partridge, S. and Drummer, T. (2004) Brown bear response to elevated viewing structures at Brooks River, Alaska. *Wildlife Society Bulletin* 32, 1132–1140.

Fitz, M. (2016) Bears of the brooks river – a guide to their identification, lives, and habits. National Park Service. US Department of the Interior. Available at: https://www.nps.gov/katm/learn/photosmultimedia/ebooks.htm (accessed 1 November 2016).

Katmai National Park and Preserve (2016) Katmai National Park and Preserve website. Available at: http://www.nps.gov/katm (accessed 9 August 2016).

Knight, R. and Gutzwiller, K. (eds) *Wildlife and Recreationists – Coexistence through Management and Research*. Island Press, Washington, DC.

Mosby, C., Anderson, S., Campbell, J., and Hamon, T. (2013) Brown bear-human conflict management at Brooks River, Katmai National Park and Preserve. *Journal of Earth Science and Engineering* 3, 583–593.

United States Geological Survey (2007) A human-dimensions review of human-wildlife disturbance: A literature review of impacts, frameworks, and management solutions. US Department of the Interior, Fort Collins, Colorado.

Whittaker, D. (1997) Capacity norms on bear viewing platforms. *Human Dimensions of Wildlife* 2, 37–49.

# 22 Don't Pick Up Aquatic Hitchhikers in Voyageurs

Visitors to Voyageurs National Park have the opportunity to boat, paddle, swim, and fish on a historic water passageway credited with "the opening of the Northwestern United States". However, the movement of visitors between water bodies within the park and larger region can harm aquatic habitats by introducing invasive species and fish disease (**Impacts to water; Impacts to wildlife**). To address these concerns, new regulations were implemented. These regulations require the use of artificial bait and prohibit private boats and float plane landings, and are enforced by park staff (**Rules/Regulations, Law enforcement**). In addition, best-management practices to reduce the spread of invasive species are promoted to anglers and boaters on lakes throughout the park through a multi-faceted public education and outreach program (**Information/ Education**). All of these management practices are designed to **Reduce the impact of use**.

## Introduction

Throughout the Great Lakes region of the USA, considerable concern has developed over the spread of invasive exotic species. Well-known examples include zebra mussels, sea lamprey, alewife, purple loosestrife, and Eurasian watermilfoil. **When introduced plants and animals succeed in their new habitats, the consequences can be devastating.** Aquatic ecosystems may be significantly altered, food webs disrupted, and biodiversity decreased. Once a species has successfully settled in a new habitat, removal can be difficult and expensive, meaning that the best approach is a proactive one: prevent the invasion in the first place. This approach is being taken within a relatively new unit of the National Park System. Voyageurs National Park has implemented an ambitious series of management actions to help prevent the introduction and spread of invasive exotic aquatic species to the park's historically significant lakes.

## Voyageurs National Park

Established in 1975, Voyageurs National Park is named after the French Canadian fur traders who paddled through its waters two centuries ago. Carrying beaver pelts and other goods, voyageurs followed a water trail that stretched more than 3000 miles from Montreal to north-west Canada, exchanging goods, trading with the Ojibwe Indians, and setting up camp in the Rainy Lake Basin of what is now northern Minnesota and southern Ontario. Well before the area was discovered by Europeans, native Americans fished, hunted, and gathered plants in the glaciated landscape. In more recent times, lands were used for logging, mining, commercial fishing, and private resorts. Today, Voyageurs is part of a larger international network of protected areas north-west of Lake Superior that includes the Boundary Waters Canoe Area Wilderness, Superior National Forest, and Quetico Provincial Park.

**Voyageurs National Park encompasses 218,054 acres of lakes, upland forest, and rocky island shoreline** (Fig. 22.1). Water is the predominant feature, with Lakes Kabetogama, Namakan, Rainy, and Sand Point, as well as 26 smaller interior lakes, covering 38% of the park's geographic area. About 250,000 people visit Voyageurs each year. Not surprisingly, most visitor activities are water-based and include boating, swimming, paddling, and fishing. Guided boat and canoe tours depart from two of the park's visitor centers in summer months. In winter, visitors participate in cross-country skiing, snowmobiling, and ice fishing.

## Managing Voyageurs' Water Resources

Given the historical, cultural, and natural importance of water in the region, protecting and managing water quality and aquatic habitats is a high priority in Voyageurs National Park. Modern recreation and surrounding uses present challenges to

**Fig. 22.1.** Voyageurs National Park features an extensive series of interconnected waterways that were used in the early European/American fur trade and are now popular for outdoor recreation. (National Park Service photo.)

lake health that were not faced during the time of the voyageurs. Septic system runoff, oil leaks from motorboats and snowmobiles, and shoreline erosion can all threaten water quality in the park. Likewise, the **movement of people throughout the park for recreation can lead to the introduction of invasive species that threaten aquatic habitats.**

Studies have shown high water quality throughout Voyageurs National Park, and the park has taken steps to monitor and protect water quality. For example, the Voyageurs National Park Clean Water Project, a partnership with surrounding communities, is focused on developing a regional wastewater collection and treatment system. Within the park, aquatic ecologists and technicians regularly test lakes for any signs of trouble. However, concerns remain about the possible spread of exotic aquatic invasive species in Voyageurs through recreational boating and fishing. Of particular concern are a small zooplankton known as the spiny waterflea, an aggressive crayfish from the Ohio River basin, and the fish disease viral hemorrhagic septicemia (VHS).

At about one-quarter to a half inch in length, spiny water fleas first arrived in the Great Lakes from Eurasia through ship ballast water. They are agile swimmers that can cling to fishing line, anchor ropes, nets, waders, and bait. Boats and fishing gear can also pick up waterflea eggs, which remain dormant and viable for long periods of time. It is the abilities to swim, reproduce asexually, and generate resting eggs that have allowed the invasive crustacean to successfully avoid predators, compete for food, reproduce, and spread to new habitats. These same abilities can, however, alter a lake's food web, as spiny waterfleas compete directly with juvenile fish and minnows for food. Spiny waterfleas have been found in Voyageurs' large lakes, but have not yet spread to the interior lakes.

Like the spiny waterflea, the rusty crayfish is a successful competitor not native to the northern Minnesota landscape. They are aggressive creatures that can displace native crayfish and decimate aquatic plants. Crayfish can spread to new lakes when used as live bait for fishing. Rusty crayfish have been found in one of the large lakes in Voyageurs, and in nearby lakes outside the park. Another potential concern for the park is possible spread of the fish disease VHS. Deadly to game fish, VHS is spread through infected water and bait. While the disease has been found in several of the Great Lakes, it has not yet spread to Lake Superior or any lakes in Minnesota.

To prevent the spread of exotic, invasive species and fish disease, Voyageurs adopted new interim boating and fishing regulations in 2007. Updated in 2010, the three regulations are specific to the park's smaller, interior lakes:

1. Private watercraft (including kayaks, canoes, tubes, and inflatable boats) are prohibited. Visitors wishing to paddle on these lakes can rent canoes and rowboats through the Boats on Interior Lakes program for $10 per day.
2. Float planes, another potential source of contamination, are not allowed to land on interior lakes.
3. Only artificial bait can be used for fishing.

To the extent possible, these regulations are enforced by park staff. For example, personal boats easily stand out when compared to the older, marked boats rented through the park, and these boats and float planes may be spotted either by rangers on the ground or by the park pilot. A fine is issued to visitors violating one of the interior lakes regulations.

In addition to new regulations, the park also partnered with the Minnesota Department of Natural Resources (DNR) to promote best management practices for both interior lakes and for the four large lakes in the park. On all lakes, visitors are asked to take steps to ensure that they won't transfer invasive species or fish disease through fishing gear or any other items that come in contact with lake water. This can be accomplished by using a separate set of gear for the interior lakes, by drying gear for 5 days or more, or by washing gear with hot water for 1 minute or more. Boaters are also asked to remove any plant or animal material from fishing equipment. Additional practices are encouraged on the four large lakes, where personal and motorized watercraft are allowed. Here, boaters are asked to inspect boats, trailers, and other equipment and to remove any aquatic plants, animals, or mud, to drain water from boats and bait containers, and to rinse or thoroughly dry boats as well as fishing gear. Lakes listed as "infected" by the DNR are subject to state invasive species law, and its "clean-drain-dispose" requirements.

**Under the slogan "Help Stop Aquatic Hitchhikers!" the park has engaged in public education and outreach to promote new regulations and best** management practices (Fig. 22.2). These efforts have taken place at boat docks, visitor centers, on the park website, through social media, and in park and Minnesota DNR publications. An interpreter hired through the Environmental Protection Agency's Great Lakes Restoration Initiative interacts with visitors at boat launches and trails, and information about aquatic invaders is also presented on boat tours. Visitors may be shown samples of exotic species, including the hard-to-see spiny waterflea, to further emphasize the importance of cleaning or drying boats and equipment. Information about invasive species and best management practices is posted on signs at boat launches, which are maintained and updated by the Minnesota DNR. (The DNR also conducts periodic boat inspections.) Interpretive efforts also extend beyond the park. With the help of a traveling, interactive kiosk, programs are presented to school groups, fishing tournament participants, and other interested groups.

Through a combination of regulation, enforcement, best practices, and interpretation, Voyageurs

**Fig. 22.2.** The National Park Service works closely with the Minnesota Department of Natural Resources to educate visitors about how to help stop the spread of invasive species. (Image by Minnesota Department of Natural Resources.)

Chapter 22

National Park has taken an aggressive approach to addressing an issue faced by parks throughout the Great Lakes region. Through the cooperation of many visitors, these efforts help to protect the biological integrity of Voyageurs' historic waters.

## Further Reading

Catton, T. and Montgomery, M. (2000) Special history: The environment and the fur trade experience in Voyageurs National Park, 1730–1870. Available at: https://www.nps.gov/parkhistory/online_books/voya/futr/index.htm (accessed 1 November 2016).

Fields, S. (2003) The environmental pain of pleasure boating. *Environmental Health Perspectives* 111, 216–223.

Gunderson, D. (2015) Tiny animals may have a big impact on Minnesota fish. MPR News. Available at: http://www.mprnews.org/story/2015/09/09/walleye-spiny-waterflea (accessed 6 July 2016).

Holmberg, K., Odde, B. and Perry, J. (2005) Voyageurs National Park water resources management plan. National Park Service, International Falls, Minnesota.

Johnson, L., Ricciardi, A. and Carlton, J. (2001) Overland dispersal of aquatic invasive species: A risk assessment of transient recreational boating. *Ecological Applications* 11, 1789–1799.

Murray, C. (2011) Recreational boating: A large unregulated vector transporting marine invasive species. *Diversity and Distributions* 17, 1161–1172.

Voyageurs National Park (2016) Available at: http://www.nps.gov/voya (accessed 6 July 2016).

# 23 A Mountain with Handrails at Yosemite

Increasingly large numbers of visitors to Yosemite National Park were choosing to hike to the summit of Half Dome, the scenic symbol of the park and one of the most distinctive and charismatic mountains in the world. The last portion of the hike ascends the steep and exposed east face of the mountain by way of a system of fixed cables. Large numbers of visitors on the cables were substantially slowing the time needed to ascend and descend the cables and some visitors were moving outside the cables to avoid this congestion (**Crowding; Impacts to trails; Impacts to attractions**). This may have contributed to a number of accidents and rescues on the mountain as well as the deaths of several hikers. Based on a program of research, a limit was placed on the number of hikers that can ascend the Half Dome cables each day (**Rationing/Allocation; Rules/Regulations**) and this limit is enforced through the presence of a park ranger at the cables (**Law enforcement**). Permits are allocated primarily through a lottery system. This management program is designed to **Limit use** of this iconic attraction site.

## Introduction

In 1919, there were few visitors to Yosemite National Park. In an attempt to make the park more attractive to potential visitors and increase its accessibility, a set of cables was installed on the steep east face of Half Dome, the mountain that is the scenic symbol of the park. This enabled the average park visitor to reach the summit by means of a day hike from Yosemite Valley, and that's when the trouble on Half Dome began. By 2008, tens of thousands of visitors annually (a group the state's newspaper, the *San Francisco Chronicle*, derisively described as "hikers wearing tennis shoes and sandals, city kids in baggy basketball garb, children, flabby tourists, and the elderly") were hiking the 16-mile round trip. After climbing nearly 5000 feet, they used the cables, pulling and dragging themselves up the last 400 vertical feet – a 100% grade, 9000 feet above sea level, exposed on all sides, jostling for position with as many as 100 or more fellow climbers. According to one breathless website "**Half Dome is the ultimate Yosemite day hike—the one you can't die without doing, and the one you're most likely to die while doing.**" On a 1-to-10 difficulty scale, this website gives Half Dome an "11," while it gets a "9" on the "insanity factor." And the website might be right about the dying part; four hikers have died climbing the mountain in the last few years. This extreme level

of crowding and the public safety issues it raises required management by the National Park Service.

## Yosemite National Park and Half Dome

Yosemite National Park was one of the first national parks in America (and the world), established in 1890. It is one of the "crown jewels" of the US national park system, receiving 3.5 million visits annually. Legendary conservationist John Muir, considered the "father" of the national park movement, spent much of his adult life exploring the park and working for its preservation. The park includes about 1200 square miles of the Sierra Nevada Mountains, which form the border between the states of California and Nevada. But most visitors consider Yosemite Valley to be the heart of the park. The valley is just 1 mile wide and 7 miles long, but it includes what may be the most amazing convergence of natural features in the national park system: sheer granite cliffs that rise 3000 feet above the valley, several of the world's highest waterfalls, and the striking Merced River which meanders through an old-growth forest of pines, firs, and oaks on the valley floor (Fig. 23.1). And towering above the valley's east end is. Half Dome, the park's most distinctive and celebrated mountain that rises to 9000 feet.

**Fig. 23.1.** The view of Yosemite Valley is one of the most iconic scenes in the US national park system; Half Dome rises nearly a mile above the east end (in the background) of the Valley. (Photo by Robert Manning.)

Half Dome is legendary in the climbing community. The first technical ascent of the vertical north face was in 1957 via a route pioneered by Royal Robbins and others, the first Grade VI climb in the USA. Today, there are nearly 50 climbing routes to the summit. However, most visitors stick to the trails. The John Muir Trail leaves Yosemite Valley at the Happy Isles trailhead and climbs by some of the most scenic and iconic features in the park, including Vernal and Nevada Falls, Liberty Cap, and Little Yosemite Valley. After about 6.5 miles, the Half Dome Trail branches off for the last 2 miles to the "subdome" (a false summit) and the shallow saddle at the base of the cables. The "cables route" consists of two parallel strands of braided steel cables approximately 2.5 feet apart and supported by metal stanchions fixed to the granite and spaced at intervals of approximately 10 feet. Wooden planks are anchored between most pairs of stanchions offering climbers a series of footholds. The cables route travels about 800 linear feet to gain the last 400 feet of elevation to reach the broad summit of Half Dome (Fig. 23.2). From the mostly flat 13-acre summit the views are astounding—west down the length of Yosemite Valley, north across the valley to Yosemite Falls, and east and south out over the vast High Sierra.

The National Park Service takes the cables "down" (removes the stanchions and lays them and the cables flat on the rock surface) at the end of the hiking season (normally Columbus Day), and puts them back "up" on Memorial Day weekend (snow and weather conditions allowing). **Getting to the top of Half Dome is on the life list of many climbers and hikers around the world.**

## Studying and Managing Use of Half Dome

The vast majority of hikers reach the summit by means of a day hike from Yosemite Valley. Most hikers start by sunrise for the 16-or-so-mile round-trip hike that takes 10–12 demanding hours. This hike poses a number of potentially serious challenges. The granite track of the cables route has been polished by the boots of all those hikers over the years and can be slippery, especially when wet. The hike can be exhausting and this can be exacerbated by dehydration. Some hikers suffer from altitude sickness. Many are afflicted with vertigo associated with the extreme exposure of climbing the cables, and this can lead to a "freeze response" when on the cables. One hiker was recently quoted as saying **"Everything in my body was shaking. I felt like I was going to vomit."** All this is made

**Fig. 23.2.** Hikers must use a set of cables to climb the last few hundred feet to attain the summit of Half Dome. (Photo by Brett Kiser.)

In 1985, five people on the summit were struck by lightning and two died. In 2007, three hikers fell to their deaths in separate incidents. Two of these cases involved hikers who were on the mountain when the cables were not "up." Another death occurred in 2009, along with a near miss. Of course, these accidents are tragic for those involved, but are also traumatic for other hikers who witness them, some of whom report enduring nightmares. Responding to these accidents can also put park rangers at risk.

Despite the very high use of Half Dome, it's important to note that it's part of the 95% of Yosemite National Park that's been designated as wilderness by Congress under the provisions of the landmark Wilderness Act of 1964. The Act stipulates that **wilderness areas are "to provide opportunities for solitude and a primitive and unconfined type of recreation."** Moreover, National Park Service wilderness policy states that "Unacceptable impacts are impacts that would...unreasonably interfere with the atmosphere of peace and tranquility... in wilderness...." Consequently, the National Park Service decided to institute a mandatory permit system for Half Dome in 2010 to limit use.

The National Park Service conducted monitoring counts of use on Half Dome in 2009. Based on these observations, the permit system limited use on weekend days and holidays to 400 hikers: 300 day hikers and 100 permits reserved for backpacking parties. A permit was not required for weekdays because monitoring data showed that use was relatively low during this period. Permits for day hikers were made available through a government website and phone number, cost a nominal US$1.50 per person (plus a $5.00 processing fee per group), and could be reserved up to 4 months in advance. On the first day of sales, permits sold out in 32 minutes. A ranger was stationed at Half Dome where permits must be presented. Climbing Half Dome via the cables route without a permit was subject to a $5000 fine and/or 6 months in jail. Use of Half Dome was monitored again in 2010 and it was found that congestion on the cables was substantially reduced on weekend days and holidays, but that congestion on weekdays had increased substantially. More specifically, the average number of hikers on weekend days and holidays (days for which permits were required) was 301 (many permit holders apparently did not do the hike as originally planned) while the average number of hikers on weekdays was 692. The 2010 monitoring report

worse by the fact that many hikers are not adequately prepared. In the kind, understated words of Yosemite ranger Mark Fincher, "Many of the hikers making their way to the cables don't hike routinely, and for many it is their first real exposure to wilderness." Once on the mountain's summit, hikers may encounter lightning storms that can develop quickly in the afternoon. All this is made worse still by extreme crowding on the cables and long delays in ascending and descending. It's been estimated that there may have been as many as 200 climbers on the cables at one time. Frustration with this slow pace, along with diminished cognitive abilities from exhaustion and vertigo and "summit fever," has led some hikers to move outside the cables to get around congested areas and bottlenecks, exposing them to a greater degree of danger from falling and a serious accident.

Over the years there have been accidents on Half Dome, most of them minor. But an increasing number require assistance from park rangers, and some of these accidents have become very serious.

concluded that "Thus, it appears that an unintended consequence of the permit system was the interchange of use levels from weekends to weekdays." Based on these findings, the permit system was extended to include all days during the 2011 Half Dome "season." **Permits for weekends in May and June 2011 sold out in 5 minutes.** Half Dome permits started showing up on Craigslist (a classified advertisement website) for as much as $100.

Meanwhile, the National Park Service commissioned a program of research to support management of recreational use on Half Dome. This program of research included several components:

**1.** A series of statistical models of use of Half Dome were developed using: (i) travel time on the cables (measured by a card that visitors carried with them and that was "stamped" with the current time by a field technician at key locations, including the base of the cables, on the summit, and then again at the bottom of the cables); and (ii) a systematic series of photographs of hikers on the cables to determine how many hikers at one time were on the cables route, and how many were climbing outside the cables. Statistically significant relationships were found between the number of hikers at one time on the cables and both the time required to climb the cables, and the number of hikers outside the cables. More specifically, **when there are more than 30 people on the cables at any one time, travel time on the cables slows significantly and some visitors move outside the cables.**

**2.** A representative sample of hikers was surveyed after they had completed their hike. The survey included many questions about the sociodemographic characteristics of hikers, their assessment of the Half Dome hike, and their attitudes toward management. Key findings were that most Half Dome hikers felt crowded, believed accidents can happen (but mostly to other hikers), report going outside the cables occasionally, but seeing others go outside the cables more often, mostly to cope with crowding.

**3.** Field technicians walked the approximately 2-mile Half Dome Trail from where it branches off the John Muir Trail to the subdome, recording the number of hikers they met along the way. On permit days in 2010, an average of 120 hikers were encountered, while on non-permit days an average of 276 hikers were encountered. These numbers are very high for a wilderness area and do not comport well with the Wilderness Act's emphasis on solitude.

**4.** A computer-based simulation model of visitor use on Half Dome was created. Data collected to construct the model included hiking times from the Happy Isles Trailhead in Yosemite Valley to the subdome, travel times to ascend and descend the cables, time spent on the summit, and behavior on the cables (i.e. whether hikers remained inside or went outside the cables). The resulting model **estimates that a maximum of 227 hikers per day can be allowed to hike to Half Dome without exceeding the 30 people-at-one-time on the cables figure noted above (the point at which some visitors begin to move outside the cables).** Under the current maximum use level of 300 hikers per day, the model estimates that it would take 47 minutes to evacuate the summit in case of a lightning storm or other emergency; under pre-permit use levels of 2008, it's estimated that it would take well over 1 hour. For safety reasons, some have proposed that hikers be required to use climbing harnesses and "clip on" to the cables in *via ferrata* ("iron road") style. But this would slow climbing to such a degree that the model estimates that only 70 hikers could be allowed to do the hike per day without exceeding the 30 people-at-one-time on the cables standard noted above. Of the 300 daily permits available, 75 are allocated to backpackers and 225 to day hikers. A lottery system is used to distribute permits.

### This Page is Intentionally Left Blank

The National Park Service has issued several reports that describe ongoing research, planning, and management efforts for Half Dome. In a sometimes stiff, bureaucratic style, pages of these documents that for some reason do not contain any printing (e.g. dividers between chapters) are marked "This Page is Intentionally Left Blank." This is a well-meaning attempt to assure readers that they're not missing anything important, but it may well be a metaphor for the future of Half Dome. Where do we go from here?

US national parks are icons of American nature and culture, but they are historical artifacts as well, the result of decisions made a century or more ago. To attract and accommodate visitors in the early years of Yosemite National Park, the National Park Service built more than 100 miles of scenic roads, a luxury hotel, a golf course, a ski resort, and cables on Half Dome. **When these artificial attractions cross the line into carnival-like distractions, like the**

Yosemite Fire Fall and roads through giant sequoias, we bring them to a well-deserved end. What shall we do with the cables on Half Dome? Of course, there's no shortage of strong public opinion. One public comment on the current permit system reads "Our group has been hiking Half Dome for years never having a problem and now cannot get permits. This sucks, whoever did this sucks!"

All of this is just one more manifestation of the use versus preservation issue that is at the heart of the national parks and our tension-filled relationship with the environment more broadly. As noted in Chapter 1 of this book, the Organic Act of the National Park Service famously directs that the agency is "to conserve the scenery and the natural and historic objects and the wild life therein and to provide for the enjoyment of the same in such manner and by such means as will leave them unimpaired for the enjoyment of future generations". In his homey wisdom, American conservation philosopher Aldo Leopold characterized the situation more generally as "How can we live on a piece of land without spoiling it?" Garrett Hardin, in his influential paper "The Tragedy of the Commons," used Yosemite as an example of common property resources, arguing that the only way to avert the tragic destruction that comes with the inevitable trend toward overuse is "mutual coercion, mutually agreed upon" (this issue is discussed in Chapter 1). And Joseph Sax, in his eloquent book, *Mountains Without Handrails*, cautions us about overdeveloping visitor attraction sites in the national parks (such as building handrails on Half Dome).

As we've seen with Half Dome, science—in this case, an impressive program of social science—can help inform the management process by providing objective information on current and likely future conditions. But decisions on the desired future of Half Dome will have to address what we want as a society for this iconic place and what we're willing to give up to get it. **Stay tuned to how the National Park Service ultimately decides how to manage Half Dome. Better yet, get involved.**

## Further Reading

Fimrite, P. (2007a) Deadly trek up Half Dome, rangers re-examine safety of popular hike after a fatal fall from cables during final ascent. *San Francisco Chronicle*, June 19.

Fimrite, P. (2007b) Danger on the dome, hikers swarming Yellowstone's Half Dome create bottleneck at the treacherously steep granite climb to the summit. *San Francisco Chronicle*, July 7.

Fimrite, P. (2010) Climbers to the top of Half Dome will require a permit. *San Francisco Chronicle*, February 10.

Manning, R. (2012) Mountains with handrails: The trouble on Half Dome. *Appalachia* Winter/Spring, 42–53.

Runte, A. (1990) *Yosemite, the Embattled Wilderness*. University of Nebraska Press, Lincoln, Nebraska.

Sax, J. (1980) *Mountains Without Handrails, Reflections on the National Parks*. University of Michigan Press, Ann Arbor, Michigan.

Yosemite National Park (2016a) Half Dome Day Hike. Available at: http://www.nps.gov/yose/planyourvisit/halfdome.htm (accessed 1 November 2016).

Yosemite National Park (2016b) Available at: http://www.nps.gov/yose (accessed 1 November 2016).

Yosemite National Park (2016c) Half Dome: Your guide to Yosemite's most demanding day hike. Available at: http://www.yosemitehikes.com/yosemite-valley/half-dome/half-dome.htm (accessed 1 November 2016).

# 24 Doing the Zion Shuttle

The road serving Zion Canyon—the scenic heart of Zion National Park—was often congested, and parking lots overflowed (**Impacts to roads/parking; Impacts to attraction sites; Crowding; Conflict**). This made the Canyon noisy (**Impacts to natural quiet**), and unauthorized parking along the road resulted in substantive degradation of soil and vegetation (**Impacts to soil; Impacts to vegetation**). Park wildlife were sometimes injured or killed while crossing the road (**Impacts to wildlife**). And the presence of so many vehicles contributed to air pollution (**Impacts to air**). A mandatory (**Rules/Regulations**) shuttle bus system (**Facility development/Site design/Maintenance**) was initiated for Zion Canyon (**Spatial zoning**) for the peak use season (**Temporal zoning**). These management practices were designed to **Reduce the impact of use** and **Harden park resources**.

## Introduction

There's an old adage that there aren't too many people in the national parks, there are too many cars. Nearly all visitors to the "crown jewel" parks such as Yellowstone, Yosemite, and Grand Canyon drive to the parks, and driving on park roads is a primary way most visitors experience the iconic features of these places. But the increasing number of visitors (and their cars) has led to a number of problems, including traffic congestion, a chronic shortage of parking (**after all, it's not the National Parking Service**), damage to soils and vegetation from improper parking, car–wildlife collisions, and increasing air pollution and noise. All of these issues recently came to a head at Zion National Park. Visitors need an attractive alternative to their cars, designed and managed specifically to their needs and those of the park. The Zion shuttle bus system, instituted in 2000, is a prototype for this approach to park management.

## Zion National Park

Zion National Park comprises 229 square miles in south-west Utah. The area was established as a national park in 1919 because of its impressive landscape of mountains, rivers, and steep sandstone canyons (Fig. 24.1). The park is part of the massive, elevated Colorado Plateau in the Southwestern USA, and is part of an impressive string of national parks that includes Arches, Canyonlands, Capitol Reef, Bryce, and the North Rim of the Grand Canyon. Elevations in the park generally range from about 4000–9000 feet. The name, Zion, is taken from the Bible and refers to "the promised land." Visitors enter the park from the east or south-west on the scenic Zion–Mt Carmel Highway, and a 6-mile spur road provides access to Zion Canyon, the park's primary scenic feature. The town of Springdale on the southern boundary of the park provides visitor facilities and services such as hotels, restaurants, and shops.

## Managing Cars at Zion National Park

Most visitors consider Zion Canyon to be the scenic heart of the park. The upper portion of the Canyon includes intimate views of its dramatic, multicolored sandstone cliffs and access to most of the favorite hikes in the park, including Emerald Pools, Weeping Rock, and the challenging Angel's Landing. The Canyon is served by a 6-mile, two-lane winding road that dead-ends at the Temple of Sinawava (referring to the coyote god of the Native Americans of the Paiute Tribe). The trail at the end of the road leads to the Zion River Narrows where hikers can walk upstream in the Virgin River (often in water that is knee-deep, or higher) and through its world-famous "slot canyon" as narrow as 20 feet with vertical cliffs as high as 2000 feet. However, by the late 1990s, the number of visitors to the national park was approaching two and half million annually and the park's scenic drive in Zion

**Fig. 24.1.** Zion National Park features some of the most scenic canyon country in the USA. (Photo by Robert Manning.)

**Fig. 24.2.** The National Park Service has developed a mandatory propane-powered bus system to serve visitors to Zion Canyon; the bus system also connects to the gateway town of Springdale. (National Park Service photo.)

Canyon was the worse for wear. **As many as 5000 cars entered the Canyon each day, competing for the area's 450 parking spaces.** The road was often severely congested, and many frustrated visitors parked in unauthorized areas, trampling vegetation, and compacting and eroding soils. The Canyon was often a noisy place and even the area's air quality was diminished. All this traffic was certainly affecting wildlife, though this is difficult to quantify.

In a bold initiative, the National Park Service introduced the Zion Canyon Transportation System in 2000. The heart of the system is 30 propane-powered "double" shuttle buses, each holding 66 people (or the equivalent of about 25 cars) (Fig. 24.2). The scenic road in Zion Canyon is now closed to private vehicles during the busy months, generally from Easter to November, and visitors must ride the shuttle buses. The transportation system was developed in partnership with the gateway town of Springdale, local businesses, and other public agencies. The system includes two loops. The Canyon Loop includes eight stops in the park at primary visitor attractions, and the Town Loop includes seven stops in Springdale at local hotels, restaurants, and related facilities and services. The two loops are connected at the park's new visitor center and transit hub. Park visitors can take a Town Loop bus from their hotel (or a parking area in town) to the visitor center/transit hub and transfer to the Park Loop. The visitor center/transit hub includes an information desk, bookstore, and open-air educational and interpretive displays, including an amphitheater for ranger-led programs. The shuttle buses run from 6:00 am to 11:00 pm daily, and serve all stops at intervals ("headways" in transit lingo) as frequent as every 6 minutes during the peak hours of the day. Riders can get on and off as many times as they want. The transit system is used by park staff and Springdale residents as well as park visitors, and the buses are fully accessible to people with physical disabilities. Buses are equipped with bike racks. Maybe best of all, the system is "free" to riders—or, more honestly, the cost of the system is included in the park entrance fee.

The many components of the transportation system were designed to be in keeping with the park context. As noted above, buses are powered by propane to be as quiet as possible. An abundance of windows allows for maximum viewing. The size of shuttle bus stops are based on visitor use studies, and include bike racks, shade shelters, stone masonry walls for site definition, and seating. Architectural elements echo the historic vernacular of the Civil Conservation Corp of the 1930s, which built many of the structures in Zion and throughout the US national park system.

There are a number of issues that challenge the continued success of the Zion Canyon Transportation System, and financing may be the most significant. Much of the start-up funding came from special grants, but long-term maintenance and ultimate replacement of the buses will be more difficult. Communicating with visitors about the shuttle bus system is also difficult. Many first-time visitors to the park aren't aware of the system and restrictions on use of automobiles, and many more visitors don't know that parking is available in Springdale or where to find it. More effective use of websites, highway advisory radio broadcasts, real-time parking messages, and signing is needed.

But the shuttle bus system in Zion is widely celebrated for its success, and for good reason. It has enhanced visitor access to Zion Canyon by eliminating the constraints of automobile congestion and limited parking. At the same time it has helped restore and protect park resources that were damaged by inappropriate parking. It has substantially reduced automobile use in the park by an estimated 50,000 vehicle miles per day or over 10 million miles per year, and this has reduced carbon ($CO_2$) emissions by an estimated 12 tons per day or 2264 tons per year. **Zion Canyon is strikingly quieter and more tranquil than it was before the shuttle bus system,** and wildlife is returning to the area. Without cars on the road, more visitors are biking into the Canyon. Business owners in Springdale like the shuttle bus system too, noting that it has reduced automobile traffic and increased foot traffic and sales.

Perhaps most importantly, the shuttle bus system offers a model of sustainability that is central to the mission of the National Park Service and that seems to resonate with most visitors. It has changed visitor behavior—taken them out of their cars and on to public transport—thereby reducing the impact of visitor use. And, according to a survey, nearly all visitors like the shuttle bus system. Accordingly, park attendance has increased steadily since initiation of the bus system. Representative quotes from visitors registered on the internet include "I was uneasy about the shuttle—no more ... way to go Nat'l Park Service!" and "More parks should have this type of frequent and efficient mode of travel to see a park." And more parks do. Thanks in part to the leadership of Zion and the town of Springdale, more than 50 units of the national park system now have some form of "alternative transportation." Way to go, indeed.

## Further Reading

Daigle, J. (2008) Transportation research needs in national parks: A summary and exploration of future trends. *The George Wright Forum* 25, 57–64.

Dunning, A. (2005) Impacts of transit in national parks and gateway communities. *Journal of the Transportation Research Board* 1931, 129–136.

Manning, R. (2009) Parks or parking lots? Hikers should vote with their feet. *Appalachia* LX, 8–14.

Marquit, J., Mace, B. and Roberts, M. (2004) Economic and environmental assessment of the Zion National Park shuttle system in the gateway community of Springdale, Utah. Environmental Psychology Symposium, Rocky Mountain Psychological Association, Reno, Nevada.

National Park Service (2008) Zion canyon transportation system technical analysis report. US Department of the Interior, Springdale, Utah.

Turnbull, K. (2003) Transports to nature: Transportation strategies enhancing visitor experience of national parks. *TR News* January–February, 15–21.

Turnbull, K. (2004) Transportation partnerships in the parks - Cooperative initiatives serve visitors, preserve the environment. *TR News* July–August, 14–23.

Zion National Park (2001) Zion National Park general management plan. US Department of the Interior, Springdale, Utah.

Zion National Park (2016a) Shuttle system. Available at: http://www.nps.gov/zion/planyourvisit/shuttle-system.htm (accessed 1 November 2016).

Zion National Park (2016b) Available at: http://www.nps.gov/zion (accessed 1 November 2016).

# 25 The Buzz from Above at Grand Canyon

Air tours provide visitors with thrilling access to the vistas at Grand Canyon National Park, but this type of visitation can interfere with the experiences of visitors on the ground, disturb wildlife, and alter the wilderness character of the park (**Impacts to natural quiet; Impacts to wildlife; Impacts to attraction sites; Impacts to trails; Impacts to campgrounds; Impacts to interpretive facilities/programs; Conflict**). Through Congressional action and collaboration between the Federal Aviation Administration and National Park Service, several measures have been taken to substantially restore "natural quiet" in the park. These efforts are directed at **Limiting use** and **Reducing the impact of use**. A Special Flights Rules Area has been established, along with four Flight Free Zones, designated routes for air tours, curfews, an annual flight allocation, and reporting requirements for tour operators (**Rationing/Allocation, Rules/Regulations, Zoning**).

## Introduction

High above the Colorado River, air tour visitors to Grand Canyon National Park are afforded an entirely different, but equally exhilarating experience to the rafters below (see the Colorado River case study, Chapter 14, p. 86). Airplane and helicopter tours, with their spine-tingling vistas, guided narration, and carefully choreographed music, are a highlight for many. Air tours have been around as long as Grand Canyon National Park, with the first recorded tour occurring several months before the park's creation in 1919. The first air tour company was established in the 1920s. Today, visitors may choose to take an airplane or helicopter tour from nearby Grand Canyon Airport, or through a tour package from Las Vegas or Phoenix, with fees ranging from US$150 to several hundred dollars. On one tour operator's website, enthusiastic tour goers describe their adventures as "a trip of a lifetime" and "worth every cent spent."

But down below, at scenic vistas, near cultural sites, along hiking trails, and at interpretive programs there are consequences to the thrilling experiences above (Fig. 25.1). **Noise from airplanes and helicopters intrude upon the experiences of visitors on the ground, disturb wildlife, and alter the wilderness character of the park** (Fig. 25.2). Addressing the impacts of aviation noise, while providing for the experiences of those viewing the canyon from high above, has required years of planning, study, collaboration, coordination, and adaptation on a national scale.

## Managing Overflights in Grand Canyon National Park

Concerns about the potential impacts of aircraft noise on natural quiet and visitor experiences in Grand Canyon were formally raised in the 1975 Grand Canyon National Park Enlargement Act. The Act recognized the need to protect natural quiet and required research into the effects of overflights. A decade later, a fatal collision between two air tours drew national attention to the issue, and the National Parks Overflights Act was passed. The 1987 legislation requires both "substantial restoration of the natural quiet" and the "protection of public health and safety" and continues to guide management of aircraft overflights in and around the park today. For the former requirement, the National Park Service has defined "substantial restoration of natural quiet" as "50% or more of the park achieving restoration of the natural quiet (i.e. no aircraft audible) 75% to 100% of the day, each and every day." Today, this goal is achieved through zoning, curfews, and a limit on the number of air tours allowed to operate each year, with plans for additional measures in review.

In the iconic Grand Canyon, with its myriad interest groups, a complex set of activities has followed the National Parks Overflights Act. A series of rules, regulations, public meetings, environmental assessments and impact statements, a congressional report, a presidential memorandum, and additional legislation, have shaped management

**Fig. 25.1.** Grand Canyon National Park attracts millions of visitors from around the world each year. (Photo by Robert Manning.)

**Fig. 25.2.** Helicopters offer thrilling views of the vast Grand Canyon, but their noise can disturb more conventional visitors on the ground. (Photo by Robert Manning.)

activities around the issue of overflights. Contributing to the complexity is the need for coordination between two disparate agencies: the National Park Service and the Federal Aviation Administration. While the National Park Service is required to recommend actions that will substantially restore natural quiet and experience, the Federal Aviation Administration is responsible for implementing these rules and regulations.

**Zoning provides a primary mechanism for regulating aircraft noise in and around Grand Canyon.** The park and surrounding area lie within a Special Flights Rules Area. Airspace below 18,000 feet mean sea level is regulated in this area, which includes designated routes for tour aircraft. Within the boundaries of the national park, four "Flight Free Zones" (FFZs) prohibit flights below certain altitudes. On the Canyon's west side, the Sanup FFZ prohibits flights below 8000 feet, while flights below 15,000 feet are prohibited in the Toroweap/Shinumo, Bright Angel, and Desert View FFZs in the central and eastern portions of the park. Within the Flight Free Zones, four General Aviation Corridors provide places for aircraft to cross above 10,500 feet.

In addition to zoning, curfews limit the times that air tours may operate. Within travel corridors in the park's east end, air tour operations are allowed from 8 am to 6 pm from May to September, and from 9 am to 5 pm from October through April. The number of air tours allowed to operate each year is also limited. An annual allocation of 93,971 flights is permitted, a number reflecting the total number of flights that occurred over a 1-year period in 1997–1998. In addition, air tour operators are required to report flight totals for each 3-month period. Under these management actions, it is estimated that natural quiet has been restored to 55% of the park, with much air tour noise occurring beneath the Dragon and Zuni Point flight corridors in the eastern portion of the park.

To further restore natural quiet in the park, the National Park Service prepared a draft Environmental Impact Statement in 2011. The draft Environmental Impact Statement reviewed a number of additional strategies that have been taken, and included a preferred alternative that would restore natural quiet to 67% of the park in 10 years.

Under the preferred alternative annual flight allocations would have been reduced to 65,000 (a number that is higher than the number of flights reported in recent years). In addition, a daily cap of 364 air tours would have been added, and tour companies would have been required to report daily flights instead of flights occurring over a 3-month period. Air tour curfews would have been adjusted to allow at least 1 hour of quiet time after sunrise and before sunset; air tour routes would have been adjusted to protect sensitive areas; and the ceiling in all Flight Free Zones would have been raised to 18,000 feet. Finally, all tour operators would have been required to use quiet technology aircraft in 10 years.

However, language added to a transportation bill passed in 2012 derailed the park's plan. After efforts that included years of intense interdisciplinary research, millions of dollars, and the compiling of almost 30,000 public comments, congress passed a bill that has left park managers with the status quo. The only remnant of the planning process incorporated into the bill was a requirement for all aircraft tour operators to use quiet technology within 15 years. Quiet technology was not only a part of the park's preferred alternative, but is also a topic addressed in the National Parks Air Tour Management Act.

Passed in 2000, the Act requires that Air Tour Management Plans (ATMPs) be developed for national park units where commercial air tour operation applications have been made. Over 100 National Park Service units fall into this category; they include those with dramatic natural features, such as Glacier National Park and Hawaii Volcanoes National Park, as well as iconic cultural parks, including Statue of Liberty National Monument and Mount Rushmore National Memorial. ATMPs may prohibit air tours altogether, or in part; they may establish tour routes, altitudes, curfews, and caps; and they are required to include incentives for quiet aircraft technology. The plans apply to tours taking place within half a mile of park boundaries. Alaskan national parks are exempt from the law. And air tours are banned completely in Rocky Mountain National Park, as a result of a presidential directive, special flight rules, and congressional action that took place in the late 1990s.

**Air tours provide an exhilarating way to experience some of the world's most spectacular natural and cultural parks, but balancing these experiences with impacts on the ground is a challenging, complex proposition requiring involvement and collaboration among many groups.** Management efforts at Grand Canyon National Park have provided a model for subsequent legislation and planning requirements. As an issue subject to continued debate, there is much yet to be determined about how the spaces above our national parks will be managed.

## Further Reading

Government Accountability Office (2006) National parks air tour management act - more flexibility and better enforcement needed. United States Government GAO-06-263, Washington, DC.

Graefe, A. and Thapa, B. (2004) Conflict in natural resource recreation. In: Manfredo, M., Vaske, B., Bruyere, B., Field, D. and Brown, P. (eds) *Society and Natural Resources: A Summary of Knowledge.* Modern Litho, Jefferson, Missouri, 209–224.

Grand Canyon National Park (2016) Available at: http://www.nps.gov/grca (accessed 22 August 2016).

Kelly, E. (2012) Congress thwarts plan to curtail Grand Canyon aircraft noise. *USA Today*, June 30.

Manning, R. (2011) *Studies in Outdoor Recreation: Search and Research for Satisfaction*, 3rd edn. Oregon State University Press, Corvallis, Oregon.

Miller, N. (2008) US National Parks and management of park soundscapes: A review. *Applied Acoustics* 69, 77–92.

National Park Service (2011) Special flight rules area in the vicinity of Grand Canyon National Park. US Department of the Interior DES 10-60, Grand Canyon, Arizona.

Natural Sounds Program (2016) Natural sounds and night skies. Available at: http://www.nature.nps.gov/naturalsounds (accessed 22 August 2016).

Park Science (2009–2010) Special issue: Soundscapes research and management - Understanding, protecting, and enjoying the acoustic environment of our national parks. *Park Science* 26, 1–72.

Williams, D. (1993) Conflict in the great outdoors. *Parks & Recreation* 28, 28–34.

# 26 Managing Monuments and Memorials at the National Mall

The National Mall contains some of the world's most iconic monuments and memorials, serving as a national symbolic space, a backdrop for civic discourse, and an attraction to visitors from across the globe. Intensive levels of use have led to challenges probably never envisioned by early planners, including trampling of lawns (**Impacts to soil; Impacts to vegetation**); degraded facilities and walking paths (**Impacts to attractions; Impacts to historical/cultural resources; Impacts to trails**); facilities and services inadequate for growing use levels (**Crowding; Impacts to roads/parking; Impacts to interpretive facilities/services**); and competing uses, including special events and demonstrations (**Conflict**). To meet these diverse challenges, the National Park Service is employing all four of the basic management strategies of **Limiting use, Increasing supply, Reducing the impact of use**, and **Hardening park resources**. To advance these strategies, the National Park Service has developed a plan to: **1.** restore and redevelop park facilities (**Facility development/Site design/Maintenance**); **2.** provide information to guide visitors to and around major attractions (**Information/Education**); **3.** prohibit activities that could degrade park resources, visitor experiences, or the integrity of memorials (**Rules/Regulations**); and **4.** require permits for organized activities (**Rationing/Allocation**). In addition, organizers of special events are required to pay for security and cleanup associated with these activities (**Law enforcement, Facility development/Site design/Maintenance**).

## Introduction

The US capital hosts some of the world's most recognizable structures—among them are the obelisk of the Washington Monument, the Lincoln Memorial, the Capitol building, and the White House. These monuments, memorials, and cultural sites of Washington, positioned among urban parks, circles, squares, and triangles, reflect more than two centuries of intentional planning and design. The framework for the National Mall dates back to the original 1791 design of commissioned city planner Pierre L'Enfant, with further development and expansion following the McMillan plan at the turn of the 20th century, plans developed around the 1976 US Bicentennial, and the 1997 Extending the Legacy plan. Today, this public space is considered a nationally important symbolic space, the front yard of the country, and a stage for democracy.

As such, **the National Mall is intensively used, receiving more than 25 million visits each year from all over the world.** (By comparison, Grand Canyon, Yosemite, and Yellowstone National Parks each receive between 3 and 4.5 million visits each year.) Visitors come to the Mall to tour monuments, to reflect at war memorials, to explore national museums, to walk and run, to rent paddle boats at the Tidal Basin, to attend festivals, and to celebrate national holidays. Beyond recreational pursuits, the Mall is a nationally important center for expressions of free speech and civic engagement, drawing huge crowds for rallies, demonstrations, protests, and other political events.

With these many and competing demands come several consequences, the nature and magnitude of which probably could not have been imagined by the city's early planners. Large crowds have trampled lawns, killing grass, compacting soils beneath, and negatively impacting irrigation and drainage systems. Sidewalks have proved to be too narrow to accommodate use levels or disability access and have become degraded over time. Similarly, the size and number of visitor facilities and services, including visitor centers; restrooms; food and water; and seating areas have not kept up with demand. During events, temporary structures block historic views and vast amounts of trash are generated. Further, the National Park Service is charged with keeping visitors informed and safe, balancing general visitation with numerous—and potentially conflicting—requests for special events. All this has to be done in a way that respects the historic significance of the National Mall.

## National Mall and Memorial Parks

The National Mall is part of a large collection of green spaces and cultural sites in Washington that are managed by the National Park Service. Features within the National Mall and Memorial Parks, which encompasses just over 1000 acres, include Ford's Theatre (site of Lincoln's assassination), Pennsylvania Avenue National Historic Park (extending from the US Capitol to the White House), Dupont Circle, Franklin Square, and the lawn at Union Station. The Mall itself stretches approximately 2 miles from the foot of the US Capitol to the Lincoln Memorial (Fig. 26.1). Constitution Avenue borders the north side, while Independence Avenue and the Thomas Jefferson Memorial mark its southern boundary. The national museums of the Smithsonian Institute are housed here. Beyond cultural and historical features, the Mall is an urban oasis, with expansive lawns, cultivated gardens, and thousands of trees, including American Elms and world-famous cherry trees gifted from Japan. Congress declared the site a "completed work of civic art" in 2003, prohibiting the development of new monuments and memorials within its borders.

## Managing the National Mall

In 2010, the National Park Service issued a new plan to address challenges faced at the National Mall (Fig. 26.2). The result of 4 years of planning, the National Mall Plan provides a framework and objectives to guide management over the next half century. The balance between the historical significance of the park and intense visitation rates is reflected in the plan's intent to "respectfully rehabilitate and refurbish the National Mall so that very high levels of use can be perpetuated." Among the provisions of the plan are: the development of flexible, multi-purpose facilities that can accommodate different types of events; addition of shaded seating at food service areas; installation of high-capacity restrooms; restoration and replacement of soils, grass, and trees; separated paths for pedestrians, bicycles, and vehicles; installation of wider, paved walkways; a nearby new welcome

**Fig. 26.1.** The National Mall commemorates US history and includes many of the country's most famous sites that honor former presidents, the sacrifices of veterans, and symbols of the nation's commitment to freedom. (National Park Service photo.)

**Fig. 26.2.** Heavy visitor use of the National Mall led to soil and vegetation damage caused by trampling. (National Park Service photo.)

center; and updated educational exhibits—with restoration, rehabilitation, and development of facilities to be done in keeping with the historical context of the site. The plan comes at a cost, with early estimates at US$700 million. Initial funding has been provided through the American Recovery and Reinvestment Act, and several projects have been supported through funding from The Trust for the National Mall—a non-profit partner of the National Park Service dedicated to the mall's restoration and improvement.

Recently, an extensive turf grass restoration project was completed on the National Mall. Damaged grass and soils were removed and replaced with durable species of grass and compaction-resistant engineered soils. A new drainage system more effectively moves rainwater off the mall, and large underground cisterns collect this water for irrigation. Visitor use is managed to prevent further lawn damage. This includes limits on the type of structures and lawn coverings allowed for organized events. Events are restricted to a certain number of days, depending on the season, and there is a required recovery period between events. Sections of lawn may also be temporarily closed for casual

public use. The US Park Police are responsible for enforcing these temporary closures, which are indicated to the public through the placement of red flags.

Information and education is used to help a diversity of visitors have enjoyable experiences at the National Mall. Effective communication is needed to help guide visitors, many of whom may be visiting for the first time, to and through major attractions. **Detailed information and maps are provided on the park website and through mobile apps.** The latter can be downloaded on a cell (mobile) phone or tablet, and feature current park news, walking directions, customized tours, and tools for wayfinding. Interpretive programs and exhibits are offered at monuments, and **in collaboration with the Trust for the National Mall, pairs of roving docents are also available to give tours, answer questions, and provide information.**

To protect park resources, visitor experiences, and the integrity of memorials, certain activities are prohibited. Among the restricted activities are: tree climbing; attaching items to trees or other park structures; flying remote model airplanes; and flying kites that have abrasive, non-biodegradable string. Jogging, picnicking, rollerblading, skating, skateboarding, bicycling, and riding on scooters are prohibited at certain memorials, including the Vietnam Veterans and Korean War Veterans Memorials and within the Jefferson, Lincoln, and Roosevelt Memorials. Given the urban location of the National Mall, parking is limited, and special provisions are made for the estimated 8 million visitors who arrive by bus each year. Bus drop-off and pick-up locations have been established at seven locations near the Mall, with parking available at six locations in other parts of the city.

Among those arriving by bus are people coming to participate in one of the thousands of organized events that take place each year. Balancing these events with general visitation is another major management activity at the National Mall. Groups wishing to host a demonstration or special event are required to obtain a permit from the National Park Service. Permits must be requested at least 2 days before an event, and can be applied for up to 1 year in advance. Special events are distinguished from demonstrations as activities that focus on entertainment or celebration. Demonstrations, on the other hand, are events intended to convey a message, and include speeches, vigils, and picketing. Applications are processed on a first-come, first-served basis, and about 4000 of the 6000 requests are permitted each year. This means that **more than 30 permitted events could be taking place on the Mall each day.**

With organized events, particularly demonstrations, comes the potential for conflict. In the permitting process, applicants are asked to indicate whether they expect any groups, organizations, or individuals to disrupt the proposed activity. If so, the applicant is asked to provide the contact information for these groups or individuals. Applicants are also required to provide a monetary bond to cover expenses associated with the event, including monitoring by the US Park Police and cleanup costs. For large events, such as Presidential inaugurations, the National Park Service may collaborate with US Capitol Police, Metropolitan Police, and

the Secret Service. Special events are also subject to the Cost Recovery Program (as at Biscayne National Park described in another case study, see Chapter 10, p. 71) and may be responsible for any damages caused during the activity, including turf grass damage. A US$120 application fee is waived for events that are determined to be "First Amendment activities." Through the permitting process, the park works to reduce conflict between these activities and to ensure that they can be accommodated safely and appropriately.

**The cultural, historical, and democratic significance of the National Mall, coupled with intensive levels of use, and uses that sometimes conflict, requires a multi-faceted management approach.** Park rules, information services, and a purposefully designed permitting system have helped the National Park Service accommodate these many uses. Thoughtful facility redevelopment and rehabilitation, as proposed in the National Mall Plan, may enable an enthusiastic modern public to be more effectively accommodated, while respecting the historic vision of the Mall's original planners.

## Further Reading

Meserve, J. (2008) National Mall in monumental disrepair, activists say. *CNN U.S.*, July 4.

National Mall and Memorial Parks (2016) Available at: http://www.nps.gov/nama (accessed 29 July 2016).

National Park Service (2010) Final National Mall plan/environmental impact statement. US Department of the Interior, Washington, DC.

National Park Service (2012) Turf management operations and maintenance guide for the mall. US Department of the Interior, Washington, DC.

Reis, P. (2010) $700M National Mall plan emphasizes water, energy conservation. *The New York Times*, July 14.

Runion, G., Rogers, H., Wood, C., Prior, S. and Mitchell, R. (1993) Effects of traffic on soil physical characteristics and vegetative resources of the National Mall. *Journal of Soil and Water Conservation* September–October, 389–393.

Trust for the National Mall (2016) Available at: http://www.nationalmall.org (accessed 29 July 2016).

# 27 Climbing Towards Common Ground at Devils Tower

Devils Tower holds an ethereal allure to many people. Rock climbers regularly challenge the monolith's signature cracks and columns. But the act of climbing is perceived as disrespectful by some Native Americans (**Conflict**) who practise traditional ceremonial activities at the sacred site. Moreover, climbers and other visitors have disturbed ceremonies and removed prayer offerings (**Depreciative behavior; Impacts to historical/cultural resources**). As climbing has continued at Devils Tower, monument managers have chosen to **Reduce the impact of use** through a pioneering Climbing Management Plan. The plan implemented a voluntary climbing closure during the month of June (**Zoning**), incorporated a cross-cultural education program to enhance visitor knowledge of significance of the site to Native Americans (**Information/Education**), and re-emphasized the importance of registering with a ranger before and after climbs (**Rules/Regulations**). A dedicated climber registration office has also been developed to provide visitors more contacts with climbing rangers (**Facility development/Site design/Maintenance**).

## Introduction

On 24 September 1906, with the inaugural use of the Antiquities Act, President Theodore Roosevelt proclaimed Devils Tower the world's first national monument. In declaring the site an "object of historic and great scientific interest" he expanded the intended use of the Act to include cultural as well as scientific significance. This executive action set in motion a dialogue over cultural resources that continues today.

**Many Native Americans consider lands within Devils Tower National Monument to be sacred.** To some, including the Crow, Lakota, and Cheyenne Tribes, the area is known as Bear Lodge (historical records suggest Devils Tower is derived from an incorrect initial translation), and more than 20 tribes have cultural affiliation with the site. Traditional ceremonial activities involve personal and group rituals and include prayer offerings (cloths, bundles, ribbons, and flags), sweat lodge ceremonies, the Sun Dance, pipe ceremonies, and vision quests. Oral histories of tribes include ecological and astronomical knowledge linked to the area, and many ceremonial activities are conducted during the summer solstice. Native Americans' principle opposition to climbing activities stem from experiencing undesirable encounters during this traditionally important time.

The history of rock climbing at Devils Tower extends over a century. The first recorded ascent of the stone sentinel was made by William Rogers and William Ripley in 1893. The pair developed a 350-foot wooden ladder in a fissure of the Tower and climbed the remaining 175 feet to the top. On 4 July of the same year, Rogers made a public climb and unfurled an American flag at the summit for the benefit of spectators. Roger's wife Linnie was the first woman to ascend the tower using the ladder 2 years later. A team led by Fritz Weissner made the first non-ladder summit in 1937, and in 1952 the first female-only ascent was made by Jan Conn and Jane Showacre. Today, Devils Tower has more than 200 named routes ranging from the popular Durrance route to those with more colorful names such as "Good Holds for Godzilla" and "Accident Victim." Devils Tower has become a world-class climbing destination and has also played a significant role in the nation's history of climbing and high angle search and rescue (Fig. 27.1).

**As a surge in the annual number of climbers occurred in the 1970s and 1980s, conflict between traditional cultural uses and climbing may have been inevitable.** From 1956 to 1968, 30–50 groups per year were ascending the Tower. By the early 1990s, there were more than 6000 registered climbers at the monument annually. During these decades of exponential growth, pitons and bolts were driven into the Towers' face and other debris left behind by climbers also began to mount. Prayer bundles were often removed from the area, and

**Fig. 27.1.** The signature cracks and columns of Devils Tower have made the site a world-class climbing destination. (National Park Service photo by Avery Locklear.)

ceremonial activities were frequently disrupted by the shouting of commands between climbing partners. The solitude sought for rituals was frequently disturbed by the photographing of Native Americans during the solemn events. In 1995, monument managers implemented an innovative plan that would attempt to address conflict and share understanding among Native Americans and the climbing community.

## Devils Tower Climbing Management Plan

In the early 1990s, amidst peak climbing use at Devils Tower, monument managers organized a working group to begin to assess and address rising tension among interested parties. The group included tribal and community leaders, climbing groups, local business representatives, environmental groups, and National Park Service officials. The collaborative process led to a preferred approach for establishing respect for cultural traditions on monument lands. Both the climbing community and Native

Americans agreed that a voluntary ban on climbing during the month of June (the time period when solstice ceremonies occur) would be a mutually beneficial outcome of a planning process, and in 1995 the voluntary ban was implemented through the Devils Tower Climbing Management Plan.

Central to the success of the plan's ban was an enhanced interpretive endeavor to educate visitors, including climbers, about Native American cultural practices and traditions. The improved education program has incorporated online outreach, interpretive site development, and increased opportunities for contacts with rangers. In addition to hard copies of brochures available on site, the park website includes information on Native American cultural connections to the Tower and regulations related to climbing it. Much of this information is also available through streaming video or audio online.

**Visitors are asked not to interfere with ceremonial activities and are advised not to touch, take, or disturb prayer offerings in any way.** Information provided explains that quiet and solitude are required for rituals, and that brightly colored pieces of cloth that may be found throughout monument lands are physical symbols of prayers made by Native American people. Visitors are also asked to refrain from taking photographs of prayer offerings, given their cultural significance.

Interpretive site development has included a sculpture entitled "Circle of Sacred Smoke" installed to increase awareness of indigenous links to the land (Fig. 27.2). The sculpture is accessible by road or trail and is also a gesture of world peace. It symbolizes the first puff of smoke from the pipe used by native people to pray. A World Peace Pole was also established near the sculpture which reads in both Lakota and English; Wólakhóta Akan Macóke, May Peace Prevail on Earth.

As part of an effort to increase climber education contacts, a dedicated climber registration office was developed in 2005. As all visitors planning to climb the Tower are required to register before and after climbing each day, this also serves as an ideal opportunity for climbing rangers to engage individuals in meaningful conversations regarding park resources and potential impacts to them. Registration is free, improves climber safety, and contributes to a historical database maintained since 1937.

**Climber registration also provides clarification of rules and regulations. These include the voluntary June closure, no new bolting, replacement bolting by permit and by hammer only, replacement of slings with neutrally colored ones or chains, and required human waste carry-out off approach routes and the Tower.** Rules and regulations applying specifically to commercial climbing guides include no guiding during the month of June and providing information on guide websites and printed materials regarding the voluntary June closure.

## Fostering Mutual Respect at Bear Lodge

Citing an 80% reduction in the number of climbers during the month of June, many consider the voluntary climbing ban at Devils Tower a resounding success. It was conceived from cooperation and collaboration, endorsed education over coercion, and has allowed parties at odds an opportunity to cultivate mutual respect. This civic effort has been a struggle, however, and may continue to be.

Upon the release of Devils Tower's Climbing Management Plan, litigation over the voluntary ban ensued for 4 years. Only in 1999, was the annual closure upheld by a ruling from the US 10th District Court of Appeals. Furthermore, monument managers have noted a trend that compliance with the June climbing closure is decreasing. As Native American spiritual values and opportunities for personal reflection have been documented by the National Park Service as fundamental to the monument, "continued climbing at Devils Tower may depend on the willingness of the climbing community to abide by their own code of climber ethics in conjunction with NPS policies and regulations."

But, the future looks promising. **Progressive models of co-management and partnerships between the National Park Service and indigenous people appear to be on the rise.** Managers at Grand Canyon National Park include 11 traditionally associated tribes in their decision making. Native farming remains active at Canyon De Chelly National Monument. At Grand Portage the monument's orientation video may be viewed in

**Fig. 27.2.** A sculpture entitled "Circle of Sacred Smoke" was installed to interpret and increase awareness of indigenous links to the land. (National Park Service photo by Avery Locklear.)

Ojibwemowin, the language of the Ojibwe people. And, in 2015, the tallest mountain in North America was officially renamed Denali (see Chapter 13, p. 82) in recognition of its sacred status to generations of Alaska Natives.

## Further Reading

Brown, M.F. (2003) *Who Owns Native Culture?* Harvard University Press, Cambridge, Massachusetts.

Devils Tower National Monument (2016) Devils Tower National Monument website. Available at: www.nps.gov/deto (accessed 16 June 2016).

Dustin, D.L., Schneider, I.E., McAvoy, L.H. and Frakt, A.N. (2002) Cross-cultural claims on Devils Tower National Monument: A case study. *Leisure Sciences* 24, 79–88.

Hanson, J.R. and Moore, D. (1999) Applied anthropology at Devils Tower National Monument. *Plains Anthropologist* 44, 53–60.

Lane-Kamahele, M. (2016) Indigenous voices. In: Manning, R.E., Diamant, R., Mitchell, N., and Harmon, D. (eds) *A Thinking Person's Guide to America's National Parks*. George Braziller Inc., New York, New York.

National Park Service (1995) Final climbing management plan/finding of no significant impact. Devils Tower National Monument. US Department of the Interior.

National Park Service (2014) Foundation document. Devils Tower National Monument. US Department of the Interior.

# 28 The Winter Wonderland of Yellowstone

In winter, Yellowstone National Park is a geothermal wonderland of steam, snow, and ice. Visitors on snowmobiles and snowcoaches are afforded remarkable opportunities to experience the park's interior in midwinter, but this type of visitation has not been without controversy. Motorized over-snow vehicles were polluting the park's air (**Impacts to air**) and soundscape (**Impacts to natural quiet**), disturbing wildlife (**Impacts to wildlife**), and threatening the health and safety of other visitors and employees (**Conflict**). The growing popularity of snowmobiling led to crowded conditions in the fragile winter landscape (**Crowding; Impacts to attraction sites; Impacts to trails**), and the actions of a few visitors venturing off trails fueled the conflict (**Depreciative behavior**). Management of winter use in Yellowstone has focused primarily on the strategies of **Limiting use** and **Reducing the impact of use**. The park grooms trails for over-snow travel (**Facility development/Site design/Maintenance**) and has taken several measures to reduce the impacts of motorized snowmobile and snowcoach access, including requiring best available technology for snowmobiles and snowcoaches (**Rules/Regulations**), setting limits on the number and type of vehicles allowed to enter the park each season (**Rationing/Allocation**), requiring visitors to travel with guides, establishing curfews, and setting speed limits (**Rules/Regulations**). A hefty fine is assessed to visitors who travel off designated trails (**Law enforcement**).

## Introduction

While many national parks boast scenery described as "outstanding," "spectacular," and "magnificent," visitors reserve a special vocabulary for Yellowstone National Park in winter. **In this frozen, harsh landscape, among vast stretches of thick snow and ice, lie steaming geysers, bubbling mud pots, and gem-toned hot springs, frozen waterfalls, ice arches, and "ghost trees."** All require a more mystical set of words—magical, ethereal, wonderland, fantasy world. It is little wonder that so many are drawn to Yellowstone during this time of year, entering its interior by snowmobile and snowcoach (Fig. 28.1). But managing for motorized winter access in Yellowstone has not come without controversy; winter use planning has taken place in the context of extensive study, multiple lawsuits, and vigorous public comment and debate.

Questions about how to manage winter visitation at Yellowstone predate the arrival of the first snowmobiles in the 1950s. Few visitors ventured into the park in wintertime in its early days, but by 1932, surrounding communities started to ask managers to plow park roads in order to allow vehicle access year-round. In 1949, the first motorized snow vehicles arrived, "snow planes" that were propelled across the landscape by a single propeller much like an Everglades airboat. Soon thereafter, the first multi-passenger snowcoaches were developed by the Bombardier company, and by 1963, the first modern private snowmobiles arrived. With the growing popularity of these winter activities, the path for active management for snowmobile and snowcoach access, including trail grooming, was established. Park managers reasoned that these types of over-snow access were preferable to plowing roads, an approach that would be difficult given the park's narrow roads and prodigious snowfall, and that would greatly alter Yellowstone's winter wilderness character.

But as winter visitation grew steadily during the following decades, a new set of problems developed. Older model snowmobiles with two-stroke engines were noisy and polluted the air. The park's wildlife, which are particularly vulnerable during these months of cold temperatures, limited food supplies, and challenging travel through deep snow, were stressed by the noise and pollution, and by inexperienced snowmobilers who were unable to pass them appropriately (Fig. 28.2). Fueling the conflict, a small number of snowmobilers engaged in thrill-seeking behaviors, traveling off designated routes to race up slopes. All of these factors were exacerbated by the number of snowmobiles in the

**Fig. 28.1.** Yellowstone National Park takes on a very different character in the winter and has become very popular for snowmobiling. (Photo by Robert Manning.)

**Fig. 28.2.** Snowmobiles can impact wildlife, including bison, at a time when they are already under stress. (Photo by Robert Manning.)

park. By the late 1990s, nearly 800 snowmobiles—with older, more polluting technology—entered the park each day, causing crowded conditions. (At the time, relatively few visitors traveled through the park by snowcoach.) **The problems at Yellowstone gained national attention when images of park personnel wearing gas masks at entrance stations reached the media.**

In 2013, Yellowstone implemented a long-term winter use plan that addresses several factors: the

---

safety and health of visitors and park employees; the quality and educational value of visitor experiences; impacts to air quality, natural quiet, and wildlife; and economic impacts to gateway communities. The winter use plan and associated collaborative adaptive management program provide flexibility in addressing challenges associated with motorized winter visitation.

## Yellowstone National Park

**The first national park in the world, Yellowstone National Park was established by an act of Congress in 1872.** More than 2 million acres in size, the park spans parts of Wyoming, Montana, and Idaho. It's famous for its geothermal features—geysers, hot springs, mudpots, and fumaroles. More than 60% of the planet's geysers are found here, including the most famous: Old Faithful. As part of the 20 million acre Greater Yellowstone Ecosystem, the park is home to an abundant diversity of wildlife species. Among them are bison, wolves, and bears; coyotes, elk, deer, and moose; eagles, bighorn sheep, and foxes. Three million or more people visit Yellowstone each year, most of them during the snow-free summer months. Opportunities to explore the park's natural features abound, and in summer possible activities include hiking, fishing, horseback riding, and camping. In winter, visitors come to experience the contrast of geothermal features against snow and ice, to watch wildlife brought down to more forgiving conditions in the park's lower elevations, and to stay in the Old Faithful Snow Lodge. While the road between the north and north-east entrances of the park is open to cars year-round, other entrances and interior destinations in Yellowstone can only be accessed by over-snow vehicle, skis, or snowshoes in winter.

## Managing Winter Visitation in Yellowstone

The approaches to managing winter use in Yellowstone have been shaped through the courts and through advances in technology. Lawsuits and petitions from environmental groups in the late 1990s challenged the idea of managing the park for over-snow access. A suit filed by the group Fund for Animals came after a particularly cold and icy winter, when hundreds of bison followed groomed trails out of the park in search of food, and were killed over suspicion that the animals would transmit the disease brucellosis to livestock. When in

2000 a National Park Service environmental impact statement proposed allowing snowcoach access but banning snowmobiles, the agency was sued by industry and state interests. What followed was a series of environmental assessments and impact statements, proposing varying limits on the number of snowmobiles allowed to enter the park each day, with caps ranging from 318 to 950. Following extensive public comment and plan revision, the park moved away from a daily vehicle cap to a system of "transportation events."

The transportation event approach is, in essence, a use limit, but one that provides some flexibility for commercial tour operators. A transportation event consists of a group of snowmobiles or a snowcoach. The park allows up to 110 transportation events per day, and 50 of these can be snowmobile groups. Within this limit, tour operators can choose whether to offer snowmobile and/or snowcoach tours and have the option of exchanging allocated events with one another. While no more than ten snowmobiles are allowed on a tour, operators can run tours of varying sizes so long as they do not exceed a seasonal average of seven snowmobiles per group. Moreover, tour operators have the opportunity to increase their seasonal average group sizes (to eight snowmobiles or 1.5 snowcoaches) if they exceed required technology standards. By setting a transportation event limit, rather than individual vehicle limit, tour operators are encouraged to send visitors into the park in larger groups. This allows similar or increased visitation, but less frequent disturbance of wildlife, natural quiet, and other visitors. The amount of air and noise pollution is reduced through set technology standards, and incentives for operators to exceed these standards.

**Technology standards are a significant component of managing for motorized winter access in Yellowstone.** Before 2002, snowmobiles were dirtier and noisier, emitting, on average, 150 g per kilowatt-hour (g/kW-h) of hydrocarbons and 400 g/kW-h of carbon monoxide into the atmosphere. Noise from these older snowmobiles averages 78 decibels. By comparison, modern snowmobiles employ four-stroke engine technology and are cleaner and somewhat quieter. Today, the National Park Service requires that snowmobiles entering the park meet standards of 15 and 90 g/kW-h for hydrocarbons and carbon monoxide emissions, respectively. The standard for noise is 67 decibels. Snowcoaches, previously not subject to best available technology requirements, must now comply with designated Environmental Protection Agency Tier 2 vehicle standards and a noise standard of 75 decibels. Since technology requirements and prohibitions on idling were first implemented, pollution and noise levels in the park have dropped significantly. Park scientists continue to monitor noise and pollution levels, so the effect of new standards and the transportation event approach remains to be seen.

A number of additional rules and requirements are in place to further minimize impacts associated with motorized winter recreation at Yellowstone. The latest winter plan allocates five transportation events to non-commercial private trips. However, all trips, commercial or private, must be guided. Non-commercial guides must complete a certification course covering park rules and regulations, safety, and environmental considerations. By requiring that trips be guided and that snow vehicles enter the park in single file, wildlife disturbance has decreased, along with the number of accidents and citations for traffic violations. Speed limits of 35 mph for snowmobiles and 25 mph for snowcoaches further improve visitor safety. **The prohibition of operating snowmobiles off designated trails is strictly enforced, with a US$5000 fine for those who travel off established routes.** Additionally, motorized snow vehicles are only allowed to operate between 7 am and 9 pm, a rule that limits the duration of soundscape impacts.

The adoption of a long-term winter use plan at Yellowstone is the culmination of an extended process of public involvement, research, and revision, but it is not the end of the process. The park has developed an adaptive management plan that will guide future management. Six working groups—focused on wildlife, air quality, human dimensions, operations and technology, and non-commercial access—have contributed their knowledge to the plan. Visitation to Yellowstone's winter wonderland will likely be a topic of continued public interest and debate for many years to come.

## Further Reading

Borrie, W., Freimund, W. and Davenport, M. (2002) Winter visitors to Yellowstone National Park: Their value orientations and support for management actions. *Human Ecology Review* 9, 41–48.

Davenport, M. and Borrie, W. (2005) The appropriateness of snowmobiling in national parks: An investigation of the meanings of snowmobiling experiences in Yellowstone National Park. *Environmental Management* 35, 151–160.

Davenport, M., Borrie, W., Freimund, W. and Manning, R. (2002) Assessing the relationship between desired experiences and support for management action at Yellowstone National Park using multiple methods. *Journal of Park and Recreation Administration* 20, 51–64.

Dustin, D. and Schneider, I. (2005) The science of politics/the politics of science: Examining the snowmobile controversy in Yellowstone National Park. *Environmental Management* 34, 761–767.

Mansfield, C., Phaneuf, D., Johnson, F., Yang, J. and Beach, R. (2008) Preferences for public lands management under competing uses: The case of Yellowstone National Park. *Land Economics* 84, 282–305.

National Park Service (2011) Yellowstone National Park winter use plan/environmental impact statement. US Department of the Interior, Yellowstone National Park, Wyoming.

Yellowstone National Park (2016) Available at: http://www.nps.gov/yell (accessed 8 July 2016).

Yochim, M. (2015) From conflict to resolution in the two big-Y parks: Ending 20 years of controversy in Yellowstone and Yosemite. *The George Wright Forum* 32, 141–150.

# 29 Alternative Transportation at Grand Teton

Roads in Grand Teton National Park were designed to accommodate visitors in automobiles, and most visitors travel through the park in this way. But with narrow or nonexistent shoulders, roads present a challenge for those wishing to travel through the park in other ways (**Conflict**). To increase opportunities for non-motorized travel—and to reduce impacts associated with vehicle traffic (road and parking lot congestion, trampled vegetation, compacted soils, air pollution) (**Impacts to roads; Crowding; Impacts to vegetation; Impacts to soil; Impacts to air**)—the park constructed an 8-mile multi-use pathway for pedestrians, bicyclists, and skaters (**Facility development/Site design/Maintenance**). The pathway provides visitors with an alternative route to the popular South Jenny Lake area, and bicycle racks are provided along the path and at attraction sites (**Facility development/Site design/Maintenance**). A number of rules and regulations are communicated to help ensure the safety of visitors and to reduce the impacts of multi-use path users on wildlife (**Rules/Regulations; Information/Education; Impacts to wildlife**). This mix of management practices uses three of the four basic management strategies: **Increasing the supply** of opportunities, **Reducing the impact of use**, and **Hardening the resource/experience**. Adaptive management will guide the future development of an extended network of multi-use paths in the park.

## Introduction

Many travel corridors in national parks have been developed with the auto tourist in mind. In Grand Teton National Park, three main roads—the Teton Park Road, Outer Highway, and North Park Road—and several smaller roads provide access to park attractions. The latter include visitor centers, campgrounds, and trailheads in the Moose, Jenny Lake, and Colter Bay Districts and the Laurance S. Rockefeller Preserve. Routed through Jackson Hole Valley with its views of the Teton Range and opportunities for wildlife viewing, these roads are traveled by hundreds of thousands of visitors in private automobiles each summer. However, for visitors wishing to travel through the park by alternative means—on foot or by bicycle—the design of these roads is less than ideal. Narrow or nonexistent road shoulders place pedestrians and cyclists close to motor vehicles, including large recreational vehicles (RVs). This scenario can reduce the enjoyment of both motorized and non-motorized travelers, in addition to raising concerns about safety, especially when families bicycling with young children and less experienced riders are involved.

Given the environmental and social impacts of automobile travel—which include congestion, full parking lots, trampled vegetation and compacted soils from unauthorized parking, and degraded air quality—**encouraging alternative means of travel is an important goal for the National Park Service.** In Grand Teton, multi-use paths have been proposed as one approach to moving toward this goal. In 2009, an 8-mile non-motorized pathway opened near a section of the Teton Park Road, allowing visitors to walk, pedal, or skate from park headquarters in Moose to the popular South Jenny Lake area. The pathway is promoted as part of the park's Healthy Families Initiative, and provides a first step in connecting the park to multi-use paths in surrounding communities. Through an adaptive management approach informed by research on wildlife-related impacts, up to 42 miles of paths may eventually be constructed in the park.

## Grand Teton National Park

Grand Teton National Park's 310,000 acres encompass the youngest mountains in the Rockies. **The towering peaks of the Teton Range—eight of which exceed 12,000 feet—rise abruptly from the valley floor below** (Fig. 29.1). The contrast is the result of powerful shifts along a 40-mile crack in the earth that has pushed the Teton peaks skyward,

**Fig. 29.1.** The Tetons rise abruptly from the surrounding plains at Grand Teton National Park. (National Park Service photo by E. Himmel.)

while plunging the valley floor down to an elevation that now averages 6800 feet. In this dramatic setting, sculpted by glaciers, landscapes range from alpine tundra to sagebrush flats. Wetlands, meadows, forests, and lakes provide habitat for a rich diversity of wildlife that includes large carnivores, ungulates (elk, pronghorn, moose, mule deer), birds of prey, and several species of smaller animals that live in the nearly intact Greater Yellowstone Ecosystem.

Originally established in 1929, Grand Teton National Park was enlarged in 1950 when combined with the adjacent Jackson Hole National Monument. The park lies just south of Yellowstone National Park and the adjacent John D. Rockefeller Jr. Memorial Parkway. It is surrounded by the Winegar Hole, Jedediah Smith, and Teton Wildernesses; Targhee and Bridger Teton National Forests; and the National Elk Refuge. About 2.5 million people visit Grand Teton each year, with most visitation occurring during the summer months. Visitors come to Grand Teton to view mountain scenery, to see wildlife, to hike, camp, mountain climb, and to take float trips on the Snake River. And many will ride a bicycle during their time in the park.

## Promoting Alternative Travel in Grand Teton

The multi-use pathway in Grand Teton is the result of transportation planning efforts that date back to 2000 (Fig. 29.2). Through an initial study, management approaches were determined that would:

1. Increase the number of ways that visitors could move through the park.
2. Better accommodate both motorized and non-motorized travel.
3. Reduce congestion in popular areas.
4. Improve the communication of transportation-related information to visitors.

The final transportation plan, completed in 2007, calls for a system of multi-use pathways, both separate from and within existing road corridors, as a major strategy for addressing these goals. Pathways will allow visitors to reach park attractions without traveling on park roads, stowing their means of transport at bicycle racks while cars and other motorized vehicles compete for parking spaces. Other elements of the plan include a study on the feasibility of developing a transit system for the park; improved road signs and visitor information about traffic conditions and transportation options;

**Fig. 29.2.** The National Park Service has developed a greenway as a form of "alternative transportation" at Grand Teton National Park. (National Park Service photo.)

and addition of a pedestrian crossing signal. Perhaps **one of the more important components of the plan is its focus on adaptive management.** This means constructing multi-use pathways in phases; conducting research before, during, and after pathway construction; and integrating research findings into subsequent pathway development phases.

Of particular concern to managers are the potential impacts that new multi-use paths might have on wildlife, and in turn, the impact that wildlife (particularly large mammals) might have on people who are traveling through the landscape in a new way. While constructed within 50 feet of the Teton Park Road, a feature that wildlife have lived among for decades, animals interact differently with people on foot or bicycle than they do with people in motor vehicles. To help minimize impacts on wildlife, and promote safe visitor interactions with park animals, several rules are in place for path users. Path use is restricted to daylight hours and pets are prohibited (except guide dogs). As in other parts of the park, visitors are required to stay at least 300 feet from large animals and are not allowed to feed or in other ways harass wildlife. Food and backpacks must be attended at all times. To further improve safety, the park recommends that path users travel in groups when possible and carry and know how to use bear spray. Studies conducted on bird and ungulate interactions with the path and its

users have confirmed the loss of some habitat, but did not show other major impacts on these species. However, a recent study found that, since the pathway has been in use, black bear activity near the travel corridor has decreased during midday and increased during mornings and evenings. The study also documented pathway crossings by black bears increased by 20–40% at night. This sound science helps reinforce the rationale for the pathway's nighttime restriction.

Beyond wildlife, a number of rules and recommendations are in place to promote safety and to reduce conflicts between users on the new path. First, only non-motorized forms of transportation are allowed on the paved multi-use path (an exception is made for electric/battery-operated transport for the disabled). Bicyclists and skaters are encouraged to travel at an appropriate speed for the number of other users and to alert others when passing. When venturing on to park roads, bicycles are required to follow the same rules as cars, and must also travel in single file, and yield to motorized vehicles. Helmets, bright-colored clothing, and reflectors to enhance visibility are recommended. The park directs cyclists to dirt roads for mountain biking, but bicycles are strictly prohibited on trails. Information about bicycle routes, the new multi-use pathway, and associated rules is provided to visitors on signs, at visitor centers, and on the park website.

The rules and regulations around bicycling and other forms of "alternative transportation" are important to protecting both visitors and wildlife, but they are secondary to the significance of constructing a new pathway in the first place. The placement of new facilities in a national park, with the associated planning, construction and maintenance costs, and the decision to impact a portion of the natural environment, is a challenging proposition. **But as with the shuttle bus system at Zion National Park (discussed in another case study, see Chapter 24, p. 127), managers at Grand Teton have tackled a big issue with a bold approach.** As park facilities change to reflect modern transportation concerns, the conventional auto tourist may become just one of many types of national park traveller.

## Further Reading

Barber, J., Fristrup, K., Brown, C., Hardy, A., Angeloni, L. and Crooks, K. (2009–2010) Conserving the wild life therein: Protecting park fauna from anthropogenic noise. *Park Science* 26, 26–31.

Chalfoun, A. (2011) Effects of pathways within Grand Teton National Park on avian diversity, abundance, distribution, nesting productivity, and breeding behaviors.

University of Montana College of Forestry and Conservation Final Report, Missoula, Montana, 1–29.

Costello, C., Cain, S., Nielson, R., Servheen, C. and Schwartz, C. (2013) Response of American black bears to non-motorized expansion of a road corridor in Grand Teton National Park. *Ursus* 24, 54–69.

Gleason, R. (2008) Guide to promoting bicycling on federal lands. Federal Lands Highway Central Federal Lands Technical Report TD-08-007, Lakewood, Colorado.

Grand Teton National Park (2006) Transportation plan final environmental impact statement. US Department of the Interior, Moose, Wyoming, 1–368.

Grand Teton National Park (2016a) Biking in the park. Available at: http://www.nps.gov/grte/planyourvisit/bike.htm (accessed 2 November 2016).

Grand Teton National Park (2016b) Available at: http://www.nps.gov/grte (accessed 2 November 2016).

Hardy, A. and Crooks, K. (2001) Ungulate responses to multi-use pathway construction and use in Grand Teton National Park, Wyoming. University of Montana College of Forestry and Conservation Final Report, Fort Collins, Colorado, 1–52.

Knight, R. and Gutzwiller, I. (eds) *Wildlife and Recreationists – Coexistence through Management and Research.* Island Press, Washington, DC.

Little, C. (1995) *Greenways for America.* Johns Hopkins University Press, Baltimore, Maryland.

# 30 No Bad Trip in Glacier

Glacier National Park is known as a backpacker's paradise, and for much of the park's history, little regulation of back-country camping existed. But as visits to the park's primitive interior increased, concerns grew about safely accommodating this use while protecting wilderness resources (**Impacts to vegetation; Impacts to soil; Impacts to wildlife; Impacts to water**). Today, backcountry camping is managed primarily through the strategies of **Limiting use; Reducing the impact of use;** and **Hardening resources/experiences**. A permit system is used to limit use throughout the backcountry (**Rationing/ Allocation**). Visitors are required to camp at designated campsites (**Facility development/Site design/Maintenance**), and are informed about rules and safety issues through a backcountry camping video, a backcountry guide, and on the park website (**Rules/Regulations; Information/Education**). In addition, backcountry rangers help to ensure visitor awareness of these issues and to enforce park rules when necessary (**Law enforcement**). Finally, a range of camping opportunities—from at-large camping to hike-in chalets—are provided to accommodate different types of backcountry experiences (**Zoning**).

## Introduction

In the early 20th century, trips into Glacier's backcountry took place on horseback. Visitors stayed in cabins and campgrounds constructed and maintained by the Great Northern Railway company. In the decades that followed, few regulations guided backcountry camping activities in the park. Visitors camped where they wanted and when they wanted—in the shadows of craggy mountain peaks; in alpine meadows, coniferous forest, and prairies; and among glaciers, lakes, and the park's abundant wildlife. **But, by the 1960s, increased visitation and growing awareness of the impacts of this visitation called for more active management of overnight use.** Initially, permits were required for campfires, and by the end of the decade, planning for a more comprehensive backcountry camping permit system began. The change followed the park's first two recorded deaths from bear attack, an event in 1967 known as the "night of the Grizzlies." Today, a sophisticated permitting system of reservations and walk-in requests is in place to manage use of the park's 65 primitive campgrounds. Several rules and regulations protect park resources and the camping experiences of visitors.

## Glacier National Park

The "Crown of the Continent," Glacier was established as the tenth national park in the USA in 1910, becoming part of the first International Peace Park (Waterton-Glacier) in 1932. Located in the northern Rocky Mountains in Montana, **Glacier is world renowned for its jagged, snow-covered mountain peaks, rich biodiversity, and glacial carved valleys.** Though shrinking in a warming climate, 25 glaciers remain; they include Blackfoot (the largest), Grinnell, Jackson, Sperry, and Rainbow. Nearly 2000 species of plants, more than 275 bird species, and 68 species of animals can be found in Glacier's 1 million acres. Among them are celebrated large mammals—grizzly bears, mountain goats, and bighorn sheep; the wolverine, lynx, and mountain lion. Along with its partner park to the north, Glacier is globally recognized as an International Biosphere Reserve (1974) and World Heritage Site (1995).

The iconic Going-to-the-Sun road, completed in 1932, carves a route through some of Glacier's most spectacular scenery, providing access to Lake McDonald, the popular Avalanche Lake hiking area, Logan Pass, and St Mary Lake. Replicas of the original red touring cars, and several historic lodges—among them, Lake McDonald Lodge, Many Glacier Hotel, and Glacier Park Lodge—are reminiscent of an earlier time of visitation in the park. But for many today, a trip to Glacier is not complete without a trip into the backcountry. **Known as a backpackers' paradise, Glacier's nearly 750 miles of trails take visitors away from roads and into the park's interior** (Fig. 30.1).

**Fig. 30.1.** Glacier National Park features its namesake ice formations along with meadows of wildflowers and hundreds of miles/kilometers of trails. (Photo by Robert Manning.)

### Managing Backcountry Camping in Glacier

On its surface, the backcountry camping policy in Glacier is straightforward: all backpackers are required to obtain and carry a permit and (with the exception of the Nyack/Coal Creek Camping Zone) to camp in designated campsites. It is an approach designed to concentrate use and prevent widespread ecological impacts. The complexity arises in the diversity of issues that need to be addressed in administering a permit program. The summer backpacking season is short, with snow covering campsites well into June or July. Campsite opening dates and challenging trail conditions (such as water hazards) are not completely predictable. During the short season, demand for popular camping locations is high. Further, backpackers have a range of physical abilities and interests to be accommodated. And there is the issue that led to the development of a formal permitting system in the first place—the presence of large and potentially dangerous wildlife species in the park, particularly, the grizzly bear.

**A Backcountry Camping Guide, along with the park's backcountry website pages provide prospective backpackers with detailed instructions for obtaining a permit.** The steps that need to be taken depend upon the time of year that a trip is proposed and how far in advance an excursion is planned. Winter campers (those intending to camp between mid-November and the end of April) can simply request a permit up to 7 days before a trip. Summer campers have two options:

1. Applying for a reservation online.
2. Checking walk-in availability within 24 hours of a proposed trip.

About half of the park's 208 campsites are reserved for each type of request.

Applications for advanced reservations are first-come, first-served, and are accepted beginning in March. In the application, trip leaders are asked to indicate the number of campers who will participate in the trip, their proposed itinerary, and up to three alternative itineraries, including proposed dates and campgrounds for up to 14 nights. Applicants are encouraged to indicate whether they would accept other options (different start/end dates, different campgrounds, reverse route, shorter trip) or a completely different itinerary than they requested. There is a three-night limit per trip for each campground. In addition, some popular campsites can only be requested for one or two nights per trip during July, August, and September. These efforts are designed to accommodate high demand and to direct campers to available alternatives when capacity is reached along popular routes. **To help** campers feel better about potential alternatives, the park emphasizes that "There is no bad trip in Glacier!"

A further challenge arises when accounting for the unpredictability of campsite conditions. Each campground is assigned an anticipated opening date—the day on which it is expected that snow will have melted at the site—and reservations can be made only after that date. (Campgrounds that become accessible before their opening date are added as options in the online advance reservation system.) Additionally, sudden trail hazards (e.g. snow cover from an avalanche) could lead to last-minute trail closures. When this happens, back-country rangers meet with campers on the trail to adjust itineraries. The park provides detailed information on its website to help campers identify potential complications. Daily trail status reports and a backcountry blog provide details about trail and campsite conditions. An online chart also helps visitors plan by providing a list of campsites that still have availability. GPS coordinates are provided for each campsite to help those wanting to incorporate this technology into their trip.

Getting campers permitted and distributed among the available campsites is just one step in managing backcountry use in Glacier. Several rules and regulations are in place to help minimize the impacts that campers have on the natural environment and on the experiences of others. These rules incorporate the principles of Leave No Trace (see the case study on Acadia National Park, Chapter 6, p. 55). Given the relative impact of large groups, the park encourages smaller group sizes by setting a maximum group size of 12 people, and permitting only five of these large groups per night. Groups must fit within the design limits of campsites, which accommodate up to two tents and four people. While in camp, visitors are required to use established cooking areas, campfire pits, and pit toilets. Only downed wood is to be collected for fires. Loud conversations are discouraged while in camp, though talking and clapping is encouraged while hiking through bear habitat as a way of minimizing encounters with bears.

On the trail, hikers are asked to urinate on rocks (to reduce impacts from animals digging for salt) and to bury solid waste in catholes away from water sources. Visitors are encouraged to hike in single file, to rest on durable surfaces, and to pick up litter that they see along the trail. Shortcutting switchbacks is prohibited, as is collecting any natural or cultural items from the park (other than

berries and fish for personal consumption). Only guide dogs are allowed on backcountry trails, and even they are discouraged because of potential interactions with wildlife.

Special precautions are required at campsites to reduce the likelihood of negative interactions with wildlife. Food must be handled carefully; no food preparation or storage is allowed at tent sites. All food and odorous items must be stored in designated containers or in bags hung out of reach of animals, and campers are required to carry rope and a hanging bag with them. Food scraps must be collected in a strainer and carried out with other garbage. Backpackers are encouraged to carry bear spray (a pepper spray for defensive purposes) and are given instructions about how to respond if they encounter a grizzly. Details about bear encounters and other rules and requirements are outlined in a 15-minute video that campers can watch online or at the backcountry camping office. Backcountry rangers interact with visitors on trails and at campsites, enforcing permits and camping rules when needed.

While rules and regulations protect park resources, different types of camping opportunities provide for different types of visitor preferences and abilities. While most camping is restricted to designated primitive campsites, the Nyack/Coal Creek Camping Zone, located on the south-west side of the park, provides an opportunity for at-large camping in this rugged and less visited area. Only the most experienced backcountry visitors are encouraged to participate in this type of camping, and they will still need a permit to do so. On the other end of the spectrum are hike-in mountain chalets that provide visitors with beds, a solid structure to sleep in, kitchen facilities, and food service (Fig. 30.2). At Sperry Chalet, visitors can send their gear to the top on a mule, while hiking the 6-mile trail with a day pack, or they may choose to arrange a ride for themselves by horse. Guide services are permitted by the park for visitors wanting to hike and camp with a resident expert.

The backcountry management and camping permit system at Glacier serves to protect an internationally recognized wilderness, while accommodating the many visitors who are eager to venture into its interior. It is exemplary in using multiple management strategies and practices to balance these two often-competing goals. While use is limited by the number of available campsites, the range of alternative itineraries that can be offered through a combination of an online reservation and walk-in

**Fig. 30.2.** Granite Park Chalet offers shelter to hikers and is one of many types of hiking experiences available in the backcountry of Glacier National Park. (Photo by Robert Manning.)

permit system also serves to expand the number of options available to visitors. By concentrating use within designated campsites, a hardened resource, the spread of impacts is minimized; and by setting and enforcing rules and regulations, impacts to the natural environment and other visitors are reduced and visitor safety is enhanced.

## Further Reading

Benedict, J. and Wagtendonk, J. (1980) Wilderness permit compliance and validity. *Journal of Forestry* 78, 399.

Cole, D. (2004) Impacts of hiking and camping on soils and vegetation: A review. In: Buckley, R. (ed.) *Environmental Impacts of Ecotourism*. CAB International, Wallingford, UK.

Cole, D. and Hall, T. (2008) Wilderness visitors, experiences, and management preferences: How they vary with use level and length of stay. US Department of Agriculture Forest Service, Fort Collins, Colorado.

Fazio, J. and Gilbert, D. (1974) Mandatory wilderness permits: Some indications of success. *Journal of Forestry* 72, 753.

Glacier National Park (2016) Available at: http://www.nps.gov/glac (accessed 24 July 2016).

Hall, T. (2001) Use limits in wilderness: Assumptions and gaps in knowledge. US Department of Agriculture, Forest Service, Rocky Mountain Research Station, Missoula, Montana.

Hammitt, W. and Cole, D. (1998) *Wildland Recreation: Ecology and Management*. 2nd edn, John Wiley, New York.

Jope, K. (1985) Implications of grizzly bear habituation to hikers. *Wildlife Society Bulletin* 13, 32–37.

Manning, R. (2011) *Studies in Outdoor Recreation: Search and Research for Satisfaction*. Oregon State University Press, Corvallis, Oregon.

Marion, J. and Stubbs, C. (1992) Campsite impact management: A survey of National Park Service backcountry managers. In: Proceedings of the Northeastern Recreation Research Symposium. US Department of Agriculture, Forest Service, Rocky Mountain Research Station, Saratoga Springs, New York.

National Park Service (1999) Glacier National Park Final General Management Plan and Environmental Impact Statement. National Park Service, West Glacier, Montana.

# Part III   Conclusions

# 31 Lessons Learned

In this book, we've seen that parks and outdoor recreation are important to society for many reasons. Outdoor recreation is the way in which millions of people enjoy and appreciate national parks and related areas each year, and this helps build a strong constituency for parks and outdoor recreation. But managing outdoor recreation is complicated by the dual mission of parks: to provide for public enjoyment, but to do so in ways that protect park resources and the quality of the visitor experience. This dual mission is at the heart of the US national park system and is embodied in the objectives of related park and outdoor recreation agencies and organizations around the world.

This challenge is also manifested and clarified in a number of long-standing conceptual frameworks in the field of parks and outdoor recreation, such as parks as common property resources, carrying capacity, and limits of acceptable change. Parks are common property resources and need to be managed proactively, an approach that Garrett Hardin termed "mutual coercion, mutually agreed upon." Carrying capacity suggests that too much or inappropriate recreational use of parks and related areas can degrade park resources and/or the quality of the visitor experience to an unacceptable degree, and that parks must be managed in accordance with their carrying capacity. The concept of limits of acceptable change acknowledges that outdoor recreation will cause change in park resources and/or the quality of the visitor experience, but demands that limits must be defined on the amount of change that is acceptable.

These concepts have given rise to several management frameworks, including Limits of Acceptable Change (LAC) (Stankey *et al.*, 1985), Visitor Experience and Resource Protection (VERP) (National Park Service, 1997; Manning, 2001), and Visitor Use Management (Interagency Visitor Use Management Council, 2016). Though these frameworks sometimes use different terminology and include other nuances, they are more alike than different (Manning, 2004). These frameworks require:

1. Formulation of management objectives and associated indicators and standards of quality.
2. Monitoring of indicator variables.
3. Management to ensure that standards of quality are maintained.

Moreover, consideration should be given to formulating indicators and standards of quality for each component of the threefold framework of parks and outdoor recreation: park resources, the visitor experience, and the management environment. Finally, indicators and standards of quality can be arrayed in a systematic way as suggested in the Recreation Opportunity Spectrum (ROS) to help ensure that there is a diverse system of park and outdoor recreation opportunities designed to meet the wide-ranging needs of society.

This book also describes the ways in which outdoor recreation can impact park resources (soil, vegetation, water, wildlife, air, natural quiet, natural darkness, and historical/cultural resources) and the quality of the visitor experience (crowding, conflict, and depreciative behavior). These impacts are often concentrated on visitor facilities and services, including attraction sites, trails, campgrounds/campsites, roads and parking areas, and interpretive facilities and services. Together, these impacts constitute 16 basic types of management problems. The impacts of individual visitors are usually small, but when multiplied by millions of visitors each year and accumulated over decades of increasing use, these impacts can be substantial and may threaten the integrity of park resources, the quality of the visitor experience, and the management capacity of park and outdoor recreation agencies.

Fortunately, there are a number of management practices that can be brought to bear on these problems, and research suggests that these management practices can be effective in reducing the impacts of outdoor recreation. These management practices can be organized into four basic strategies:

- limiting use;
- increasing supply;
- reducing the impact of use; and
- hardening the resource and/or the visitor experience;

and into six categories of management practices:

- information/education;
- rationing/allocation;
- rules/regulations;
- law enforcement;
- zoning; and
- facility development/site design/maintenance.

A series of four matrices (see Chapter 5) can be constructed, using the 16 management problems and the four management strategies and six management practices identified and described in this book. These matrices can be useful in thinking systematically, comprehensively, and creatively about the range of practices that might be used to manage outdoor recreation. The management practices that might be applicable to each problem are presented in Appendices A1–A4, and readers are challenged to think creatively about additional management practices that might be applicable.

Finally, a series of 25 case studies presented in Part II of this book illustrate the ways in which the management strategies and practices outlined in this book are being successfully used in diverse units of the US national park system. These case studies address all 16 of the problems associated with outdoor recreation and all four of the management strategies and six categories of management practices that might be used to address these problems.

## Principles of Managing Outdoor Recreation

What lessons can be learned from this survey of the scientific and professional literature and the 25 case studies presented in the first two parts of this book? Integration and synthesis of the material suggest a series of principles that have emerged for managing outdoor recreation in a broad range of contexts. This chapter presents and briefly discusses each of these principles and illustrates these principles using examples from the case studies.

### Principle 1: Parks and related outdoor recreation areas must be managed in ways that provide outdoor recreation opportunities but also protect park resources and the quality of the visitor experience

The dual mission of parks embodied in the outdoor recreation profession requires that parks be made available for outdoor recreation but that recreation is managed in ways that protect vital park resources and the quality of the visitor experience. The 1916 Organic Act of the US National Park Service is an important manifestation of this dual mission. Parks as common property resources, carrying capacity of parks, and the limits of acceptable change are closely related concepts that address the dual mission of parks and related outdoor recreation areas. Parks are good examples of "commons" and must be protected by a program of management that represents the concept of "mutual coercion, mutually agreed upon." Similarly, carrying capacity suggests that there are limits to the amount of recreation that can be accommodated in parks without unacceptable impacts. Implicit in the concept of carrying capacity is the notion that recreation will inevitably cause change in parks and related areas, but that "limits of acceptable change" must be established and respected. Management of outdoor recreation must address the dual mission of parks and related areas.

All of the case studies presented in Part II of this book represent diverse examples of how the inherent tension between use and protection of parks and outdoor recreation areas is manifested, such as: hikers at Acadia trampling fragile soils and vegetation; boaters at Biscayne damaging coral reefs; extreme crowding on Half Dome; theft of artifacts at Petrified Forest; visitors disturbing firefly habitat at Great Smoky Mountains; parking lot runoff threatening Carlsbad Caverns; traffic congestion at Zion; visitors overtaxing interpretive tours at Mesa Verde; snowmobiles polluting the air and soundscape at Yellowstone.

They also include the creative ways in which managers have addressed this issue, including: a bus system at Denali to limit conflicts between park visitors and wildlife; design of campsites on the Appalachian Trail that are more resistant to expansion; use of volunteers to conduct interpretive walks at the National Mall; sensitizing visitors at Muir Woods to human-caused noise; potential requirements for use of quiet technology for air tours over Grand Canyon; development of a greenway for bikers and pedestrians at Grand Teton; and a requirement that visitors must be accompanied by uniformed rangers to minimize their impacts at Mammoth Cave.

### Principle 2: Outdoor recreation management should be guided by a management-by-objectives framework

Management of parks and outdoor recreation can be complex and even contentious. For example, striking the proper balance between use and protection as described in Principle 1 can be difficult as it often involves decisions about the use of public lands: allocating recreation opportunities among competing demands; mediating potential conflicts among visitors; and imposing management restrictions, sometimes including limits on public use. A structured framework should be used to help guide these management decisions. Several such frameworks have been developed in the park and outdoor recreation literature and include Limits of Acceptable Change, Visitor Experience and Resource Protection, and Visitor Use Management. These frameworks rely on core elements of:

1. Formulating management objectives and associated indicators and standards of quality.
2. Monitoring indicators of quality.
3. Taking management action to maintain standards of quality (as illustrated in Fig. 1.4).

This constitutes a rational, transparent, and traceable framework for managing outdoor recreation. Several of the case studies presented in Part II of this book are good manifestations of this approach. For example, a standard of quality for the maximum number of people-at-one-time was set for Delicate Arch (as well as other experiential and resource-related indicators and standards of quality for other sites at Arches National Park), and the park monitors these indicators and takes management action (e.g. limits the amount of parking at the Delicate Arch trailhead) to ensure that standards of quality are maintained. Standards of quality have also been formulated for resource and social conditions on the Colorado River (e.g. campsite degradation, number of groups of boaters seen on the river each day), and these conditions are monitored to ensure that standards of quality are maintained. The wilderness management plan at Denali has adopted standards of quality for condition of campsites and the number of groups encountered per day, and a mandatory permit system is used to help maintain these standards. It's likely that more parks and outdoor recreation areas will adopt this management approach in the future as the impacts and associated problems described in this book become more urgent, and as this management approach becomes more deeply embedded in the profession.

### Principle 3: Outdoor recreation management is an iterative, adaptive process

The contemporary management-by-objectives framework in the field of parks and outdoor recreation outlined in Principle 2 and illustrated in Fig. 1.4 is an iterative approach that relies on a long-term program of monitoring and adaptive management. As described in Chapter 1 and Principle 2, management of parks and outdoor recreation involves three primary steps:

1. Formulating management objectives and associated indicators and standards of quality.
2. Monitoring of indicators of quality.
3. Taking management action designed to maintain standards of quality.

Thus, monitoring is a process that is applied periodically to determine if standards of quality are being maintained and if management practices are being applied successfully. This approach to outdoor recreation management requires a long-term commitment to monitoring. Findings from the program of monitoring are used to determine the effectiveness of management: if standards of quality are being maintained, then current management may not need to be revised. However, if standards of quality have been violated, or if trends in monitoring data suggest that standards of quality are in danger of being violated, then alternative management practices should be considered. In this way, managers learn from the success or failure of management actions and adapt their program of management accordingly. The monitoring and management programs at Arches, the Colorado River, and Denali (as described above in Principle 2) are good examples of this management approach, and management of alternative transportation at Grand Teton relies explicitly on a program of adaptive management. Likewise, collaborative adaptive management now guides winter use management at Yellowstone.

### Principle 4: Outdoor recreation should be managed within a threefold framework of concerns: resources, experiences, and management

Outdoor recreation has potential impacts on park resources and the quality of the visitor experience, and these impacts occur primarily at a variety of management facilities and services (as illustrated in Fig. 1.2). All three of these components of parks and outdoor recreation—resources, experiences, and management—should receive explicit attention in designing and implementing management programs. Moreover, there can be important interrelationships among these three components of outdoor recreation. For example, impacts to park resources can also degrade the quality of the recreation experience and require implementation of management action. Failure to give explicit attention to all three components of parks and outdoor recreation and the potential interactions among them may leave outdoor recreation unmanaged in important ways. This threefold framework is a useful way to consider and analyse outdoor recreation in a comprehensive, multidisciplinary fashion. The case studies presented in Part II of this book address all three components of outdoor recreation as illustrated in Table 5.1: all eight categories of resource impacts are represented, as well as all three categories of experiential impacts, and all five categories of park facilities and services.

### Principle 5: The Recreation Opportunity Spectrum should be used to help ensure diversity in outdoor recreation opportunities

The Recreation Opportunity Spectrum (ROS) uses ranges of potential indicators and standards of quality to help define a diverse system of outdoor recreation opportunities (as illustrated in Fig. 1.3). A range of recreation opportunities is needed to meet the increasingly diverse demands of society. ROS can be a useful management framework in several ways, including conducting an inventory of recreation opportunities at a park or group of parks and related areas, suggesting the types of recreation opportunities that may be in short supply at a park or group of parks and related areas,

and suggesting the types of indicators and standards of quality that may be most appropriate for selected types of outdoor recreation opportunities.

The case studies presented in Part II of this book represent many types of park and recreation opportunities that might be found in an ROS framework. These opportunities range from urban parks such as the National Mall to wilderness parks like Katmai; from crown jewel parks like Yosemite to lesser-known places such as Voyageurs; from water-based parks like Biscayne to mountains like Mt. Whitney; from natural areas like Grand Canyon to historical/cultural areas like Chaco; and from small sites like Muir Woods to vast reserves such as Denali. All of these parks contribute in important ways to the larger spectrum of the nation's outdoor recreation opportunities. Even at the individual park level, many types of outdoor recreation experiences can and should be found. The backcountry zoning system at Glacier National Park is a good example where opportunities range from chalets to at-large camping. Similarly, the extensive cave system at Carlsbad Caverns offers high-capacity viewing opportunities for most first-time visitors and more limited access to low-capacity backcountry or more "wild" caves.

### Principle 6: Outdoor recreation can impact parks and related areas in many ways, including park resources, visitor experiences, and park facilities and services

Chapter 2 outlined how outdoor recreation can impact parks and related areas. As suggested by the threefold framework of parks and outdoor recreation outlined in Principle 4, these impacts can affect park resources, the quality of the visitor experience, and can be found across a range of park facilities and services. For the purposes of this book, impacts to park resources were organized into eight categories, including soil, vegetation, water, wildlife, air, natural quiet, natural darkness, and historical/cultural resources. Impacts to the quality of the visitor experience were organized into three categories, including crowding, conflict, and depreciative behavior. These resource and social impacts can occur at five categories of management facilities and services, including attraction sites, trails, campsites/campgrounds, roads and parking lots, and interpretive facilities and services. For the purposes of this book, these impacts can occur in 16 basic ways or places.

The case studies presented in Part II represent all of these impacts and problems as illustrated in Table 5.1. Together, the 25 case studies addressed all eight types of park resources, though impacts to soil, vegetation, wildlife, and historical/cultural resources were most common. Impacts to water and air were not as common, probably due to their often ephemeral character. Impacts to natural quiet and natural darkness were less common, but these are only emerging in the public and professional conscience as increasingly scarce, but important "resources." Crowding is a nearly ubiquitous social impact, though it is manifested in many different ways: encounters with other groups on the trails to the summits of Mt. Whitney and Half Dome; traffic congestion on the road into Zion Canyon; competition for campsites on the Colorado River; or standing room on the bear-viewing platforms at Katmai. Conflict among park users is also common: motorized and non-motorized boaters on the Colorado River; "flightseeing" tours and wilderness hikers at Grand Canyon; cars and bikes at Grand Teton; demonstrators of different political persuasions at the National Mall; and mountain climbers and Native Americans at Devils Tower. Depreciative behavior of visitors is less common, but no less important in its implications: hikers tampering with rock cairns on the trails at Acadia; careless boat groundings at Biscayne; and theft of bits of petrified trees at Petrified Forest. Of course, all of these impacts and related problems are found most often at visitor attraction sites such as iconic natural features, viewpoints, historic and cultural sites, rivers and lakes, and mountain summits. Impacts at trails and interpretive facilities and programs are also common. Impacts on roads and parking areas, and at campsites and campgrounds are less common. Of course, the 25 case studies presented in Part II are not necessarily representative of the vast and diverse system of more than 400 units of the US national park system, and impacts associated with recreational use are as varied as the parks themselves.

### Principle 7: Outdoor recreation can be managed using four basic strategies

Strategies are fundamental approaches to management; they describe the basic means that managers might take to solve problems. Four basic strategies can be used to manage outdoor recreation (as illustrated in Fig. 3.1): limit use, increase supply, reduce the impact of use, and harden park resources and/or the visitor experience. For example, excessive recreation-related impact to soil and vegetation at a recreation site might be managed by:

**1.** Reducing the amount of use (e.g. through a permit system).
**2.** Increasing the supply of recreation opportunities to disperse use (e.g. constructing a new trail).
**3.** Reducing the impact of use (e.g. by encouraging visitors to adopt Leave No Trace (LNT) behaviors).
**4.** Hardening the resource (e.g. paving a trail) or the visitor experience (e.g. creating realistic visitor expectations).

These four strategic approaches are quite different and each has potential advantages and disadvantages.

As illustrated in Table 5.1, the case studies in Part II of this book offer examples of all four of these management strategies. Use is limited at Delicate Arch by sizing the trailhead parking lot to help ensure that no more than 30 people-at-one-time are at the arch; the number of bus trips per year at Denali is limited to minimize disturbance of wildlife; the number of visitors on interpretive tours of Cliff Palace is limited to ensure that all visitors can hear the ranger and ask questions; the number of backcountry campers at Glacier is limited to prevent excessive trampling of fragile soils and vegetation; and the daily number of hikers on the Half Dome cables is limited to prevent extreme crowding and related safety issues. Increasing the supply of recreation opportunities is more challenging, but has been successfully accomplished by building more bear-viewing platforms at Katmai; offering bits of petrified wood (collected outside the park) at the souvenir shop at Petrified Forest; developing a non-motorized greenway at Grand Teton; plowing park roads and opening visitor centers in the winter at Apostle Islands and using trained volunteers to conduct tours on the National Mall. Reducing the impact of use is nearly universally embraced because of its inherent attractiveness: reducing impact without reducing public access. Hikers are taught the principles of LNT on the trails at Acadia; boaters are taught how to avoid environmentally destructive groundings (and how to dislodge a boat when groundings occur) at Biscayne; visitors are sensitized to the values of natural quiet at Muir Woods and how to reduce human-caused noise; hikers are asked to remove their own human waste on Mt. Whitney; visitors to the synchronous firefly phenomenon at Great

Smoky Mountains are taught the "light show etiquette" of using flashlights to reduce their impact on fireflies and the ability of other visitors to see them; and anglers at Voyageurs are taught how to clean boats and other equipment to minimize the spread of exotic species. Hardening park resources and the visitor experience are less commonly used, at least in the case studies included in Part II, but can be an effective strategy. A new campsite design on the Appalachian Trail restricts the potential for campsite expansion; visitors are informed of how to prepare for viewing the ice caves at Apostle Islands, including the large number of visitors that are likely to be encountered; ancient ruins at Mesa Verde are rebuilt and stabilized to resist disturbance by visitors; and the shuttle buses at Zion absorb the use that thousands of cars each day exerted on the park road and parking lots. All four of these basic strategies can be useful in addressing and minimizing the potential impacts of outdoor recreation.

### Principle 8: Outdoor recreation can be managed using six basic categories of management tactics or practices

There are many tactics or practices that can be used to manage outdoor recreation as described in Chapter 3. These management practices can be grouped into six basic categories:

**1.** Information/education (e.g. a website that describes the seven principles of the LNT program).
**2.** Rationing/allocation (e.g. a mandatory permit system with a fixed number of permits).
**3.** Rules/regulations (e.g. a ban on campfires above tree line).
**4.** Law enforcement (e.g. the presence of a uniformed ranger who has the authority to issue citations).
**5.** Zoning (e.g. designating one trail for hikers and another for bikers).
**6.** Facility development/site design/maintenance (e.g. development of wooden tent pads).

These six categories of management practices are quite different and each has potential advantages and disadvantages. Chapter 4 outlines the efficacy of these six categories of management practices as documented in the scientific and professional literature.

The case studies in Part II of this book offer examples of all six of these management practices as illustrated in Table 5.1. Given its indirect and light-handed approach, it should be no surprise that information/education is used in nearly all of these case studies: hikers at Arches are informed about the damage to fragile soils and vegetation caused by walking off maintained trails; bus riders on the Denali Park Road are taught how to avoid disturbing wildlife; campers at Chaco are educated about the significance of natural darkness and night-sky viewing and how to minimize human-introduced light; and boaters at Voyageurs are taught how to minimize the chances of contributing to the spread of exotic invasive plants and animals. Rationing of use often appears in case studies and takes many different forms: hikers to Half Dome can reserve a permit on the internet; non-commercial boaters on the Colorado River in Grand Canyon participate in a lottery system; limited parking at Delicate Arch is first-come, first-served; peak season visitors to Mesa Verde may purchase a ticket for only one of the park's two most popular tours each day. Of course, rules and regulations are nearly pervasive among the case studies and are needed to bring order to growing demand for outdoor recreation. No overflow parking is allowed at Arches; group sizes are limited on the Colorado River in Grand Canyon; air tours must follow prescribed routes at Grand Canyon; snowmobilers at Yellowstone must use machines equipped with less polluting and quieter technology. Rules and regulations must ultimately be enforced and law enforcement is found throughout the case studies: a caretaker is stationed at the popular Annapolis Rocks camping area on the Appalachian Trail; rangers patrol the entrances to caves that have been closed to public use at Carlsbad Caverns; park rangers are stationed at all cliff dwellings open to the public at Mesa Verde; park rangers ask visitors as they leave Petrified Forest if they have picked up any petrified wood; and rangers check for required hiking and/or camping permits at Half Dome, Denali, Mt. Whitney, and on the Colorado River. Zoning is also a staple of park and outdoor recreation management. The Colorado River is zoned in both space and time to offer visitors an array of recreation opportunities; the Denali Road is zoned into areas where personal cars are allowed and where park buses must be used; Muir Woods includes a quiet zone; temporal zoning is applied at Devils Tower; the extensive backcountry of Glacier is zoned to provide a range of outdoor recreation experiences; and the sky over Grand Canyon is zoned into areas that allow air tours and areas where air tours are prohibited.

Finally, facility development/site design/maintenance is widely used to address potential impacts of outdoor recreation: the parking lot serving Delicate Arch has been resized to help avoid unacceptable levels of crowding; the shuttle buses at Zion reduce the impacts of private automobiles; downward-directed lighting has been installed at Chaco; the boardwalks and viewing platforms at Katmai minimize disturbance to bears; and new walkways, turf grass panels, and underground cisterns on the National Mall are designed to minimize damage to soils and vegetation.

## Principle 9: Outdoor recreation management problems can be addressed by more than one management strategy or practice

Most of the recreation-related impacts and problems associated with outdoor recreation can be addressed by more than one management strategy and/or practice. Crowding, for example, can be addressed by the strategy of limiting use (e.g. using the practice of raising fees or the practice of conducting a lottery for use permits), increasing the supply of recreation opportunities (e.g. using the practice of informing visitors about substitute recreation opportunities or the practice of developing additional facilities such as trails), and reducing the impact of use (e.g. using the practice of education about LNT principles or a regulation against cell phones to limit visitor-caused noise that can contribute to perceived crowding). The case studies presented in Part II describe how a variety of recreation-related impacts and associated problems were addressed using a range of recreation management strategies and practices. For example, the problem of crowding at Arches was addressed using the management practices of information/education (suggesting lesser-used places and times to visitors who inquire at the visitor center), rationing/allocation (limiting the number of parking spaces at the trailhead to Delicate Arch), rules/regulations (prohibiting overflow parking), and law enforcement (enforcing the ban on overflow parking when and where needed).

## Principle 10: Outdoor recreation management strategies and practices can address multiple problems

Principle 9 suggests that recreation management problems can be addressed by more than one management strategy and practice. The converse of this is true as well: recreation management strategies and practices can address multiple problems. For example, the strategy of reducing the impact of use and the associated practice of information/education can be used to address impacts to a number of park resources, including soils, vegetation, water, wildlife, and air; the LNT program has been designed specifically for this purpose. Information/education can also be used to reduce crowding by dispersing use to other sites/parks, minimize conflict by suggesting appropriate visitor behavior, limit depreciative behaviors by explaining why littering and graffiti are inappropriate, and "hardening" the visitor experience to the impacts visitors encounter by helping to shape realistic expectations about park conditions.

All four management strategies and all six categories of recreation management practices can be used to address many of the impacts and problems associated with outdoor recreation, and the case studies in Part II offer a number of examples. For instance, at Denali the strategy of reducing the impact of use and the associated practice of information/education are used to minimize conflict between bus riders and wildlife (by communicating appropriate visitor behavior), and to minimize impacts to soil and vegetation caused by wilderness campers (by communicating LNT guidelines). Similarly, the regulation banning private vehicles in Zion Canyon is used to minimize impacts to wildlife (by reducing the potential for cars injuring or killing animals), and to minimize crowding, traffic congestion, and conflict among visitors (by reducing competition for parking spaces and the danger of having both cars and bicycles on the road).

## Principle 11: Outdoor recreation management practices can be used to advance more than one management strategy

This book suggests that there are four basic strategies for managing outdoor recreation and six basic categories of management practices. Each of the six categories of management practices can be used to advance more than one of the four management strategies, and this effectively expands management options exponentially. For example, following the discussion in Principle 8, the management practice of information/education could be used to reduce use at a problem site or park (by informing visitors of the problems being experienced at the site or park or by informing them of advantages of alternative sites or parks, for instance), or to reduce the impact of use (by educating visitors about LNT behaviors). It's important to design and apply management practices in ways that will advance the strategies that are chosen to solve management problems. It's also important to take advantage of the ways in which one management practice might be used to advance more than one management strategy.

The case studies illustrate ways in which management practices can be used to advance more than one management strategy. For example, the management practice of information/education is used to support the management strategy of reducing the impact of use at a number of parks, including hiking at Acadia and boating at Biscayne. But information/education is also used to communicate and explain the rationale for the management strategy of limiting use at a number of parks, including hiking at Half Dome and rafting on the Colorado River.

### Principle 12: Outdoor recreation management strategies can be advanced by more than one management practice

Principle 11 suggests that management practices can be used to advance more than one management strategy. The converse of this is true as well: management strategies can be advanced by more than one management practice. For example, the management strategy of limiting use can be advanced by informing visitors of alternative outdoor recreation opportunities, rationing use through a permit system, and implementing a rule that limits group size. The management strategy of reducing the impact of use can be advanced by educating visitors about LNT practices, rationing use through a permit system, implementing a rule against the use of campfires above tree line, and developing tent pads to harden fragile soils and vegetation.

The case studies illustrate this principle. For example, the strategy of reducing the impact of use at campsites along the Appalachian Trail was accomplished by adopting a new design for campsites that was more "resistant" to spatial expansion, and by stationing a caretaker in the vicinity to educate campers and enforce regulations. Reducing visitor impacts to wildlife in the wilderness of Denali was accomplished by rationing use and educating visitors about proper behavior and food storage.

### Principle 13: Where possible, a reinforcing program of outdoor recreation management practices should be used

A suite of management practices can be used to reinforce each other and maximize the likelihood of successfully resolving a management problem. For example, campfires in wilderness areas can have ecological impacts, including sterilization of soil, removal of down wood, and development of social trails caused by visitors searching for firewood. They can also cause aesthetic impacts. These impacts can be especially pronounced at high elevations where firewood is scarce. A coordinated, reinforcing management program to address this problem might include:

**1.** An information/education campaign about the impacts of campfires, asking visitors to carry and use portable stoves.
**2.** A regulation against campfires above tree line.
**3.** Occasional patrols of trails and campsites to enforce the regulation when needed.

The case studies presented in Part II include a number of examples of reinforcing programs of management practices. At Arches, the parking lots servicing the park's most iconic attractions are sized to prevent unacceptable levels of crowding. A regulation against overflow parking has been adopted and is communicated to visitors at the park's visitor center, in the park newspaper, and on park signs, and this rule is enforced by park rangers when needed. On the Colorado River, resource and social impacts of boaters are minimized by educating visitors through the park's website about minimum impact camping behaviors. This educational program is extended on the river by means of contractual arrangements with commercial river guides, limiting the number of boat launches each day, adopting a temporal zoning system to provide a period in which motorized boats are not allowed, and enforcing regulations through regular river patrols.

### Principle 14: Managers should think systematically, comprehensively, and creatively about the range of practices that might be used to manage outdoor recreation

Given the range of potential impacts of outdoor recreation and the variety of management strategies and practices available, a concerted effort is needed to think about management in a systematic, comprehensive, and creative manner. The matrices developed in Chapter 5 and illustrated in Appendices A1 through A4 offer an approach that can support this thinking. These matrices array the impacts of outdoor recreation against available management strategies and practices and challenge managers to think about the ways in which each management alternative might be useful in addressing each impact or management problem. Chapter 5 describes the alternative ways the matrices and associated appendices can be used or "entered": the type of problem encountered, the location or context of the problem, the type of management strategy and/or practice considered, the 96 cells contained in each of the four matrices (Fig. 5.1 through Fig. 5.4), or the more detailed listing of management practices contained in Appendices A1 through A4. As illustrated in Table 5.1, the case studies in Part II of the book demonstrate many of the ways in which the four management strategies and six management practices can be (and have been) creatively employed to address the array of impacts caused by outdoor recreation in a diversity of park contexts.

## Principle 15: Outdoor recreation management practices should not be used simply because they are familiar or administratively expedient

The management matrices developed in Chapter 5, along with their associated appendices, suggest that there are many potential management options to address outdoor recreation-related impacts and problems. Managers should think creatively about this range of management alternatives and resist the temptation of relying on management practices that are familiar, administratively easy, or commonly used. For example, it may be common to implement limits on use when managers see park resources being degraded and the quality of the visitor experience diminished. But these problems may be caused by inappropriate types of use or behavior, and in these cases limits on use may be less effective than management efforts to change offending behaviors. Moreover, limiting use in these circumstances may be a disservice to the public as it doesn't address the root cause of the problem and unnecessarily denies public access to parks and related areas.

Many of the case studies in Part II represent this creative, innovative approach to management. For example, instead of limiting use at Zion Canyon, the park instituted a mandatory shuttle bus system that has eliminated or drastically reduced resource

and experiential impacts while maintaining visitor access. Katmai has added several webcams at Brooks Camp to allow "virtual" access to this iconic natural phenomenon. Hikers on Mt. Whitney carry and use waste allocation and gelling (WAG) bags to minimize impacts to fragile soils and vegetation and to maximize public access. At Carlsbad Caverns park staff and volunteers remove lint unknowingly deposited by park visitors from cave walls during an annual "lint camp."

## Principle 16: Potential unintended and undesirable consequences of outdoor recreation management practices should be identified and avoided

Application of recreation management practices to address selected problems can have unintended side effects. For example, rationing use at selected sites or parks may lead to similar problems at other sites or parks. For instance, the substantial reduction in use implemented on Half Dome in Yosemite National Park described in one of the case studies may cause an increase in use at substitute sites in the park, and managers should be sure that these other sites or parks are prepared for this increase in use. As another example, assignment of fixed itineraries for backpackers in wilderness areas (requiring backpackers to camp in assigned sites for each night of their trip) can substantially reduce camp encounters and associated crowding, but can also limit the sense of freedom and spontaneity that may be important to wilderness users. Assigning campsites to parties floating the Colorado River in Grand Canyon National Park as described in one of the case studies would allow for an increase in river use without a concomitant increase in campsite crowding. But this management practice was not applied because research found that visitors value the opportunity to adjust their trip based on the conditions experienced and other considerations. Potential side effects and unintended consequences of management actions should be considered when selecting and applying recreation management practices.

## Principle 17: Good information is needed to manage outdoor recreation effectively

Outdoor recreation management should be as informed as possible by several types of information. As illustrated in the first part of this book, there is a considerable body of research on outdoor recreation, including the types of impacts and problems associated with this activity, and this body of knowledge is outlined in Chapter 2. This information can help managers anticipate potential problems and understand how these impacts occur and the problems they create. And, of course, there is a growing professional literature on the broad range of management practices that might be applied, including their potential effectiveness, and this body of knowledge is outlined in Chapters 3 and 4. This type of information can stimulate systematic and creative thinking about management practices. Finally, information is needed about the specific context of the area under consideration. Some park resources are more fragile than others: for example, fine-textured soils (e.g. clay) are more susceptible to compaction than soils with large particle sizes (e.g. sand); broad-leaf vegetation (e.g. ferns) tends to be more susceptible to trampling than narrow-leaf vegetation (e.g. grass). Visitors can also be quite different; some are motivated to meet new people while others are seeking solitude. Parks can be quite different as well; some are near population centers and may be used most effectively in an intensive manner, while others are remote and may be managed more appropriately as wilderness. Information on all these issues will help ensure that management of outdoor recreation is as effective as possible.

Many of the case studies presented in Part II are especially good examples of the ways in which information has been used to design and implement informed outdoor recreation management. For example, designation of a quiet zone at Cathedral Grove in Muir Woods National Monument was based—at least partially—on a program of research on visitor support for this type of management action, and confirmation that visitors were behaving appropriately in response to this management practice. A substantive program of research on the relationship between crowding and visitor safety contributed to design and implementation of the permit system for hiking to the summit of Half Dome. A program of research on the ecological and social impacts of boating on the Colorado River helped guide development of the new river management plan.

## Principle 18: Management of outdoor recreation should be as informed as possible by understanding the cause of the impact or problem

Impacts and associated problems caused by outdoor recreation can have many potential causes. For example, excessive trail erosion might be caused by too much visitor use. However, it might also be caused by inappropriate visitor behavior (e.g. visitors walking off the maintained portion of the trail), unwise siting of the trail (e.g. on too steep a slope), or by inadequate maintenance (e.g. failure to clear water bars periodically and so allow water to accumulate on a trail). Management is unlikely to be effective if the cause of the problem is not adequately understood. For example, if the cause of the problem (e.g. soil erosion) is unwise siting of a trail, then a reduction in visitor use will probably have little effect in addressing the problem.

The case study of camping on the Appalachian Trail offers a good example of this principle. Much of the impact to the original camping area at Annapolis Rocks was caused by its location in a flat and open area, and not necessarily the amount of use or the number of Appalachian Trail hikers. This allowed extreme spatial expansion of the camping area, and associated impacts such as trampling of soils and vegetation. Movement of the camping area and adoption of the new side-hill campsite design has substantially reduced the amount of impact to soils and vegetation, a result that could not have been attained with a simple cap on the number of campers allowed.

## Principle 19: Outdoor recreation management decisions should be considered within the context of larger geographic scales

Parks and related outdoor recreation areas consist of a number of sites, and parks themselves are part of a larger system of outdoor recreation opportunities. Formulation of park and outdoor recreation management objectives and associated indicators and standards of quality, as well as the management practices used to maintain standards of quality, should consider the potential contribution of each site and park to the larger system of outdoor recreation opportunities. This is in keeping with the objectives of the Recreation Opportunity Spectrum (ROS), and the latter can be a useful tool in helping to design a diverse spectrum of recreation opportunities (see Principle 5). In keeping with the threefold framework of outdoor recreation (see Principle 4), management practices are an important component of outdoor recreation opportunities, and this suggests that management practices should be selected, designed, and applied in ways that add needed diversity to recreation opportunities at the park, regional, and even national and international levels.

Several of the case studies in Part II reflect management consideration at a large geographic perspective.

For example, the Colorado River represents nearly 300 river-miles in Grand Canyon National Park and the river has been divided into three spatial zones, each offering a different kind of recreation opportunity and each managed in quite different ways. At Arches, a relatively liberal crowding-related standard of quality was set for the iconic feature of Delicate Arch because of the high demand at this site, but standards of quality place more emphasis on solitude at other sites in the park. Moreover, Arches is part of a large system of parks and public lands in southern Utah, and consideration was given to the most appropriate role Arches might play in this regional mix of park and outdoor recreation opportunities.

## Principle 20: Outdoor recreation management should focus on the impacts of recreation use, not use itself

It's not necessarily recreation use that is the root of the problems described in this book, it's the **impacts** of this use: soil compaction and erosion, disturbance of wildlife, crowding, and other problems often associated with outdoor recreation. This suggests that management should focus on limiting the impacts of outdoor recreation, not necessarily limiting recreation itself. In fact, limiting the amount of recreation runs counter to the mandate of most parks to accommodate recreation. Moreover, in some contexts, limiting the amount of use may not be as effective in reducing the impacts of use as information/education programs designed to encourage low-impact behavior of visitors. There are a number of management practices designed to limit the impacts of outdoor recreation, and this is the most appropriate focus of management efforts. Of course, limiting recreation use can be a valid and effective approach to managing the impacts of outdoor recreation (it's one of the four basic outdoor recreation management strategies and there are a number of management practices that can be used to limit or ration use), but it should be used only in the context of limiting the impact of recreation. Nearly all of the case studies presented in Part II illustrate ways in which recreation impacts can be reduced without limiting the amount of recreation use. Ridge runners at Acadia educate hikers about the importance of staying on maintained trails. Boaters at Biscayne are taught how to "read" the water and avoid environmentally damaging groundings. Visitors to Mammoth Cave are required

to change their clothes if they have been worn in other caves as part of an effort to stop the spread of disease among bats. Hikers at Muir Woods are asked to reduce the noise they make in Cathedral Grove. Visitors to Voyageurs are required to clean their boats and fishing gear to reduce the potential spread of invasive species. All of these case studies are examples of the ways in which the impacts of visitor use can be minimized while maximizing public access.

## Principle 21: Limiting use is generally a last management option in outdoor recreation

As discussed in Principle 1, most parks and associated areas have been established at least partially to provide opportunities for outdoor recreation. This is evident in the dual mission statement embodied in the Organic Act of the US National Park Service (as outlined in Chapter 1) and most other park and outdoor recreation management agencies and organizations. It follows that management agencies should give full consideration to management practices that do not limit use, before choosing to ration use. As an example from the case studies in Part II, the shuttle bus system at Zion National Park doesn't restrict visitation to Zion Canyon, but it reduces much of the impact of use that was attributed to use of private automobiles, including congestion on roads and parking lots, resource impacts from unauthorized parking, injuries to wildlife from collisions with cars, and noise from motorized traffic. Similarly, an educational program at Muir Woods limited the amount of human-caused noise without limiting the number of visitors. However, in some cases restrictions on the amount of recreation are needed and constitute a valid and appropriate management approach. For example, too many backpackers in the wilderness portion of Denali National Park are likely to disturb sensitive wildlife and diminish the quality of the wilderness experience to an unacceptable degree. In this case, a limitation on visitor use must be imposed.

## Principle 22: Limiting or rationing outdoor recreation use requires consideration of how limited opportunities for use will be allocated

By definition, placing limits on the amount of use a park or related area can accommodate necessitates implementation of a mechanism to allocate available opportunities for outdoor recreation. Because most parks and related areas are established on public lands, outdoor recreation managers must be especially thoughtful about how to allocate scarce recreation opportunities in ways that are fair and equitable. As discussed in Chapter 4, there are five basic management practices that can be used to allocate outdoor recreation:

- reservation systems;
- lotteries;
- first-come first-served or queuing;
- pricing; and
- merit.

Each of these practices has advantages and disadvantages, and these must be taken into consideration when developing and implementing a use rationing system.

The case studies in Part II suggest that use rationing is an important part of managing outdoor recreation in the national parks. Examples include the number of day hikers at Half Dome, the number of boat launches on the Colorado River, bus and overnight wilderness trips at Denali, the number and size of interpretive tours at Mesa Verde, the number of visitors allowed on viewing platforms at Katmai, the number of hikers on Mt. Whitney, the number of visitors at the synchronous firefly displays at Great Smoky Mountains, the number of visitors at one time at Delicate Arch, the number of air tours at Grand Canyon, the number of overnight hikers at Glacier, and the number of snowmobile and snowcoach "transportation events" at Yellowstone. In each case, an allocation system has been developed and implemented and some of these systems are very sophisticated, employing reservations, first-come first-served, lotteries (weighted and non-weighted), websites, toll-free reservation numbers, fees, and combinations of these systems. Reservations and first-come first-served systems are most common, lotteries are used occasionally, and pricing and merit are used only rarely. Though fees are often charged for use permits, the fees are usually nominal because of concern over discriminating among visitors based on income. Merit systems may see increasing use as they have the potential advantage of limiting not just the amount of use but the impact of use as well, if merit is judged on knowledge and practice of low-impact outdoor recreation uses.

## Principle 23: Indirect outdoor recreation management practices are generally preferred over direct management practices

Chapter 3 suggested that management practices can be classified as either direct or indirect (as illustrated in Fig. 3.2). As suggested by the terminology, indirect management practices are aimed at influencing visitor behavior through practices such as information and education. Direct management practices do not allow freedom of choice for visitors, and include practices such as rules and regulations, and law enforcement. Indirect management practices are generally favored as they are more in keeping with the freedom conventionally associated with outdoor recreation. But direct management practices are justified when needed to attain management objectives. A combination of indirect and direct management practices can be applied in a complementary way and may be needed to achieve maximum effectiveness. For example, a regulation is not likely to be effective if it hasn't been communicated and justified to visitors. Direct management practices may be needed more often in a number of situations such as high use levels, fragile or scarce natural/cultural resources, and when visitor behavior may cause substantial impacts to park resources and/or the quality of the visitor experience. The topic of direct and indirect management practices is discussed further in Principle 34.

The case studies in Part II reflect these ideas. As illustrated in Table 5.1, the indirect management practice of information/education is used almost universally because of its appeal to both visitors and managers. However, the direct management practices of rationing/allocation, rules/regulations, and law enforcement are also commonly used, suggesting that managers use these approaches when and where warranted.

## Principle 24: Intensive outdoor recreation use usually demands intensive management

Visits to national parks and related areas have increased dramatically over the past several decades and are now often counted in the millions for individual parks, and even hundreds of millions across the US national park system. Moreover, much of this use is concentrated in peak-use periods and at developed facilities, including attraction sites, trails, campsites/campgrounds, roads and parking lots, and interpretive facilities and services. This intensive use can have substantial impacts on park resources and the quality of the visitor experience. This suggests that intensive management will also be needed to meet the responsibility of park management to protect park resources and the quality of the visitor experience.

All of the case studies in Part II describe intensive programs of outdoor recreation management that bring to bear many of the management strategies and practices outlined in this book. For example, relatively large-scale public transit programs have been designed and implemented at Denali and Zion. A sophisticated weighted lottery system allocates permits to non-commercial boaters on the Colorado River. Backcountry permits at Glacier include reservation and walk-in components. A new system of campsites has been designed and constructed at a popular camping area along the Appalachian Trail. Airspace above the Grand Canyon is tightly regulated by the Federal Aviation Administration in cooperation with the National Park Service. Some caves at Mammoth Cave have been closed due to their especially fragile character. As outdoor recreation continues to increase in popularity, increasingly intensive and sophisticated programs of management will be required.

### Principle 25: When and where warranted, outdoor recreation management should be designed to reach visitors before they arrive at parks and outdoor recreation areas

Many management practices can be more effectively applied if their reach can be felt by visitors long before they arrive at the park. Examples include some of the more common management practices, including information/education, rules/regulations, and rationing/allocation. For instance, an educational program addressing the impacts of campfires above the tree line will, by definition, be more effective if visitors receive this message at home, thereby allowing them the opportunity to bring a portable stove. A regulation restricting pets from sensitive wildlife areas is more likely to be effective if visitors are aware of and prepared for this requirement before they arrive at the park. And visitors are more likely to be able to successfully cope with use rationing programs if they're familiar with them and tailor their use in a strategic way. Fortunately, electronic media offer managers unprecedented options to reach potential visitors before they arrive at the gates.

Several of the case studies in Part II illustrate the ways in which parks are reaching out to potential visitors, and electronic media are a favored approach. All units of the US national park system have relatively sophisticated websites that include information and education aimed at potential visitors. Apostle Islands uses a dedicated phone line (the "Ice Line") to inform visitors when the ice caves are open and how to prepare for visiting them. Some parks are using cutting-edge media: Arches uses Facebook and Twitter to help prepare potential visitors, and Grand Canyon has developed video podcasts for potential boaters on the Colorado River, as well as a DVD designed specifically for non-commercial boaters.

### Principle 26: The list of outdoor recreation activities and other uses of parks that need management consideration continues to evolve and expand

Outdoor recreation in parks and related areas includes conventional activities such as hiking, camping, and scenic driving. However, the list of activities has expanded greatly in recent years to include many unconventional uses such as off-road recreation vehicles and jet skis, trail running, and extreme sports. New recreation activities may result in new types of recreation impacts and associated problems, and managers need to stay abreast of these trends and anticipate where management attention will be needed. Several of the case studies presented in Part II offer examples of these relatively new recreation and related activities, including snowmobiles in Yellowstone, air tours over Grand Canyon, and public demonstrations at the National Mall.

### Principle 27: The list of park and outdoor recreation "resources" that need protection continues to evolve and expand

All parks are established to protect the resources that make them so valuable to society. For example, the 1872 legislation establishing Yellowstone National Park—generally considered to be the world's first national park—focused on protecting the area's natural "wonders," "curiosities," and "decorations." This terminology reflects a focus on static objects of great aesthetic and recreational appeal, and only a nascent appreciation of contemporary ecology. It was not until 1947 when Everglades National Park was established that management of national parks began to recognize the more modern and dynamic values of parks. The Antiquities Act of 1906 extended public concern from natural to historical and cultural resources.

The 1916 Organic Act of the US National Park Service embraced both natural and cultural resources when it directed the National Park Service to protect "the natural and historical objects and the wildlife therein" as found in the national parks. Traditionally, natural resources have included the conventional landscape components of soil, vegetation, water, wildlife, and air.

But more recently, the list of important park resources that might be threatened by too much or inappropriate types of outdoor recreation has been extended to include natural quiet and natural darkness—the ability to hear, see, and appreciate the sounds of nature and the celestial environment as our ancestors did. Natural quiet and natural darkness are beginning to be recognized as increasingly scarce and important park resources that need protection and management action. The case studies at Muir Woods National Monument (addressing natural quiet) and Chaco Culture National Historical Park (addressing natural darkness) are good examples of the ways in which diverse units of the US national park system are addressing these emerging resources. It seems likely that the list of park resources will continue to grow as we become more ecologically and culturally literate and sophisticated. For example, interactions among components of the environment that together comprise ecosystems, as well as landscape and global level processes such as climate stability and change, may be the most important resources of the parks of the future. Park managers need to be sensitive to these changes and adapt their management regimes accordingly.

### Principle 28: Variations in outdoor recreation management practices continue to evolve and expand

Research, new technology, and management innovation continue to contribute to evolution and expansion of recreation management practices. Managers need to keep abreast of these changes through networking and keeping up with the professional literature. The case studies presented in Part II of this book highlight several innovations in management practices. For example, the campsite design used in the Annapolis Rocks location on the Appalachian Trail works well as a way to minimize the impacts of camping on soil and vegetation. "Alternative transportation" systems have been developed at Denali, Zion, and Grand Teton.

Ecological and social science research has helped park managers formulate indicators and standards of quality, develop monitoring protocols, and test the potential acceptability of management practices at Arches, Denali, Half Dome, and the Colorado River. Computer simulation modeling of visitor use has helped inform management practices at Arches and on the Colorado River. Finally, several case studies have developed and used sophisticated websites (Arches), podcasts (Colorado River), apps (National Mall) and other electronic media as a means of providing information/education to visitors as they plan their trips.

### Principle 29: Outdoor recreation management can impact the quality of the visitor experience both positively and negatively

Recreation management practices are generally aimed at maintaining or enhancing the quality of outdoor recreation. For example, trails and campsites are built to enable visitors to use parks and related areas; and information and education, especially in the form of interpretation, are used to enhance appreciation of parks and related areas. But, paradoxically, management actions can sometimes diminish the quality of outdoor recreation. (This issue was introduced in the discussion of Principle 16, but warrants fuller treatment as a principle of its own.) In some cases, this is obvious: if recreation is substantially limited or even prohibited based on environmental or other considerations (for example, the closure of the backcountry of Mesa Verde due to sensitive cultural resources), then the recreational values of these areas are diminished. But in other cases, this issue may be less clear. For example, when use of a backcountry or wilderness area is limited to help ensure opportunities for solitude, managers should have evidence that visitors (or some segment of visitors) value opportunities for solitude at least as much as they value access and use of the area under consideration. Otherwise, the management action of limiting use may be more negative than positive, at least as it applies to the quality of the outdoor recreation experience. The example of the efficiency inherent in fixed itineraries for wilderness use versus the values of freedom and spontaneity as described in Principle 16 is another example of how this issue can be manifested. In developing the Colorado River Management Plan, it was found (through use of a computer simulation model) that requiring boaters to camp at specified beaches for each night of their trip would allow more groups of boaters to use the river, while maintaining a desired level of campsite solitude. However, this management option was not favored by boaters because it would substantially diminish the sense of freedom that boaters so closely associate with a Colorado River trip. In this case, most boaters would rather give up some access to the river to help ensure that the river trip meets their expectations. For this reason, a management system of fixed itineraries was not adopted as part of the management program.

### Principle 30: Caution should be used when dispersing visitor use as an outdoor recreation management practice

Dispersing recreation use is an inherently attractive management practice to address problems of resource and/or experiential degradation. It's a form of the basic management strategy of limiting use, but doesn't necessarily limit the amount of use; rather, it just spreads out use to areas or times that are underutilized (or, at least, less heavily used). Dispersing use can be effective, but can also cause a number of unintended side effects (see Principle 16). Managers should be careful that the places and/or times to which use is dispersed are indeed underutilized and that they are capable of accommodating increased use without important undesirable consequences. Moreover, it's important that the greater system of parks and outdoor recreation areas include sites and experiences that are explicitly defined to be low in use and associated impacts. This notion is at the heart of the concept of ROS (see Principle 5) and argues against a system of park and outdoor recreation opportunities that are relatively homogeneous.

### Principle 31: Partnerships between park and related outdoor recreation management agencies and other groups and entities can be helpful in managing outdoor recreation

Parks and related areas are not isolated entities, but are embedded in local, regional, and even national and international contexts. This means that park and outdoor recreation managers should work with a wide range of stakeholders, including gateway communities, associations of recreational users, equipment manufacturers and retailers, outdoor writers, environmental organizations, and

friends groups. Developing strong partnerships with these stakeholders can be mutually beneficial and extend the reach of park management. The case studies presented in Part II of this book offer a number of innovative examples of such partnerships. The shuttle bus system at Zion National Park was designed in collaboration with the gateway community of Springdale, Utah, and the resulting bus system provides a seamless transportation network for park visitors that benefits both the park and local businesses. The Museum Association at Mesa Verde National Park helps organize special tours for park visitors. Friends of Acadia helps fund the Ridge Runners program at Acadia National Park. The Minnesota Department of Natural Resources provides boaters in Voyageurs National Park with information about preventing the spread of aquatic invasive species. Snowplow services are provided by a local town at Apostle Islands to allow visitor use in the winter. The National Park Service and the US Forest Service manage recreational use at Mt. Whitney in a collaborative and coordinated way. Park staff at Devils Tower and Grand Canyon work directly with local Native American tribes to help determine appropriate and acceptable park uses. Chaco Culture National Historical Park, along with other Southwestern parks, successfully lobbied for passage of the New Mexico Night Sky Protection Act, which prohibits sale of mercury vapor lights in the state. These types of partnerships are extending the effectiveness of park and outdoor recreation management, and are likely to become even more important in the future.

### Principle 32: Responsibility for managing outdoor recreation should be shared jointly by managers and researchers

Principle 31 addressed the need for partnerships as a way to extend the reach and efficacy of park and outdoor recreation management. One of the most potentially important and powerful partnerships is between managers and researchers, and this relationship can be mutually beneficial: managers can offer researchers the opportunities they covet for applied research, and researchers can offer managers the information they need to make informed management decisions. But this relationship doesn't always work as smoothly as this. Research is sometimes viewed by managers as too basic (rather than applied), too driven by abstract disciplinary theory and inscrutable statistical methods, defined by narrow limits on subject matter, oriented toward purely academic colleagues and publications, and conducted on time lines oriented to an academic year schedule. On the other hand, researchers may feel the needs of managers are too immediate to allow for a fully thoughtful scientific approach, too broadly defined to allow needed focus, and too oriented toward variables that are under the control of managers (rather than those that are of statistical significance). Clearly, communication, collaboration, and compromise are needed between managers and researchers. Managers must offer meaningful incentives for research, including an opportunity for researchers to help define the topic under consideration, logistical field support, and, of course, assistance in the form of funding and/or in-kind services. Researchers must appreciate the demands under which managers operate, fully develop the management implications of research, and pursue more directly management-oriented types of research when and where feasible, including review and synthesis of existing literature, development of monitoring protocols, and testing the efficacy of management practices.

Several of the case studies in Part II are suggestive of meaningful relationships between managers and researchers. As outlined in Principle 17, research has played an important role in informing and shaping management programs, including helping to define standards of quality for crowding at Arches, the maximum acceptable levels of use on the Colorado River, and the maximum acceptable level of visitor-caused noise at Muir Woods. Research has also helped inform the most effective methods to prevent the spread of exotic species at Voyageurs, and development of educational programs to minimize human–wildlife conflict at Denali and Katmai. Expanded opportunities for collaborative work between managers and researchers will lead to more informed and effective outdoor recreation management.

### Principle 33: Quality in outdoor recreation is most appropriately defined as the degree to which recreation opportunities meet the objectives for which they are managed

There's a conventional tendency to manage the experiential dimension of parks based on measures of visitor satisfaction. However, this may be deceptively simple and work against sound park and outdoor recreation management. The problem is that there is great demand for outdoor recreation experiences of all kinds, but some kinds of uses are not compatible. For instance, there is a long-standing tendency for conflict between motorized and non-motorized recreation, including motor boaters and canoeists; snowmobilers and cross-country skiers; and automobile drivers and bikers. Moreover, these types of conflict are often asymmetric; that is, one group (the latter in the pairs above) objects to the presence of the other, but the reverse is not necessarily true. In these cases, without appropriate management, one group of visitors is likely to drive away the other. Thus, if managers rely solely on visitor satisfaction, they are likely to continue to find satisfied groups of motorized visitors, but non-motorized users may no longer be there to register their dissatisfaction. In the scientific and professional literature this process is often called "displacement" (Manning, 2011).

A more informed approach to management is to employ the contemporary management-by-objectives framework for outdoor recreation as outlined in Chapter 1 and Principle 2. This involves defining the types of outdoor recreation opportunities that are to be provided through a system of management objectives and associated indicators and standards of quality, and then measuring the degree to which these management objectives have been attained by monitoring indicators of quality. In this way, the quality of outdoor recreation is not defined simply by visitor satisfaction, but by the degree to which recreation opportunities meet the objectives for which they've been designed. As noted in Principle 2, the case studies at Arches and Grand Canyon (for both the Colorado River and air tours) offer good examples of using indicators and standards of quality as the primary mechanism for defining, measuring, and managing quality in outdoor recreation.

### Principle 34: Management of outdoor recreation should be conducted proactively, not reactively

The management-by-objectives framework outlined in Chapter 1 and Principle 2 and illustrated in Fig. 1.4 might be interpreted as reactive in that it suggests that management action is needed only when monitoring finds that standards of quality are in danger of being violated. However, this should not mean that management cannot be applied earlier in the process. This can be addressed in two ways:

1. It was noted in Chapter 3 and Principle 23 that management practices can be classified as either indirect or direct. It may be most appropriate to use indirect management practices to keep standards of quality high, even when monitoring suggests that standards of quality are not in danger of being violated. In this way, the management practices themselves are not likely to diminish the quality of the visitor experience. When monitoring suggests that standards of quality are in danger of being violated, then direct management practices may also be warranted.

2. A variation on this approach has been suggested; this posits standards of quality in terms of "yellow light" and "red light" (Whittaker *et al.*, 2010). Yellow light standards suggest caution that standards of quality are declining and that indirect management practices should be employed. Red light standards suggest that standards of quality are in imminent danger of being violated and that both indirect and direct management practices should be used as needed.

The case studies in Part II offer good examples of this issue. In some of these cases (e.g. trail management at Acadia, management of natural quiet at Muir Woods), managers are relying primarily on indirect management practices (principally information/education) because impacts of visitor use have not reached unacceptable levels, or standards of quality are not in imminent danger of being violated. These indirect management approaches are proactive efforts designed to minimize visitor impacts, but not at the expense of visitor access or other desired elements of the quality of the visitor experience. In other cases (hiking to the summit of Half Dome, boating on the Colorado River, hiking to Delicate Arch), managers are relying on direct management practices (use limits, rules and regulations, law enforcement) because impacts of visitor use have reached (or soon will reach) unacceptable levels, or standards of quality are in imminent danger of being violated. These direct management approaches are proactive efforts designed to minimize visitor impacts, and must be implemented despite their potential effects on public access or other desirable elements of the quality of the visitor experience.

## Principle 35: Managers must exercise their professional judgment in outdoor recreation management

Principle 17 suggests that recreation management should be as informed as possible, but there are inherent limits to our knowledge base at any point in time. After attempting in good faith to make reasonable efforts to inform themselves of the problems facing parks and outdoor recreation areas and the context in which they work, park and recreation managers must ultimately exercise their professional judgment. Unfortunately, there will rarely be perfect knowledge about the types of problems that exist in parks and their seriousness, the causes of these problems, and the effectiveness of alternative management practices. Nevertheless, managers should find courage in their knowledge of the burgeoning scientific and professional literature, the conceptual and management frameworks that have arisen, the inherently adaptive nature of park and outdoor recreation management, and in the responsibilities with which they have been entrusted. Management programs can be revisited and revised based on monitoring and advances in scientific and professional knowledge. Of course, management judgment should be as informed as possible by science and related considerations (Manning and Lawson, 2002). All of the case studies in Part II of this book are manifestations of the exercise of management judgment on the part of managers across a diverse set of national parks.

## Principle 36: A strong program of management is vital to maintaining the quality of parks and outdoor recreation

The contemporary management-by-objectives framework described in Chapter 1 and referenced in Principle 2 and Fig. 1.4 relies on development and implementation of a strong program of management. In fact, **management** constitutes the final component of this management-by-objectives framework (though the framework can also be seen as iterative and adaptive as described in Principle 3, relying on an ongoing program of monitoring and corresponding revisions and refinements in management). It is management (of park resources, visitors, and park facilities and services) that provides the necessary link between the visionary management objectives and associated indicators and standards of quality formulated at the beginning of the management-by-objectives framework, and the ultimate protection of park resources and the quality of the visitor experience. And it's management that must respond to the data derived from the periodic program of monitoring. For all of these reasons, management is vital to protecting park resources and the quality of the visitor experience.

The case studies included in Part II offer good examples of the ways in which strong programs of management have been designed and implemented in the national parks.

## Conclusion

Management of parks and outdoor recreation is a relatively new field of study. Demand for outdoor recreation in national parks and related areas began to expand dramatically in the post-World War II period, and research on outdoor recreation began in earnest in the 1960s. The field has made substantial progress in identifying and understanding the impacts of outdoor recreation, and associated problems and developing and testing a range of management practices.

This book reviews and synthesizes this scientific and professional literature and applies it in ways that can help guide management in systematic, comprehensive, and creative ways. A number of conceptual frameworks to help guide management of outdoor recreation have been developed in the professional literature, and are outlined in Chapter 1. Chapter 2 categorizes and describes the impacts and associated problems caused by outdoor recreation. Chapters 3 and 4 outline the range of strategies and practices available to manage outdoor recreation, along with a review of their effectiveness.

Chapter 5 and Appendices A1–A4 organize information on management problems and practices into a series of matrices that help guide systematic, comprehensive, and creative thinking about management. The chapters in Part II of the book offer a series of case studies that illustrate how a broad range of management problems are being successfully addressed in diverse units of the US national park system. These case studies use a wide range of management practices. Finally, this chapter builds on the first two parts of the book by suggesting a series of principles that might help to guide park and outdoor recreation management.

This book is designed to be both helpful and hopeful. While knowledge about outdoor recreation is far from perfect (and is never likely to approach this purely theoretical point), knowledge has advanced to the point that managers—in partnership with stakeholders and researchers where possible—should move ahead directly in managing parks and associated areas for outdoor recreation. Only in this way are park resources and the quality of the recreation experience likely to be protected for present and future generations. Outdoor recreation should be managed by design, not by default; perhaps that should be the most important principle of managing outdoor recreation. The case studies presented in Part II of this book are good models for the park and outdoor recreation profession.

# Appendix A   Management Practices

# Appendix A1    Management Practices for Limiting Use

## Problem: Impacts to Soil

### Strategy: Limit use

#### Information/Education

**1a.** Promote alternative sites (e.g. within park, other parks)
**1b.** Promote alternative times to use site/park (e.g. seasons when soil is not wet)
**1c.** Inform visitors of current impacts/conditions at site/park (e.g. soil compaction, erosion)

#### Rationing/Allocation

**2a.** Set capacity (for site, park) and allocate access by reservation system
**2b.** Set capacity (for site, park) and allocate access by queuing system
**2c.** Set capacity (for site, park) and allocate access by fee system
**2d.** Set capacity (for site, park) and allocate access by lottery system
**2e.** Set capacity (for site, park) and allocate access by merit system
**2f.** Implement differential fee system (e.g. temporally, spatially)

#### Rules/Regulations

**3a.** Set capacity and require a use permit
**3b.** Require a reservation for entry/use
**3c.** Require a fee for entry/use
**3d.** Require special knowledge/skills for entry/use
**3e.** Institute a maximum length of stay
**3f.** Limit group size
**3g.** Close site/park (e.g. temporarily, seasonally, permanently)

#### Law enforcement

**4a.** Establish presence of a uniformed ranger
**4b.** Require visitors to show a use permit
**4c.** Sanction (e.g. fine) visitors for unauthorized use

#### Zoning

**5a.** Zone site/park for lower use
**5b.** Zone site/park for no use

#### Facility development/Site design/Maintenance

**6a.** Set capacity (for site, park) and design visitor facilities (e.g. parking lots at trailheads) and services accordingly
**6b.** Make access to site/park more difficult (e.g. lower-standard roads, trails, transit)
**6c.** Improve access (e.g. higher-standard roads, trails, transit) to alternative sites/parks

## Problem: Impacts to Vegetation

### Strategy: Limit use

#### Information/Education

**7a.** Promote alternative sites (within park, other parks)
**7b.** Promote alternative times to use site/park (e.g. seasons)
**7c.** Inform visitors of current impacts/conditions (e.g. trampled vegetation) at site/park

#### Rationing/Allocation

**8a.** Set capacity (for site, park) and allocate access by reservation system
**8b.** Set capacity (for site, park) and allocate access by queuing system
**8c.** Set capacity (for site, park) and allocate access by fee system
**8d.** Set capacity (for site, park) and allocate access by lottery system
**8e.** Set capacity (for site, park) and allocate access by merit system
**8f.** Implement differential fee system (e.g. seasons)

### Rules/Regulations

**9a.** Set capacity (for site, park) and require a use permit
**9b.** Require a reservation for entry/use
**9c.** Require a fee for entry/use
**9d.** Require special knowledge/skills for entry/use
**9e.** Institute a maximum length of stay
**9f.** Limit group size

### Law enforcement

**10a.** Establish presence of a uniformed ranger
**10b.** Require visitors to show a use permit
**10c.** Sanction (e.g. fine) visitors for unauthorized use

### Zoning

**11a.** Zone site/park for lower use
**11b.** Zone site/park for no use

### Facility development/Site design/Maintenance

**12a.** Set capacity (for site, park) and design visitor facilities (e.g. parking lots) and services accordingly
**12b.** Make access to site/park more difficult (e.g. lower-standard roads, trails, transit)
**12c.** Improve access (e.g. higher-standard roads, trails, transit) to alternative sites/parks

## Problem: Impacts to Water

### Strategy: Limit use

#### Information/Education

**13a.** Promote alternative sites (e.g. within park, other parks)
**13b.** Promote alternative times to use site/park (e.g. seasons)
**13c.** Inform visitors of current impacts/conditions at site/park (e.g. polluted water)

#### Rationing/Allocation

**14a.** Set capacity (for site, park) and allocate access by reservation system
**14b.** Set capacity (for site, park) and allocate access by queuing system
**14c.** Set capacity (for site, park) and allocate access by fee system

**14d.** Set capacity (for site, park) and allocate access by lottery system
**14e.** Set capacity (for site, park) and allocate access by merit system
**14f.** Implement differential fee system (e.g. temporally, spatially)

### Rules/Regulations

**15a.** Set capacity (for site, park) and require a use permit
**15b.** Require a reservation for entry/use
**15c.** Require a fee for entry/use
**15d.** Require special knowledge/skills for entry/use
**15e.** Institute a maximum length of stay
**15f.** Limit group size
**15g.** Close site/park (e.g. temporarily, seasonally, permanently)

### Law enforcement

**16a.** Establish presence of a uniformed ranger
**16b.** Require visitors to show a use permit
**16c.** Sanction (e.g. fine) visitors for unauthorized use

### Zoning

**17a.** Zone site/park for lower use
**17b.** Zone site/park for no use

### Facility development/Site design/Maintenance

**18a.** Set capacity (for site, park) and design visitor facilities (e.g. parking lots) and services accordingly
**18b.** Make access to site/park more difficult (e.g. lower-standard roads, trails, transit)
**18c.** Improve access (e.g. higher-standard roads, trails, transit) to alternative sites/parks

## Problem: Impacts to Wildlife

### Strategy: Limit use

#### Information/Education

**19a.** Promote alternative sites (e.g. within park, other parks)
**19b.** Promote alternative times to use site/park (e.g. hours, days, seasons)
**19c.** Inform visitors of current impacts/conditions at site/park (e.g. threatened/endangered species, habituation)

### Rationing/Allocation

**20a.** Set capacity (for site, park) and allocate access by reservation system

**20b.** Set capacity (for site, park) and allocate access by queuing system

**20c.** Set capacity (for site, park) and allocate access by fee system

**20d.** Set capacity (for site, park) and allocate access by lottery system

**20e.** Set capacity (for site, park) and allocate access by merit system

**20f.** Implement differential fee system (e.g. temporally, spatially)

### Rules/Regulations

**21a.** Set capacity (for site, park) and require a use permit

**21b.** Require a reservation for entry/use

**21c.** Require a fee for entry/use

**21d.** Require special knowledge/skills for entry/use

**21e.** Institute a maximum length of stay

**21f.** Limit group size

**21g.** Prohibit recreation activities/uses with high impacts to wildlife (e.g. motorized uses)

**21h.** Close site/park (e.g. temporarily, seasonally, permanently)

### Law enforcement

**22a.** Require visitors to show a use permit

**22b.** Sanction (e.g. fine) visitors for unauthorized use

### Zoning

**23a.** Zone site/park for lower use

**23b.** Zone site/park for no use

### Facility development/Site design/Maintenance

**24a.** Set capacity (for site, park) and design visitor facilities (e.g. parking lots) and services accordingly

**24b.** Make access to site/park more difficult (e.g. lower-standard roads, trails, transit)

**24c.** Improve access (e.g. higher-standard roads, trails, transit) to alternative sites/parks

**24d.** Eliminate attractions/facilities/services in problem site/park

**24e.** Provide attractions/facilities/services in alternative sites (e.g. within park, other parks)

## Problem: Impacts to Air

### Strategy: Limit use

### Information/Education

**25a.** Promote alternative sites (e.g. within park, other parks)

**25b.** Promote alternative times to use site/park (e.g. seasons)

**25c.** Inform visitors of current impacts/conditions at site/park (e.g. polluted air)

### Rationing/Allocation

**26a.** Set capacity (for site, park) and allocate access by reservation system

**26b.** Set capacity (for site, park) and allocate access by queuing system

**26c.** Set capacity (for site, park) and allocate access by fee system

**26d.** Set capacity (for site, park) and allocate access by lottery system

**26e.** Set capacity (for site, park) and allocate access by merit system

**26f.** Implement differential fee system (e.g. temporally, spatially)

### Rules/Regulations

**27a.** Set capacity (for site, park) and require a use permit

**27b.** Require a reservation for entry/use

**27c.** Require a fee for entry/use

**27d.** Require special knowledge/skills for entry/use

**27e.** Institute a maximum length of stay

**27f.** Limit group size

**27g.** Close site/park (e.g. temporarily, seasonally, permanently)

### Law enforcement

**28a.** Establish presence of a uniformed ranger

**28b.** Require visitors to show a use permit

**28c.** Sanction (e.g. fine) visitors for unauthorized use

### Zoning

**29a.** Zone site/park for lower use

**29b.** Zone site/park for no use

### Facility development/Site design/Maintenance

**30a.** Set capacity (for site, park) and design visitor facilities (e.g. parking lots) and services accordingly
**30b.** Make access to site/park more difficult (e.g. lower-standard roads, trails, transit)
**30c.** Improve access (e.g. higher-standard roads, trails, transit) to alternative sites/parks

## Problem: Impacts to Natural Quiet

### Strategy: Limit use

#### Information/Education

**31a.** Promote alternative areas (e.g. within park, other parks)
**31b.** Promote alternative times to use area (e.g. hours, days, seasons)
**31c.** Inform visitors of current impacts/conditions (e.g. prevalence of anthropogenic noise)

#### Rationing/Allocation

**32a.** Set capacity and allocate access by reservation system
**32b.** Set capacity and allocate access by queuing system
**32c.** Set capacity and allocate access by fee system
**32d.** Set capacity and allocate access by lottery system
**32e.** Set capacity and allocate access by merit system
**32f.** Implement differential fee system (e.g. temporally, spatially)

#### Rules/Regulations

**33a.** Set capacity and require a use permit
**33b.** Require a reservation for entry/use
**33c.** Require a fee for entry/use
**33d.** Require special knowledge/skills for entry/use
**33e.** Institute a maximum length of stay
**33f.** Close area (e.g. temporarily, seasonally, permanently)

#### Law enforcement

**34a.** Establish presence of a uniformed ranger
**34b.** Require visitors to show a use permit
**34c.** Sanction (e.g. fine) visitors for unauthorized use

### Zoning

**35a.** Zone site/park for lower use
**35b.** Zone site/park for no use

### Facility development/Site design/Maintenance

**36a.** Set capacity (for site, park) and design visitor facilities (e.g. parking lots at trailheads) and services accordingly
**36b.** Make access more difficult (e.g. lower-standard roads, trails, transit)
**36c.** Improve access (e.g. higher-standard roads, trails, transit) to alternative sites/parks

## Problem: Impacts to Natural Darkness

### Strategy: Limit use

#### Information/Education

**37a.** Promote alternative areas (e.g. within park, other parks)
**37b.** Promote alternative times to use area (e.g. days, seasons)
**37c.** Inform visitors of current impacts/conditions (e.g. light pollution/reduced visibility of stars)

#### Rationing/Allocation

**38a.** Set capacity (for site, park) and allocate access by reservation system
**38b.** Set capacity (for site, park) and allocate access by queuing system
**38c.** Set capacity (for site, park) and allocate access by fee system
**38d.** Set capacity (for site, park) and allocate access by lottery system
**38e.** Set capacity (for site, park) and allocate access by merit system
**38f.** Implement differential fee system (e.g. temporally, spatially)

#### Rules/Regulations

**39a.** Set capacity (for site, park) and require a use permit
**39b.** Require a reservation for entry/use
**39c.** Require a fee for entry/use
**39d.** Require special knowledge/skills for entry/use
**39e.** Institute a maximum length of stay

**39f.** Limit group size
**39g.** Close site/park (e.g. temporarily, seasonally, permanently)

### Law enforcement

**40a.** Establish presence of a uniformed ranger
**40b.** Require visitors to show a use permit
**40c.** Sanction (e.g. fine) visitors for unauthorized use

### Zoning

**41a.** Zone site/park for lower use
**41b.** Zone site/park for no use

### Facility development/Site design/Maintenance

**42a.** Set capacity for site/park and design visitor facilities (e.g. parking lots) and services accordingly
**42b.** Make access to site/park more difficult (e.g. lower-standard roads, trails, transit)
**42c.** Improve access (e.g. higher-standard roads, trails, transit) to alternative sites/parks

## Problem: Impacts to Historical/Cultural Resources

### Strategy: Limit use

#### Information/Education

**43a.** Promote alternative sites (e.g. within park, other parks)
**43b.** Promote alternative times to use site/park (e.g. hours, days, seasons)
**43c.** Inform visitors of current impacts/conditions at site/park (e.g. deterioration of historic buildings, loss of cultural artifacts)

#### Rationing/Allocation

**44a.** Set capacity (for site, park) and allocate access by reservation system
**44b.** Set capacity (for site, park) and allocate access by queuing system
**44c.** Set capacity (for site, park) and allocate access by fee system
**44d.** Set capacity (for site, park) and allocate access by lottery system
**44e.** Set capacity (for site, park) and allocate access by merit system
**44f.** Implement differential fee system (e.g. temporally, spatially)

### Rules/Regulations

**45a.** Set capacity (for site, park) and require a use permit
**45b.** Require a reservation for entry/use
**45c.** Require a fee for entry/use
**45d.** Require special knowledge/skills for entry/use
**45e.** Institute a maximum length of stay
**45f.** Limit group size
**45g.** Close site/park (e.g. temporarily, permanently)

### Law enforcement

**46a.** Establish presence of a uniformed ranger
**46b.** Require visitors to show a use permit
**46c.** Sanction (e.g. fine) visitors for unauthorized use

### Zoning

**47a.** Zone site/park for lower use
**47b.** Zone site/park for no use

### Facility development/Site design/Maintenance

**48a.** Set capacity (for site, park) and design visitor facilities (e.g. parking lots) and services accordingly
**48b.** Make access to site/park more difficult (e.g. lower-standard roads, trails, transit)
**48c.** Improve access (e.g. higher-standard roads, trails, transit) to alternative sites (within park, other parks)

## Problem: Crowding

### Strategy: Limit use

#### Information/Education

**49a.** Promote alternative sites (e.g. within park, other parks)
**49b.** Promote alternative times to use site/park (e.g. hours, days, seasons)
**49c.** Inform visitors of current impacts/conditions at site/park (e.g. crowding)

#### Rationing/Allocation

**50a.** Set capacity (for site, park) and allocate access by reservation system
**50b.** Set capacity (for site, park) and allocate access by queuing system

**50c.** Set capacity (for site, park) and allocate access by fee system
**50d.** Set capacity (for site, park) and allocate access by lottery system
**50e.** Set capacity (for site, park) and allocate access by merit system
**50f.** Implement differential fee system (e.g. temporally, spatially)

### Rules/Regulations

**51a.** Set capacity (for site, park) and require a use permit
**51b.** Require a reservation for entry/use
**51c.** Require a fee for entry/use
**51d.** Require special knowledge/skills for entry/use
**51e.** Institute a maximum length of stay
**51f.** Limit group size
**51g.** Prohibit selected activities/uses (e.g. activities/uses with high resource and/or social impacts)
**51h.** Close site/park (e.g. temporally, seasonally, permanently)

### Law enforcement

**52a.** Establish presence of a uniformed ranger
**52b.** Require visitors to show a use permit
**52c.** Sanction (e.g. warn, fine) visitors for unauthorized use

### Zoning

**53a.** Zone site/park for lower use
**53b.** Zone site/park for no use

### Facility development/Site design/Maintenance

**54a.** Set capacity (for site, park) and design visitor facilities (e.g. parking lots) and services accordingly
**54b.** Make access to site/park more difficult (e.g. lower-standard roads, trails, transit)
**54c.** Improve access (e.g. higher-standard roads, trails, transit) to alternative sites (within park, other parks)
**54d.** Eliminate attractions/facilities/services at problem site/park
**54e.** Provide attractions/facilities/services at alternative sites (e.g. within park, other parks)

## Problem: Conflict

### Strategy: Limit use

#### Information/Education

**55a.** Promote alternative sites (e.g. within park, other parks)
**55b.** Promote alternative times to use site/park (e.g. hours, days, seasons)
**55c.** Inform visitors of current impacts/conditions (e.g. conflict among uses/groups)

### Rationing/Allocation

**56a.** Set capacity (for site, park) and allocate access by reservation system
**56b.** Set capacity (for site, park) and allocate access by queuing system
**56c.** Set capacity (for site, park) and allocate access by fee system
**56d.** Set capacity (for site, park) and allocate access by lottery system
**56e.** Set capacity (for site, park) and allocate access by merit system
**56f.** Implement differential fee system (e.g. temporally, spatially)

### Rules/Regulations

**57a.** Set capacity (for site, park) and require a use permit
**57b.** Require a reservation for entry/use
**57c.** Require a fee for entry/use
**57d.** Require special knowledge/skills for entry/use
**57e.** Institute a maximum length of stay
**57f.** Limit group size
**57g.** Prohibit selected activities/uses (e.g. activities/uses with high resource and/or social impacts)
**57h.** Close site/park (temporarily, seasonally, permanently)

### Law enforcement

**58a.** Establish presence of a uniformed ranger
**58b.** Require visitors to show a use permit
**58c.** Sanction (e.g. fine) visitors for unauthorized use

### Zoning

**59a.** Zone site/park for lower use
**59b.** Zone site/park for no use

### Facility development/Site design/Maintenance

**60a.** Set capacity for site/park and design visitor facilities (e.g. parking lots) and services accordingly
**60b.** Make access to site/park more difficult (e.g. lower-standard roads, trails, transit)
**60c.** Improve access (e.g. higher-standard roads, trails, transit) to alternative sites/parks
**60d.** Eliminate attractions/facilities/services at problem site
**60e.** Provide attractions/facilities/services at alternative sites (e.g. within park, other parks)

## Problem: Depreciative Behavior
### Strategy: Limit use
#### Information/Education

**61a.** Promote alternative sites (e.g. within park, other parks)
**61b.** Promote alternative times to use site/park (e.g. hours, days, seasons)
**61c.** Inform visitors of current impacts/conditions at site/park (e.g. litter, vandalism)

#### Rationing/Allocation

**62a.** Set capacity (for site, park) and allocate access by reservation system
**62b.** Set capacity (for site, park) and allocate access by queuing system
**62c.** Set capacity (for site, park) and allocate access by fee system
**62d.** Set capacity (for site, park) and allocate access by lottery system
**62e.** Set capacity (for site, park) and allocate access by merit system
**62f.** Implement differential fee system (e.g. temporally, spatially)

#### Rules/Regulations

**63a.** Set capacity (for site, park) and require a use permit
**63b.** Require a reservation for entry/use
**63c.** Require a fee for entry/use
**63d.** Require special knowledge/skills for entry/use
**63e.** Require visitors to show a use permit
**63f.** Institute a maximum length of stay
**63g.** Limit group size
**63h.** Close site/park (e.g. temporarily, seasonally, permanently)

### Law enforcement

**64a.** Establish presence of a uniformed ranger
**64b.** Require visitors to show a use permit
**64c.** Sanction (e.g. fine) visitors for unauthorized use

### Zoning

**65a.** Zone site/park for lower use
**65b.** Zone site/park for no use

### Facility development/Site design/Maintenance

**66a.** Set capacity (for site, park) and design visitor facilities (e.g. parking lots) and services accordingly
**66b.** Make access to site/park more difficult (e.g. lower-standard roads, trails, transit)
**66c.** Improve access (e.g. higher-standard roads, trails, transit) to alternative sites (within park, other parks)

## Problem: Impacts to Attraction Sites
### Strategy: Limit use
#### Information/Education

**67a.** Promote alternative attraction sites (e.g. within park, other parks)
**67b.** Promote alternative times to visit attraction site/park (e.g. hours, days, seasons)
**67c.** Inform visitors of current impacts/conditions at attraction site (e.g. impacts to resources, crowding)

#### Rationing/Allocation

**68a.** Set capacity (for attraction site, park) and allocate access by reservation system
**68b.** Set capacity (for attraction site, park) and allocate access by queuing system
**68c.** Set capacity (for attraction site, park) and allocate access by fee system
**68d.** Set capacity (for attraction site, park) and allocate access by lottery system
**68e.** Set capacity (for attraction site, park) and allocate access by merit system
**68f.** Implement differential fee system (e.g. temporally, spatially)

#### Rules/Regulations

**69a.** Set capacity (for attraction site, park) and require a use permit
**69b.** Require a reservation for entry/use
**69c.** Require a fee for entry/use

**69d.** Require special knowledge/skills for entry/use
**69e.** Institute a maximum length of stay
**69f.** Limit group size
**69g.** Prohibit selected activities/uses (e.g. activities/uses with high resource and/or social impacts)
**69h.** Close attraction site/park (e.g. temporarily, seasonally, permanently)

### Law enforcement

**70a.** Establish presence of a uniformed ranger
**70b.** Require visitors to show a use permit
**70c.** Sanction (e.g. fine) visitors for unauthorized use

### Zoning

**71a.** Zone attraction site/park for lower use
**71b.** Zone attraction site/park for no use

### Facility development/Site design/Maintenance

**72a.** Set capacity (for attraction site, park) and design visitor facilities (e.g. parking lots) and services accordingly
**72b.** Make access to attraction site/park more difficult (e.g. lower-standard roads, trails, transit)
**72c.** Improve access (e.g. higher-standard roads, trails, transit) to alternative attraction sites/parks
**72d.** Eliminate attractions/facilities/services at problem attraction site/park
**72e.** Provide attractions/facilities/services at alternative attraction sites (e.g. within park, other parks)

## Problem: Impacts to Trails
### Strategy: Limit use
#### Information/Education

**73a.** Promote alternative trails (e.g. within park, other parks)
**73b.** Promote alternative times to use trails (e.g. hours, days, seasons)
**73c.** Inform visitors of current impacts/conditions on trails (e.g. soil erosion, crowding)

#### Rationing/Allocation

**74a.** Set capacity (for trail, trail system) and allocate access by reservation system
**74b.** Set capacity (for trail, trail system) and allocate access by queuing system
**74c.** Set capacity (for trail, trail system) and allocate access by fee system
**74d.** Set capacity (for trail, trail system) and allocate access by lottery system
**74e.** Set capacity (for trail, trail system) and allocate access by merit system
**74f.** Implement differential fee system (e.g. temporally, spatially)

### Rules/Regulations

**75a.** Set capacity (for trail, trail system) and require a use permit
**75b.** Require a reservation for entry/use
**75c.** Require a fee for entry/use
**75d.** Require special knowledge/skills for entry/use
**75e.** Institute a maximum length of stay
**75f.** Close trail/trail system (temporarily, seasonally, permanently)

### Law enforcement

**76a.** Establish presence of a uniformed ranger
**76b.** Require visitors to show a use permit
**76c.** Sanction (e.g. fine) visitors for unauthorized use

### Zoning

**77a.** Zone trail/trail system for lower use
**77b.** Zone trail/trail system for no use

### Facility development/Site design/Maintenance

**78a.** Set capacity (for trail, trail system) and design visitor facilities (e.g. parking lots at trailheads) and services accordingly
**78b.** Make access to trail/trail system more difficult (e.g. lower-standard roads, trails, transit)
**78c.** Improve access (e.g. higher-standard roads, trails, transit) to alternative trails/trail systems (within park, other parks)

## Problem: Impacts to Campgrounds/Campsites
### Strategy: Limit use
#### Information/Education

**79a.** Promote alternative campgrounds/campsites (e.g. within park, other parks)
**79b.** Promote alternative times to use campgrounds/campsites (e.g. days, seasons)

**79c.** Inform visitors of current impacts/conditions at campground/campsites (e.g. resource degradation, crowding)

### Rationing/Allocation

**80a.** Set capacity (for campground, campsites) and allocate access by reservation system
**80b.** Set capacity (for campground, campsites) and allocate access by queuing system
**80c.** Set capacity (for campground, campsites) and allocate access by fee system
**80d.** Set capacity (for campground, campsites) and allocate access by lottery system
**80e.** Set capacity (for campground, campsites) and allocate access by merit system
**80f.** Implement differential fee system (e.g. temporally, spatially)

### Rules/Regulations

**81a.** Set capacity (for campground, campsites) and require a use permit
**81b.** Require a reservation for use
**81c.** Require a fee for use
**81d.** Require special knowledge/skills for use
**81e.** Institute a maximum length of stay
**81f.** Limit group size
**81g.** Close area (e.g. temporarily, seasonally, permanently)

### Law enforcement

**82a.** Establish presence of a uniformed ranger
**82b.** Require visitors to show a use permit
**82c.** Sanction (e.g. fine) visitors for unauthorized use

### Zoning

**83a.** Zone campground/campsite for lower use
**83b.** Zone campground/campsite for no use

### Facility development/Site design/Maintenance

**84a.** Set capacity (for campground, campsites) and design visitor facilities (e.g. parking lots) and services accordingly
**84b.** Make access to campground/campsites more difficult (e.g. lower-standard roads, trails, transit)
**84c.** Improve access (e.g. higher-standard roads, trails, transit) to alternative campgrounds/campsites (within park, other parks)

## Problem: Impacts to Roads/Parking
### Strategy: Limit use
#### Information/Education

**85a.** Promote alternative roads/parking areas (e.g. within park, other parks)
**85b.** Promote alternative times to use roads/parking areas (e.g. hours, days, seasons)
**85c.** Inform visitors of current impacts/conditions (e.g. traffic congestion, lack of parking) on roads/parking areas

### Rationing/Allocation

**86a.** Set capacity (for roads, parking areas) and allocate access by reservation system
**86b.** Set capacity (for roads, parking areas) and allocate access by queuing system
**86c.** Set capacity (for roads, parking areas) and allocate access by fee system
**86d.** Set capacity (for roads, parking areas) and allocate access by lottery system
**86e.** Set capacity (for roads, parking areas) and allocate access by merit system
**86f.** Implement differential fee system (e.g. temporally, spatially)

### Rules/Regulations

**87a.** Set capacity (for roads, parking areas) and require a use permit
**87b.** Require a reservation for entry/use
**87c.** Require a fee for entry/use
**87d.** Require special knowledge for entry/use
**87e.** Institute a maximum length of stay
**87f.** Limit group size
**87g.** Close roads/parking areas (e.g. temporarily, seasonally, permanently)

### Law enforcement

**88a.** Establish presence of a uniformed ranger
**88b.** Require visitors to show a use permit
**88c.** Sanction (e.g. fine) visitors for unauthorized use

### Zoning

**89a.** Zone roads/parking areas for lower use
**89b.** Zone roads/parking areas for no use

### Facility development/Site design/Maintenance

**90a.** Set capacity (for road, parking areas) and design visitor facilities (e.g. parking lots) and services accordingly

**90b.** Make access to road/parking area more difficult (e.g. lower-standard roads, trails, transit)

**90c.** Improve access (e.g. higher-standard roads, trails, transit) to alternative roads/parking areas (within park, other parks)

## Problem: Impacts to Interpretive Facilities/Programs

### Strategy: Limit use

#### Information/Education

**91a.** Promote alternative interpretive facilities/programs (e.g. within park, other parks)

**91b.** Promote alternative times to participate in interpretive facilities/programs (e.g. hours, days, seasons)

**91c.** Inform visitors of current impacts/conditions at interpretive facilities/programs (e.g. crowding, shortage of tickets)

#### Rationing/Allocation

**92a.** Set capacity interpretive facilities/programs and allocate access by reservation system

**92b.** Set capacity for interpretive facilities/programs and allocate access by queuing system

**92c.** Set capacity for interpretive facilities/programs and allocate access by fee system

**92d.** Set capacity for interpretive facilities/programs and allocate access by lottery system

**92e.** Set capacity for interpretive facilities/programs and allocate access by merit system

**92f.** Implement differential fee system (e.g. temporally, spatially)

### Rules/Regulations

**93a.** Set capacity for interpretive facilities/programs and require a use permit/ticket

**93b.** Require a reservation for interpretive facilities/programs

**93c.** Require a fee for interpretive facilities/programs

**93d.** Require special knowledge/skills for interpretive facilities/programs

**93e.** Institute a maximum length of stay

**93f.** Limit group size

**93g.** Close interpretive facilities/programs (e.g. temporally, seasonally, permanently)

### Law enforcement

**94a.** Establish presence of a uniformed ranger

**94b.** Require visitors to show a use permit/ticket

**94c.** Sanction (e.g. fine) visitors for unauthorized use

### Zoning

**95.** Zone interpretive facilities/programs for lower use

### Facility development/Site design/Maintenance

**96a.** Set capacity of interpretive facilities/programs and design visitor facilities (e.g. parking lots) and services (interpretive rangers) accordingly

**96b.** Make access to interpretive facilities/programs more difficult (e.g. lower-standard roads, trails, transit)

**96c.** Improve access (e.g. higher-standard roads, trails, transit) to alternative interpretive facilities/programs (within park, other parks)

# Appendix A2 Management Practices for Increasing Supply

## Problem: Impacts to Soil

### Strategy: Increase supply

#### Information/Education

**1a.** Inform visitors of the range of recreation areas and opportunities available
**1b.** Promote use of low-use areas

#### Rationing/Allocation

2. Not applicable

#### Rules/Regulations

3. Extend time that area is open to visitor use (hour, days, seasons)

#### Law enforcement

4. Not applicable

#### Zoning

5. Zone alternative areas for higher use

#### Facility development/Site design/Maintenance

**6a.** Improve attractions, facilities, services in alternative areas
**6b.** Develop attractions, facilities, services in new areas
**6c.** Improve access to new/alternative areas

## Problem: Impacts to Vegetation

### Strategy: Increase supply

#### Information/Education

**7a.** Inform visitors of the range of recreation areas and opportunities available
**7b.** Promote use of low-use areas

#### Rationing/Allocation

8. Not applicable

#### Rules/Regulations

9. Extend time that area is open to visitor use (hours, days, seasons)

#### Law enforcement

10. Not applicable

#### Zoning

11. Zone alternative areas for higher use

#### Facility development/Site design/Maintenance

**12a.** Improve attractions, facilities, services in alternative areas
**12b.** Develop attractions, facilities, services in new areas
**12c.** Improve access to new/alternative areas

## Problem: Impacts to Water

### Strategy: Increase supply

#### Information/Education

**13a.** Inform visitors of the range of recreation areas and opportunities available
**13b.** Promote use of low-use areas

#### Rationing/Allocation

14. Not applicable

#### Rules/Regulations

15. Extend time that area is open to visitor use (hours, days, seasons)

### Law enforcement

**16.** Not applicable

### Zoning

**17.** Zone alternative areas for higher use

### Facility development/Site design/Maintenance

**18a.** Improve attractions, facilities, services in alternative areas
**18b.** Develop attractions, facilities, services in new areas
**18c.** Improve access to new/alternative areas

## Problem: Impacts to Wildlife
### Strategy: Increase supply
### Information/Education

**19a.** Inform visitors of the range of recreation areas and opportunities available
**19b.** Promote use of low-use areas
**19c.** Promote visitor behavior that will increase wildlife (e.g. don't approach wildlife too closely)

### Rationing/Allocation

**20.** Not applicable

### Rules/Regulations

**21a.** Extend time that area is open to visitor use (hours, days, seasons)
**21b.** Require visitors to adopt behavior that will increase wildlife (e.g. visitors must not approach wildlife too closely)

### Law enforcement

**22a.** Establish presence of a uniformed ranger
**22b.** Sanction (e.g. fine) visitors for violating rules (e.g. approaching wildlife too closely)

### Zoning

**23.** Zone alternative areas for higher use

### Facility development/Site design/Maintenance

**24a.** Improve attractions, facilities, services in alternative areas
**24b.** Develop attractions, facilities, services in new areas
**24c.** Improve access to new/alternative areas
**24d.** Design facilities that will encourage increased wildlife presence (e.g. wildlife viewing blinds)

## Problem: Impacts to Air
### Strategy: Increase supply
### Information/Education

**25a.** Inform visitors of the range of recreation areas and opportunities available
**25b.** Promote use of low-use areas

### Rationing/Allocation

**26.** Not applicable

### Rules/Regulations

**27.** Extend time that area is open to visitor use (hours, days, seasons)

### Law enforcement

**28.** Not applicable

### Zoning

**29.** Zone alternative areas for higher use

### Facility development/Site design/Maintenance

**30a.** Improve attractions, facilities, services in alternative areas
**30b.** Develop attractions, facilities, services in new areas
**30c.** Improve access to new/alternative areas

## Problem: Impacts to Natural Quiet
### Strategy: Increase supply
### Information/Education

**31a.** Inform visitors of the range of recreation areas and opportunities available
**31b.** Promote use of low-use areas
**31c.** Educate visitors about natural quiet
**31d.** Promote visitor behavior that reduces human-caused noise

### Rationing/Allocation

**32.** Not applicable

### Rules/Regulations

**33a.** Extend time that area is open to visitor use (hours, days, seasons)
**33b.** Require visitors to reduce noise

### Law enforcement

**34a.** Establish presence of a uniformed ranger
**34b.** Sanction (e.g. fine) visitors for making unacceptable noise

### Zoning

**35a.** Zone alternative areas for higher use
**35b.** Zone areas for natural quiet

### Facility development/Site design/Maintenance

**36a.** Improve attractions, facilities, services in alternative areas
**36b.** Develop attractions, facilities, services in new areas
**36c.** Improve access to new/alternative areas
**36d.** Design facilities to reduce visitor-caused noise (e.g. use vegetative screening)

## Problem: Impacts to Natural Darkness

### Strategy: Increase supply

#### Information/Education

**37a.** Inform visitors of the range of recreation areas and opportunities available
**37b.** Promote use of low-use areas
**37c.** Educate visitors about the importance of night skies
**37d.** Promote visitor behavior designed to protect night sky viewing (e.g. no lights after 10:00 PM)

### Rationing/Allocation

**38.** Not applicable

### Rules/Regulations

**39a.** Extend time that area is open to visitor use (hours, days, seasons)
**39b.** Require visitors to adopt behaviors that protect night sky viewing (e.g. no lights after 10:00 pm)

### Law enforcement

**40a.** Establish a uniformed ranger presence
**40b.** Sanction (e.g. fine) visitors for behavior that degrades night sky viewing (e.g. using lights after 10:00 pm)

### Zoning

**41a.** Zone alternative areas for higher use
**41b.** Zone areas for night sky viewing

### Facility development/Site design/Maintenance

**42a.** Improve attractions, facilities, services in alternative areas
**42b.** Develop attractions, facilities, services in new areas
**42c.** Improve access to new/alternative areas
**42d.** Design facilities and services that reduce light pollution (e.g. use lighting that minimizes glare)

## Problem: Impacts to Historical/Cultural Resources

### Strategy: Increase supply

#### Information/Education

**43a.** Inform visitors of the range of recreation areas and opportunities available
**43b.** Promote use of low-use areas

### Rationing/Allocation

**44.** Not applicable

### Rules/Regulations

**45.** Extend time that area is open to visitor use (hours, days, seasons)

### Law enforcement

**46.** Not applicable

### Zoning

**47.** Zone alternative areas for higher use

### Facility development/Site design/Maintenance

**48a.** Improve attractions, facilities, services in alternative areas
**48b.** Develop attractions, facilities, services in new areas
**48c.** Improve access to new/alternative areas

## Problem: Crowding

### Strategy: Increase supply

#### Information/Education

**49a.** Inform visitors of the range of recreation areas and opportunities available
**49b.** Promote use of low-use areas

#### Rationing/Allocation

**50.** Not applicable

#### Rules/Regulations

**51.** Extend time that area is open to visitor use (hours, days, seasons)

#### Law enforcement

**52.** Not applicable

#### Zoning

**53.** Zone alternative areas for higher use

#### Facility development/Site design/Maintenance

**54a.** Improve attractions, facilities, services in alternative areas
**54b.** Develop attractions, facilities, services in new areas
**54c.** Improve access to new/alternative areas

## Problem: Conflict

### Strategy: Increase supply

#### Information/Education

**55a.** Inform visitors of the range of recreation areas and opportunities available
**55b.** Promote use of low-use areas
**55c.** Educate visitors about the potential for conflict
**55d.** Promote behavior that reduces conflict (e.g. educate visitors about behaviors that can cause conflict)

#### Rationing/Allocation

**56.** Not applicable

#### Rules/Regulations

**57a.** Extend time that area is open to visitor use (hours, days, seasons)
**57b.** Prohibit activities/behavior that causes conflict (e.g. boisterous behavior)

#### Law enforcement

**58a.** Establish presence of a uniformed ranger
**58b.** Sanction (e.g. fine) visitors for behavior that causes conflict (e.g. boisterous behavior)

#### Zoning

**59a.** Zone alternative areas for higher use
**59b.** Zone areas to separate conflicting uses

#### Facility development/Site design/Maintenance

**60a.** Improve attractions, facilities, services in alternative areas
**60b.** Develop attractions, facilities, services in new areas
**60c.** Improve access to new/alternative areas

## Problem: Depreciative Behavior

### Strategy: Increase supply

#### Information/Education

**61a.** Inform visitors of the range of recreation areas and opportunities available
**61b.** Promote use of low-use areas
**61c.** Educate visitors about inappropriate activities/behaviors (e.g. carry out all trash)
**61d.** Promote appropriate visitor behavior (e.g. carry out all trash)

#### Rationing/Allocation

**62.** Not applicable

#### Rules/Regulations

**63a.** Extend time that area is open to visitor use (hours, days, seasons)
**63b.** Require visitors to refrain from depreciative behaviors (e.g. don't litter)

### Law enforcement

**64a.** Establish presence of a uniformed ranger
**64b.** Sanction (e.g. fine) visitors for depreciative behavior (e.g. littering)

### Zoning

**65.** Zone alternative areas for higher use

### Facility development/Site design/Maintenance

**66a.** Improve attractions, facilities, services in alternative areas
**66b.** Develop attractions, facilities, services in new areas
**66c.** Improve access to new/alternative areas
**66d.** Design facilities that are resistant to depreciative behavior (e.g. use surfaces that are resistant to graffiti)
**66e.** Maintain areas in good condition (e.g. remove graffiti)

## Problem: Attraction Sites

### Strategy: Increase supply

#### Information/Education

**67a.** Inform visitors of the range of recreation areas and opportunities available
**67b.** Promote use of low-use areas

#### Rationing/Allocation

**68.** Not applicable

#### Rules/Regulations

**69.** Extend time that area is open to visitor use (hours, days, seasons)

#### Law enforcement

**70.** Not applicable

#### Zoning

**71.** Zone alternative areas for higher use

### Facility development/Site design/Maintenance

**72a.** Improve attractions, facilities, services in alternative areas
**72b.** Develop attractions, facilities, services in new areas
**72c.** Improve access to new/alternative areas

## Problem: Trails

### Strategy: Increase supply

#### Information/Education

**73a.** Inform visitors of the range of recreation areas and opportunities available
**73b.** Promote use of low-use areas

#### Rationing/Allocation

**74.** Not applicable

#### Rules/Regulations

**75.** Extend time that area is open to visitor use (hours, days, seasons)

#### Law enforcement

**76.** Not applicable

#### Zoning

**77.** Zone alternative areas for higher use

#### Facility development/Site design/Maintenance

**78a.** Improve attractions, facilities, services in alternative areas
**78b.** Develop attractions, facilities, services in new areas
**78c.** Improve access to new/alternative areas

## Problem: Campgrounds/Campsites

### Strategy: Increase supply

#### Information/Education

**79a.** Inform visitors of the range of recreation areas and opportunities available
**79b.** Promote use of low-use areas

#### Rationing/Allocation

**80.** Not applicable

### Rules/Regulations

**81.** Extend time that area is open to visitor use (hours, days, seasons)

### Law enforcement

**82.** Not applicable

### Zoning

**83.** Zone alternative areas for higher use

### Facility development/Site design/Maintenance

**84a.** Improve attractions, facilities, services in alternative areas
**84b.** Develop attractions, facilities, services in new areas
**84c.** Improve access to new/alternative areas

## Problem: Roads/Parking

### Strategy: Increase supply

#### Information/Education

**85a.** Inform visitors of the range of recreation areas and opportunities available
**85b.** Promote use of low-use areas

#### Rationing/Allocation

**86.** Not applicable

#### Rules/Regulations

**87.** Extend time that area is open to visitor use (hours, days, seasons)

#### Law enforcement

**88.** Not applicable

### Zoning

**89.** Zone alternative areas for higher use

### Facility development/Site design/Maintenance

**90a.** Improve attractions, facilities, services in alternative areas
**90b.** Develop attractions, facilities, services in new areas
**90c.** Improve access to new/alternative areas

## Problem: Interpretive Facilities/Programs

### Strategy: Increase supply

#### Information/Education

**91a.** Inform visitors of the range of recreation areas and opportunities available
**91b.** Promote use of low-use areas

#### Rationing/Allocation

**92.** Not applicable

#### Rules/Regulations

**93.** Extend time that area is open to visitor use (hours, days, seasons)

#### Law enforcement

**94.** Not applicable

#### Zoning

**95.** Zone alternative areas for higher use

### Facility development/Site design/Maintenance

**96a.** Improve attractions, facilities, services in alternative areas.
**96b.** Develop attractions, facilities, services in new areas
**96c.** Improve access to new/alternative areas

# Appendix A3 Management Practices for Reducing the Impact of Use

## Problem: Impacts to Soil

### Strategy: Reduce the impact of use

#### Information/Education

**1a.** Promote alternative sites (e.g. within park, other parks) to disperse use
**1b.** Promote alternative times to use site (e.g. seasons when soils are not wet)
**1c.** Promote resistant/hardened sites to concentrate use
**1d.** Inform visitors of acceptable and unacceptable recreation activities (e.g. pedestrian use only, no motorized uses)
**1e.** Inform visitors of acceptable and unacceptable behavior (e.g. Leave No Trace program, stay on designated trails)
**1f.** Educate visitors about why selected behaviors are unacceptable (e.g. walking off-trail can compact fragile soil)

#### Rationing/Allocation

**2.** Not applicable

#### Rules/Regulations

**3a.** Prohibit high-impact uses (e.g. no motorized activities)
**3b.** Prohibit high-impact behavior (e.g. no walking off-trail)
**3c.** Limit group size

#### Law enforcement

**4a.** Establish presence of a uniformed ranger
**4b.** Sanction (e.g. warn, fine) visitors for inappropriate use/behavior (e.g. walking off-trail)

#### Zoning

**5a.** Zone area for low-impact uses only (e.g. pedestrian use only)

#### Facility development/Site design/Maintenance

**6a.** Provide facilities/services for low-impact uses only (e.g. pedestrian use only)
**6b.** Locate/concentrate facilities and services on impact-resistant soil
**6c.** Design facilities and services to minimize impact (e.g. install waterbars along trail)
**6d.** Maintain facilities to minimize impact (e.g. clear waterbars regularly)

## Problem: Impacts to Vegetation

### Strategy: Reduce the impact of use

#### Information/Education

**7a.** Promote alternative sites (e.g. within park, other parks) to disperse use
**7b.** Promote alternative times to use site (e.g. seasons when vegetation is less fragile)
**7c.** Promote resistant/hardened sites to concentrate use
**7d.** Inform visitors of acceptable and unacceptable recreation activities (e.g. pedestrian use only, no motorized uses)
**7e.** Inform visitors of acceptable and unacceptable behavior (e.g. Leave No Trace program, stay on designated trails)
**7f.** Educate visitors about why selected behaviors are unacceptable (e.g. walking off-trail can trample fragile vegetation)

#### Rationing/Allocation

**8.** Not applicable

#### Rules/Regulations

**9a.** Prohibit high-impact uses (e.g. no motorized activities)
**9b.** Prohibit high-impact behavior (e.g. no walking off-trail)
**9c.** Limit group size

### Law enforcement

**10a.** Establish presence of a uniformed ranger
**10b.** Sanction (e.g. warn, fine) visitors for inappropriate use/behavior (e.g. walking off-trail)

### Zoning

**11a.** Zone area for low-impact uses only (e.g. pedestrian use only)

### Facility development/Site design/Maintenance

**12a.** Provide facilities/services for low-impact uses only (e.g. pedestrian use only)
**12b.** Locate/concentrate facilities and services on impact-resistant vegetation
**12c.** Design facilities and services to minimize impact (e.g. install barriers along margins of trail)
**12d.** Maintain facilities to minimize impact (e.g. clear waterbars regularly)

## Problem: Impacts to Water

### Strategy: Reduce impact of use

#### Information/Education

**13a.** Promote alternative sites (e.g. within park, other parks) to disperse use
**13b.** Promote alternative times to use site (e.g. seasons when water levels are low)
**13c.** Promote resistant/hardened sites to concentrate use
**13d.** Inform visitors of acceptable and unacceptable recreation activities (e.g. no motorized uses)
**13e.** Inform visitors of acceptable and unacceptable behavior (e.g. Leave No Trace program, no camping within 100 feet of lakes)
**13f.** Educate visitors about why selected behaviors are unacceptable (e.g. camping close to lakes can cause siltation and eutrophication)

#### Rationing/Allocation

**14.** Not applicable

#### Rules/Regulations

**15a.** Prohibit high-impact uses (e.g. no motorized activities)
**15b.** Prohibit high-impact behavior (e.g. washing too close to lakes)
**15c.** Limit group size

### Law enforcement

**16a.** Establish presence of a uniformed ranger
**16b.** Sanction (e.g. warn, fine) visitors for inappropriate use/behavior (e.g. camping too close to lakes)

### Zoning

**17.** Zone area for low-impact uses only (e.g. no motorized uses)

### Facility development/Site design/Maintenance

**18a.** Provide facilities/services for low-impact uses only (e.g. canoe/kayak landings)
**18b.** Locate/concentrate facilities and services away from fragile bodies of water
**18c.** Design facilities and services to minimize impact (e.g. locate campsites at least 200 feet from streams and lakes)
**18d.** Maintain facilities to minimize impact (e.g. clear waterbars along trails regularly)

## Problem: Impacts to Wildlife

### Strategy: Reduce impact of use

#### Information/Education

**19a.** Promote alternative sites (e.g. within park, other parks) to disperse use
**19b.** Promote alternative times to use site (e.g. seasons when wildlife are not reproducing)
**19c.** Promote resistant/hardened sites to concentrate use
**19d.** Inform visitors of acceptable and unacceptable recreation activities (e.g. no motorized uses)
**19e.** Inform visitors of acceptable and unacceptable behavior (e.g. Leave No Trace program, no feeding wildlife)
**19f.** Educate visitors about why selected behaviors are unacceptable (e.g. feeding wildlife leads to habituation)

#### Rationing/Allocation

**20.** Not applicable

#### Rules/Regulations

**21a.** Prohibit high-impact uses (e.g. no motorized activities)
**21b.** Prohibit high-impact behavior (e.g. no feeding wildlife, no walking through nesting areas)
**21c.** Limit group size

### Law enforcement

**22a.** Establish the presence of a uniformed ranger
**22b.** Sanction (e.g. warn, fine) visitors for inappropriate use/behavior (e.g. feeding wildlife)

### Zoning

**23a.** Zone area for low-impact uses only (e.g. no motorized uses)

### Facility development/Site design/Maintenance

**24a.** Provide facilities/services for low-impact uses only (e.g. build blinds for watching wildlife)
**24b.** Locate/concentrate facilities and services away from wildlife habitat
**24c.** Design facilities and services to reduce impact (e.g. provide wildlife-resistant trash cans)
**24d.** Maintain facilities to minimize impact (e.g. maintain wildlife enclosures)

## Problem: Impacts to Air

### Strategy: Reduce impact of use

### Information/Education

**25a.** Promote alternative sites (e.g. within park, other parks) to disperse use
**25b.** Promote alternative times to use site (e.g. when atmospheric inversions are less likely)
**25c.** Promote resistant/hardened sites to concentrate use (e.g. sites that are less subject to atmospheric inversions)
**25d.** Inform visitors of acceptable and unacceptable recreation activities (e.g. no motorized uses)
**25e.** Inform visitors of acceptable and unacceptable behavior (e.g. no campfires)
**25f.** Educate visitors about why selected behaviors are unacceptable (e.g. campfires can cause air pollution)

### Rationing/Allocation

**26.** Not applicable

### Rules/Regulations

**27a.** Prohibit high-impact uses (e.g. no motorized activities)
**27b.** Prohibit high-impact behavior (e.g. no campfires)
**27c.** Limit group size

### Law enforcement

**28a.** Establish presence of a uniformed ranger
**28b.** Sanction (e.g. warn, fine) visitors for inappropriate use/behavior (e.g. campfires when prohibited)

### Zoning

**29a.** Zone area for low-impact uses only (e.g. no motorized uses)

### Facility development/Site design/Maintenance

**30a.** Provide facilities/services for low-impact uses only (e.g. pedestrian use only)
**30b.** Locate/concentrate facilities and services away from sites susceptible to air pollution
**30c.** Design facilities and services to minimize impact (e.g. no fire grates provided at campsites)
**30d.** Maintain facilities to minimize impact (e.g. clear campground of down wood to discourage campfires)

## Problem: Impacts to Natural Quiet

### Strategy: Reduce impact of use

### Information/Education

**31a.** Promote alternative sites (e.g. within park, other parks) to disperse use
**31b.** Promote alternative times to use site (e.g. hours, days, seasons)
**31c.** Promote selected sites to concentrate use
**31d.** Inform visitors of acceptable and unacceptable recreation activities (e.g. no motorized uses)
**31e.** Inform visitors of acceptable and unacceptable behavior (e.g. no boisterous activity)
**31f.** Educate visitors about why selected behaviors are unacceptable (e.g. human caused noise can disturb wildlife and reduce the opportunity of visitors to hear the sounds of nature)

### Rationing/Allocation

**32.** Not applicable

### Rules/Regulations

**33a.** Prohibit high-impact uses (e.g. no motorized activities)
**33b.** Prohibit high-impact behavior (e.g. radios, cell phones)
**33c.** Limit group size

### Law enforcement

**34a.** Establish the presence of a uniformed ranger
**34b.** Sanction (e.g. warn, fine) visitors for inappropriate use/behavior (e.g. boisterous activity)

### Zoning

**35a.** Zone as "quiet area"
**35b.** Zone area for low-impact uses only (e.g. no motorized uses)

### Facility development/Site design/Maintenance

**36a.** Provide facilities/services for low-impact uses only (e.g. trails for walking only)
**36b.** Locate/concentrate facilities and services away from sensitive areas (e.g. old-growth forests)
**36c.** Design facilities and services to minimize impact (e.g. use only quiet technology for park administration)

## Problem: Impacts to Natural Darkness

### Strategy: Reduce impact of use

### Information/Education

**37a.** Promote alternative sites (e.g. within park, other parks) to disperse use
**37b.** Promote alternative times to use site (e.g. days, seasons)
**37c.** Promote selected sites to concentrate use
**37d.** Inform visitors of acceptable and unacceptable recreation activities (e.g. no motorized use requiring lights)
**37e.** Inform visitors of acceptable and unacceptable behavior (e.g. minimize use of lights)
**37f.** Educate visitors about why selected behaviors are unacceptable (e.g. some visitors enjoy looking at the night sky)

### Rationing/Allocation

**38.** Not applicable

### Rules/Regulations

**39a.** Prohibit high-impact uses (e.g. no motorized use requiring lights after dark)
**39b.** Prohibit high-impact behavior (e.g. unnecessary use of lights)

**39c.** Require "lights out" time
**39d.** Limit group size

### Law enforcement

**40a.** Establish the presence of a uniformed ranger
**40b.** Sanction (e.g. warn, fine) visitors for inappropriate use/behavior (e.g. using lights after "lights out" time)

### Zoning

**41a.** Zone area for dark sky
**41b.** Zone area for low-impact uses only (e.g. no campfires)

### Facility development/Site design/Maintenance

**42a.** Provide facilities/services for low-impact uses only (e.g. no campfire interpretive programs)
**42b.** Locate/concentrate facilities and services away from sensitive areas (e.g. popular/designated night sky viewing areas)
**42c.** Design facilities and services to minimize impact (e.g. use of low-glow lights)
**42d.** Maintain facilities to minimize impact (e.g. maintain downward orientation of park lighting)

## Problem: Impacts to Historical/Cultural Resources

### Strategy: Reduce impact of use

### Information/Education

**43a.** Promote alternative sites (e.g. within park, other parks) to disperse use
**43b.** Promote alternative times to use site (e.g. hours, days, seasons)
**43c.** Promote selected sites to concentrate use
**43d.** Inform visitors of acceptable and unacceptable recreation activities (e.g. do not take historical artifacts, no photography of sensitive art works)
**43e.** Inform visitors of acceptable and unacceptable behavior (e.g. do not disturb/remove cultural artifacts)
**43f.** Educate visitors about why selected behaviors are unacceptable (e.g. cultural artifacts are important to archeologists, visitors like to see cultural artifacts)

### Rationing/Allocation

**44.** Not applicable

### Rules/Regulations

**45a.** Prohibit high-impact uses (e.g. no rubbings of pictographs)
**45b.** Prohibit high-impact behavior (e.g. no disturbance of cultural artifacts)
**45c.** Limit group size

### Law enforcement

**46a.** Establish the presence of a uniformed ranger
**46b.** Sanction (e.g. warn, fine) visitors for inappropriate use/behavior (e.g. removing cultural artifacts)

### Zoning

**47.** Zone area for low-impact uses only (e.g. no large groups)

### Facility development/Site design/Maintenance

**48a.** Provide facilities/services for low-impact uses only (e.g. set maximum group size)
**48b.** Locate/concentrate facilities and services away from sensitive areas (e.g. archeological sites)
**48c.** Design facilities and services to minimize impact (e.g. place cultural resources in protective cases)
**48d.** Maintain facilities to minimize impact (e.g. maintain the integrity of barriers to keep visitors away from sensitive resources)

## Problem: Crowding

### Strategy: Reduce impact of use

### Information/Education

**49a.** Promote alternative sites (e.g. within park, other parks) to disperse use
**49b.** Promote alternative times to use site (e.g. hours, days, seasons) to disperse use
**49c.** Promote sites (e.g. attraction sites) that are designed to accommodate large numbers of visitors
**49d.** Inform visitors of acceptable and unacceptable recreation activities (e.g. no motorized use, no stock use, no pets, no large groups)
**49e.** Inform visitors of acceptable and unacceptable behavior (e.g. no boisterous behavior, dogs must be on leash)
**49f.** Educate visitors about why selected activities/behaviors are unacceptable (e.g. some visitors are searching for solitude, large groups tend to increase perceived crowding)
**49g.** Inform visitors of existing impacts/conditions (e.g. crowding)

### Rationing/Allocation

**50.** Not applicable

### Rules/Regulations

**51a.** Prohibit recreation activities that tend to minimize crowding (e.g. commercial tours)
**51b.** Prohibit behavior that tends to exacerbate crowding (e.g. boisterous behavior)
**51c.** Limit group size
**51d.** Institute a maximum length of stay

### Law enforcement

**52a.** Establish the presence of a uniformed ranger
**52b.** Sanction (e.g. warn, fine) visitors for inappropriate use/behavior (e.g. boisterous behavior)

### Zoning

**53.** Zone area for recreation activities that tend to minimize crowding (e.g. pedestrian activities)

### Facility development/Site design/Maintenance

**54a.** Provide facilities/services only for recreation activities that tend to minimize crowding (e.g. pedestrian activities)
**54b.** Locate/concentrate facilities and services away from areas designed to provide opportunities for solitude (e.g. wilderness areas)
**54c.** Design facilities and services to minimize crowding (e.g. provide adequate restrooms)
**54d.** Maintain facilities to minimize crowding (e.g. remove litter regularly)

## Problem: Conflict

### Strategy: Reduce impact of use

### Information/Education

**55a.** Promote alternative sites (e.g. within park, other parks) to separate conflicting uses
**55b.** Promote alternative times to use site (e.g. hours, days, seasons) to separate conflicting uses

**55c.** Inform visitors of acceptable and unacceptable recreation activities (e.g. no motorized use, no stock use, no large groups)

**55d.** Inform visitors of acceptable and unacceptable behavior (e.g. no boisterous behavior, dogs must be on leash)

**55e.** Educate visitors about why selected behaviors are unacceptable (e.g. dogs can scare away wildlife, some visitors want to hear the sounds of nature)

### *Rationing/Allocation*

**56.** Not applicable

### *Rules/Regulations*

**57a.** Prohibit recreation activities that tend to cause conflict (e.g. motorized uses)

**57b.** Prohibit high-impact behavior (e.g. boisterous activity)

**57c.** Limit group size

### *Law enforcement*

**58a.** Establish the presence of a uniformed ranger

**58b.** Sanction (e.g. warn, fine) visitors for inappropriate use/behavior (e.g. motorized use, boisterous behavior)

### *Zoning*

**59a.** Separate conflicting activities by spatial zoning (e.g. one site for motorized activities and a different site for non-motorized activities)

**59b.** Separate conflicting activities by temporal zoning (hours, days, seasons) (e.g. a site is zoned for motorized activities during one season and non-motorized activities during another season)

**59c.** Zone area for recreation activities that tend not to cause conflict (e.g. pedestrian activities)

### *Facility development/Site design/Maintenance*

**60a.** Provide facilities/services only for recreation activities that tend not to cause conflict (e.g. pedestrian activities)

**60b.** Locate/concentrate facilities and services for recreation activities that tend to cause conflict (e.g. motorized activities) away from facilities and services for other recreation activities

**60c.** Design facilities and services to minimize conflict (e.g. provide separate trails for hikers and bikers)

## Problem: Depreciative Behavior
### Strategy: Reduce impact of use
#### *Information/Education*

**61a.** Inform visitors of acceptable and unacceptable recreation activities (e.g. no motorized use)

**61b.** Inform visitors of acceptable and unacceptable behavior (e.g. do not litter)

**61c.** Educate visitors about why selected behaviors are unacceptable (e.g. litter is unsightly and can harm wildlife)

#### *Rationing/Allocation*

**62.** Not applicable

#### *Rules/Regulations*

**63.** Prohibit depreciative acts (e.g. littering, graffiti)

#### *Law enforcement*

**64a.** Establish the presence of a uniformed ranger

**64b.** Sanction (e.g. warn, fine) visitors for inappropriate use/behavior (e.g. littering, graffiti)

#### *Zoning*

**65.** Not applicable

#### *Facility development/Site design/Maintenance*

**66a.** Design facilities to minimize depreciative behavior (e.g. provide for waste disposal, use construction materials that are unfavorable for graffiti)

**66b.** Maintain facilities to minimize depreciative behavior (e.g. remove litter, graffiti)

## Problem: Impacts to Attraction Sites
### Strategy: Reduce the impact of use
#### *Information/Education*

**67a.** Promote alternative sites (e.g. within park, other parks) to disperse use

**67b.** Promote alternative times to use site (e.g. hours, days, seasons) to disperse use

**67c.** Promote resistant/hardened sites to concentrate use

**67d.** Inform visitors of current impacts/conditions (e.g. resource impact, crowding)

**67e.** Inform visitors of acceptable and unacceptable recreation activities (e.g. no climbing on attraction site features)

**67f.** Inform visitors of acceptable and unacceptable behavior (e.g. stay on developed facilities)

**67g.** Educate visitors about why selected activities/behaviors are unacceptable (e.g. walking off developed facilities can damage fragile vegetation)

### Rationing/Allocation

**68.** Not applicable

### Rules/Regulations

**69a.** Prohibit high-impact uses (e.g. no motorized activities)

**69b.** Prohibit high-impact behavior (e.g. no walking off developed facilities)

**69c.** Limit group size

**69d.** Institute a maximum length of stay

### Law enforcement

**70a.** Establish presence of a uniformed ranger

**70b.** Sanction (e.g. warn, fine) visitors for inappropriate use/behavior (e.g. walking off developed facilities)

### Zoning

**71.** Zone area for low-impact uses only (e.g. pedestrian use only)

### Facility development/Site design/Maintenance

**72a.** Provide facilities/services for low-impact uses only (e.g. pedestrian use only)

**72b.** Locate/concentrate facilities and services on impact-resistant sites (e.g. impact-resistant soils and vegetation, away from sensitive wildlife habitat)

**72c.** Design facilities and services to minimize impact (e.g. boardwalks over wet areas)

**72d.** Maintain facilities to minimize impact (e.g. maintain the integrity of fencing at viewpoints)

## Problem: Impacts to Trails

### Strategy: Reduce the impact of use

#### Information/Education

**73a.** Promote alternative trails (e.g. within park, other parks) to disperse use

**73b.** Promote alternative times to use trails (e.g. hours, days, seasons) to disperse use

**73c.** Promote resistant/hardened trails to concentrate use

**73d.** Inform visitors of current impacts/conditions (e.g. resource impact, crowding)

**73e.** Inform visitors of acceptable and unacceptable recreation activities (e.g. no mountain biking)

**73f.** Inform visitors of acceptable and unacceptable behavior (e.g. do not walk off-trail)

**73g.** Educate visitors about why selected activities/behaviors are unacceptable (e.g. walking off-trail can damage fragile vegetation)

#### Rationing/Allocation

**74.** Not applicable

#### Rules/Regulations

**75a.** Prohibit high-impact uses (e.g. no pack stock)

**75b.** Prohibit high-impact behavior (e.g. no walking off-trail)

**75c.** Limit group size

**75d.** Institute a maximum length of stay

#### Law enforcement

**76a.** Establish presence of a uniformed ranger

**76b.** Sanction (e.g. warn, fine) visitors for inappropriate use/behavior (e.g. walking off-trail)

#### Zoning

**77a.** Zone area for low-impact uses only (e.g. pedestrian use only)

**77b.** Separate conflicting activities by spatial zoning (e.g. one trail for motorized activities and a different trail for non-motorized activities)

**77c.** Separate conflicting activities by temporal zoning (hours, days, seasons) (e.g. a trail is zoned for motorized activities during one season and non-motorized activities during another season)

### Facility development/Site design/Maintenance

**78a.** Provide facilities/services for low-impact uses only (e.g. pedestrian use only)

**78b.** Locate trails on impact-resistant sites (e.g. impact resistant soils and vegetation, away from sensitive wildlife habitat)

**78c.** Design trails to minimize impact (e.g. use switchbacks on steep slopes, construct waterbars along trail, designate trail margins)

**78d.** Maintain facilities to minimize impact (e.g. clean out waterbars regularly)

## Problem: Impacts to Campgrounds/ Campsites

### Strategy: Reduce the impact of use

#### Information/Education

**79a.** Promote alternative campsites (e.g. within park, other parks) to disperse use

**79b.** Promote alternative times to use campsites (e.g. days, seasons) to disperse use

**79c.** Promote resistant/hardened campsites to concentrate use

**79d.** Inform visitors of current impacts/conditions (e.g. resource impact, conflict)

**79e.** Inform visitors of acceptable and unacceptable recreation activities (e.g. no recreational vehicles)

**79f.** Inform visitors of acceptable and unacceptable behavior (e.g. store food properly, respect quiet hours, no campfires, carry bear cannisters)

**79g.** Educate visitors about why selected activities/ behaviors are unacceptable (e.g. unattended food can attract animals)

#### Rationing/Allocation

**80.** Not applicable

#### Rules/Regulations

**81a.** Prohibit high-impact uses (e.g. no recreational vehicles)

**81b.** Prohibit high-impact behavior (e.g. no campfires/collecting wood, no boisterous behavior)

**81c.** Limit group size

**81d.** Institute a maximum length of stay

**81e.** Allow camping at designated campsites only

### Law enforcement

**82a.** Establish presence of a uniformed ranger

**82b.** Sanction (e.g. warn, fine) visitors for inappropriate use/behavior (e.g. unattended food, boisterous behavior)

### Zoning

**83a.** Zone area for low-impact uses only (e.g. walk-in campsites only)

**83b.** Separate conflicting activities by spatial zoning (e.g. one campground for recreational vehicles and a different campground for tent camping)

**83c.** Separate conflicting activities by temporal zoning (hours, days, seasons) (e.g. a campground/ campsite is zoned for recreational vehicles during one season and tent camping during another season)

### Facility development/Site design/Maintenance

**84a.** Provide facilities/services for low-impact uses only (e.g. no electricity, showers)

**84b.** Locate campsite on impact-resistant sites (e.g. impact resistant soils and vegetation, away from sensitive wildlife habitat)

**84c.** Provide firewood

**84d.** Design campsite to minimize impact (e.g. install tent platforms, designate margins of campsites, provide bear boxes, fire grates)

**84e.** Maintain facilities to minimize impact (e.g. maintain the integrity of fences around campsites)

## Problem: Impacts to Roads/Parking Lots

### Strategy: Reduce the impact of use

#### Information/Education

**85a.** Promote (e.g. intelligent transportation systems—ITS) alternative roads/parking lots (e.g. within park, other parks) to disperse use

**85b.** Promote (e.g. ITS) alternative times to use roads/parking lots (e.g. hours, days, seasons) to disperse use

**85c.** Promote (e.g. ITS) resistant/hardened roads/ parking lots to concentrate use

**85d.** Inform visitors (e.g. ITS) of current impacts/ conditions (e.g. resource impact, congestion, lack of available parking)

**85e.** Inform visitors (e.g. ITS) of acceptable and unacceptable recreation activities (e.g. no oversize vehicles)

**85f.** Inform visitors (e.g. ITS) of acceptable and unacceptable behavior (e.g. respect speed limit, no unauthorized parking)

**85g.** Educate visitors about why selected activities/behaviors are unacceptable (e.g. oversize vehicles cause excessive congestion, speeding endangers wildlife, unauthorized parking damages fragile soil and vegetation)

**85h.** Promote (e.g. ITS) alternative transportation/public transit (e.g. biking, shuttle buses)

**85i.** Educate visitors about advantages of alternative transportation/public transit (e.g. less congestion, less environmental impact, more convenient)

### Rationing/Allocation

86. Not applicable

### Rules/Regulations

**87a.** Prohibit high-impact uses (e.g. oversize vehicles, private vehicles)

**87b.** Prohibit high-impact behavior (e.g. no speeding, no unauthorized parking)

**87c.** Institute a maximum length of stay in parking lots

### Law enforcement

**88a.** Establish presence of a uniformed ranger

**88b.** Sanction (e.g. warn, fine) visitors for inappropriate use/behavior (e.g. oversize vehicles, speeding, unauthorized parking)

### Zoning

89. Not applicable

### Facility development/Site design/Maintenance

**90a.** Zone area for low-impact uses only (e.g. passenger cars only, public transit)

**90b.** Separate conflicting activities by spatial zoning (e.g. separate travel lane for bicycles)

**90c.** Separate conflicting activities by temporal zoning (hours, days, seasons) (e.g. road closed to private vehicles and open to biking during selected hours)

**90d.** Provide facilities/services for low-impact uses only (e.g. public transit)

**90e.** Locate roads/parking lots on impact-resistant sites (e.g. impact-resistant soils and vegetation, away from wildlife habitat)

**90f.** Design roads/parking lots to minimize impact (e.g. locate roads in non-sensitive resource areas)

**90g.** Maintain roads/parking lots to minimize impact (e.g. maintain the integrity of fencing around parking areas)

## Problem: Impacts to interpretive facilities/programs

### Strategy: Reduce the impact of use

#### Information/Education

**91a.** Promote alternative interpretive facilities/programs (e.g. within park, other parks) to disperse use

**91b.** Promote alternative times to use interpretive facilities/programs (e.g. hours, days, seasons) to disperse use

**91c.** Inform visitors of current impacts/conditions (e.g. resource impact, crowding)

**91d.** Inform visitors of acceptable and unacceptable activities/behavior (e.g. no boisterous behavior during interpretive programs)

**91e.** Educate visitors about why selected activities/behaviors are unacceptable (e.g. boisterous behavior can disturb other visitors)

#### Rationing/Allocation

92. Not applicable

#### Rules/Regulations

**93a.** Prohibit high-impact uses (e.g. no large groups)

**93b.** Prohibit high-impact behavior (e.g. no boisterous behavior)

**93c.** Limit group size

**93d.** Institute a maximum length of stay

#### Law enforcement

**94a.** Establish presence of a uniformed ranger

**94b.** Sanction (e.g. warn, fine) visitors for inappropriate use/behavior (e.g. vandalizing interpretive signs)

### Zoning

**95.** Zone area for low-impact uses only (e.g. no commercial groups)

### Facility development/Site design/Maintenance

**96a.** Provide facilities/services for low-impact uses only (e.g. no school groups)

**96b.** Locate/concentrate facilities/programs on impact-resistant sites (e.g. impact-resistant soils and vegetation, away from wildlife habitat)

**96c.** Design facilities/programs to minimize impact (e.g. set maximum group size)

**96d.** Maintain facilities to minimize impact (e.g. maintain audio/visual equipment)

# Appendix A4    Management Practices for Hardening Resources and the Visitor Experience

## Problem: Impacts to Soil

### Strategy: Harden resource/experience

#### Information/Education

**1.** Inform visitors of current conditions (i.e. soil compaction, erosion)

#### Rationing/Allocation

**2.** Not applicable

#### Rules/Regulations

**3.** Not applicable

#### Law enforcement

**4.** Not applicable

#### Zoning

**5.** Not applicable

#### Facility development/Site design/Maintenance

**6a.** Locate visitor attractions/facilities (e.g. trails, campsites) on durable soils (e.g. soils that are resistant to compaction and erosion)
**6b.** Develop facilities (e.g. rock steps, wooden boardwalks) to "shield" fragile soils
**6c.** Design facilities to concentrate use on naturally resistant or hardened soils
**6d.** Maintain and/or rehabilitate impacted locations (e.g. add soil cement to composted areas)
**6e.** Close and rehabilitate impacted area
**6f.** Maintain/repair damage to compacted and eroded soils

## Problem: Impacts to Vegetation

### Strategy: Harden resource/experience

#### Information/Education

**7.** Inform visitors of current conditions (i.e. trampled vegetation)

#### Rationing/Allocation

**8.** Not applicable

#### Rules/Regulations

**9.** Not applicable

#### Law enforcement

**10.** Not applicable

#### Zoning

**11.** Not applicable

#### Facility development/Site design/Maintenance

**12a.** Locate visitor attractions/facilities (e.g. trails, campsites) on durable vegetation (e.g. vegetation that is resistant to trampling)
**12b.** Develop facilities (e.g. viewing platforms, boardwalks) to "shield" fragile vegetation
**12c.** Design facilities to concentrate use on naturally resistant vegetation
**12d.** Maintain and/or rehabilitate impacted locations (e.g. thin tree canopy to encourage regrowth of trampled understory)
**12e.** Close and rehabilitate impacted area
**12f.** Revegetate area with trampling-resistant vegetation
**12g.** Maintain/repair damage to sensitive vegetation

## Problem: Impacts to Water

### Strategy: Harden resource/experience

#### Information/Education

**13.** Inform visitors of current conditions (i.e. water pollution)

#### Rationing/Allocation

**14.** Not applicable

#### Rules/Regulations

**15.** Not applicable

#### Law enforcement

**16.** Not applicable

#### Zoning

**17.** Not applicable

#### Facility development/Site design/Maintenance

**18a.** Locate visitor attractions/facilities (e.g. trails, campsites) away from water bodies
**18b.** Develop facilities (e.g. piers, bridges) to "shield" fragile shorelines
**18c.** Design facilities to concentrate use on areas away from water bodies
**18d.** Maintain and/or rehabilitate impacted locations (e.g. plant vegetation along shoreline to "buffer" stormwater runoff)
**18e.** Close and rehabilitate impacted area
**18f.** Develop toilets to keep human waste away from water bodies
**18g.** Remove human waste that has been disposed of improperly

## Problem: Impacts to Wildlife

### Strategy: Harden resource/experience

#### Information/Education

**19.** Inform visitors of current conditions (i.e. habituated, extirpated wildlife)

#### Rationing/Allocation

**20.** Not applicable

#### Rules/Regulations

**21.** Not applicable

#### Law enforcement

**22.** Not applicable

#### Zoning

**23.** Not applicable

#### Facility development/Site design/Maintenance

**24a.** Locate visitor attractions/facilities (e.g. trails, campsites) away from sensitive wildlife habitat
**24b.** Develop facilities (e.g. wildlife blinds) to minimize disturbance of wildlife
**24c.** Design facilities to concentrate use away from important wildlife habitat
**24d.** Maintain and/or rehabilitate prime wildlife habitat
**24e.** Close and rehabilitate impacted area

## Problem: Impacts to Air

### Strategy: Harden resource/experience

#### Information/Education

**25.** Inform visitors of current conditions (i.e. air pollution)

#### Rationing/Allocation

**26.** Not applicable

#### Rules/Regulations

**27.** Not applicable

#### Law enforcement

**28.** Not applicable

#### Zoning

**29.** Not applicable

#### Facility development/Site design/Maintenance

**30a.** Locate visitor attractions/facilities (e.g. trails, campsites) away from areas susceptible to air pollution

**30b.** Close areas susceptible to air pollution
**30c.** Remove firegrates from campsites
**30d.** Remove evidence of campfires

## Problem: Impacts to Natural Quiet
### Strategy: Harden resource/experience
#### Information/Education

**31.** Inform visitors of current conditions (i.e. prevalence of human-caused noise)

#### Rationing/Allocation

**32.** Not applicable

#### Rules/Regulations

**33.** Not applicable

#### Law enforcement

**34.** Not applicable

#### Zoning

**35.** Not applicable

#### Facility development/Site design/Maintenance

**36a.** Locate visitor attractions/facilities (e.g. trails, campsites) away from sensitive soundscapes
**36b.** Develop facilities (e.g. vegetative barriers) to buffer human-caused sound
**36c.** Adopt quiet technology (e.g. electric trimmers) for maintenance

## Problem: Impacts to natural darkness
### Strategy: Harden resource/experience
#### Information/Education

**37.** Inform visitors of current conditions (i.e. prevalence of light pollution)

#### Rationing/Allocation

**38.** Not applicable

#### Rules/Regulations

**39.** Not applicable

#### Law enforcement

**40.** Not applicable

#### Zoning

**41.** Not applicable

#### Facility development/Site design/Maintenance

**42a.** Locate visitor attractions/facilities (e.g. trails, campsites) away from sensitive night sky areas
**42b.** Develop/retrofit facilities (e.g. downward oriented lighting) to minimize light pollution
**42c.** Design facilities to concentrate use in areas that are not night sky sensitive

## Problem: Impacts to Historical/Cultural Resources
### Strategy: Harden resource/experience
#### Information/Education

**43.** Inform visitors of current conditions (i.e. missing artifacts)

#### Rationing/Allocation

**44.** Not applicable

#### Rules/Regulations

**45.** Not applicable

#### Law enforcement

**46.** Not applicable

#### Zoning

**47.** Not applicable

#### Facility development/Site design/Maintenance

**48a.** Locate visitor attractions/facilities (e.g. trails, campsites) away from sensitive historical/cultural resources
**48b.** Develop facilities (e.g. viewing platforms, walkways) to "shield" sensitive historical/cultural resources
**48c.** Design facilities to concentrate use on naturally resistant or hardened historical/cultural resources

**48d.** Stabilize/reconstruct sensitive historical/cultural resources
**48e.** Maintain/repair damage to sensitive historical/cultural resources

## Problem: Crowding

### Strategy: Harden resource/experience

#### Information/Education

**49a.** Inform visitors of current conditions (i.e. crowding at attraction sites)
**49b.** Encourage visitors to wear clothing and use equipment that blends with the environment
**49c.** Educate visitors about how to avoid conflict with other groups (e.g. no boisterous behavior)

#### Rationing/Allocation

**50.** Set limit on amount of use

#### Rules/Regulations

**51.** Regulate use levels

#### Law enforcement

**52a.** Establish a uniformed presence to enforce use limit
**52b.** Establish a uniformed presence to reduce conflict among visitors

#### Zoning

**53.** Separate conflicting uses spatially or temporally

#### Facility development/Site design/Maintenance

**54a.** Develop additional facilities/services (e.g. trails, attraction sites) to disperse use
**54b.** Maintain high environmental quality

## Problem: Conflict

### Strategy: Harden resource/experience

#### Information/Education

**55a.** Inform visitors of current conditions (i.e. conflict among recreation activities)
**55b.** Educate visitors about how to avoid conflict with other groups (e.g. no boisterous behavior)

#### Rationing/Allocation

**56.** Not applicable

#### Rules/Regulations

**57.** Regulate activities/behaviors (e.g. motorized uses) that may lead to conflict

#### Law enforcement

**58.** Establish a uniformed presence to reduce conflict among visitors

#### Zoning

**59.** Separate conflicting uses spatially or temporally

#### Facility development/Site design/Maintenance

**60.** Develop facilities/services (e.g. trails) for conflicting groups in separate areas

## Problem: Depreciative Behavior

### Strategy: Harden resource/experience

#### Information/Education

**61a.** Inform visitors of current conditions (e.g. presence of litter)
**61b.** Educate visitors about depreciative behavior

#### Rationing/Allocation

**62.** Not applicable

#### Rules/Regulations

**63.** Regulate depreciative behaviors (e.g. no littering, removal of artifacts)

#### Law enforcement

**64.** Establish a uniformed presence to enforce regulations

#### Zoning

**65.** Not applicable

#### Facility development/Site design/Maintenance

**66a.** Provide facilities/services (e.g. trash cans) to discourage littering
**66b.** Maintain the area regularly (e.g. remove litter)

## Problem: Impacts to Attraction Sites

### Strategy: Harden resource/experience

#### Information/Education

**67.** Inform visitors of current conditions (i.e. resource degradation, crowding at attraction sites)

#### Rationing/Allocation

**68.** Not applicable

#### Rules/Regulations

**69.** Not applicable

#### Law enforcement

**70.** Not applicable

#### Zoning

**71.** Not applicable

#### Facility development/Site design/Maintenance

**72a.** Locate visitor attractions/facilities on durable areas (e.g. soils that are resistant to compaction and erosion)
**72b.** Develop facilities (e.g. viewing platforms) to "shield" fragile resources
**72c.** Design facilities to concentrate use on naturally resistant or hardened areas
**72d.** Maintain or rehabilitate impacted locations
**72e.** Close and rehabilitate impacted areas
**72f.** Maintain/repair damage to impacted areas
**72g.** Clean/maintain area regularly

## Problem: Impacts to Trails

### Strategy: Harden resource/experience

#### Information/Education

**73.** Inform visitors of current conditions (i.e. resource degradation, crowding on trails)

#### Rationing/Allocation

**74.** Not applicable

#### Rules/Regulations

**75.** Not applicable

#### Law enforcement

**76.** Not applicable

#### Zoning

**77.** Not applicable

#### Facility development/Site design/Maintenance

**78a.** Locate trails in durable areas (e.g. soils that are resistant to compaction and erosion)
**78b.** Develop facilities (e.g. boardwalks) to "shield" fragile resources
**78c.** Design trails to concentrate use on naturally resistant or hardened areas
**78d.** Maintain or rehabilitate impacted trails
**78e.** Close and rehabilitate impacted trails
**78f.** Maintain/repair damage to impacted trails
**78g.** Clean/maintain trails regularly

## Problem: Impacts to campgrounds/ campsites

### Strategy: Harden resource/experience

#### Information/Education

**79.** Inform visitors of current conditions (i.e. resource degradation, crowding at campgrounds/ campsites)

#### Rationing/Allocation

**80.** Not applicable

#### Rules/Regulations

**81.** Not applicable

#### Law enforcement

**82.** Not applicable

#### Zoning

**83.** Not applicable

#### Facility development/Site design/Maintenance

**84a.** Locate campgrounds/campsites in durable areas (e.g. soils that are resistant to compaction and erosion)

**84b.** Develop facilities (e.g. tent platforms) to "shield" fragile resources

**84c.** Design campgrounds/campsites to concentrate use on naturally resistant or hardened areas

**84d.** Maintain or rehabilitate impacted campgrounds/campsites

**84e.** Close and rehabilitate impacted campgrounds/campsites

**84f.** Maintain/repair damage to impacted campgrounds/campsites

**84g.** Clean/maintain campgrounds/campsites regularly

## Problem: Impacts to Roads/Parking

### Strategy: Harden resource/experience

#### Information/Education

**85.** Inform visitors of current conditions (i.e. resource degradation, congestion on roads and at parking lots)

#### Rationing/Allocation

**86.** Not applicable

#### Rules/Regulations

**87.** Not applicable

#### Law enforcement

**88.** Not applicable

#### Zoning

**89.** Not applicable

#### Facility development/Site design/Maintenance

**90a.** Locate roads/parking lots in durable areas (e.g. soils that are resistant to compaction and erosion)

**90b.** Develop facilities to "shield" fragile resources

**90c.** Design roads/parking lots to concentrate use on naturally resistant or hardened areas

**90d.** Maintain or rehabilitate impacted roads/parking lots

**90e.** Close and rehabilitate impacted roads/parking lots

**90f.** Maintain/repair damage to impacted roads/parking lots

**90g.** Clean/maintain roads/parking lots regularly

## Problem: Impacts to Interpretive Facilities/Programs

### Strategy: Harden resource/experience

#### Information/Education

**91.** Inform visitors of current conditions (i.e. crowding at interpretive facilities/programs)

#### Rationing/Allocation

**92.** Not applicable

#### Rules/Regulations

**93.** Not applicable

#### Law enforcement

**94.** Not applicable

#### Zoning

**95.** Not applicable

#### Facility development/Site design/Maintenance

**96a.** Locate interpretive facilities/resources in durable areas (e.g. soils that are resistant to compaction and erosion)

**96b.** Develop facilities to "shield" fragile resources

**96c.** Design interpretive facilities/services to concentrate use on naturally resistant or hardened areas

**96d.** Maintain or rehabilitate impacted interpretive facilities

**96e.** Close and rehabilitate impacted interpretive facilities

**96f.** Maintain/repair damage to impacted interpretive facilities

**96g.** Clean/maintain interpretive facilities regularly

# Appendix B   Teaching and Management Tools

Powerpoint presentations for each of the 25 case studies included in Part II of this book and an interactive version of the matrices in Chapter 5 and the management strategies and practices in Appendices A1–A4 can be found at http://www.cabi.org/openresources/91018.

# Bibliography

Absher, J., McCollum, D. and Bowker, J. (1999) The value of research in recreation fee project implementation. *Journal of Park and Recreation Administration* 17, 116–120.

Akabua, K., Adamowicz, W., Phillips, W. and Trelawny, P. (1999) Implications of realization uncertainty on random utility models: The case of lottery rationed hunting. *Canadian Journal of Agricultural Economics* 47, 165–179.

Alder, J. (1996) Effectiveness of education and enforcement: Cairns section of the Great Barrier Reef Marine Park. *Environmental Management* 20, 541–551.

Alpert, L. and Herrington (1998) An interactive information kiosk for the Adirondack Park visitor interpretive center, Newcomb, NY. Proceedings of the 1997 Northeastern Recreation Research Symposium, *USDA Forest Service General Technical Report NE-241*, Radnor, Pennsylvania, pp. 265–267.

Anderson, D. and Manfredo, M. (1986) Visitor preferences for management actions. *Proceedings - National Wilderness Research Conference: Current Research, USDA Forest Service General Technical Report INT-212*, Fort Collins, Colorado, pp. 314–319.

Anderson, D., Lime, D. and Wang, T. (1998) Maintaining the quality of park resources and visitor experiences. A handbook for managers. University of Minnesota Cooperative Park Studies Unit, St. Paul, Minnesota, pp. 1–134.

Bamford, T., Manning, R., Forcier, L. and Koenemann, E. (1988) Differential campsite pricing: An experiment. *Journal of Leisure Research* 20, 324–342.

Barker, N. and Roberts, C. (2004) Scuba diver behavior and the management of diving impacts on coral reefs. *Biological Conservation* 120, 481–489.

Barringer, F. (2013) As vandals deface U.S. parks, some point to online show-offs. *The New York Times*, June 5, p. A1.

Basman, C., Manfredo, M., Barro, S., Vaske, J. and Watson, A. (1996) Norm accessibility: An exploratory study of backcountry and frontcountry recreational norms. *Leisure Sciences* 18, 177–191.

Becker, R. (1981) User reaction to wild and scenic river designation. *Water Resources Bulletin* 17, 623–626.

Becker, R., Berrier, D. and Barker, G. (1985) Entrance fees and visitation levels *Journal of Park and Recreation Administration* 3, 28–32.

Behan, R. (1974) Police state wilderness: A comment on mandatory wilderness permits. *Journal of Forestry* 72, 98–99.

Behan, R. (1976) Rationing wilderness use: An example from Grand Canyon. *Western Wildlands* 3, 23–26.

Biscombe, J., Hall, J. and Palmer, J. (2001) Universal campsite design: An opportunity for adaptive management. *Proceedings of the 2000 Northeastern Recreation Research Symposium, USDA Forest Service General Technical Report NE-276*, Newtown Square, Pennsylvania, pp. 150–154.

Borrie, W. and Harding, J. (2002) Effective recreation visitor communication strategies: Rock climbers in the Bitterroot Valley, Montana. *USDA Forest Service Research Note RMRS-15*, Fort Collins, Colorado, pp. 1–11.

Bowker, J., Cordell, H. and Johnson, C. (1999) User fees for recreation services on public lands: A national assessment. *Journal of Park and Recreation Administration* 17, 1–14.

Bowman, E. (1971) The cop image. *Parks and Recreation* 6, 35–36.

Bradford, L. and McIntyre, N. (2007) Off the beaten track: Messages as a means of reducing social trail use at St. Lawrence Islands National Park. *Journal of Park and Recreation Administration* 25, 1–21.

Bright, A. (1994) Information campaigns that enlighten and influence the public. *Parks and Recreation* 29, 49–54.

Bright, A. and Manfredo, M. (1995) Moderating effects of personal importance on the accessibility of attitudes toward recreation and participation. *Leisure Sciences* 17, 281–294.

Bright, A., Manfredo, M., Fishbein, M. and Bath, A. (1993) Application of the theory of learned action to the National Park Service's controlled burn policy. *Journal of Leisure Research* 25, 263–280.

Brown, C., Halstead, J. and Luloff, A. (1992) Information as a management tool: An evaluation of the Pemigewasset Wilderness Management Plan. *Environmental Management* 16, 143–148.

Brown, P. and Hunt, J. (1969) The influence of information signs on visitor distribution and use. *Journal of Leisure Research* 1, 79–83.

Brown, P., Driver, B. and McConnell, C. (1978) The opportunity spectrum concept in outdoor recreation supply inventories: Background and application. *Proceedings of the Integrated Renewable Resource Inventories Workshop, USDA Forest Service General Technical Report RM-55*, Fort Collins, Colorado, pp. 73–84.

Brown, P., Driver, B., Burns, D. and McConnell, C. (1979) The outdoor recreation opportunity spectrum in wildland recreation planning: Development and application. *First Annual National Conference on Recreation Planning and Development: Proceedings of the Speciality Conference* 2, Snowbird, Utah, pp. 1–12.

Brown, P., McCool, S. and Manfredo, M. (1987) Evolving concepts and tools for recreation user management in wilderness. *Proceedings of the National Wilderness Research Conference: Issues, State-of-knowledge, Future Directions, USDA Forest Service General Technical Report INT-220*, Fort Collins, Colorado, pp. 320–346.

Budruk, M. and Manning, R. (2006) Indicators and standards of quality at an urban-proximate park: Litter and graffiti at Boston Harbor Islands National Recreation Area. *Journal of Park and Recreation Administration* 24, 1–23.

Burde, J., Peine, J., Renfro, J. and Curran, K. (1988) Communicating with park visitors: Some successes and failures at the Great Smoky Mountains National Park. *National Association of Interpretation 1988 Research Monograph*, Fort Collins, Colorado, pp. 7–12.

Burgess, R., Clark, R. and Hendee, J. (1971) An experimental analysis of anti-litter procedures. *Journal of Applied Behavior Analysis* 4, 71–75.

Cable, S. and Watson, A. (1998) Recreation use allocation: Alternative approaches for the Bob Marshall Wilderness Complex. *USDA Forest Service Research Note RMRS-1*, Missoula, Montana, pp. 1–7.

Cable, T., Knudson, D., Udd, E. and Stewart, D. (1987) Attitude changes as a result of exposure to interpretive messages. *Journal of Park and Recreation Administration* 5, 47–60.

Campbell, F., Hendee, J. and Clark, R. (1968) Law and order in public parks. *Parks and Recreation* 3, 51–55.

Cannon, C. (1991) Ranger or stranger? *Earth Works* 1, 5–9.

Carroll, M. (1988) A tale of two rivers: Comparing NPS-local interactions in two areas. *Society and Natural Resources* 1, 317–333.

Charles, M. (1982) The Yellowstone ranger: The social control and socialization of federal law enforcement officers. *Human Organization* 41, 216–226.

Chavez, D. (1996) Mountain biking direct, indirect, and bridge building management styles. *Journal of Park and Recreation Administration* 14, 21–35.

Chavez, D. (2000) Invite, include, and involve! Racial groups, ethnic groups, and leisure. In: Allison, M. and Schneider, I. (eds) *Diversity and the Recreation Profession*. Venture Publishing, State College, Pennsylvania.

Christensen, H. (1981) Bystander intervention and litter control: an experimental analysis of an appeal to help program. *USDA Forest Service General Research Paper PNW-287*, Portland, Oregon.

Christensen, H. (1986) Vandalism and depreciative behavior. *A Literature Review: The President's Commission on Americans Outdoors*. US Government Printing Office, M-73-M-87, Washington, DC.

Christensen, H. and Clark, R. (1983) Increasing public involvement to reduce depreciative behavior in recreation settings. *Leisure Sciences* 5, 359–378.

Christensen, H. and Dustin, D. (1989) Reaching recreationists at different levels of moral development. *Journal of Park and Recreation Administration* 7, 72–80.

Christensen, H., Johnson, D. and Brookes, M. (1992) Vandalism: Research, Prevention, and Social Policy. *USDA Forest Service General Technical Report PNW-293*, Portland, Oregon.

Christensen, N. and Cole, D. (2000) Leave no trace practices: Behaviors and preferences of wilderness visitors regarding use of cookstoves and camping away from lakes. *Wilderness Science in a Time of Change Conference—Volume 4: Wilderness Visitors, Experiences, and Visitor Management.* USDA Forest Service Proceedings RMRS-15, Missoula, Montana, pp. 77–85.

Clark, R. and Stankey, G. (1979) The Recreation Opportunity Spectrum: A Framework for Planning, Management, and Research. *USDA Forest Service General Research Paper PNW-98*, Portland, Oregon.

Clark, R., Hendee, J. and Campbell, F. (1971) Depreciative Behavior in Forest Campgrounds: An Exploratory Study. *USDA Forest Service Research Paper PNW-161*, Portland, Oregon.

Clark, R., Burgess, R. and Hendee, J. (1972a) The development of anti-litter behavior in a forest campground. *Journal of Applied Behavior Analysis* 5, 71–75.

Clark, R., Hendee, J. and Burgess, R. (1972b) The experimental control of littering. *Journal of Environmental Education* 4, 22–28.

Cockrell, D. and McLaughlin, W. (1982) Social influences on wild river recreationists. *Forest and River Recreation: Research Update.* University of Minnesota Agricultural Experiment Station Miscellaneous Publication 18, St. Paul, Minnesota, pp. 140–145.

Cohen, J. (1995) How many people can the Earth support? *The Sciences* 35, 18–23.

Cole, D. (1993) Wilderness recreation management. *Journal of Forestry* 91, 22–24.

Cole, D. (2004) Impacts of hiking and camping on soils and vegetation: A review. In: Buckley, R. (ed.) *Environmental Impacts of Ecotourism.* CAB International, Wallingford, UK, pp. 41–60.

Cole, D. (2005) Computer simulation modeling of recreation use: Current status, case studies, and future directions. *USDA Forest Service General Technical Report RMRS-143*, Fort Collins, Colorado.

Cole, D. and Hall, T. (2006) Wilderness zoning: Should we purposely manage to different standards? *The 2005 George Wright Society Conference Proceedings*, Hancock, Michigan, pp. 33–38.

Cole, D. and Hall, T. (2008) Wilderness visitors, experiences, and management preferences: How they vary with use level and length of stay. *USDA Forest Service General Research Paper RMRS-71*, Fort Collins, Colorado.

Cole, D. and Rang, B. (1983) Temporary campsite closure in the Selway-Bitterroot Wilderness. *Journal of Forestry* 81, 729–732.

Cole, D., Watson, A. and Roggenbuck, J. (1995) Trends in Wilderness Visitors and Visits: Boundary Waters Canoe Area, Shining Rock, and Desolation Wilderness. *USDA Forest Service General Research Paper INT-483*, Ogden, Utah.

Cole, D., Watson, A., Hall, T. and Spildie, D. (1997a) High-Use Destinations in Wilderness: Social and Bio-Physical Impacts, Visitor Responses, and Management Options. *USDA Forest Service General Research Paper INT-496*, Ogden, Utah.

Cole, D., Hammond, T. and McCool, S. (1997b) Information quality and communication effectiveness: Low-impact messages on wilderness trailhead bulletin boards. *Leisure Sciences* 19, 59–72.

Confer, J., Mowen, A., Graefe, A. and Absher, J. (2000) Magazines as wilderness information sources: Assessing users' general wilderness knowledge and specific leave no trace knowledge. *Wilderness Science in a Time of Change Conference—Volume 4: Wilderness Visitors, Experiences, and Visitor Management.* USDA Forest Service Proceedings RMRS-15, Ogden, Utah, pp. 193–197.

Connors, E. (1976) Public safety in park and recreation settings. *Parks and Recreation* 11, 20–21, 55–56.

Crompton, J. (2002) The rest of the story. *Journal of Leisure Research* 34, 93–102.

Crompton, J. and Lue, C. (1992) Patterns of equity preferences among Californians for allocating park and recreation resources. *Leisure Sciences* 14, 227–246.

Crompton, J. and Wicks, B. (1988) Implementing a preferred equity model for the delivery of leisure services in the U.S. context. *Leisure Sciences* 7, 287–304.

Crompton, J. (2015) Complementing Scott: Justifying discounts for low-income groups through an economic lens. *Journal of Park and Recreation Administration* 33, 1–15.

Daniels, M. and Marion, J. (2006) Visitor evaluations of management actions at a highly impacted Appalachian Trail camping area. *Environmental Management* 38, 1006–1019.

Day, J. (2002) Zoning – lessons from the Great Barrier Reef Marine Park. *Ocean & Coastal Management* 45, 139–156.

Dimara, E. and Skuras, D. (1998) Rationing preferences and spending behavior of visitors to a scarce recreational resource with limited carrying capacity. *Land Economics* 74, 317–327.

D'Luhosch, P., Kuehn, D. and Schuster, R. (2009) Behavioral intentions within off-highway vehicle communities in the northeastern U.S.: An application of the theory of planned behavior. *Proceedings of the 2008 Northeastern Recreation Research Symposium, USDA Forest Service General Technical Report NRS-P-42*, Newtown Square, Pennsylvania, pp. 258–265.

Doucette, J. and Cole, D. (1993) Wilderness Visitor Education: Information About Alternative Techniques. *USDA Forest Service General Technical Report INT-295*, Ogden, Utah.

Doucette, J. and Kimball, K. (1990) Passive trail management in northeastern alpine zones: A case study. *USDA Forest Service General Technical Report NE-145*, Radnor, Pennsylvania, pp. 195–201.

Dowell, D. and McCool, S. (1986) Evaluation of a wilderness information dissemination program. *USDA Forest Service General Technical Report INT-212*, Fort Collins, Colorado, pp. 494–500.

Driver, B. (2002) Reality testing. *Journal of Leisure Research* 34, 79–88.

Driver, B. and Brown, P. (1978) The opportunity spectrum concept in outdoor recreation supply inventories: A rationale. *USDA Forest Service General Technical Report RM-55*, Fort Collins, Colorado, pp. 24–31.

Duncan, G. and Martin, S. (2002) Comparing the effectiveness of interpretive and sanction messages for influencing wilderness visitors' intended behavior. *International Journal of Wilderness* 8, 20–25.

Dustin, D. (2002) One dog or another: Tugging at the strands of social science. *Journal of Leisure Research* 34, 89–92.

Dustin, D. and Knopf, R. (1989) Equity issues in outdoor recreation. *USDA Forest Service General Technical Report SE-52*, Asheville, North Carolina, pp. 467–471.

Dustin, D. and McAvoy, L. (1980) Hardening national parks. *Environmental Ethics* 2, 29–44.

Dustin, D. and McAvoy, L. (1984) The limitation of the traffic light. *Journal of Park and Recreation Administration* 2, 8–32.

Dwyer, W., Huffman, M. and Jarratt, L. (1989) A comparison of strategies for gaining compliance with campground regulations. *Journal of Park and Recreation Administration* 7, 21–30.

Echelberger, H., Leonard, R. and Hamblin, M. (1978) The trail guide system as a backcountry management tool. *USDA Forest Service Research Note NE-266*, Upper Darby, Pennsylvania.

Echelberger, H., Leonard, R. and Adler, S. (1983) Designated-dispersed tentsites. *Journal of Forestry* 81, 90–91, 105.

Ehrlich, P. (1968) *The Population Bomb*. Ballantine Books, New York.

Fay, S., Rice, S. and Berg, S. (1977) Guidelines for design and location of overnight backcountry facilities. *USDA Forest Service*, Broomall, Pennsylvania.

Fazio, J. (1979a) Agency literature as an aid to wilderness management *Journal of Forestry* 77, 97–98.

Fazio, J. (1979b) *Communicating with the Wilderness User*. Wildlife and Range Science Bulletin Number 28, University of Idaho College of Forestry, Moscow, Idaho.

Fazio, J. and Gilbert, D. (1974) Mandatory wilderness permits: Some indications of success. *Journal of Forestry* 72, 753–756.

Fazio, J. and Ratcliffe, R. (1989) Direct-mail literature as a method to reduce problems of wild river management. *Journal of Park and Recreation Administration* 7, 1–9.

Feldman, R. (1978) Effectiveness of audio-visual media for interpretation to recreating motorists. *Journal of Interpretation* 3, 14–19.

Fesenmeier, D. and Schroeder, H. (1983) Financing public outdoor recreation: A study of user fees at Oklahoma state parks. *Review of Regional Economics and Business* 2, 29–35.

Fix, P. and Vaske, J. (2007) Visitor evaluations of recreation user fees at Flaming Gorge National Recreation Area. *Journal of Leisure Research* 39, 611–622.

Fleming, C. and Manning, M. (2015) Rationing access to protected natural areas: an Australian case study. *Tourism Economics* 21, 995–1014.

Forsyth, C. (1994) Bookers and peacemakers: Types of game wardens. *Sociological Spectrum* 14, 47–63.

Fractor, D. (1982) Evaluating alternative methods for rationing wilderness use. *Journal of Leisure Research* 14, 341–349.

Frauman, E. and Norman, W. (2003) Managing visitors via "mindful" information services: One approach in addressing sustainability. *Journal of Park and Recreation Administration* 21, 87–104.

Frost, J. and McCool, S. (1988) Can visitor regulation enhance recreational experiences? *Environmental Management* 12, 5–9.

Gilbert, G., Peterson, G. and Lime, D. (1972) Towards a model of travel behavior in the

Boundary Waters Canoe Area. *Environment and Behavior* 4, 131–157.

Gilligan, C. (1982) *In a Different Voice*. Harvard University Press, Cambridge, Massachusetts.

Gimblett, R. and Skov-Petersen, H. (eds) (2008) *Monitoring, Simulation, and Management of Visitor Landscapes*. The University of Arizona Press, Tucson, Arizona.

Glass, R. and More, T. (1992) Satisfaction, Valuation, and Views Toward Allocation of Vermont Goose Hunting Opportunities. *USDA Forest Service Research Paper NE-668*, Radnor, Pennsylvania.

Godin, V. and Leonard, R. (1976) Guidelines for managing backcountry travel and usage. *Trends* 13, 33–37.

Godin, V. and Leonard, R. (1977) Permit compliance in eastern wilderness: Preliminary results. *USDA Forest Service Research Note NE-238*, Radnor, Pennsylvania.

Graefe, A. and Thapa, B. (2004) Conflict in natural resource recreation. *Society and Natural Resources: A Summary of Knowledge*. Modern Litho, Jefferson, Missouri, pp. 209–224.

Graefe, A., Vaske, J., and Kuss, F. (1984) Social carrying capacity; an integration and synthesis of twenty years of research. *Leisure Sciences* 6, 395–431.

Gramann, J. and Vander Stoep, G. (1987) Prosocial behavior theory and natural resource protection: A conceptual synthesis. *Journal of Environmental Management* 24, 247–257.

Greist, D. (1975) Risk zone management: A recreation area management system and method of measuring carrying capacity. *Journal of Forestry* 73, 711–714.

Griffin, C. (2005) Leave no trace and national park wilderness areas. *Proceedings of the 2004 Northeastern Recreation Research Symposium, USDA Forest Service General Technical Report NE-326*, Newton Square, Pennsylvania, pp. 152–157.

Haas, G., Driver, B., Brown, P. and Lucas, R. (1987) Wilderness management zoning. *Journal of Forestry* 85, 17–22.

Hadley, L. (1971) Perspectives on law enforcement in recreation areas. *Recreation Symposium Proceedings*. USDA Forest Service Northeastern Forest Experiment Station, Upper Darby, Pennsylvania, pp. 156–160.

Hadwen, S. and Palmer, L. (1922) Reindeer in Alaska. US Department Agricultural Bulletin 1089, p. 74.

Hammitt, W., Cole, D. and Monz, C. (2015) *Wildland Recreation: Ecology and Management*. 3rd edn, Wiley-Blackwell, Chichester, UK.

Hanley, N., Alvarez-Farizo, B. and Shaw, W. (2002) Rationing an open-access resource: mountaineering in Scotland. *Land Use Policy* 19, 167–176.

Hardin, G. (1968) The tragedy of the commons. *Science* 162, 1243–1248.

Harmon, D. (1992) Using an interactive computer program to communicate with the wilderness visitor. *Proceedings of the Symposium on Social Aspects and Recreation Research. USDA Forest Service General Technical Report PSW-132*, Albany, California, p. 60.

Harmon, L. (1979) How to make park law enforcement work for you. *Parks and Recreation* 14, 20–21.

Harwell, R. (1987) A "no-rescue" wilderness experience: What are the implications? *Parks and Recreation* 22, 34–37.

Heinrichs, J. (1982) Cops in the woods. *Journal of Forestry* 11, 722–725,748.

Hendee, J. and Lucas, R. (1973) Mandatory wilderness permits: A necessary management tool. *Journal of Forestry* 71, 206–209.

Hendee, J. and Lucas, R. (1974) Police state wilderness: A comment on a comment. *Journal of Forestry* 72, 100–101.

Hendee, J., Stankey, G. and Lucas, R. (1990) *Wilderness Management*. North American Press, Golden, Colorado.

Hendricks, B., Ruddell, E. and Bullis, C. (1993) Direct and indirect park and recreation resource management decision making: A conceptual approach. *Journal of Park and Recreation Administration* 11, 28–39.

Hendricks, W., Ramthun, R. and Chavez, D. (2001) The effects of persuasive message source and content on mountain bicyclists' adherence to trail etiquette guidelines. *Journal of Park and Recreation Administration* 19, 38–61.

Hepcan, S. (2000) A methodological approach for designating management zones in Mount Spil National Park, Turkey. *Environmental Management* 26, 329–338.

Heywood, J. (1985) Large recreation group and party size limits. *Journal of Park and Recreation Administration* 3, 36–44.

Hope, J. (1971) Hassles in the park. *Natural History* 80, 20–23, 82–91.

Horsley, A. (1988) The unintended effects of a posted sign on littering attitudes and stated intentions. *Journal of Environmental Education* 19, 10–14.

Huffman, M. and Williams, D. (1986) Computer versus brochure information dissemination as a backcountry management tool. *USDA Forest Service General Technical Report INT-212*, Ogden, Utah, pp. 501–508.

Huffman, M. and Williams, D. (1987) The use of microcomputers for park trail information dissemination. *Journal of Park and Recreation Administration* 5, 35–46.

Huhtala, A. and Pouta, E. (2008) User fees, equity and the benefits of public outdoor recreation services. *Journal of Forest Economics* 14, 117–132.

Hulbert, J. and Higgins, J. (1977) BWCA visitor distribution system. *Journal of Forestry* 75, 338–340.

Hultsman, W. (1988) Applications of a touch-sensitive computer in park settings: Activity alternatives and visitor information. *Journal of Park and Recreation Administration*, Bloomington, Indiana, p. 6.

Hultsman, W. and Hultsman, J. (1989) Attitudes and behaviors regarding visitor-control measures in fragile environments: Implications for recreation management. *Journal of Park and Recreation Administration* 7, 60–69.

Hunt, J. and Brown, P. (1971) Who can read our writing? *Journal of Environmental Education* 2, 27–29.

Hvenegaard, G. (2016) Visitors' perceived impacts of interpretation on knowledge, attitudes, and behavioral intentions at Miquelon Lake Provincial Park, Alberta, Canada. *Tourism and Hospitality Research* 0, 1–12.

Hwang, Y.-H., Kim, S.-I. and Jeng, J.-M. (2000) Examining the causal relationships among selected antecedents of responsible environmental behavior. *The Journal of Environmental Education* 31, 19–25.

Interagency Visitor Use Management Council (2016) Framework & Guidebooks. Available at: http://www.visitorusemanagement.nps.gov/vum/framework (accessed 29 August 2016).

Jacob, G. and Schreyer, R. (1980) Conflict in outdoor recreation: A theoretical perspective. *Journal of Leisure Research* 12, 368–380.

Jacobi, C. (2003) Leave the rocks for the next glacier - Low impact education in a high use national park. *International Journal of Wilderness* 9, 30–31.

Johnson, D. and Vande Kamp, M. (1996) Extent and control of resource damage due to noncompliant visitor behavior: A case study from the U.S. National Parks. *Natural Areas Journal* 16, 134–141.

Jones, P. and McAvoy, L. (1988) An evaluation of a wilderness user education program: A cognitive and behavioral analysis. *Natural Association of Interpretation 1988 Research Monograph*, St. Louis, Missouri, 13–20.

Kerkvliet, J. and Nowell, C. (2000) Tools for recreation management in parks: the case of the greater Yellowstone's blue-ribbon fishery. *Ecological Economics* 34, 89–100.

Kernan, A. and Drogin, E. (1995) The effect of a verbal interpretive message on day user impacts at Mount Rainier National Park. *Proceedings of the 1994 Northeast Recreation Research Symposium. USDA Forest Service General Technical Report NE-198*, Saratoga Springs, New York, pp. 127–129.

Kidd, A., Monz, C., D'Antonio, A., Manning, R., Reigner, N., Goonan, K. and Jacobi, C. (2015) The effect of minimum impact education on visitor spatial behavior in parks and protected areas: An experimental investigation using GPS-based tracking. *Journal of Environmental Management* 162, 53–62.

Knopf, R. and Andereck, K. (2004) Managing depreciative behavior in natural settings. *Society and Natural Resources: A Summary of Knowledge.* Modern Litho, Jefferson, Missouri, pp. 305–314.

Kohlberg, L. (1976) Moral stages and moral development. *Moral Development and Behavior: Theory, Research and Social Issues.* Holt, Rinehart and Winston, New York.

Krannich, R., Eisenhauer, B., Field, D., Pratt, C. and Luloff, A. (1999) Implications of the National Park Service recreation fee demonstration program for park operations and management: Perceptions of NPS managers. *Journal of Park and Recreation Administration* 17, 35–52.

Krumpe, E. and Brown, P. (1982) Using information to disperse wilderness hikers. *Journal of Forestry* 80, 360–362.

Kuo, I.-L. (2002) The effectiveness of environmental interpretation at resource-sensitive tourism destinations. *International Journal of Tourism Research* 4, 87–101.

Lahart, D. and Barley, J. (1975) Reducing children's littering on a nature trail. *Journal of Environmental Education* 7, 37–45.

LaPage, W., Cormier, P., Hamilton, G. and Cormier, A. (1975) Differential Campsite Pricing and Campground Attendances. *USDA Forest*

*Service Research Paper NE-330*, Upper Darby, Pennsylvania.

Lawhon, B., Newman, P., Taff, D., Vaske, J., Vagias, W., Lawson, S. and Monz, C. (2013) Factors influencing behavioral intentions for Leave No Trace behavior in national parks. *Journal of Interpretation Research* 18, 23–38.

Lawson, S. and Manning, R. (2003a) Research to inform management of wilderness camping at Isle Royale National Park: Part 1 descriptive research. *Journal of Park and Recreation Administration* 21, 22–42.

Lawson, S. and Manning, R. (2003b) Research to inform management of wilderness camping at Isle Royale National Park: Part 2 prescriptive research. *Journal of Park and Recreation Administration* 21, 43–55.

Lawson, S., Moldovanyi, A., Roggenbuck, J. and , Hall, T. (2006) Reconciling tradeoffs in wilderness management: A comparison of day and overnight visitors' attitudes and preferences concerning management of the Okefenokee swamp wilderness. *The 2005 George Wright Society Conference Proceedings*, Hancock, Michigan, pp. 39–47.

Lawson, S., Hallo, J. and Manning, R. (2008) Measuring, monitoring, and managing visitor use in parks and protected areas using computer-based simulation modeling. In: Gimblett, R. and Skov-Petersen, H. (eds) *Monitoring, Simulation, and Management of Visitor Landscapes*. University of Arizona Press, Tucson, Arizona, pp. 175–188.

Leave No Trace (2012) Available at: http://www.lnt.org (accessed 1 September 2016).

Lee, K. (1993) *Compass and Gyroscope: Integrating Science and Politics for the Environment*. Island Press, Washington, DC.

Leopold, A. (1934) Conservation economics. *Journal of Forestry* 32, 537–544.

Leung, Y. and Marion, J. (2000) Recreation impacts and management in wilderness: A state-of-knowledge review. *USDA Forest Service Proceedings RMRS-P-15-Vol-5*, Ogden, Utah.

Leung, Y.-F. and Marion, J. (1999) Spatial strategies for managing visitor impacts in national parks. *Journal of Park and Recreation Administration* 17, 20–38.

Leuschner, W., Cook, P., Roggenbuck, J. and Oderwald, R. (1987) A comparative analysis for wilderness user fee policy. *Journal of Leisure Research* 19, 101–114.

Lime, D. (1977) Alternative strategies for visitor management of western whitewater river recreation. *Managing Colorado River Whitewater: The Carrying Capacity Strategy*. Utah State University, Logan, Utah, 146–155.

Lime, D. (1979) Carrying capacity. *Trends* 16, 37–40.

Lime, D. and Lorence, G. (1974) Improving estimates of wilderness use from mandatory travel permits. *USDA Forest Service Research Paper NC-101*, St. Paul, Minnesota.

Lime, D. and Lucas, R. (1977) Good information improves the wilderness experience. *Naturalist* 28, 18–20.

Lindberg, K. and Aylward, B. (1999) Price responsiveness in the developing country nature tourism context: Review and Costa Rican case study. *Journal of Leisure Research* 31, 281–299.

Little, J., Grimsrud, K., Champ, P. and Baerrens, R. (2006) Investigation of stated and revealed preferences for an elk hunting raffle. *Land Economics* 82, 623–640.

Lucas, R. (1964) The recreational capacity of the Quetico-Superior Area. *USDA Forest Service Research Paper LS-15*, St. Paul, Minnesota.

Lucas, R. (1970) User evaluation of campgrounds on two Michigan National Forests. *USDA Forest Service Research Paper NC-44*, St. Paul, Minnesota.

Lucas, R. (1980) Use patterns and visitor characteristics, attitudes, and preferences in nine wilderness and other recreation areas. *USDA Forest Service Research Paper INT-253*, Ogden, Utah.

Lucas, R. (1981) Redistributing wilderness use throughout information supplied to visitors. *USDA Forest Service Research Paper INT-277*, Ogden, Utah.

Lucas, R. (1982) Recreation regulations: When are they needed? *Journal of Forestry* 80, 148–151.

Lucas, R. (1983) The role of regulations in recreation management. *Western Wildlands* 9, 6–10.

Lucas, R. (1985) Recreation trends and management of the Bob Marshall Wilderness Complex. Proceedings of the 1985 National Outdoor Recreation Trends Symposium, U.S. National Park Service, Atlanta, Georgia, pp. 309–316.

Magill, A. (1976) Campsite reservation systems: The campers' viewpoint. *USDA Forest Service Research Paper PSW-121*, Berkeley, California.

Malthus, T. (1798) *An Essay on the Principle of Population*. W.W. Norton & Co., New York.

Manfredo, J. (1992) *Influencing Human Behavior: Theory and Applications in Recreation Tourism, and Natural Resources Management*. Sagamore Publishing, Inc., Champaign, Illinois.

Manfredo, M. (1989) An investigation of the basis for external information search in recreation and tourism. *Leisure Sciences* 11, 29–45.

Manfredo, M. and Bright, A. (1991) A model for assessing the effects of communication on recreationists. *Journal of Leisure Research* 23, 1–20.

Manfredo, M., Yuan, S. and McGuire, F. (1992) The influence of attitude accessibility on attitude-behavior relationships: Implications for recreation research. *Journal of Leisure Research* 24, 157–170.

Manning, R. (1979) Strategies for managing recreational use of national parks. *Parks* 4, 13–15.

Manning, R. (1987) *The Law of Nature: Park Rangers in Yosemite Valley*. Umbrella Films, Brookline, Massachusetts.

Manning, R. (1999) Crowding and carrying capacity in outdoor recreation: From normative standards to standards of quality. In: Jackson, E. and Burton, T. (eds) *Leisure Studies: Prospects for the Twenty-First Century*. Venture Press, State College, Pennsylvania, pp. 323–334.

Manning, R. (2001) Experience and resource protection: A framework for managing carrying capacity of National Parks. *Journal of Park and Recreation Administration* 19, 93–108.

Manning, R. (2003) Emerging principles for using information/education in wilderness management. *International Journal of Wilderness* 9, 20–12.

Manning, R. (2004) Recreation Planning Frameworks. *Society and Natural Resources: A Summary of Knowledge*. Modern Litho, Jefferson, Missouri, pp. 83–96.

Manning, R. (2007) *Parks and Carrying Capacity: Commons Without Tragedy*. Island Press, Washington, DC.

Manning, R. (2011) *Studies in Outdoor Recreation: Search and Research for Satisfaction*. 3rd edn, Oregon State University Press, Corvallis, Oregon.

Manning, R. and Baker, S. (1981) Discrimination through user fees: Fact or fiction? *Parks and Recreation* 16, 70–74.

Manning, R. and Ciali, C. (1979) The computer hikes the Appalachian trail. *Appalachia* 43, 75–85.

Manning, R. and Cormier, P. (1980) Trends in the temporal distribution of park use. *Proceedings of the 1980 Outdoor Recreation Trends Symposium, Volume II. USDA Forest Service General Technical Report NE-57*, Broomall, Pennsylvania, pp. 81–87.

Manning, R. and Lawson, S. (2002) Carrying capacity as "informed judgment": The values of science and the science of values. *Environmental Management* 30, 157–168.

Manning, R. and Potter, F. (1982) Wilderness encounters of the third kind. *Proceedings of the Third Annual Conference of the Wilderness Psychology Group*. West Virginia University, Morgantown, West Virginia, pp. 1–14.

Manning, R. and Potter, F. (1984) Computer simulation as a tool in teaching park and wilderness management. *Journal of Environmental Education* 15, 3–9.

Manning, R., Powers, L. and Mock, C. (1982) Temporal distribution of forest recreation: Problems and potential. *Forest and River Recreation: Research Update*. University of Minnesota Agricultural Experiment Station Miscellaneous Publication 18, St. Paul, Minnesota, pp. 26–32.

Manning, R., Callinan, E., Echelberger, H., Koenemann, E. and McEwen, D. (1984) Differential fees: Raising revenue, distributing demand. *Journal of Park and Recreation Administration* 2, 20–38.

Manning, R., LaPage, W., Griffall, K. and Simon, B. (1996a) Suggested principles for designing and implementing user fees and charges in the National Park System. Recreation Fees in the National Park System, University of Minnesota Cooperative Park Studies Unit, St. Paul, Minnesota, pp. 134–136.

Manning, R., Lime, D., Freimund, W. and Pitt, D. (1996b) Crowding norms at frontcountry sites: A visual approach to setting standards of quality. *Leisure Sciences* 18, 39–59.

Manning, R., Rovelstad, E., Moore, C., Hallo, J., and Smith, B. (2015) Indicators and standards of quality for viewing the night sky in the national parks. *Park Science* 32, 9–17.

Marion, J. and Farrell, T. (2002) Management practices that concentrate visitor activities: Camping impact management at Isle Royale National Park, USA. *Journal of Environmental Management* 66, 201–212.

Marion, J. and Reid, S. (2001) Development of the United States Leave No Trace programme: A historical perspective. In: Usher, M.B. (ed.) *Enjoyment and Understanding of the Natural Heritage*. The Stationery Office Ltd, Scottish Natural Heritage, Edinburgh, pp. 81–92.

Marion, J. and Reid, S. (2007) Minimising visitor impacts to protected areas: The efficacy of low impact education programmes. *Journal of Sustainable Tourism* 15, 5–27.

Marion, J., Dvorak, R. and Manning, R. (2008) Wildlife feeding in parks: Methods for monitoring the effectiveness of educational interventions and wildlife food attraction behaviors. *Human Dimensions of Wildlife* 13, 429–442.

Marler, L. (1971) A study of anti-letter messages. *Journal of Environmental Education* 3, 52–53.

Marsinko, A. (1999) The effect of fees on recreation site choice: Management/agency implications. *Proceedings of the 1999 Northeastern Recreation Research Symposium. USDA Forest Service General Technical Report NE-269*, Bolton Landing, New York, pp. 164–171.

Marsinko, A., Dwyer, J. and Schroeder, H. (2004) Attitudes toward fees and perceptions of costs of participating in day-use outdoor recreation. *Proceedings of the 2003 Northeastern Recreation Research Symposium. USDA Forest Service General Technical Report NE-317*, Radnor, Pennsylvania, pp. 278–284.

Martin, S. (1999) A policy implementation analysis of the recreation fee demonstration program: Convergence of public sentiment, agency programs, and policy principles? *Journal of Park and Recreation Administration* 17, 15–34.

McAvoy, L. (1990) *Rescue-free Wilderness Areas.* Venture Publishing, State College, Pennsylvania.

McAvoy, L. and Dustin, D. (1981) The right to risk in wilderness. *Journal of Forestry* 79,150–152.

McAvoy, L. and Dustin, D. (1983a) Indirect versus direct regulation of recreation behavior. *Journal of Park and Recreation Administration* 1, 12–17.

McAvoy, L. and Dustin, D. (1983b) In search of balance: A no-rescue wilderness proposal. *Western Wildlands* 9, 2–5.

McCool, S. (2001) Limiting recreational use in wilderness: Research issues and management challenges in appraising their effectiveness. *Visitor Use Density and Wilderness Experience. USDA Forest Service Proceedings RMRS-20*, Ogden, Utah, pp. 49–55.

McCool, S. and Christensen, N. (1996) Alleviating congestion in parks and recreation areas through direct management of visitor behavior. *Crowding and Congestion in the National Park System: Guidelines for Management and Research* 86, 67–83.

McCool, S. and Cole, D. (2000) Communicating minimum impact behavior with trailside bulletin boards: Visitor characteristics associated with effectiveness. *Wilderness Science in a Time of Change Conference Volume 4: Wilderness Visitors, Experiences, and Visitor Management. USDA Forest Service Proceedings RMRS-15*, Ogden, Utah, pp. 208–216.

McCool, S. and Lime, D. (1989) Attitudes of visitors toward outdoor recreation management policy. *Outdoor Recreation Benchmark 1988: Proceedings of the National Outdoor Recreation Forum. USDA Forest Service General Technical Report SE-52*, Athens, Georgia, pp. 401–411.

McCool, S. and Utter, J. (1981) Preferences for allocating river recreation use. *Water Resources Bulletin* 17, 431–437.

McCool, S. and Utter, J. (1982) Recreation use lotteries: Outcomes and preferences. *Journal of Forestry* 80, 10–11, 29.

McEwen, D. and Tocher, S. (1976) Zone management: Key to controlling recreational impact in developed campsites. *Journal of Forestry* 74, 90–91.

McLean, D. and Johnson, R. (1997) Techniques for rationing public recreation services. *Journal of Park and Recreation Administration* 15, 76–92.

Meadows, D., Randers, J. and Behrens, W. (1972) *The Limits to Growth.* Universe Books, New York.

Monz, C., Roggenbuck, J., Cole, D., Brame, R. and Yoder, A. (2000) Wilderness party size regulations: Implications for management and a decisionmaking framework. *Wilderness Science in a Time of Change Conference Volume 4: Wilderness Visitors, Experiences, and Visitor Management. USDA Forest Service Proceedings RMRS-15*, Missoula, Montana.

Monz, C., Cole, D., Leung, Y. and Marion, J. (2010) Sustaining visitor use in protected areas: Future opportunities in recreation ecology research based on the USA experience. *Environmental Management* 45, 551–562.

Monz, C., Pickering, C. and Hadwen, W. (2013) Recent advances in recreation ecology and the implications of different relationships between recreation use and ecological impacts. *Frontiers in Ecology and the Environment* 11(8), 441–446.

More, T. (1999) A functionalist approach to user fees. *Journal of Leisure Research* 31, 227–244.

More, T. (2002) The marginal user as the justification for public recreation: A rejoinder to Cropton, Driver and Dustin. *Journal of Leisure Research* 34, 103–118.

More, T. and Stevens, T. (2000) Do user fees exclude low-income people from resource-based recreation? *Journal of Leisure Research* 32, 341–357.

Morehead, J. (1979) The ranger image. *Trends* 16, 5–8.

Moscardo, G. (1999) Supporting ecologically sustainable tourism in the Great Barrier Reef. *Proceedings of the 1990 CAUTHE national research conference.* Bureau of Tourism Research, Canberra, pp. 236–253.

Muth, R. and Clark, R. (1978) Public participation in wilderness and backcountry litter control: A review of research and management experience. *USDA Forest Service General Technical Report PNW-75*, Portland, Oregon.

Nash, R. (2014) *Wilderness and the American Mind.* 5th Edn. Yale University Press, New Haven, Connecticut.

National Park Service (1997) VERP: The visitor experience and resource protection (VERP) framework - A handbook for planners and managers. Denver Service Center, Denver, Colorado.

National Trails (2011) National Trails System Annual Report for FY 2010. Available at: http://www.nps.gov/nts/2010%20Annual%20Report.pdf (accessed 4 November 2016).

Newman, P., Manning, R., Bacon, J., Graefe, A. and Kyle, G. (2002) An evaluation of Appalachian Trailhikers' knowledge of minimum impact skills and practices. *Proceedings of the 2001 Northeastern Recreation Research Symposium. USDA Forest Service General Technical Report NE-289*, Newtown Square, Pennsylvania, pp. 163–167.

Newman, P., Manning, R., Bacon, A., Graefe, A. and Kyle, G. (2003) An evaluation of Appalachian Trail hikers' knowledge of minimum impact skills and practices. *International Journal of Wilderness* 9, 34–38.

Newsome, D., Cole, D. and Marion, J. (2004) Environmental impacts associated with recreational horse-riding. In: Buckley, R. (ed.) *Environmental Impacts of Ecotourism.* CAB International, Wallingford, UK.

Nielson, C. and Buchanan, T. (1986) A comparison of the effectiveness of two interpretive programs regarding fire ecology and fire management. *Journal of Interpretation* 1, 1–10.

NPS Air Resources (2016) National Park Service Air Resources Division. Available at: http://www.nature.nps.gov/air (accessed 15 August 2016).

NPS Archaeology Program (2016) Available at: http://www.nps.gov/archeology/ (accessed 15 August 2016).

NPS Natural Sounds (2016) Available at: https://www.nps.gov/subjects/sound/index.htm (accessed 15 August 2016).

NPS Night Skies (2016) Available at: https://www.nps.gov/subjects/nightskies/index.htm (accessed 15 August 2016).

NPS Stats (2016) Available at: https://irma.nps.gov/Stats/ (accessed 15 August 2016).

Nyaupane, G., Graefe, A. and Burns, R. (2007) Understanding equity in the recreation user fee context. *Leisure Sciences* 29, 425–442.

Odum, E. (1953) *Fundamentals of Ecology.* W.B. Saunders, Philadelphia, Pennsylvania.

Oliver, S., Roggenbuck, J. and Watson, A. (1985) Education to reduce impacts in forest campgrounds. *Journal of Forestry* 83, 234–236.

Olson, E., Bowman, M. and Roth, R. (1984) Interpretation and nonformal education in natural resources management. *Journal of Environmental Education* 15, 6–10.

Ostergren, D., Solop, F. and Hagen, K. (2005) National Park Service fees: Value for the money or barrier to visitation? *Journal of Park and Recreation Administration* 23, 18–36.

Park, L., Manning, R., Marion, J., Lawson, S. and Jacobi, C. (2008) Managing visitor impacts in parks: A multi-method study of the effectiveness of alternative management practices. *Journal of Park and Recreation Administration* 26, 97–121.

Park Science (2009–2010) Special issue: Soundscapes research and management - Understanding, protecting, and enjoying the acoustic environment of our national parks. *Park Science* 26, 1–72.

Parsons, D., Stohlgren, T. and Fodor, P. (1981) Establishing backcountry use quotas: The example from Mineral King, California. *Environmental Management* 5, 335–340.

Parsons, D., Stohlgren, T. and Kraushaar, J. (1982) Wilderness permit accuracy: Differences between reported and actual use. *Environmental Management* 6, 329–335.

Pendleton, M. (1996) Crime, criminals and guns in "natural settings": Exploring the basis for disarming federal rangers. *American Journal of Police* 4, 3–25.

Pendleton, M. (1998) Policing the park: Understanding soft enforcement. *Journal of Leisure Research* 30, 552–571.

Perry, M. (1983) Controlling crime in the parks. *Parks and Recreation* 18, 49–51, 67.

Peters, N. and Dawson, C. (2005) Estimating visitor use and distribution in two Adirondack wilderness areas. *Proceedings of the 2004 Northeastern Recreation Research Symposium, USDA Forest Service GTR-NE-326*, Newtown Square, Pennsylvania.

Peterson, D. (1987) Look ma, no hands! Here's what's wrong with no-rescue wilderness. *Parks and Recreation* 22, 39–43, 54.

Peterson, G. and Lime, D. (1979) People and their behavior: A challenge for recreation management. *Journal of Forestry* 77, 343–346.

Philley, M. and McCool, S. (1981) Law enforcement in the National Park system: Perceptions and practices. *Leisure Sciences* 4, 355–371.

Plager, A. and Womble, P. (1981) Compliance with backcountry permits in Mount McKinley National Park. *Journal of Forestry* 79, 155–156.

Potter, F. and Manning, R. (1984) Application of the wilderness travel simulation model to the Appalachian Trail in Vermont. *Environmental Management* 8, 543–550.

Powers, R., Osborne, J. and Anderson, E. (1973) Positive reinforcement of litter removal in the natural environment. *Journal of Applied Behavior Analysis* 6, 579–580.

Puttkammer, A. and Wright, V. (2001) Linking wilderness research and management-Volume 3. Recreation fees in wilderness and other public lands: an annotated reading list. *USDA Forest Service General Technical Report RMRS-79*, Fort Collins, Colorado.

Ramthun, R. (1996) Information sources and attitudes of mountain bikers. *Proceedings of the 1995 Northeastern Recreation Research Symposium. USDA Forest Service General Technical Report NE-218*, Radnor, Pennsylvania.

Ready, R., Delavan, W. and Epp, D. (2004) The impact of license fees on Pennsylvania trout anglers' participation. *Proceedings of the 2003 Northeastern Recreation Research Symposium, USDA Forest Service General Technical Report NE-317*, Radnor, Pennsylvania, pp. 410–416.

Rechisky, A. and Williamson, B. (1992) Impact of user fees on day use attendance in New Hampshire State Parks. *Proceedings of the 1991 Northeastern Recreation Research Symposium. USDA Forest Service General Technical Report NE-160*, Radnor, Pennsylvania, pp. 106–108.

Reid, S. and Marion, J. (2004) Effectiveness of a confinement strategy for reducing campsite impacts in Shenandoah National Park. *Environmental Conservation* 31, 274–282.

Reid, S. and Marion, J. (2005) A comparison of campfire impacts and policies in seven protected areas. *Environmental Management* 36, 48–58.

Reiling, S., Cheng, H. and Trott, C. (1992) Measuring the discriminatory impact associated with higher recreational fees. *Leisure Sciences* 14, 121–137.

Reiling, S., McCarville, R. and White, C. (1994) *Demand and Marketing Study at Army Corps of Engineers Day-Use Areas.* U.S. Army Corps of Engineers Waterways Experiment Station, Vicksburg, Mississippi.

Reiling, S., Cheng, H., Robinson, C., McCarville, R. and White, C. (1996) Potential equity effects of a new day-use fee. *Proceedings of the 1995 Northeastern Recreation Research Symposium, USDA Forest Service General Technical report NE-218*, Radnor, Pennsylvania, pp. 27–31.

Robertson, R. (1982) Visitor knowledge affects visitor behavior. *Forest and River Recreation: Research Update.* University of Minnesota Agricultural Experiment Station Miscellaneous Publication 18, St. Paul, Minnesota, pp. 49–51.

Rodgers, J. and Schwikert, S. (2002) Buffer-zone distances to protect foraging and loafing waterbirds from disturbance by personal watercraft and outboard-powered boats. *Conservation Biology* 16, 216–224.

Roggenbuck, J. (1992) Use of persuasion to reduce resource impacts and visitor conflicts. *Influencing Human Behavior: Theory and Applications in Recreation, Tourism, and Natural Resources.* Sagamore Publishing, Champaign, Illinois, pp. 149–208.

Roggenbuck, J. and Berrier, D. (1981) Communications to disperse wilderness campers. *Journal of Forestry* 75, 295–297.

Roggenbuck, J. and Berrier, D. (1982) A comparison of the effectiveness of two communication strategies in dispersing wilderness campers. *Journal of Leisure Research* 14, 77–89.

Roggenbuck, J. and Ham, S. (1986) Use of information and education in recreation management. *A literature review: the President's commission on Americans outdoors.* U.S. Government Printing Office, M-59, M-71, Washington, DC.

Roggenbuck, J. and Passineau, J. (1986) Use of the field experiment to assess the effectiveness of interpretation. *Proceedings of the Southeastern Recreation Research Conference.* University of Georgia Institute of Community and Area Development, Athens, Georgia, pp. 65–86.

Roggenbuck, J. and Schreyer, R. (1977) Relations between river trip motives and perception of crowding, management preference, and experience satisfaction. *Proceedings: River Recreation Management and Research Symposium. USDA*

*Forest Service General Technical Report NC-28*, St. Paul, Minnesota, pp. 359–364.

Roggenbuck, J., Williams, D. and Bobinski, C. (1992) Public-private partnership to increase commercial tour guides' effectiveness as nature interpreters. *Journal of Park and Recreation Administration* 10, 41–50.

Roman, G., Dearden, P. and Rollins, R. (2007) Application of zoning and limits of acceptable change to manage snorkeling tourism. *Environmental Management* 39, 819–830.

Ross, T. and Moeller, G. (1974) Communicating rules in recreation areas. *USDA Forest Service Research Paper NE-297*, Darby, Pennsylvania.

Runte, A. (2010) *National Parks: The American Experience*. Taylor Trade Publishing, Boulder, Colorado.

Schechter, M. and Lucas, R. (1978) *Simulation of Recreational Use for Park and Wilderness Management*. Johns Hopkins University Press, Baltimore, Maryland.

Schneider, I. and Budruk, M. (1999) Displacement as a response to the federal recreation fee program. *Journal of Park and Recreation Administration* 17, 76–84.

Schomaker, J. and Leatherberry, E. (1983) A test for inequity in river recreation reservation systems. *Journal of Soil and Water Conservation* 38, 52–56.

Schroeder, H. and Louviere, J. (1999) Stated choice models for predicting the impact of user fees at public recreation sites. *Journal of Leisure Research* 31, 300–324.

Schuett, M. (1993) Information sources and risk recreation: The case of whitewater kayakers. *Journal of Park and Recreation Administration* 11, 67–72.

Schwartz, E. (1973) Police services in the parks. *Parks and Recreation* 8, 72–74.

Schwartz, Z. and Lin, L.-C. (2006) The impact of fees on visitation of national parks. *Tourism Management* 27, 1386–1396.

Scott, D. (2013) Economic inequality, poverty, and park and recreation delivery. *Journal of Park and Recreation Administration* 31, 1–11.

Scrogin, D. (2005) Lottery-rationed public access under alternative tariff arrangements: Changes in quality, quantity, and expected utility. *Journal of Environmental Economics and Management* 50, 189–211.

Scrogin, D. and Berrens, R. (2003) Rationed access and welfare: The case of public resource lotteries. *Land Economics* 79, 137–148.

Scrogin, D., Berrens, R. and Bohara, A. (2000) Policy changes and the demand for lottery-rationed big game hunting licenses. *Journal of Agricultural and Resource Economics* 25, 501–519.

Shanks, B. (1976) Guns in the parks. *The Progressive* 40, 21–23.

Shelby, B. and Heberlein, T. (1984) A conceptual framework for carrying capacity determination. *Leisure Sciences* 6, 433–451.

Shelby, B. and Heberlein, T. (1986) *Carrying Capacity in Recreation Settings*. Oregon State University Press, Corvallis, Oregon.

Shelby, B., Danley, B., Gibbs, M. and Peterson, M. (1982) Preferences of backpackers and river runners for allocation techniques. *Journal of Forestry* 80, 416–360.

Shelby, B., Whittaker, D. and Danley, M. (1989a) Idealism versus pragmatism in user evaluations of allocation systems. *Leisure Sciences* 11, 61–70.

Shelby, B., Whittaker, D. and Danley, M. (1989b) Allocation currencies and perceived ability to obtain permits. *Leisure Sciences* 11, 137–144.

Shindler, B. and Shelby, B. (1993) Regulating wilderness use: An investigation of user group support. *Journal of Forestry* 91, 41–44.

Shore, D. (1994) Bad lands. *Outside* 19, 56–71.

Siderelis, C. and Moore, R. (2006) Examining the effects of hypothetical modifications in permitting procedures and river conditions on whitewater boating behavior. *Journal of Leisure Research* 38, 558–574.

Sieg, G., Roggenbuck, J. and Bobinski, C. (1988) The effectiveness of commercial river guides as interpreters. *Proceedings of the 1987 Southern Recreation Research Conference*. University of Georgia, Athens, Georgia, pp. 12–20.

Sorice, M., Oh, C.-O. and Ditton, R. (2007) Managing scuba divers to meet ecological goals for coral reef conservation. *Ambio* 36, 316–322.

Spildie, D., Cole, D. and Walker, S. (2000) Effectiveness of a confinement strategy in reducing pack stock impacts at campsites in the Selway-Bitterroot Wilderness, Idaho. *Wilderness Science in a Time of Change Conference Volume 4: Wilderness Visitors, Experiences, and Visitor Management. USDA Forest Service Proceedings RMRS-15*, Ogden, Utah, pp. 199–208.

Stankey, G. (1973) Visitor perception of wilderness recreation carrying capacity. *USDA Forest Service Research Paper INT-142*, Ogden, Utah.

Stankey, G. (1979) Use rationing in two southern California wilderness. *Journal of Forestry* 77, 347–349.

Stankey, G. and Baden, J. (1977) Rationing wilderness use: Methods, problems, and guidelines. *UDSA Forest Service Research Paper INT-192*, Ogden, Utah.

Stankey, G. and Manning, R. (1986) Carrying capacity of recreation settings. *A literature review: The President's commission on Americans outdoors*. U.S. Government Printing Office, M-47, M-57, Washington, DC.

Stankey, G. and Schreyer, R. (1987) Attitudes toward wilderness and factors affecting visitor behavior: A state-of-knowledge review. *Proceedings: National Wilderness Research Conference: Issues, State-of-Knowledge, Future Directions. USDA Forest Service General Technical Report INT-220*, Ogden, Utah, pp. 246–293.

Stankey, G., Cole, D., Lucas, R., Peterson, M., Frissell, S. and Washburne, R. (1985) The limits of acceptable change (LAC) system for wilderness planning. *USDA Forest Service General Technical Report INT-176*, Ogden, Utah.

Stankey, G., Clark, R. and Bormann, B. (2005) Adaptive management of natural resources: Theory, concepts and management institutions. *USDA Forest Service General Technical Report PNW-654*, Portland, Oregon.

Steidl, R. and Powell, B. (2006) Assessing the effects of human activities on wildlife. *The George Wright Forum* 23, 50–58.

Stewart, W. (1989) Fixed itinerary systems in backcountry management *Journal of Environmental Management* 29, 163–171.

Stewart, W. (1991) Compliance with fixed itinerary systems in water-based parks. *Environmental Management* 15, 235–240.

Stewart, W., Cole, D., Manning, R., Valliere, W., Taylor, J. and Lee, M. (2000) Preparing for a day hike at Grand Canyon: What information is useful? *Wilderness Science in a Time of Change Conference Volume 4: Wilderness Visitors, Experiences, and Visitor Management. USDA Forest Service Proceedings RMRS-15*, Ogden, Utah.

Steidl, R. and Powell, B. (2006) Assessing the effects of human activities on wildlife. *The George Wright Forum* 23(2), 50–58.

Swearington, T. and Johnson, D. (1995) Visitors' responses to uniformed park employees. *Journal of Park and Recreation Administration* 13, 73–85.

Taff, D., Newman, P., Vagias, W. and Lawhon, B. (2014a) Comparing day-users' and overnight visitors' attitudes concerning leave no trace. *Journal of Outdoor Recreation, Education, and Leadership* 6, 133–146.

Taff, D., Newman, P., Lawson, S., Bright, A., Marin, L., Gibson, A. and Archie, T. (2014b) The role of messaging on acceptability of military aircraft sounds in Sequoia National Park. *Applied Acoustics* 84, 122–128.

Taylor, D. and Winter, P. (1995) Environmental values, ethics, and depreciative behavior in wildland settings. *Proceedings of the Second Symposium on Social Aspects and Recreation Research. USDA Forest Service General Technical Report PSW-156*, Ontario, California, 59–66.

Taylor, J., Vaske, J., Shelby, L., Donnelly, M. and Browne-Nunez, C. (2002) Visitor response to demonstration fees at National Wildlife Refuges. *Wildlife Society Bulletin* 30, 1238–1244.

Thede, A., Haider, W. and Rutherford, M. (2014) Zoning in national parks: are Canadian zoning practices outdated? *Journal of Sustainable Tourism* 22, 626–645.

Trainor, S. and Norgaard, R. (1999) Recreation fees in the context of wilderness values. *Journal of Park and Recreation Administration* 17, 100–115.

Tucker, W. (2001) Minimum group sizes: Allowing public access and increasing safety. *Crossing Boundaries in Park Management: Proceedings of the 11th Conference on Research and Resource Management in Parks and Public Lands*. The George Wright Society, Hancock, Michigan, pp. 187–192.

Underhill, H., Xaba, A. and Borkan, R. (1986) The wilderness use simulation model applied to Colorado River Boating in Grand Canyon National Park, USA. *Environmental Management* 10, 367–374.

Utter, J., Gleason, W. and McCool, S. (1981) User perceptions of river recreation allocation techniques. *Some Recent Products of River Recreation Research. USDA Forest Service General Technical Report NC-63*, St. Paul, Minnesota, pp. 27–32.

Uysal, M., McDonald, C. and Reid, L. (1990) Sources of information used by international visitors to U.S. parks and natural areas. *Journal of Park and Recreation Administration* 8, 51–59.

Van Wagtendonk, J. (1981) The effect of use limits on backcountry visitation trends in Yosemite National Park. *Leisure Sciences* 4, 311–323.

Van Wagtendonk, J. and Benedict, J. (1980) Wilderness permit compliance and validity. *Journal of Forestry* 78, 399–401.

Van Wagtendonk, J. and Colio, P. (1986) Trailhead quotas: Rationing use to keep wilderness wild. *Journal of Forestry* 84, 22–24.

Vander Stoep, G. and Gramann, J. (1987) The effect of verbal appeals and incentives on depreciative behavior among youthful park visitors. *Journal of Leisure Research* 19, 69–83.

Vander Stoep, G. and Roggenbuck, J. (1996) Is your park being "loved to death?": Using communication and other indirect techniques to battle the park "love bug". *Crowding and Congestion in the National Park System: Guidelines for Research and Management*, University of Minnesota Agricultural Experiment Station, St. Paul, Minnesota.

Vogt, C. and Williams, D. (1999) Support for wilderness recreation fees: The influence of fee purpose and day versus overnight use. *Journal of Park and Recreation Administration* 17, 85–99.

Vork, M. (1998) Visitor response to management regulation – A study among recreationists in southern Norway. *Environmental Management* 22, 737–746.

Wade, J. (1979) Law enforcement in the wilderness. *Trends* 16, 12–15.

Wagar, J. (1964) The carrying capacity of wild lands for recreation. *Forest Science Monograph 7*, Society of American Foresters, Washington, DC.

Wagar, J. (1968) The place of carrying capacity in the management of recreation lands. *Third Annual Rocky Mountain-High Plains Park and Recreation Conference Proceedings*, Colorado State University, Fort Collins, Colorado.

Wagstaff, M. and Wilson, B. (1988) The evaluation of litter behavior modification in a river environment. In: *Proceedings of the 1987 Southeastern Recreation Research Conference*, University of Georgia, Asheville, North Carolina, pp. 21–28.

Walmsley, S. and White, A. (2003) Influence of social, management and enforcement factors on the long-term ecological effects of marine sanctuaries. *Environmental Conservation* 30, 388–407.

Wang, B. and Manning, R. (1999) Computer simulation modeling for recreation management: A study on carriage road use in Acadia National Park, Maine, USA. *Environmental Management* 23, 193–203.

Watson, A. (1993) Characteristics of visitors without permits compared to those with permits at the Desolation Wilderness, California. *USDA Forest Service General Research Note INT-414*, Ogden, Utah.

Watson, A. and Niccolucci, M. (1995) Conflicting goals of wilderness management: Natural conditions vs. natural experiences. *Proceedings of the Second Symposium on Social Aspects and Recreation Research. USDA Forest Service*

*General Technical Report PSW-156*, Ogden, Utah, pp. 11–15.

Watson, A., Niccolucci, M. and Williams, D. (1993) Hikers and recreational packstock users: predicting and managing recreation conflicts in Three Wildernesses. *USDA Forest Service Research Paper INT-468*, Ogden, Utah.

Westover, T., Flickenger, T. and Chubb, M. (1980) Crime and law enforcement. *Parks and Recreation* 15, 28–33.

Whittaker, D. and Shelby, B. (2008) *Allocating river use: A review of approaches and existing systems for river professionals*. River Management Society, Missoula, Montana.

Whittaker, D., Shelby, B., Manning, R., Cole, D. and Haas, G. (2010) *Capacity reconsidered: Finding consensus and clarifying differences*. National Association of Recreation Resource Planners, Marienville, Pennsylvania.

Whittaker, D., Shelby, B., Manning, R., Cole, D. and Haas, G. (2011) Capacity reconsidered: Finding consensus and clarifying differences. *Journal of Park and Recreation Administration* 29, 1–20.

Wicker, A. and Kirmeyer, S. (1976) What the rangers think. *Parks and Recreation* 11, 28–42.

Wicks, B. (1987) The allocation of recreation and park resources: The courts' intervention. *Journal of Park and Recreation Administration* 5, 1–9.

Wicks, B. and Crompton, J. (1986) Citizen and administrator perspectives of equity in the delivery of park services. *Leisure Sciences* 8, 341–365.

Wicks, B. and Crompton, J. (1987) An analysis of the relationships between equity choice preferences, service type and decision making groups in a U.S. city. *Journal of Leisure Research* 19, 189–204.

Wicks, B. and Crompton, J. (1989) Allocation services for parks and recreation: A model for implementing equity concepts in Austin, Texas. *Journal of Urban Affairs* 11, 169–188.

Wicks, B. and Crompton, J. (1990) Predicting the equity preferences of park and recreation department employees and residents of Austin, Texas. *Journal of Leisure Research* 22, 18–35.

Wikle, T. (1991) Comparing rationing policies used of rivers. *Journal of Park and Recreation Administration* 9, 73–80.

Williams, D., Vogt, C. and Vitterso, J. (1999) Structural equation modeling of users' response to wilderness recreation fees. *Journal of Leisure Research* 31, 245–268.

Williams, P. and Black, J. (2002) Issues and concerns related to the USDA Forest Service's recreational fee demonstration program: A synthesis of published literature, critical reports, media reports, public comments, and likely knowledge gaps. Report submitted to Recreation, Heritage, and Wilderness Program, USDA Forest Service, Washington, DC.

Willis, C., Canavan, J. and Bond, R. (1975) Optimal short-run pricing policies for a public campground. *Journal of Leisure Research* 7, 108–113.

Winter, P., Palucki, L. and Burkhardt, R. (1999) Anticipated responses to a fee program: The key is trust. *Journal of Leisure Research* 31, 207–226.

World Tourism Organization (2006) Global Code of Ethics for Tourism. Resolution 406 (XIII), World Tourism Organization, Madrid.

# Index

Note: **bold** page numbers indicate figures and tables.

Abbey, Edward 67
Acadia National Park (Maine) 15, 16, 27–28, 44, **50**, **51**, **56**, **57**, 152
    depreciative behavior in 55, 56–57, 161
    managing hiking in 55–58, **57**, 158, 161, 164, 173
    ridgerunners in 57–58, 167, 171
Acadia Trails Forever 56, 57
adaptive management 8, 144, 145, 146, 148, 159–160
air quality 12, 13, **46**, **47**, **48**, 79, 127, 128, 157, 160, 163
    and four basic strategies 179–180, 188–189, 195, 204–205
    and snow vehicles 142, 144, 145
air tours 130–133, **131**
    and regulations 130–131, 132
Alaska Range 82, 83
alcohol 59, 60, 61
Allegheny National Forest (Pennsylvania) 29
amphibians 12, 63, 110
Annapolis Rocks (Appalachian National Scenic Trail) 59–61, **60**, 162
    campfires/littering at 59–60
    redevelopment of 60–61, 170
Antiquities Act (1906) 100, 107, 169
Apostle Islands National Lakeshore (Wisconsin) 50, **51**, 91–94, 162
    crowding at 91
    ice caves at 91, 92–93, **92**, **93**
    information/education at 91, 92–93, 169
    partnerships at 93
    rules/regulations at 93
    visitor access to 91, 161, 171
Appalachian National Scenic Trail 29, 43–44, **50**, **51**, 63, 158, 162
    maintenance of 59
    redesigned campsite on 59–61, **60**, 162, 164, 166, 169, 170
Appalachian Trail Conservancy 59
applying management practices 45–50
aquatic environment 28, 41, 160
    and invasive species 118
    *see also* Biscayne National Park; Voyageurs National Park
archeoastronomy 79–80
archeological sites 99–102
Arches National Park (Utah) 50, **51**, 66–70, **67**, 170, 172
    carrying capacity of 67–69, **68**, **69**

cryptobiotic soil in 67–68
education/information in 69, 162, 163
historic cabin in 67
indicators of quality in 67, 68, 159, 167
parking at 68–69, 162, 163, 164
permit systems in 69, 163
VERP framework in 67, 69
    *see also* Delicate Arch
attraction sites 15, **46**, **47**, **48**, 79, 82, 91, 103, 110, 114, 127, 157, 160
    and four basic strategies 183–184, 191, 198–199, 207
ATVs (all-terrain vehicles) 15
Australia 35

backcountry recreation *see* wilderness
backpackers *see* hiking/hikers
Banff National Park (Canada) 40
bats 75–78, **76**, 79, 110
Bear Lake (Rocky Mountain National Park) 15
bears 11, 40, 82, 85, 104, 144, 148, 150, 152
    viewing 114–117, **115**, **116**
bicycles/cycling 15, 27, 147, 148–149, **148**
bighorn sheep 11, 144, 150
biodiversity 63, 71, 72, 118, 150
birds 11–12, 42, 96, 144
Biscayne National Park (Florida) 50, **51**, 71–74, 160, 164
    biodiversity of 71, 72
    boat groundings at 71–72, 73, 158, 161
    buoys/markers in 73
    and Columbus Day weekend 72, 74
    education at 72–73, 161, 167
    law enforcement in 74
    managing recreational boating at 72–74
    marine reserve zone in 73–74
bison 144
Blue Ridge Parkway 16
boardwalks 15, 43, 114, 115, 116, 117, 163
boating, recreational 71–74
    damage caused by 71–72, **73**
    management of 72–74
Boundary Waters Canoe Area (Minnesota) 25, 27, 28
Boy Scouts 27, 55
Bright Angel Trail (Grand Canyon National Park) 15
Brooks River (Alaska) *see* Katmai National Park and Preserve

brown bears 114, **115**
Bubble Rock (Acadia National Park) 57
bulletin boards 24, 26–27, 31
bus systems 16, **64**, 91, 93, 114, **128**
    and information/education 84, 101, 163
    and limiting use strategy 64
    and partnerships 128, 171
    and reduction of impact 62, 83–84, 158, 165, 167
    and traffic congestion 127, 128–129, 162, 163, 167
    VTS 82, 83–84, **83**, 85


Cadillac Mountain (Acadia National Park) 15
cairns 15, 56, 57
California 35, 39
campfires 10, 12, 15, 16, 59
    and direct/indirect management practices 20, 21, **21**, 22
    and information/education **23**, 27, 169
    and rules/regulations 40–41, 164
    see also firewood
campsites/campgrounds 9, 12, 14, 15–16, **17**, 20, 59–61,
    **60**, 76, 79, 86, 157, 160, 161
    caretakers at 59, 60
    design/redesign of 43–44, **43**, 158, 162
    and direct/indirect management practices 20, 21, **21**
    and four basic strategies 184–185, 191–192, 200,
        207–208
    and information/education **23**, 25–26, 29, 59
    and management matrices **46**, **47**, **48**
    monitoring 60, 61
    permits for 16
    and wildlife 82, 84, 85
car parks 16, **46**, **47**, **48**, 68–69, 137, 160, 161
    charges 36
    permits 64
    and pollution 111, 158
    see also parking
caribou 82
Carlsbad Caverns National Park (New Mexico) **50**, **51**,
    110–113, **111**, **112**, 160, 162
    above-ground trails at 111
    bats in 110
    lint pollution/clean-up in 110, 111–112, 165
    managing contaminants at 110, 111–113, 158
    permit systems at 110, 111, 112
    redesign of parking at 111
    restrictions on use at 112–113
    variety of speleothems in 110
Carriage Roads (Acadia National Park) 15
carrying capacity 4–5, 6, 66, 157, 158
Cathedral Grove (Muir Woods National
    Monument) 95–97, **97**
    quiet zone in 95, 97, 166, 170
    Roosevelt commemoration in 95–96, 97
Chaco Culture National Historical Park (New Mexico)
    **50**, **51**, 79–81, **80**, 160, 162, 163
    and archeoastronomy 79–80

in lobbying partnership 171
    managing natural darkness in 80–81, 170
    observatory at **81**
Cherokee Indians 63
children 39, 57, 58, 97, 146
choice, freedom of 4, 20, 168
Civilian Conservation Corps 56, 129
Cliff Palace (Mesa Verde National Park) 99, 100, **100**,
    101, 161
climate change 93
Colorado River (Grand Canyon National Park) 50, 51,
    86–90, **87**, 159, 164, 170, 172
    campsites on 88, **88**, 161, 165, 171
    carrying capacity of 87–88, 172
    commercial/non-commercial use on 89
    crowding on 86, 87, 173
    history of river rafting on 86
    information/education on 86, 88, 89, 169
    launch numbers/calendar for 88
    law enforcement on 88, 89, 162
    lottery system for 89, 162, 168, 169
    Management Plan for 87–89, 166, 170–171
    motorized/non-motorized use of 88, 89, 161, 164
    and National Park Service 86, 87, 88, 89
    rules/regulations on 88–89, 162
    TAOT/PAOT on 88
    website 89, 164
    zoning of 89, 162, 164, 167
common property resources, parks as 4, 157, 158
coral reefs 28, 41, 71–72, **72**, 73, 158
Costa Rica 37
crayfish, rusty 119
crowding 5, 8, 9, 13–14, 15, 16, 17, 35, 59, 62, 63–65,
    66, 91, 103, 114, 157, 160, 161, 163
    and four basic strategies 181–182,
        190, 197, 206
    and management matrices **46**, **47**, **48**, 49
    measurement of 14, **14**
    on mountains 122, 125, 158, 166
    on rivers 86
    standards of quality for 68, **68**, **69**
    and vehicles 127–129
    see also carrying capacity
cryptobiotic soil 67
curfews 132, 142


Dall sheep 82
deer 11, 144
Delicate Arch (Arches National Park) 66, 68, **68**, **69**,
    159, 161, 162, 163, 167, 173
Denali, Mount 82, 83, **83**, 141
Denali National Park and Preserve (Alaska) 16, **50**, **51**,
    82–85, 160, 163, 172
    Backcountry Information Center in 84, 85
    camping/cooking in 84, 85
    hikers in 83, 84–85, **84**

information/education in 83, 84, 162, 164
    landscapes of 82–83
    and National Park Service 83, 84, 85
    permit system in 84, 85, 162, 164, 167, 168
    quality indicators/standards in 85, 159
    road/bus service in 83–84, **83**, 158, 161, 162,
        169, 170
    wilderness area in 84–85
    wildlife of 82, 83, 85
depreciative behavior 13, 15, 17, 59–60, 142, 157,
    160, 161
    at archeological/ancient sites 99, 106
    at sacred sites 138
    classification of 22
    and educational programs 22–24, 25, 29, 55
    and four basic strategies 183, 190–191, 198, 206
    and management matrices 46–47, **46, 47, 48**
    noise-making 95, 96
    off-trail hiking 29, 41, 56–57, 69, 142, 166
    punishment for 22, 27
    theft 106, 107–109, 161, 162
Devil's Garden (Arches National Park) 67, 68
Devils Tower National Monument (Wyoming) 50, **51**,
    138–141, **139**
    climber registration at 140
    Climbing Management Plan for 138, 139–140
    education/information program at 139–140
    future of 140–141
    impacts of climbing at 138–139
    as sacred site 138, 139, 140–141, 161
    sculpture at 140, **140**
    voluntary climbing ban at 139, 140
    zoning at 138, 162
dispersing recreation use 19, 25–26, 42–43, 45–46, 161,
    163, 171
distributive justice 34
diving/divers 28, 73
dual mission of national parks 3–4, 157, 158–159


eagles 11–12, 144
Eastern Sierra Interagency Visitor Center 104
education *see* information/education
elasticity of demand 37, 38
Elkmont Campground (Great Smoky Mountains
    National Park) 62
entrance fees *see* pricing systems
environmental/social impacts 5, 15, 16, 17, 19, 146
    and information/education 25
    and use rationing/allocation 34
equity 34–35, 39, 40, 89
evaluation of management practices 25–44
    and depreciative behavior 29
    facility development/site design/maintenance
        42–44, **43**
    information/education programs 25–31
    law enforcement 41

    pricing 36–39
    use patterns 25–26, 39
    use rationing/allocation *see* recreation use rationing/
        allocation
    and visitor attitudes 29
    and visitor knowledge 26–29
    zoning 41–42
experience component 6, 7


Facebook 69, 92, 169
facility development/site design/maintenance 42–44, **43**,
    71, 99, 134, 146, 158, 162, 163
    and backcountry camping 150
    buses *see* bus systems
    car parks *see* car parks
    and contaminants 110
    fencing 66, 69
    and hardening resources strategy 203–206, 207–208
    and increasing supply strategy 187, 188, 189, 190,
        191, 192
    and limiting use strategy 177, 178, 179, 180, 181,
        182, 183, 184, 185, 186
    and management matrices 46, 47, 48
    and natural darkness 79, 80
    and reducing impact of use strategy 193, 194, 195,
        196, 197, 198, 199, 200, 201, 202
    sanitation 16, 59–60, 75
    and wildlife viewing 114, 115, 116, 117
    winter facilities 142
fairness criterion 34–35
Federal Aviation Administration 131
fee systems *see* pricing
fencing 66, 69, 114
fertilizer use 6
Fiery Furnace (Arches National Park) 67, 69
fire, controlled 29
fireflies 79, 158, 161–162, 168
    *see also Photinus carolinus*
firewood 10, 15, 22, **23**, 40–41, 59, 99, 152, 164
first-come, first-served 31–34, **32–33**, 35, 151–152,
    162, 168
fishing 12, **21**, 117, 120, 144
    fees 36–37
Flaming Gorge National Recreation Areas
    (Utah/Wyoming) 38
Florida 28, 72
fungi 10, 62, 67
    *see also* WNS


Gilligan, C. 22, **23**
Glacier National Park (Montana) 50, **51**, 132, 150–153,
    **151**, 161, 162
    backcountry camping in 150, 151–153, 160, 169
    Going-to-the-Sun road in 16, 150
    mountain chalets in 152, **153**

Glacier National Park (Montana) (*continued*)
    permit/reservation system in 150, 151–153, 169
    rules/regulations in 152, 153
    trail hazards in 150, 151, 152
    wildlife in 150, 152
Global Code of Ethics for Tourism 22
goal interference 14
Going-to-the-Sun road (Glacier National Park) 16, 150
GPS technology 28, 152
graffiti 13, 15, 17
Grand Canyon National Park (Arizona) 3, 15, 26, 41,
        50, **51**, 86, 160, 161, 162, 167
    curfews in 132
    Flight Free Zones in 132
    history/resources of 147
    managing overflights in 130–133, 159, 162,
        169, 172
    noise pollution in 96, 130–131, **131**
    promotion of alternative travel in 147–149, **148**
    *see also* Colorado River
Grand Teton National Park (Wyoming) 50, **51, 147**
    impacts of visitors on wildlife in 146, 148
    multi-use path in 146–149, 159, 161, 170
    promotion of alternative travel in 147–149, 159–160
    rules/regulations in 148–149
Great Barrier Reef Marine Park (Australia) 42
Great Lakes region 118, 119, 120, 121
Great Smoky Mountains National Park (North Carolina/
        Tennessee) 28, 50, **51**, 62–65
    biodiversity of 63
    historical/cultural resources of 63
    information/education in 64–65
    management of firefly displays in 63–65, **63, 64,**
        158, 161–162, 168
    website 64, 65
Greece 35
grizzly bears 40, 82, 83, 150
group size limits 39–40, 59, 152, 162

Half Dome (Yosemite National Park) 122–126, **123**, 161,
        165, 170
    cable route on 123, 124, **124**, 125, 126
    crowding on 122, 125, 158, 161, 166, 173
    danger for hikers on 122, 123–124
    as designated wilderness 124
    future of 125–126
    monitoring use of 124–125
    National Park Service research on 125
    permit/lottery system for 124, 125, 162, 164,
        166, 168
hardening resources strategy 19–20, 41, 43, 59, 71, 99,
        114, 127, 134, 146, 158, 161, 162, 163, 203–208
    management matrix for 48, **48**
Hardin, G. 4, 126
Hawaii Volcanoes National Park 132
Hell's Canyon (Idaho) 34

hiking/hikers 9, 10, 15, **16**, 83
    information/education for 26–29
    off-trail 29, 41, 56–57, 69, 142, 166
    and pets 57, 82, 85, 117, 148, 169
    rules/regulations for 40
    surveys of 125
    *see also* campsites/campgrounds; trails
historical/cultural resources 3, 9, 13, 56, 63, 83, 86, 99,
        106, 157, 160–161
    and Antiquities Act (1906) 100
    and four basic strategies 181, 189, 196–197,
        205–206
    and management matrices **46, 47, 48**
    sacred sites 138–141
    *see also* archeological sites; Chaco Culture
        National Historical Park; National Mall
horse-riding 15, **16**, 27, 76, 144, 150, 152
human waste 11, 16, 103, 104, **105**, 161, 165
    and education programs 22, **23**
hunting 11, 12, 14, **21, 32**, 36

increase supply strategy 79, 106, 134, 146, 158, 161
Indiana bat **76**
information brochures 25–26, 27, 28, 30, 31, 55, 77
information/education 6, 8, 21, **21**, 22–24, **23**, 44, 62,
        64–65, 66, 69, 114, 158, 162
    at historical/cultural sites 101, 106, 108–109, **108**,
        134, 136
    and attitudes/beliefs/norms 23, 24
    and communication theory 23–24
    and crowding 163
    and depreciative behavior 25, 29
    effectiveness of, evaluating 25–31
    electronic media 64, 65, 89, 136, 164, 169, 170
    guidelines for using 30–31
    and hardening resources strategy 48, 203, 204,
        205, 206, 207, 208
    and increasing supply strategy 187, 188, 189, 190,
        191, 192
    and invasive species 118, 120, **120**
    Leave No Trace *see* Leave No Trace program
    and limiting use strategy 177, 178, 179, 180, 181,
        182, 183, 184, 185, 186
    and management matrices 46–47, **46, 47, 48, 48**, 49
    and multi-use paths 146
    for natural darkness 79, 80
    for natural quiet 95, 97
    and peripheral route to persuasion 24
    and pricing 38
    and recreation use patterns 25–26
    and reducing impact of use strategy 164, 193, 194,
        195, 196, 197–198, 199, 200, 201
    and ridgerunners 55, 57–58, 60
    and sacred sites 138, 139–140
    and theories of moral development 22, **23**
    and trip planning 30, 169, 170

and use rationing/allocation 34
and visitor attitudes 25, 29
and visitor knowledge 25, 26–29
International Biosphere Reserves 76
International Dark Sky Parks 80
interpretive facilities/programs 16–17, **46, 47, 48**, 158–159
and four basic strategies 186, 192, 201–202, 208
*see also* information/education; signage
invasive species 118, 119–121
preventative strategy for 118
Inyo National Forest (California/Nevada) 103
irrigation 6, 134, 136

Katmai National Park and Preserve (Alaska) **50, 51,**
114–117, 160, 161, 172
"Bear Etiquette" course at 116–117
boardwalk/viewing platforms at 115–116, **116**, 117,
161, 163, 168
history/resources of 114–115
remoteness/popularity of 115
visitor safety at 114, 115, 116, 117
webcams/discussions/blogs at 116, 165
Kings Canyon National Park (California) 103
Koh Chang National Marine Park (Thailand) 42
Kohlberg, L. 22, **23**

LAC (Limits of Acceptable Change) framework 7, 8,
157, 159
Lakes Cave (Greece) 35
law enforcement 7, 41, 44, **46, 47, 48**, 66, 71, 77, 88,
89, 103, 134, 142, 150, 158, 162, 206
at archeological/ancient sites 99, 100, 106, 107
and increasing supply strategy 189, 190
and invasive species 118
and limiting use strategy 177, 178, 179, 180, 181,
182, 183, 184, 185, 186
and reducing impact of use strategy 193, 194, 195,
196, 197, 198, 199, 200, 201
Leave No Trace (LNT) program 22, 30, 56, 57, 58, 60,
152, 161, 163, 164
seven principles of 55, 58
Lechuguilla Cave (Carlsbad Caverns National
Park) 112–113
Lee's Ferry (Colorado River) 87, 88
Leopold, Aldo 126
light pollution 13, 65, 79, 80–81
limiting use strategy 59, 62, 66, 86, 99, 103, 110, 114,
130, 134, 142, 158, 161, 177–186
as limit of impact 167
limits of acceptable change 5, **5**, 8, 157, 158
Limits of Acceptable Change (LAC) framework 7, 8, 157, 159
litter layer 10
littering 9, 25, 29, 60
lottery systems 31, **32–33**, 36, 62, 64, 86, 89, 104, 122,
125, 162, 168, 169

McKenzie, Lake (Australia) 35
McKinley, Mount *see* Denali, Mount
Malthus, Thomas 4
Mammoth Cave National Park (Kentucky) 50, **51,**
75–78, 159
closure of caves in 75, 77, 169
clothing/caving gear in 77, 78, 167
educational materials in 77
gates in 77
regulation of visitors to 76–77
safety measures in 77–78
management matrices 45–51, 158, 165, 177–208
and categories of management practices 48
finer divisions in 49
for hardening resource/visitor experience 48, **48**,
203–208
for increasing recreation supply 45–46, **47**, 187–192
for limiting use 45, **46**, 177–186
number/variety of management options with 48–49
online 49
for reducing impact of use 46–48, **47**, 48–49,
193–202
management-by-objectives framework 7–8, **8**, 66, 67,
159, 172, 173
manatees 28, 71
Maryland 43–44
media 30, 31, 80
park newspapers 26, 31, 69, 164
merit systems 31, **32–33**, 34, 168
Mesa Verde National Park (Colorado) 50, **51**, 99–102, 158
and Antiquities Act 100–101
cliff dwellings in 100, **100**, 101
history of 99
information/education in 101
management practices in 100, 162
Museum Association 101, 171
as Native American ancestral home 99–100
ranger-led tours at 100, 101, **101**, 168
rules/regulations in 100, 101, 162
site closures in 100, 170
zoning in 100, 101–102
military aircraft 28
monitoring 7, 8, 34, 60, 61, 108, 109, 124–125,
159–160, 170
Montana 28
moose 82, 144
moral development, theories of 22, **23**
Mount Rainier National Park (Washington) 41
Mount Rushmore National Memorial (South
Dakota) 132
Mount Spil National Park (Turkey) 4
mountain biking 15, 27, 147, 148–149, **148**
Muir, John 95, 122
Muir Woods National Monument (California) 50, **51,**
95–98, **96**, 159, 160, 170, 173
education program in 95, 97, 161, 167
redwoods in 95

Muir Woods National Monument (California) (*continued*)
    visitor surveys in 95, 96–97, 172
    zoning in 95, 97, **97**, 162, 167
    *see also* Cathedral Grove

National Mall (Washington, DC) **50**, **51**, 134–137, **135**,
    **136**, 159, 160
    crowding at 134
    development of facilities at 135–136
    importance/popularity of 134
    information/education at 136, 170
    lawn restoration at 136, 163
    management framework/objectives for 135–137
    organized events/demonstrations at 137,
        161, 169
    parking at 137
    permit system at 137
    restricted activities at 136–137
    volunteer guides at 158–159, 161
National Outdoor Leadership School 55
national parks 3–8
    as environmental commons 4, 157, 158
    growing list of resources in 169–170
    importance of 3
    and threefold framework 6, 7, 157, 160, 166
National Parks Air Tour Management Act (2000) 132
National Parks Overflights Act (1987) 130
National Parks and Recreation Act (1978) 66
National Wilderness Preservation System 6
National Wildlife Refuges 38
Native Americans 63, 67, 79, 86, 99–100
    in co-management/partnership scheme 140–141
    and sacred sites 138–141, 161
natural darkness 9, 13, **46**, **47**, **48**, 79–81, 157, 160,
    161, 170
    and four basic strategies 180–181, 189, 196, 205
natural quiet 9, 12–13, **46**, **47**, **48**, 95–98, 127, 157,
    159, 160, 161, 170, 173
    and aircraft 28, 130–131
    educational program on 95
    and four basic strategies 180, 188–189, 195–196, 205
    and snow vehicles 142, 144
Natural Sounds Program Office (National Park
    Service) 96
New Hampshire 38–39
New York 26
noise pollution 95, 96, 127, 128, 142, 163
Norway 41

off-road vehicles 9, 10, **23**, 169
off-trail hiking 29, 41, 56–57, 69, 142, 166
Old Faithful Geyser (Yellowstone National Park) 15
Organic Act (1916) 126, 158, 167, 170
outdoor recreation 3–8
    growing list of activities 169

management framework 7–8, **8**
management principles *see* principles of managing
    outdoor recreation
threefold framework for 6, 7, 157, 160, 166
Owl, Northern Spotted 96

Pacific Rim National Park (Canada) 41
Painted Desert Visitor Center (Petrified Forest National
    Park) 107
PAOT (people-at-one-time) 88
Park Loop Road (Acadia National Park) 16
park managers 4, 7–8, **9**, 55
    and comprehensive/creative thinking 18
    education techniques used by 30
    professional judgement of 173
    and researchers 171–172
    *see also* recreation management practices
park newspapers 26, 31, 69, 164
park rangers
    climbing 138
    and information/education 16, 26, 29, 30, 41
    and law enforcement 29, 89, 107, 108, 122, 162, 164
    as role models 30
    tours led by 16, 66, 75, 77, 99, 101
parking 62, 66, 91, 127–129, 159, 164
    and four basic strategies 185–186, 192, 200–201, 208
    *see also* car parks
partnerships 56, 80, 81, 93, 103, 104, 119, 128,
    140–141, 171
Pemigewasset Wilderness (New Hampshire) 26
permit systems 25, 26, 28, 34, 36, 62, 66, 69, 84, 134, 164
    and backcountry camping 150, 151
    and caves 110, 111, 112
    and historical/cultural sites 137
    and mountains 103, 104, 124–125, 162
Petrified Forest National Park (Arizona) **50**, **51**, 106–109,
    158, 161
    information/education program at 106, 108–109, **108**
    monitoring at 108, 109
    prevention of theft from 106, 107–109, 161, 162
    resources of 107
    visitor center at 107
Philippines 41
*Photinus carolinus* 62, 63–65, **63**, 168
podcasts 89, 169, 170
pollution 9, 11, 12, 110, 111–113
    *see also* air quality; runoff
population growth 4
Powell, John Wesley 86
pricing systems 18, 21, 31, **32–33**, 35, 168
    acceptability of **32**, 36, 38
    differential 39
    and discrimination 34, 35, 38–39
    and elasticity of demand 37, 38
    evaluation of 36–39, 40
    and free access principle 36

overview of issues with 37
principles of 39, 40
principles of managing outdoor recreation 158–174
  Principle 1 (dual mission of parks) 158–159
  Principle 2 (management-by-objectives framework) 159
  Principle 3 (monitoring/adaptive management) 159–160
  Principle 4 (threefold framework) 160
  Principle 5 (Recreation Opportunity Spectrum) 160
  Principle 6 (impacts to park resources) 160–161
  Principle 7 (four basic strategies) 161–162
  Principle 8 (management tactics/practices) 162–163
  Principle 9 (multiple strategies/practices) 163
  Principle 10 (multiple problems) 163
  Principle 11 (multiple strategies advanced by management practices) 163–164
  Principle 12 (strategies advanced by multiple practices) 164
  Principle 13 (reinforcing programs of management practices) 164
  Principle 14 (management matrices) 164–165
  Principle 15 (appropriateness of management practices) 165
  Principle 16 (avoiding undesirable consequences of management practices) 165
  Principle 16 (use of information) 165–166
  Principle 18 (causes of impacts/problems) 166
  Principle 19 (consideration of larger geographic scales) 166–167
  Principle 20 (consideration of impacts, not use) 167
  Principle 21 (limiting use as last management option) 167
  Principle 22 (allocating limited opportunities for use) 167–168
  Principle 23 (direct/indirect management practices) 268
  Principle 24 (intensive use/management) 168–169
  Principle 25 (reaching visitors before they arrive) 169
  Principle 26 (growing list of recreation activities) 169
  Principle 27 (growing list of resources to protect) 169–170
  Principle 28 (expansion/evolution of management practices) 170
  Principle 29 (impact on visitor experience) 170–171
  Principle 30 (dispersing recreation use) 171
  Principle 31 (partnerships) 171
  Principle 32 (manager–researcher relationship) 171–172
  Principle 33 (measurement of quality) 172
  Principle 34 (proactive management) 172–173
  Principle 35 (managers' professional judgement) 173
  Principle 36 (strong management program) 173–174

problem behavior *see* depreciative behavior
Puebloan people 99–100

quality indicators/standards 5–6, 85, 170, 172, 173
  monitoring 7, 8, 67, 159
  red/yellow light system 17
  and ROS 7, 7, 8, 157, 160, 166, 171

Rainbow Forest Museum (Petrified Forest National Park) 107
rationing/allocation 31–39, **32–33**, **46**, 64, 82, 122, 158, 162, 167
  and aircraft 130
  and allocation of use 167–168
  at archeological sites 99
  effectiveness of 35–36, 44
  fairness of 34–35, 168
  five management practices for 31–34, **32–33**
  and lotteries *see* lottery systems
  and management matrices **46, 47, 48**
  monitoring 34
  permits *see* permit systems
  and pricing *see* pricing systems
  and wildlife viewing 114
  and winter activities 142
  *see also* limiting use strategy
recreation ecology 9, 11, 13
recreation management agencies 7–8, 30, 167
recreation management objectives 5–6, 8
  frameworks for 7–8, 8
recreation management practices 6, 17, 18–44, 157–158, 162–165
  adaptive management 8, 144, 145, 146, 148, 159, 160
  appropriateness of 165
  avoiding undesirable consequences of 165
  in case studies, overview of 50, 51
  direct/indirect 20–22, **20, 21**, 168, 173
  dispersing use 19, 25–26, 42–43, 45–46, 161, 163, 171
  evaluation of *see* evaluation of management practices
  expansion/evolution of 170
  for hardening resources *see* hardening resources strategy
  for increasing supply *see* increasing supply strategy
  intensive 168–169
  and larger geographic scales 166–167
  for limiting use *see* limiting use strategy
  modification of recreation activities 19
  pricing *see* pricing systems
  principles of *see* principles of managing outdoor recreation
  and problem behaviors, classification of 22
  reach of 169
  and real/effective areas 19
  and recreation management research 165–166
  and recreation supply/demand 18–19, **19**, 24

recreation management practices (*continued*)
  for reducing impact of use *see* reducing impact of
    use strategy
  and resistance/resilience of resources 18, 19–20, 24
  six categories of 25, 44, 45, 47–49, 158
  use rationing/allocation *see* recreation use rationing/
    allocation
  *see also* management matrices
recreation management strategies 18–20, **19**, 24, 163–164
  in case studies, overview of 50
  *see also* hardening resources strategy; increase
    supply strategy; limiting use strategy;
    reducing impact of use strategy
recreation opportunities 18, 20, **21**, 24, 166
  and use rationing/allocation 34
  and zoning 42
Recreation Opportunity Spectrum (ROS) 7, 7, 8, 157,
  160, 166, 171
recreation supply/demand 18–19, **19**, 24
recreation use patterns 25–26
recreation use rationing *see* rationing/allocation
reducing impact of use strategy 1, 55, 62, 66, 79, 86,
  91, 99, 103, 106, 114, 118, 127, 130, 134, 138,
  142, 146, 158, 161–162, 163, 167, 193–202
  and information/education 164
  and management matrices 46–48, **47**, 48–49, 193–202
Redwoods, Coast (*Sequoia sempervirens*) 95
reinforcing management programs 164
reservation systems 31, **32–33**, 35, 168
resistance/resilience of resources 18, 19–20, 24
rest/rotation of impact sites 6, **21**
ridgerunners 55, 57–58, 60, 167, 171
rivers/streams 11, 12
roads 12, 16, **21**, **46**, **47**, **48**, 91, 127, 128, 150, 157,
  160, 161
  conflicts over use of 146
  and four basic strategies 185–186, 192, 200–201, 208
  *see also* traffic congestion
rock climbing 28, 36, 138–139, 161
rock paintings/carvings 13
Rocky Mountain National Park (Colorado) 15, 26, 30, 132
Roosevelt, Theodore 95–96, 107
ROS *see* Recreation Opportunity Spectrum
rules/regulations 6, 15, 21, **21**, 55, 60, 62, 64–65, 66,
  75, 82, 88–89, 91, 158, 162
  at archeological/ancient sites 99, 106, 107
  and campfires 20, 22, 40–41
  effectiveness of, evaluating 29, 39–41, 44
  enforcement of *see* law enforcement
  given to visitors before arrival 169
  group size limits 39–40, 59, 152, 162
  and human waste 103
  and increasing supply strategy 187, 188, 189, 190,
    191, 192
  and invasive species 118
  and limiting use strategy 177, 178, 179, 180–181,
    182, 183–184, 185, 186

and management matrices **46**, **47**, **48**
and multi-use paths 148–149
on overflights 130–131
permits *see* permit systems
on pets 57, 82, 85, 117, 148, 169
and reducing impact of use strategy 193, 194, 195,
  196, 197, 198, 199, 200, 201
visitors' awareness of 39
*see also* recreation use rationing/allocation
runoff 10, **11**, 111, 119, 158

sanitation 16, 59–60, 75
Sargent Mountain (Acadia National Park) 28
Sax, Joseph 126
school programs 17
Scotland 36
seagrass beds 71, 72, 73, **73**, 74
Selway-Bitterroot Wilderness Area (Idaho/Montana) 26, 29
Sequoia National Park (California) 28
  *see also* Whitney, Mt.
*Sequoia sempervirens* 95
sequoia trees 95, 103, 126
Shining Rock Wilderness Area (North Carolina) 25–26
Sierra Nevada Mountains (California) 103, 122
signage 16–17, 26, 27–28, 30, 31, **43**, 57, **57**, 60
  as deterrent of theft 107–108, 109
site closures 75, 77, 99, 100, 169, 170
slide/sound exhibits 26, 89
Snake River (Hell's Canyon) 34
snowmobiles 96, 142–143, **143**, 158, 168, 169
  regulations/technology standards for 144–145, 162
social media 15, 69, 92, 116, 169
social trails 15, 27–28, 43, 69, 164
soil 9–10, **10**, **11**, 12, 15, 19, 55, 56, 59, 66, 103, 134,
  157, 160–161, 163, 166
  cryptobiotic 67–68
  and four basic strategies 161, 177, 187, 193, 203
  protection 43, 45, 46–47, **46**, **47**, 48, **48**, 49
  and vehicles 62, 127, 146
solitude 6, 7, **7**, 13, 14, 42, 124, 125, 170–171
  and Native American rituals 139, 140
souvenirs 108
spiny water fleas 119
staff training 30, 89
Statue of Liberty National Monument 3, 15, 132
Stegner, Wallace 3
Steller's Jays 95
Sugarlands Visitor Center (Great Smoky Mountains
  National Park) 64

Tamalpais, Mount (California) 27
TAOT (trips-at-one-time) 88
tent pads 43, 61, 164
theft, preventing/reducing 106, 107–109, 161, 162
threefold framework 6, 7, 157, 160, 166

toilets 16, 60, 93
traffic congestion 14, 16, 127, 128, 129, 158, 161, 167
"Tragedy of the Commons" 4
trails 9, 14, **16**, 66, 103, 150, 157, 160
    and direct/indirect management practices 20, **21**
    and four basic strategies 184, 191, 199–200, 207
    impacts of hiking on 9, 10, 15, **16**, 55, 161, 166
    and information/education 26–27, 55–58
    and management matrices **46**, 47, **47**, **48**, 49
    natural quiet on 91
    quotas for 36
    social 15, 27–28, 43, 69, 164
    and zoning 42
    *see also* hiking/hikers; mountain biking
trees
    impacts on 10, **10**, 15, 29, 59
    and spirituality 95
trips-at-one-time (TAOT) 88
Tuolumne Meadows Campground (Yosemite
      National Park) 16
turtles 71, 79
Twitter 69, 116, 169

US Forest Service 7, 8, 36, 103, 171
US National Park Service 3, 7, 8, 12, 63–64, 66, 83, 103
    and archeological sites 101
    and Federal Aviation Administration 131
    mountains managed by 125, 139
    and Organic Act (1916) 126, 158, 167, 170
    in partnerships 171
    policies on noise 96
    trails managed by 15, 55, 56
    and Washington 136
US Park Police 136, 137

vandalism 13, 15, 25, 29
vegetation 9, 10–11, **10**, 56, 59, 62, 66, 103, 127, 134,
      146, 150, 157, 160–161, 163, 166
    and four basic strategies 161, 177–178, 187,
      193–194, 203
    and management matrices **46**, **47**, **48**
    resilience of 19, 20
    restoration projects 136, 163
    *see also* trees
VHS (viral hemorrhagic septicemia) 119–120
visitor attitudes 23, 24, 29
visitor behavior
    and information/education 27–29, 163
    and management practices 18, 20, 23–24
    and use rationing/allocation **33**
    *see also* depreciative behavior
visitor centers 16, 24, 76, 79, 92, 128
visitor conflict 13, 14, 15, 88, 137, 142, 146, 157, 159, 160, 161
    and four basic strategies 182–183, 190, 197–198, 206
    and management matrices **46**, **47**, **48**

visitor experience 5, 9, 13–15, 29, 40, **50**, 87, 88, 96,
      144, 157
    hardening *see* hardening resources strategy
    resistance/resilience of 19–20
    and use rationing/allocation 35
Visitor Experience and Resource Protection (VERP)
      framework 7–8, 67, 69, 157, 159
visitor knowledge 25, 26–29, 30, 138
visitor safety 26, 64, 89, 91, 92–93, 115, 148–149, 153, 166
visitor satisfaction 6, 44, 48, 172
Visitor Use Management 8, 157, 159
volunteers 30, 59, 106, 108, 158–159
Voyageurs National Park (Minnesota) **50**, **51**, 118–121,
      **119**, 160
    information/education in 120, **120**, 161, 162, 171, 172
    invasive species/fish disease in 118, 119–121
    management practices in 120–121
    regulations/law enforcement in 120, 167
    resources of 118
    wastewater collection/treatment in 119
    water quality in 118–119

WAG (waste allocation and gelling) bags 104, **105**, 165
Wagar, J. 6
wastewater collection/treatment 119
water 6, 9, **10**, 11, 110, 157, 160, 163
    and management matrices **46**, **47**, **48**
    pollution 11, 27, 118–119
    runoff 10, **11**, 111
    *see also* aquatic environment
websites 64, 65, 89, 164, 169, 170
white-nose syndrome *see* WNS
Whitney, Mt. (Sequoia and Kings National Park) **50**, **51**,
      103–105, **104**, 160, 161, 162
    human waste regulations at 103, 104, **105**,
      161, 165
    National Park Service–US Forest Service partnership
      in 103, 104
    rationing/allocation system at 104, 168
    visitor center at 104
wilderness 6, 84–85, **86**–90, 124, 160, 170
    and aircraft 130
    and camping 150, 151–153, 165
    fees in 37, 38
    and information/education 25–26, 27
    and off-road vehicles **23**
    rules/regulations in 20, 41, 88–89
    and use rationing/allocation 28, 31, **32**, 35
    and visitor knowledge 29
    zoning in 42
Wilderness Act (1964) 6, 124
wildfires 12
wildlife 6, 7, 9, **10**, 11–12, 13, 15, 16, 57, 62, 63, 71, 82,
      114, 157, 160–161, 163
    and four basic strategies 161, 178–179, 188,
      194–195, 204

wildlife (*continued*)
 and information/education 28
 invasive species 118
 and management matrices
  **46, 47, 48**
 and multi-use paths 146, 148
 and noise pollution 95, 96
 as quality indicator 85
 and vehicles 127, 142, 144, 145
 and zoning 42
 *see also specific species*
Windows, The (Arches National Park) 67, 68
winter activities 18, 142–145
 *see also* snowmobiles
WNS (white-nose syndrome) 75, 76–78
wolves 144
workshops 27, 55
World Heritage Sites 76, 79, 99


Yellowstone National Park (Wyoming/Montana/
  Idaho) 3, 15, 26, 29, 50, **51**
 lawsuits/environmental assessments/impact
  statements over 144
 long-term winter use plan for 142–144, 160
 noise pollution in 96
 pricing in 36–37
 resources of 144
 snowmobiles in 142–143, **143**, 144–145, 158, 162,
  168, 169

transportation events approach in 144
 in winter 142–145
Yosemite National Park (California) 3, 16, 50, **51**, 122,
  **123**, 124, 160
 *see also* Half Dome


Zion Canyon (Zion National Park) 127–129, **128**, 163, 167
Zion National Park (Utah) 28, 50, **51**, **128**
 bus system in 128–129, 149, 162, 163, 165, 167,
  169, 170, 171
 collaboration in 130, 132–133, 171
 managing cars at 127–129, 158, 161
 visitor center at 128
zoning 19, **21**, 24, 66, 71, 82, 84, 103, 138, 150, 158
 and aircraft 130, 131
 and archaeological sites 100, 101–102
 and caves 110, 113–114
 evaluation of 41–42, 44
 and increasing supply strategy 187, 188, 189, 190,
  191, 192
 and limiting use strategy 177, 178, 179, 180, 181,
  182, 183, 184, 185, 186
 and management matrices **46, 47, 48**
 for natural quiet 95, 97, **97**, 162, 167
 and reducing impact of use strategy 193, 194, 195,
  196, 197, 198, 199, 200
 "rescue"/"no-rescue" 42
 of rivers 86, 88, 89, 162, 164, 167
 temporal 89, 127, 162, 164